Just Trade

Just Trade

*A New Covenant Linking Trade
and Human Rights*

Berta Esperanza Hernández-Truyol
and Stephen J. Powell

NEW YORK UNIVERSITY PRESS

New York and London

NEW YORK UNIVERSITY PRESS
New York and London
www.nyupress.org

Library of Congress Cataloging-in-Publication Data
Hernández-Truyol, Berta Esperanza.
Just trade : a new covenant linking trade and human rights /
Berta Esperanza Hernández-Truyol and Stephen J. Powell.
p.   cm.
Includes bibliographical references and index.
ISBN–13: 978–0–8147–3693–7 (cl : alk. paper)
ISBN–10: 0–8147–3693–9 (cl : alk. paper)
1. Human rights—Economic aspects. 2. Foreign trade regulation—
Political aspects. 3. International trade—Social aspects.   I. Powell,
Stephen J., 1942– II. Title.
K3240.H43   2008
341.4'8—dc22   2008031667

New York University Press books are printed on acid-free paper,
and their binding materials are chosen for strength and durability.
We strive to use environmentally responsible suppliers and materials
to the greatest extent possible in publishing our books.

Manufactured in the United States of America

10 9 8 7 6 5 4 3 2 1

To Vivian and Nikolai in the hope that they may enjoy a better world. —BEHT

To my grandfather, "Pop," whose strength and resourcefulness in starting a family in a new country humbles me still. —SJP

Contents

Acknowledgments   xiii

Acronyms   xv

Getting Started: A General Introduction   1
    Nature of the Intersections   2
    Human Rights Criticism of Trade Rules   4
    Origin of This Volume   7

1   Global Concepts: International Law Primer   13
    1.1   *Overview*   13
    1.2   *International Law and International Law-Making:*   13
        General Concepts
    1.3   *International Law-Making: Specific Provisions*   18
    1.4   *International Law as U.S. Law*   20

2   Pillars and Escape Hatches: Basic Concepts   26
    of International Trade Law in the Americas
    2.1   *Overview of the GATT and WTO*   26
    2.2   *Economic Underpinnings: Comparative Advantage*   27
    2.3   *Four Pillars of GATT*   30
    2.4   *Exceptions to the Pillars*   36
    2.5   *WTO Dispute Settlement*   39
    2.6   *Trade in the Americas*   41

3   Global Laws, Local Lives: Basic Concepts and Legal   49
    Regimes of Human Rights Law in the Americas
    3.1   *Introduction*   49
    3.2   *Theoretical Underpinnings of Human Rights Law*   50
    3.3   *Origins of International Human Rights Law:*   52
        General Concepts
    3.4   *Modern Human Rights Developments*   55
    3.5   *Classification of Specific Human Rights*   58
    3.6   *Human Rights and Trade*   61

4   Splendid Isolation's Progeny: The Intersections   62
    of Trade and Human Rights
    4.1   *Central Dilemma: Lack of Purposeful Correlation*   62
    4.2   *Philosophical and Structural Divides*   62
    4.3   *Legal Hierarchy of Trade and Human Rights Norms*   66
    4.4   *Indispensable Role of Government*   73

5   Who Belongs, Who Rules: Citizenship—Voice   75
    and Participation in the Global Marketplace
    5.1   *Overview*   75
    5.2   *Human Rights Framework*   75
    5.3   *Citizenship in a Globalized World*   77
    5.4   *Transnationalization of the Individual*   79
    5.5   *The Transnational Corporation*   83
          and the Rise of Economic Citizenship
    5.6   *Final Thoughts*   84

6   Ecosystem Degradation and Economic Growth: 86
    Trade's Unexploited Power to Improve Our Environment
    6.1   *Overview*   86
    6.2   *Human Rights Framework*   86
    6.3   *International Trade Framework*   88
    6.4   *Processes or Production Methods (PPMs)*   89
    6.5   *GATT's Public Health and Welfare Clause*   94
    6.6   *Harmonization of Product Standards:*   103
          TBT Agreement
    6.7   *From Rio to Johannesburg: Sustainable*   108
          Development Sues for Peace with Trade Rules
    6.8   *Natural Capitalism and the Equator Principles*   110
    6.9   *Final Thoughts*   112

7   Not Just a Question of Capital: 114
    Health and Human Well-Being
    7.1   *Overview*   114
    7.2   *Human Rights Framework*   114
    7.3   *International Trade Framework*   115
    7.4   *SPS Agreement*   116
    7.5   *Cartagena Protocol on Biosafety*   123
    7.6   *Using the WTO and Biosafety Protocol's*   129
          Health Provisions for Human Rights Ends

7.7   Health in the Americas and   130
       WTO's TRIPS Agreement
7.8   Colorism and Health in the Americas   133
7.9   GATT's General Exceptions and the Right to Health   134
7.10 Final Thoughts   135

8   Exploitation or Progress? Terms and Conditions of Labor   136
8.1   Overview   136
8.2   Human Rights Framework   136
8.3   International Trade Framework   142
8.4   How May GATT's General Exceptions   143
       Heighten Labor Rights Compliance?
8.5   Relevance of the TBT Agreement   149
8.6   Trade and Labor in the Americas   150
8.7   Trade and Immigration   156
8.8   Colorism and Labor Rights   160
8.9   Role of Corporate Governance   162
8.10 Soft Landings: Retraining Assistance   167
8.11 Final Thoughts   168

9   Human Bondage: Trafficking   170
9.1   Overview   170
9.2   Human Rights Framework   170
9.3   International Trade Framework   173
9.4   The Reality of Trafficking   175
9.5   The Ubiquity of Trafficking   180
9.6   The Faces of Trafficking   183
9.7   Final Thoughts   186

10   Bebel Redux: The Woman Question   192
10.1 Overview   192
10.2 Human Rights Framework   193
10.3 International Trade Framework   194
10.4 The Woman Question   198
10.5 Women and Culture in the Americas   200
10.6 Women and Work   201
10.7 Final Thoughts   203

11   First Peoples First: Indigenous Populations   206
11.1 Overview   206
11.2 Human Rights Framework   206

11.3 International Trade Framework 211
11.4 Enter WTO's TRIPS Agreement: From Bad to Worse? 213
11.5 Role of TRIPS in the Abuse of Traditional Knowledge 216
11.6 Convention on Biological Diversity to the Rescue 220
11.7 Trade Causes Overuse of Resources 223
on Which Indigenous Peoples Rely
11.8 Modernization: Not Always the Best Approach 225
11.9 Efforts to Bridge the Divide 226
11.10 Final Thoughts 229

12 From Excess to Despair: The Persistence of Poverty 231
12.1 Overview 231
12.2 Human Rights Framework 231
12.3 International Trade Framework 234
12.4 The Reality of Poverty 235
12.5 Agricultural Reform Integral to Reducing Poverty 241
12.6 Poverty and Immigration 247
12.7 Final Thoughts: Changing Paradigms 248

13 Freedom from Famine and Fear: Democracy 250
13.1 Overview 250
13.2 Human Rights Framework 251
13.3 International Trade Framework 253
13.4 Democracy, Trade, and Human Rights 254
13.5 Final Thoughts 259

14 Imperial Rules: Economic Sanctions 261
14.1 Overview 261
14.2 Human Rights Framework 262
14.3 International Trade Framework 263
14.4 Judging Economic Sanctions 264
14.5 Human Rights Impact of Economic Sanctions 265
14.6 Conundrum of Cuba 267
14.7 Final Thoughts: Value of Economic Sanctions 273

15 Recognizing Indivisibility, Bridging Divides: 275
Visions and Solutions for the Future of the
Trade and Human Rights Relationship
15.1 Overview 275
15.2 Human Rights Approach to Trade, 277
Trade Approach to Human Rights

15.3 *Small Steps: Ending Trade's Splendid*   281
Isolation from Human Rights
15.4 *Reparations for Human Rights Violations*   286
15.5 *Mr. Ricardo, Meet the 21st Century*   294
15.6 *Linking Trade and Human Rights in the Americas*   296
15.7 *Afterword*   297

Notes   299
Index   367
About the Authors   391

Documents Annex available online at
http://www.nyupress.org/webchapters/
9780814736937_Hernandez_Appendix.pdf

Acknowledgments

We wish to thank the many friends, colleagues, and students—too many to name individually—who contributed to the development of the ideas presented in this book through their support, research, and innumerable hallway, conference, classroom, and restaurant discussions. We also thank the numerous communities, including the human rights and trade communities around the world, that have provided the support and inspiration that made this project a reality.

We owe special gratitude to the unique team of Richard Delgado and Jean Stefancic—both dear friends and valued colleagues—who encouraged us to pursue the idea of the human rights/trade intersection in a critical and self-critical way. We also owe special thanks to our research assistants Veronica Arenas, Vatrice Perrin, Paola Chavarro, Joshua Clark, Joanna Theiss, Robert Bowser, Reka Toth, Trisha Low, and Geraldine Rosso. We owe exceptional gratitude to Cindy Zimmerman, a faculty assistant and word processing and editing genius, whose work has been invaluable in the production and completion of this book.

At NYU Press, Deborah Gershenowitz helped us launch the project, kept in close touch throughout the process, and saw the book to completion. She deserves special mention.

We have produced this work at the University of Florida Levin College of Law. Dean Robert Jerry has been generous with his support and personal encouragement.

Finally we want to thank our family and friends for unselfishly providing time, understanding, emotional support, nourishment, and much-needed reality checks.

Acronyms

AAWH	American Association for World Health
ABA	American Bar Association
ACHR	American Convention on Human Rights
ATCA/ ATS	Alien Tort Claims Act/ Alien Tort Statute
BFOQ	Bonafide Occupational Qualification
CAFC	Commission for Assistance to a Free Cuba
CAFTA–DR–US	Central American–Dominican Republic– United States Free Trade Agreement
CAHR	Center for the Advancement of Human Rights
CAN	Andean Community of Nations (in Spanish)
CBD	Convention on Biological Diversity
CCIC	Canadian Council for International Cooperation
CDA	Cuban Democracy Act
CEDAW	Convention on the Elimination of All Forms of Discrimination Against Women
CERD	Convention on the Elimination of All Forms of Racial Discrimination
CEWFCL	Convention Concerning the Prohibition and Immediate Action for the Elimination of the Worst Forms of Child Labour
CFC	Chlorofluorocarbon
CIEL	Center for International Environmental Law
Codex	Codex Alimentarius Commission
CRC	Convention on the Rights of the Child
CRDS	Convention on Rights and Duties of States
CSI	Center for Study of Intelligence
DEVAW	Declaration on the Elimination of Violence Against Women
DHHS	Department of Health and Human Services
DRRP	Declaration on Race and Racial Prejudice
DSU	Dispute Settlement Understanding

EC	European Communities
EPZ	Export Processing Zone
EU	European Union
FDA	Food and Drug Administration
FLSA	Fair Labor Standards Act
FTA	Free Trade Agreement
FTAA	Free Trade Area of the Americas
GATS	General Agreement on Trade in Services
GATT	General Agreement on Tariffs and Trade
GDP	Gross Domestic Product
GMO	Genetically Modified Organism
GSP	Generalized System of Preferences
HRC	Human Rights Center
HRW	Human Rights Watch
IACHR	Inter-American Commission on Human Rights
IATP	Institute for Agriculture and Trade Policy
ICCPR	International Covenant on Civil and Political Rights
ICESCR	International Covenant on Economic, Social, and Cultural Rights
ICJ	International Court of Justice
IDB	Inter-American Development Bank
IFC	International Finance Corporation
IIE	Institute of International Economics
ILO	International Labour Organization
IMF	International Monetary Fund
IPR	Intellectual Property Rights
ISO	International Organization for Standardization
ITC	(U.S.) International Trade Commission
LDC	Less-developed Country
Libertad	Cuban Liberty and Democratic Solidarity Act
LMO	Living Modified Organism
MCCA	Central American Common Market (in Spanish)
MERCOSUR	Common Market of the South (in Spanish)
MFN	Most-favored Nation
MIF	Multilateral Investment Fund
MMPA	Marine Mammal Protection Act
MSPA	Migrant and Seasonal Agricultural Worker Protection Act
NAAEC	North American Agreement on Environmental Cooperation
NAALC	North American Agreement on Labor Cooperation

NAFTA	North American Free Trade Agreement
NGO	Nongovernmental Organization
OAS	Organization of American States
OECD	Organisation for Economic Co-operation and Development
OSAGI	Office of the Special Adviser on Gender Issues and Advancement of Women
OUSGA	Office of the Under Secretary for Global Affairs
PCIJ	Permanent Court of International Justice
PPM	Processes or Production Methods
PPP	Purchasing Power Parity
PVA	Polyvinyl Alcohol
SPS	Sanitary and Phytosanitary Measures
TBT	Technical Barriers to Trade
TNC	Transnational Corporation
TRIPS	Trade-related Aspects of Intellectual Property Rights
UNCESCR	UN Committee on Economic, Social, and Cultural Rights
UNCHR	UN Commission on Human Rights
UNDP	UN Development Programme
UNESCO	UN Educational, Scientific, and Cultural Organisation
UNIFEM	UN Development Fund for Women
USTR	U.S. Trade Representative
VTVPA	Victims of Trafficking and Violence Protection Act
WEDO	Women's Environment and Development Organization
WIPO	World Intellectual Property Organization
WTC	World Trade Court (the authors' more descriptive term for the WTO's Appellate Body)
WTO	World Trade Organization

Getting Started
A General Introduction

For the Cyclops have no ships
    with crimson prows,
  No shipwrights there to build them
    good trim craft
that could sail them out to foreign
    ports of call
as most men risk the seas to trade
    with other men.
Such artisans would have made
    this island too a decent place to live in.
                    —Homer, *The Odyssey*

Just as Homer identified trade with the very concept of civilization, we seek by our analysis to identify just trade: specific paths that governments must follow to use trade's enormous power for the advancement of human rights. The realities and the consequences of leaving undisturbed the profound disconnect between human rights law and international trade law are heartbreaking. For example, India's historic opening to freer international trade in the 1980s brought huge gains to a middle class that in essence did not exist in the 1960s and now numbers more than three hundred million[1] newly prosperous Indians. Against this inarguably positive economic growth must be seen the indifference of trade rules to one of a dozen foreseeable costs of India's realization of Ricardo's conception of comparative advantage—thousands of young Indian girls and boys chained to textile looms day and night to meet world demand for inexpensive apparel.

In Bolivia, while trade with Brazil in natural gas blossoms to enrich the country's European-descended "white" elite, 90 percent of rural and predominantly Amerindian Bolivians live in utter poverty, unable to satisfy even basic requirements for sanitation, much less receive a secondary education.[2] Families in Nicaragua and other poor Latin nations participate in globalization's export boom by keeping their young children out of school to pick pesticide-laden tobacco, bananas, and vegetables. In El Salvador, the 2004 trade agreement among the United States and Central American countries promises increased employment in sugarcane production for the U.S. market, but at the cost of the education of more than the twenty-five thousand children as young as eight who work in the most dangerous job in agriculture, planting and cutting cane with sharp machetes and hazardous chemicals.[3] Virtually all the children of La Oroya in the Peruvian Andes suffer from lead poisoning and other consequences of severe air, soil, and water pollution, including sulfur dioxide levels between 80 and 300 percent of those permitted by the World Health Organization. The cause is unfiltered, unlimited, uncontrolled pollution from the copper and lead smelter of transnational Doe Run, whose exports have earned the company hundreds of millions of Peruvian nuevos soles and the town the title of one of the ten most polluted cities on earth.[4] In Papua New Guinea, the black islanders on Bougainville worked under slave-like conditions for the London-based mining company Rio Tinto to extract gold and copper, leaving behind tons of waste material. The resulting pollution of the air and water damned residents to decades of physical and mental health ills. When the islanders revolted, the army intervened to protect the government's 20 percent of the mine's profits, commencing a ten-year civil war. The legacy of Rio Tinto's and the government's insatiable appetites is the thousands of villagers killed, thousands more raped, burned villages, and other "atrocious human rights abuses."[5]

Nature of the Intersections

A recent World Bank study poignantly summarized the troubling dilemma that this volume addresses: "Globalization is already a powerful force for poverty reduction as societies and economies around the world are becoming more integrated. Although this international integration presents considerable opportunities for developing countries, it also contains significant risks. Associated with international integration are concerns about increasing inequality, shifting power, and cultural uniformity."[6] In small countries whose comparatively advantaged goods capture profitable shares of world exports, trade can actually worsen already-underdeveloped governmental institutions. Elite groups of large exporters with political sway prefer the freedom from regulation and oversight that weak ministries ensure.[7] Globalization shifts power from governments and civil society to huge transnational corporations whose decisions take on global force.

What Amy Chua in *World on Fire* called the "market-dominant minorities" have disproportionately benefited from globalization and have disenfranchised the very majorities empowered by democracy.[8] Globalization creates cultural uniformity by rewarding only those who traverse the global market, producing what that market requires, rather than what might ensure food security for a country or preservation of indigenous lifestyles. Globalization also has increased inequality in many ways. On one scale, the three richest people in the world have assets that exceed the combined gross domestic product of the forty-eight least developed countries. These indirect effects explain much of the basis for the burgeoning backlash against globalization, successfully articulated by massive protests of environmental, labor, and development advocates against the World Trade Organization ministerial meetings in Seattle in 1999, in Cancun in 2003, and in Hong Kong in 2005.

Protestors against globalization also have caused melees in various Central and South American capitals to protest free trade agreements with the United States. They staged demonstrations in Mar del Plata, Argentina, during the 2005 Summit of the Americas, which brought together the heads of state of hemispheric nations in an unsuccessful attempt to restart negotiations for a Free Trade Area of the Americas.[9] Trade added terrorism as an unwanted intersection when Colombia's second-largest guerrilla group, which has engaged in decades of pillaging and holds some five hundred hostages, announced in 2007 that it will agree to a cease-fire if the FTA with the United States is scrapped.[10]

These protestors oppose globalization in all its forms, not only its most visible international trade aspects—the movement of goods and services across borders (imports and exports)—but also the many other inevitable ways in which economies, and societies, are growing closer. This often-forced intimacy has resulted from the telescoping both of distance and time by advanced communication and transportation technologies, control by multinational corporations of financial markets that affect our daily lives, cross-border investment and the outsourcing of jobs, and liberalization of exchange and capital controls. These activities have lessened government influence, transnationalized citizenship, and in general divested discretion from individual citizens through bestowal of power on anonymous and unaccountable actors.

For those who prefer numbers,[11] consider the following: while world trade has increased at the astounding rate of nearly 400 percent in the past thirty years, fully one-fourth of the world's population subsists on less than one dollar per day and one-half survives on less than two dollars per day. Even as international trade expands to account for at least 20 percent of the GDP of every developed nation, the World Food Program of the United Nations has expanded operations to feed twice as many hungry people in 2005 as in the previous year.[12] As trade in the United States was expanding at three times the rate of its population increase, petroleum use—and with it climate-changing carbon emissions—grew by 20 percent. Virgin forests are fast disappearing. One child in five between the ages of five and fourteen remains in the workplace. The gap between the richest and poorest nations has increased by more than 100 percent in the last forty years. Someone dies of hunger every four seconds.[13]

Human Rights Criticism of Trade Rules

Human rights advocates direct three main criticisms at globalization in general and international trade in particular. First, critics claim that trade exacerbates human rights concerns, among other ways by encouraging sweatshops and child labor. Trade, its detractors argue, also results in overuse of the natural resources that give developing countries their comparative advantage. For example, tropical hardwoods of the Amazon rain forest and oil from beneath the Nigerian plains quickly are disappearing; this trade result encourages governments and multinational corporations to suppress indigenous peoples who try to protect their ancestral lands from financial exploitation.

Second, trade rules at best complicate and at worst prevent government use of economic sanctions to penalize governments that condone genocide, practice torture, or commit other human rights violations. As explained in chapter 2, GATT's Four Pillars command unconditional nondiscrimination in the treatment of imports from other Members. The principal and most effective enforcement tool of many human rights treaties and policies is precisely to discriminate among countries based on their human rights performance, to deny market access to the goods of these countries, or even to prohibit trade with them altogether.[14] Trade rules require that WTO Members treat products that share similar physical characteristics and uses alike, even if one product (for example, a blouse) was produced using indentured child labor, while the other was not; or if one product (for example, a tropical hardwood armoire) was produced using unsustainable forestry methods, while the other was not; or if one product (petroleum, for example) was obtained by depriving indigenous peoples of their economic future, while the other was not. These contradictory approaches create important and unnecessary obstacles to just trade: using trade's power to realize human rights objectives.

Third, and we believe most tellingly, human rights proponents complain that trade rules, by distancing themselves from responsibility for improving the human rights record, fail to take advantage of trade's vast power by making compliance with human rights law a condition of participation in trade's bounty. Beginning at the regional economic integration level and ultimately spreading to global rules of the WTO, trade instruments must, both from a legal and a policy perspective, command purposeful integration of trade law with human rights law. Globalization thus is faulted both for making the human rights situation worse through its activities and for not improving the human rights record through its ubiquitous presence and enormous power.

For example, human rights activists and workers in the North often hold the view that the developing economies of Latin America, in order to attract investment, engage in a "race to the bottom." That is, they sacrifice human rights standards to provide lower costs for foreign investors.[15] Most economic studies of why foreign investors choose certain countries for their operations discount these fears, noting that environmental costs, and even wage rates, cohabit a long list of factors that contribute to a corporate decision to invest. Nonetheless, the fear of a race to the bottom is so widespread that it affects the motivation of a developing country in decisions to protect the environment and to improve the conditions of workers. Thus, it is not surprising that the most fervent reaction against the Washington Consensus—that philosophical perspective that promotes industrialization and free trade by the private sector along with the reduction of government spending and regulation—has come from environmental and labor activists.[16]

There is an obverse to this coin. As the World Bank study notes, globalization is a powerful force for reducing poverty. It literally creates money. As Clive Crook has written in the *Economist*, "Globalisation, far from being the greatest cause of poverty, is its only feasible cure."[17] In developing countries, trade creates jobs that did not previously exist and that raise living standards. For example, during the last three decades of the 20th century, while the world's population was increasing by two-thirds, the percentage of that population living on less than an adjusted two dollars per day decreased from 44 percent to 8 percent.[18] Whether an econometric formula accurately can measure poverty is widely contested, however. The World Bank itself recognizes that poverty is a complex problem of which financial deprivation is but one component (see chapter 12 on poverty).

Trade also increases company profits, which theoetically allows lowering of prices, in turn raising real incomes of all consumers, rich or poor. Trade leads to technological innovation, which allows industries in developing countries to produce more efficiently, enabling people in these nations to buy more goods and services with less income. With increased living standards, governments and civil society can afford to focus on more than preventing starvation, which can lead to greater worker rights, improved health, broader freedom of association, and increases in other human rights.

To be sure, while trade's compelling economic growth indeed has driven absolute poverty downward, some areas of the globe have longer resisted trade's loud knock of opportunity, with unhappy results. For example, while Asia's poor dropped dramatically as India, China, Japan, and others opened their trade doors, Africa's poverty levels increased, with the result that, while thirty years ago 11 percent of the world's poor lived in Africa and 76 percent in Asia, now Africa hosts 66 percent of the poor and Asia's share has declined to 15 percent.[19] Latin America, breaking loose from protectionist trade policies that lasted into the 1990s, has also seen sizeable decreases in poverty levels, although none as dramatic as in most Asian nations.[20]

Other data show a correlation between an increase in trade followed by a decrease in human rights concerns. Perversely, data exist that support the opposite conclusion. For example, some studies indicate that there is an increase in indentured child labor in some countries with fast-rising trade numbers. Other data reveal a decrease in food security in developing nations that keyed agricultural production to exportable commodities, and then suffered from a drop in world prices combined with competition from heavily subsidized imports. There is also evidence of the splitting of families by Mexican women forced to travel to squalid shantytowns adjoining the border assembly-for-export industry (maquila-doras) that mushroomed to meet the demand created by Mexico's signing of the NAFTA. What we cannot do, and herein lies a principal premise of the trade and human rights debate, is demonstrate purposeful correlation, much less integration or even coordination, between human rights policies and international trade policies.

Professor Powell elsewhere has discussed the "splendid isolation"[21] that characterized the parallel growth of modern human rights and global trade law beginning in the mid-1940s.[22] The same atrocities of the Second World War inspired rapid evolution of both legal disciplines. The UN's Universal Declaration of Human Rights and the World Trade Organization's General Agreement on Tariffs and Trade, each of which continues as the key governing document in its field, celebrated their fiftieth anniversaries in the same year at the end of the last century. Each document also has inspired an unending series of negotiations leading to increasingly broader jurisdictional reach, a complex web of regional and global institutions, and ever-tighter limitations on state action.

Yet, as their subject matter increasingly overlapped and their dependency progressively tightened, treaties in these two fundamental fields of human endeavor gave, with rare exception, no hint of the existence of the other and even less do they show a coordinated effort by the states negotiating them to make the world not only a richer, but a better place.

The exceptions are protection of the environment, identified early on as directly intersecting with trade rules, and promotion of public health. Ironically, the result of recognition in these two phases of the trade and human rights intersection has been far from euphoric. In fact, the episodic, often pro forma mention of the environment in trade treaties and of trade in multilateral environmental agreements has led to direct conflict in treaty terms, as compared with simple indifference to other human rights areas. For example, as we discuss in section 7.5, if a WTO Member bans imports of genetically modified soybeans for health reasons based on incomplete evidence, its action likely would be consistent with the Convention on Biological Diversity's Protocol on Biosafety, but likely would be inconsistent with the WTO's Agreement on Sanitary and Phytosanitary Measures.

Origin of This Volume

Our inspiration and felt necessity for this volume proceeds from our research and student interactions while separately teaching law courses on human rights and on international trade and, especially, from our co-teaching over the years of courses that explore the intersection of these disciplines. While we hope that it will be of interest to any student of this intriguing intersection, the book is designed in particular to serve as the text for a trade and human rights seminar or course that explores the premises of the trade and human rights debate from the perspectives both of free trade advocates and of human rights activists, with the purpose of imparting a better understanding of the rationales for both systems of law and the ways that each is—or should be—attempting to avoid a clash that could have profound impact on the protection of human rights and on the global market.

The book examines in depth human rights policies involving conscripted child labor, sustainable development, promotion of health, equality of women, human trafficking, indigenous peoples, poverty, citizenship, and economic sanctions. We hope to aid the reader's understanding of our message through actual examples from the thirty-five nations of the Western Hemisphere. We close this study by looking to the future. Our focus on the myriad intersections of these fields in the Americas aims to recognize weaknesses and potentials in each so that conversations can be had between the trade and human rights borderlands. Our goal is nothing less than an integrated regional trade order seeking both richer and more citizen-sensitive nations.

The *2005 Human Development Report* of the United Nations glumly summarizes the blessings and curses of international trade:

> Trade is at the heart of the interdependence that binds countries together. That interdependence has contributed to some highly visible human development advances, enabling millions of people to escape poverty and share in the prosperity generated by globalization. Yet many millions more have been left behind. The costs and benefits of trade have been unevenly distributed across and within countries, perpetuating a pattern of globalization that builds prosperity for some amid mass poverty and deepening inequality for others. The rules of the game are at the heart of the problem. Developed country governments seldom waste an opportunity to emphasize the virtues of open markets, level playing fields and free trade, especially in their prescriptions for poor countries. Yet the same governments maintain a formidable array of protectionist barriers against developing countries. They also spend billions of dollars on agricultural subsidies. Such policies skew the benefits of globalization in

favour of rich countries, while denying millions of people in developing countries a chance to share in the benefits of trade. Hypocrisy and double standards are not strong foundations for a rules-based multilateral system geared towards human development.[23]

Viable alternatives exist to create structures and craft dialogues to bridge a seemingly impassable divide toward an era of splendid integration of human rights and trade. We ask the reader to see with new eyes the many intersections of human rights law and trade law that the chapters that follow will describe in detail. Our hope is that by unearthing purposeful linkages between trade and human rights, this project will cause decision-makers to recognize their indivisible nature and begin to build the bridges and close the chasms that a half century of unconscionable isolation has created.

We will share our personal story to underscore the necessity and desirability of building those bridges across the present trade and human rights divide. It also drives home the seemingly insurmountable challenge that this task presents because of the differences in language, processes, and cultures in the two fields. This volume is, in a way, a narrative of the authors' personal journey in challenging the splendid isolation of trade and human rights. We first met in the spring of 2000 at the University of Florida Levin College of Law's First Annual Law and Policy in the Americas Conference, sponsored by the college's Center for Governmental Responsibility. Berta had just joined the faculty to focus on international law and international human rights; Steve had just left the U.S. Department of Commerce after a distinguished career as the federal government's principal legal adviser on the unfair trade laws and had been named the director of international trade law programs at the college. After introductions, Berta started chatting with Steve about the exciting international programs at the law school and suggested collaborating in some way to do work on the human rights and trade intersection. Although our paths crossed at faculty events over the coming year, we did not discuss the subject further until Berta, at the Second Annual Conference, again suggested a project on the myriad connections between trade and human rights. Others joined the conversation and the topic moved into the background for another year. At the Third Annual Conference, Berta again talked with Steve about a holistic approach to both of their fields of law. When she took a breath, he stated that "you cannot simply jumble several unrelated topics together and call the result a 'holistic' approach; trade law and human rights law are separate fields for good reason." In addressing the "holistic" nature of law idea, Steve simply said, "Berta, your proposal is enigmatic." And so began the real conversations that have taken us to the journey on which we have embarked to produce this joint volume, delayed because of the intrinsic reluctance of Steve's trade law schooling to allow other disciplines to inform its progress.

This time we did talk more, and the following year we taught a trade and human rights seminar together for the first time. We have modified our materials and our format as our perspectives converged. The course, since its second offering, has been cross-listed with the Center for Latin American Studies and the Center for Women's Studies and Gender Research as well as the business school. The cross-disciplinary enrollment and consequent discussions have enriched the course for students and faculty alike. Imagine the Peace Corps volunteer talking to the aspiring CEO or Wall Street lawyer about issues such as labor rights, environmental degradation, cultural sensitivity, and indigenous rights to medical knowledge. The interplay of disciplines is rich in cross-tested learning.

To be sure, the journey has not been a simple one. We hit many bumps in the road, ranging from materials for the course to what might be realistic solutions to the myriad problems confronted in the advance of trade. These problems included use of and compensation for traditional knowledge to aid humankind, the role of culture, the role of trade in women's subordination, and so on—the discussions were endless. Sometimes these discussions took place in the classroom, as a result of which, one year, students started calling us Mom and Dad and referring to the conversations as "the folks are having another one of their arguments."

The discussions and learning are ongoing. More than once Steve expressed consternation at Berta's generalized solutions of "conversations with all participants around the table." He would say, "We need concrete ideas, concrete solutions, what can trade do? What does trade offer as a possible solution to the problem?" So just as Steve has become holistic, Berta has become more practical. The end result is an enrichment of both.

The significance in sharing our personal journey is that we both are passionate believers in the connection of our respective fields; we believe that they are mutually enriching—a reality we hope this volume underscores for both human rights and trade advocates. The beautiful irony in this narrative is Steve's transformation from considering as weird the holistic everything's-connected approach to a full embrace of that approach in the endeavor to make trade's promise of prosperity a reality for all. This expansion in the trade horizon suggests that it is not lack of care or disregard for human rights that keep the fields separate, but rather trade officials' isolation in their view of trade's reality and human rights advocates' view of trade as the irredeemable spoiler. We hope that this volume works to bring the advocates of both fields together so that they can utilize the idealism of the human rights model and the pragmatism of the trade model to broaden the reach of the economic well-being that, to date, the systems in their splendid isolation have brought to too few.

In order to attain this admittedly ambitious end, we have structured the book so that advocates, professionals, and academics in all fields, as well as students, may benefit from it. The first three chapters are introductions to the governing law in the fields that we study. The chapter after the present introduction is a basic primer on international law—the umbrella under which both trade law and human rights law fall. The second and third chapters are introductions to trade law and human rights law, respectively. Experts in any of those fields may want to skim or skip them and start with chapter 4, which presents an overview of the intersections of human rights and trade, including principles that provide insight as to the hierarchy in the ordering of their sometimes conflicting norms.

In chapters 5 through 13, we focus on specific intersections of trade and human rights, some more evident in popular discourse than others. For example, chapter 6 on the environment, chapter 8 on labor, chapter 10 on women, and chapter 11 on indigenous populations cover the more visible trade intersections, brought to the public eye mostly by civil society protests at meetings of trade ministers and the World Bank. Because most people learn of the clash of these subjects of human rights law with trade rules only through these outcries, popular opinion is that integration of these intersections faces an insurmountable divide. In this volume, we show how states can deploy rules of the powerful trade system to continue the path of economic prosperity while also improving the human condition. Not all solutions are ideal, but we have used Steve's knowledge of the instruments and instrumentalities of trade to recommend viable beginnings to the splendid integration that this volume seeks.

Chapters 5 on citizenship, 7 on health, 9 on trafficking, 12 on poverty, and 13 on democracy touch on intersections that are less evident, perhaps because trade's influence on these human rights is more difficult to capture in a two-second sound bite with a poignant image that can be carried on television stations around the globe. For example, trade is transforming the very idea of citizenship as a method of participation in the decision-making of the government. Trade is empowering massive trans-national entities that, because of their purchasing power, can sway government policy on employment and the environment. Similarly, the concept of democracy, when analyzed in the framework of economic rights, entails much more than the ballot box. Trade in the context of democracy can be a double-edged sword. While the West has deployed its economic power to insist on democracy, sometimes taking a narrow view that over-simplistically equates democracy with elections, it has in so doing eroded democracy, wearing thin the social safety net that the most marginalized sorely need. As the chapter on poverty shows, trade's promise of prosperity has not been realized for all, requiring measures to be adopted to ensure that those who have fallen through the cracks are also afforded some opportunity. Lastly, the trafficking chapter shows how trade, if carried out with blinders on, as a field in a vacuum, can unwittingly contribute to the most egregious of human rights abuses.

Chapter 14 on economic sanctions explains how a tool to enforce human rights sometimes causes human rights deprivations. This ostensible contradiction occurs because of the primacy given by the North/West to civil and political rights over social and economic rights. Inevitably, as in the case of Cuba, this divide creates apparently insurmountable conflicts.

In our conclusion, chapter 15, we try to pave the way for the future, where human rights and trade coexist as parts of a whole and thus must be cognizant and supportive of each other. Trade and human rights cannot possibly be perceived as isolated, as they have been for too long. Yet, the integration must be purposeful and proactive so that trade's powerful reach can work not only for economic expansion and well-being but also for the flourishing of human rights. Well fed, healthy, educated, and fairly compensated workers are good for business. Trade can be good for people; people are necessary for trade. Social, cultural, economic thriving of the individual ought to be one of the focal points of trade—the best result trade can offer to confirm its promise of prosperity.

1

Global Concepts
International Law Primer

1.1 Overview

This chapter provides an overview of the sources of international law and the practice of international rule formation. These principles are central to the making both of trade and of human rights agreements, as well as to the development and evolution of trade and human rights norms, and thus serve as a prerequisite for the reader unfamiliar with, or in need of a refresher lesson in, the basic rules of understanding international law.

1.2 International Law and International Law-Making: General Concepts

In this first chapter, we aim to introduce international law and international law-making. This information is important because both human rights and trade treaties are international agreements that must be concluded pursuant to, as well as comport with, established international norms. We do not anticipate that readers will need to develop an expertise in international law to engage our materials, but we find this basic introduction advisable in order to provide a foundation for all readers, especially those not versed in international law. This is a straightforward and basic introduction; readers with a background or training in the international field may well opt to skip this opening chapter and start with chapter 2.

History traces the development of rules governing relations between or among different peoples to the end of the Roman Empire when the independent and separate states that emerged needed to develop rules for interaction. The system that emerged was largely founded on the Roman system. In fact, the Roman Empire developed a set of rules—the *jus gentium*—to govern the relations between Roman and non-Roman citizens, in contrast to the *jus civile*, which applied exclusively among Roman citizens. The *jus gentium* system incorporated principles of equity in natural law that contemporary scholars analogize to the source of international law called "general principles of law recognized by civilized nations" contained in Article 38(1)(c) of the Statute of the International Court of Justice (ICJ).[1] Thus, one can trace the roots of international law to the need that arose when the formerly unified Roman Empire splintered into diverse nation-states that had to interact on a basis of sovereign equality and mutual respect. Thereafter, increased trade, improvements in navigation, and the discovery of new lands accelerated the development of the new law of nations.[2]

The Thirty Years War (1618-48) in central Europe is a significant event in the history of international law as it signified the end of one imperial reign over all of Europe. Additionally, it marked the emergence of independent nation-states as the primary actors in the global setting. Such advent of independent sovereigns was key to the evolution of international legal principles as it exposed the need to create norms to govern interactions between and among equals.[3]

In *The Law of Nations*, Brierly defined international law as "the body of rules and principles of action which are binding upon civilized states in their relations with one another."[4] This definition reflected the early view that international law applies exclusively to states. The American Law Institute's *Restatement of the Law Third, Foreign Relations Law of the United States* defines international law as "rules and principles of general application dealing with the conduct of states and of international organizations and with their relations inter se, as well as with some of their relations with persons, whether natural or juridical."[5] This definition reveals that international law no longer is the exclusive province of states and international organizations, but also deals with their relationships with individuals and corporations.

Article 92 of the United Nations Charter, itself a treaty ratified by Member states, establishes the ICJ as the principal judicial organ of the United Nations. The provisions of the Statute of the ICJ, a treaty to which all members of the UN are parties, set out the principles that constitute the ICJ and pursuant to which it functions.

Article 38 of the Statute sets out the four sources of international law:

a. international conventions, whether general or particular, establishing rules expressly recognized by the contesting states;
b. international custom, as evidence of a general practice accepted as law;
c. the general principles of law recognized by civilized nations; [and]
d. . . . judicial decisions and the teachings of the most highly qualified publicists of the various nations, as subsidiary means for the determination of rules of law.

Treaties and custom are deemed to be primary sources of law. General principles of law and judicial decisions and treatises are secondary sources.

The *Restatement* also identifies the sources of international law: custom, international agreement, "general principles common to the major legal systems of the world."[6] While treaties and custom are primary sources, general principles are supplementary rules.

Customary law comprises the "general and consistent" practice of states followed from a sense of legal obligation. Such practice may include diplomatic acts, official policy statements, and other governmental acts. Until recently, international law was mostly customary law, with agreements being limited to particular arrangements between states, but rarely used for general law-making. Although customary law evolves from the practice of states, for such practice to become a rule of law states must abide by the conduct out of a sense of legal obligation—*opinion juris sive necessitatis*. A practice that states follow but have no sense of obligation to do so does not constitute a customary norm.

The practice of states can be found in both what states say and what they do (commission) or fail to do (omission) under circumstances in which failure to act may indicate acceptance of the acts of another state that have an impact on another state's legal rights. In addition, for state practice to become customary law, the state practice must be general and consistent over time, with no major alterations or deviations. Significantly, although the general, consistent practice of states results in a binding customary norm, such principles may not be binding on states that are "persistent objectors" (i.e., states that during the development of the norm object to it).[7]

Two observations are appropriate regarding custom and persistent-objector status. One, a state cannot be insulated, as a persistent objector, from being bound by a peremptory norm (*jus cogens*) as such norms hold a superior status and permit no derogation.[8] Significant for this project is that not all customary human rights norms are *jus cogens*—the prohibitions against genocide; slavery and the slave trade; causing disappearances of persons; torture and cruel, inhuman, and degrading treatment; prolonged arbitrary detention; and systematic racial discrimination constitute peremptory norms.[9] Two, a new state coming into the international legal world will be bound by existing custom, without the opportunity to become a persistent objector. That status is only available to states in existence at the time that the norm is being created. This reality has subjected customary international norms to criticism by newly emerging states that are bound by existing rules although they had no part in their development and are given no opportunity to opt out of their application. In Article I, § 8, the U.S. Constitution refers to the "law of nations," and U.S. Supreme Court case law has made clear that customary law is part of U.S. law.[10]

Treaties, the first listed source in Article 38 of the Statute of the ICJ, are very significant in the international realm and are, in modern times, the most frequently used tool for international law-making. Whereas custom is grounded in the practice of states, treaties are rooted in the consent of states. It is important to observe that the requisite technicalities for a document to be labeled a treaty are different in the international realm and under U.S. constitutional law, although one instrument may satisfy the requirements of both. Thus, what is properly called a treaty in international law may or may not qualify as a treaty under the U.S. domestic system.

In the international realm, the Vienna Convention on the Law of Treaties is the principal source of the law of treaties. At Article 2(1)(a), it defines a "treaty" as "an international agreement concluded between States in written form and governed by international law, whether embodied in a single instrument or in two or more related instruments and whatever its particular designation." Article II, § 2, of the U.S. Constitution provides that "the President . . . shall have Power, by and with the Advice and Consent of the Senate, to make Treaties, provided two thirds of the Senators present concur." Thus, under the Constitution, an international agreement, concluded by the United States with another nation, in written form, and governed by international law—factors sufficient to make the instrument a treaty pursuant to the Vienna Convention requirements—is not a "treaty" in the domestic sense unless two-thirds of the Senate gives its advice and consent to the document. We will further address treaties and U.S. law later in the chapter, but first we need further to develop the concept of treaties in the international realm.

In the international sphere, in order to decide what constitutes an "international agreement," one must first analyze the text. Ultimately, whether an instrument is a treaty depends on the intent of the parties. Thus, when there is doubt as to whether an instrument is a treaty, one analyzes the negotiating history, the formalities observed, and the expectations induced. The more formal the process, and the more formal the law-making authority of the government involved, the stronger the case for finding an "agreement."

Treaties share critical characteristics as parliamentary and contractual instruments. For example, in terms of "who" can enter into a treaty, treaties are similar to domestic laws because only sovereigns can make treaties. On the other hand, like contracts, treaties apply only to those who are signatories.

Having first defined treaties and then described some basic characteristics, it is important to turn to the rules applicable to treaties that are set out in the Vienna Convention. The Convention is considered a codification of existing customary law.[11] Therefore, non-signatories may be bound to its terms. For example, the United States has signed, but the Senate has not given its advice and consent to, the Vienna Convention. Yet the U.S. State Department has acknowledged that the United States is bound to its terms as they reflect binding customary norms.[12]

Because this is a volume on trade and human rights, it is important to emphasize that the Vienna Convention's definition of *treaty* limits those instruments to written agreements concluded between states. This definition excludes agreements between a state and a private entity, although, through interpretation, the definition has been modified in practice to include agreements between a state and an international organization because such organizations are considered subjects of international law. In all cases, it is only the trade compacts concluded between and among states that qualify as treaties.

It is also important to note at this juncture that not all agreements between states are necessarily treaties. To be treaties, the agreements must be governed by international law. Thus, an agreement between State A and State B for the purchase by State A of State B's beef using a standard form contract of the meat trade will not be deemed a treaty. Similarly, the purchase of a building or a piece of land by a state, when the contract is subject to the law of the municipality or a third state, will not be deemed a treaty.

1.3   *International Law-Making: Specific Provisions*

Let us now turn to some provisions of the Vienna Convention to ascertain what determines whether an instrument is a "treaty." Part II of the Convention lays out the requirements for the "Conclusion and Entry into Force of Treaties" with Section 1 addressing the conclusion of treaties and Section 2 addressing reservations.

Regarding conclusion of treaties, Article 6 of the Vienna Convention provides that all states have the capacity to enter into a treaty. To be a state in international law, an entity must satisfy four requirements: it must have (a) defined territory; (b) permanent population; (c) a government capable of controlling the territory; and (d) a government with the ability to enter into international relations.[13] One significant article in the first section of the Convention is Article 18, which imposes on signatories an obligation not to act in a way that "would defeat the object and purpose of a treaty."

Section 2, "Reservations," articulates an important concept in treaty-making. Reservations are "unilateral statement[s] . . . made by a state, when signing, ratifying, accepting, approving or acceding to a treaty, whereby it purports to exclude or to modify the legal effect of certain provisions of the treaty in their application to that State" (art. 2(d)). Thus, reservations allow states unilaterally to modify the terms of a treaty or the legal effect of the terms of a treaty. However, the Vienna Convention prohibits reservations that are "incompatible with the object and purpose of the treaty" (art. 19(c)). To ascertain incompatibility, the analysis scrutinizes the reservation in light of the purpose of the treaty. Reservations that frustrate the purpose of a treaty are invalid, even if in theory a state can object to whatever it wants based on its sovereignty.

Articles 20-23 detail the rules regarding reservations, including, respectively, states' acceptance of and objection to reservations, the legal effect of reservations, withdrawals of reservations and objections thereto, and procedural requirements in making or accepting reservations, including that they be in writing. A state decides whether it deems the reserving party a party to Convention. In essence, these details emphasize that contracting states want to keep alive the "basics" of the Convention. With bilateral agreements, for instance, a reservation is the equivalent of a counteroffer to a contract in U.S. domestic law. While going into further detail on reservations is outside the scope of this chapter, it is important to note that the processes of making reservations and of objecting to or accepting reservations leads to complicated analyses about what states are bound by what terms of a treaty. The complexity is underscored when parties to multilateral instruments make multiple reservations.

Part III of the Vienna Convention focuses on the "Observance, Application, and Interpretation" processes. Article 26 sets out a basic principle of international law: *pacta sunt servanda,* which means that parties are bound by treaties and have an obligation to perform their terms in good faith. Parties cannot invoke internal law as grounds to fail to comply with a treaty obligation (art. 27). Treaties are not retroactive (art. 28), are binding on parties within their entire territory (art. 29), and their terms are to be interpreted in good faith in accordance with "the ordinary meaning to be given to the terms of the treaty in their context and in light of its object and purpose" (art. 31(1)). Article 32 allows use of the *travaux preparatoires*—preparatory works—developed during negotiations to assist in the interpretation of treaties. Significantly, the allowance of the use of *travaux preparatoires* might be a disadvantage to states that did not participate in negotiation of the treaty but became signatories later, as their voices are absent from the *travaux.*

Two other parts round out the substantive provisions of the Vienna Convention: Part IV addresses "Amendment and Modification of Treaties" and Part V focuses on the "Invalidity, Termination, and Suspension of the Operation of Treaties." Part V specifically articulates error (art. 48), fraud (art. 49), corruption of a state representative (art. 50), coercion of a representative of a state (art. 51), and coercion of a state by threat of use of force (art. 52) as grounds for invalidating a treaty.

Part V also contains two articles that are important for purposes of this work. One is Article 53, which provides that if, at the time that it is concluded, a treaty conflicts with a peremptory norm of general international law—a norm from which no derogation is permitted—the treaty is void. Related to Article 53 is Article 64, which provides that if a new peremptory norm emerges, "any existing treaty which is in conflict with that norm becomes void and terminates."

The *jus cogens* principle is particularly relevant to this volume as it is a concept of critical importance in human rights law. A rule of *jus cogens* can be derived from custom and treaties but not from other sources. In early international law this principle was articulated by writers saying that a treaty would be void if it was contrary to morality or to basic principles of international law: a treaty could not override natural law. *Jus cogens,* thus, prohibits states from contracting out of peremptory norms that are deemed binding customary norms. The concept has been adopted in several human rights contexts internationally and domestically alike.

Significantly, the Vienna Convention does not itself identify any such norms, and scholars are not in full agreement regarding precisely what norms are peremptory. As noted above, however, it is generally accepted that, for example, the prohibitions against genocide; slavery; murder or causing the disappearance of persons; torture or other cruel, inhuman, or degrading treatment or punishment; prolonged arbitrary detention; systematic racial discrimination; and consistent patterns of gross violations of recognized human rights norms are all deemed be peremptory norms against which no state may derogate. Thus, a treaty to commit genocide, or a treaty to legalize any form of a slave trade, would be void as in contravention of *jus cogens*. This signifies that although a trade agreement might not directly address human rights issues, all such agreements are, by necessity, concluded in a context of universal acceptance that they cannot derogate from peremptory norms and a general agreement as to what some such norms are.

1.4   *International Law as U.S. Law*

The following overview of international law-making and its relation to domestic law (using the United States as an example) is intended to familiarize the reader with general international law-making, as all the themes that we will engage in this volume are "binding law" by virtue of both international norms—be they conventional or customary—and domestic norms. The trade agreements, bodies, and processes that will be introduced in chapter 2 and the human rights agreements, bodies, and processes that are introduced in chapter 3 all are either custom- or treaty-based.

With the international rules in mind, it is instructive to review U.S. domestic law on treaties. As briefly noted above, the U.S. Constitution requires the president to make treaties and then obtain the advice and consent of a two-thirds majority of the Senate. Thus, in the United States, the treaty-making power is one of executive-congressional codetermination. It is noteworthy that, contrary to popular usage, the Senate's role is not one of ratification—rather, the Senate's role is to give advice and consent. Ratification takes place when the parties formally exchange ratification instruments. We often witness the exchange of ratification instruments in Rose Garden ceremonies when the president signs the instrument after

obtaining the requisite senatorial advice and consent. It is always a pleni-
potentiary who signs the instrument's ratification.

Although treaty power is one of executive-congressional codetermination, in recent years it effectively has moved, at least outside the trade regime, toward becoming a presidential monopoly by executive use of other
types of agreements that have been considered the functional equivalent
of treaties. The most notable of the alternatives is the sole executive agreement. The other is the executive agreement pursuant to legislation or joint
resolution. Both of these alternatives satisfy the Vienna Convention definition of "treaty," although they fall short of U.S. constitutional requirements because they lack the advice and consent of two-thirds of the Senate. It is undisputable that before and after adoption of the Constitution,
however, the president signed international agreements that were binding
without the Senate's advice and consent.

Effectively, the president utilizes the sole executive agreement to bypass
the Senate. There is constitutional authority for such agreements, however, if they are based on express presidential powers such as commander
in chief, authority to receive ambassadors, or implied powers to conduct
foreign relations. It thus becomes simply an undeclared treaty that seeks
to avoid paying constitutional dues by changing its name. It is an agreement between the president or his or her subordinates and a foreign
counterpart; this agreement, because it is not submitted to the Senate for
its advice and consent, cannot be a treaty for constitutional purposes.

In the early days pure executive agreements were rare, and when they
existed they were limited in scope. For instance, there might be an executive agreement for the exchange of prisoners of war. But they became
much more frequently used in the 20th century. The high-water mark for
such agreements came with President Franklin Delano Roosevelt's recognition of the communist regime in Moscow and the transfer of title to
Russian properties in the United States to compensate U.S. citizens who
had lost on investments in Russia. The U.S. Supreme Court held that the
executive agreement recognizing Russia and effecting the transfer of property was constitutional because it constituted the exercise of president ple-
nary power to recognize foreign governments.[14]

One problem with this sole executive agreement approach is that it
avoids constitutional checks and balances. The country cannot be sure
about what obligations are being assumed and foreign nations cannot
be certain what obligations Congress will consider binding. A unilateral
executive approach also has the potential for causing difficulties for the

executive in carrying out the agreement's obligations should any funds be needed, as it is Congress that possesses the power of the purse. To be sure, the trend toward executive agreements has caused concern in the Senate, which feels squeezed out of its advice and consent function.

In fact, as a result of the proliferation of executive agreements in 1972, Congress, relying on the "necessary and proper" clause, passed the Case-Zablocki Act,[15] which requires regular reporting to the Senate about ongoing international negotiations.[16] It provides Congress with surveillance power over executive agreements as the secretary of state must send to Congress the text of any international agreement to which the United States is a party, including oral ones, other than a treaty (by constitutional standards), within sixty days of the agreement coming into force. Moreover, the president under his or her own signature, "not later than March 1, 1979, and at yearly intervals thereafter," must transmit to Congress a report concerning what agreements were negotiated after the expiration of the sixty-day period with an explanation for the delay.[17]

Early executive agreements were mostly made pursuant to legislation or joint resolution of Congress. The executive agreement pursuant to legislation avoids having to obtain the advice and consent of a supermajority of the Senate. Today, executive officials cite the early cases to conclude that such historical reality legitimizes the use of executive agreements.

In the original draft of the Constitution, the Committee of Detail assigned the treaty power solely and exclusively to the Senate. The shift to a shared executive-Senate function requiring a supermajority vote in the Senate reveals a desire for a higher degree of consensus for passage of an international agreement than for ordinary law. In fact, a proposal at the Constitutional Convention that international law be made by the president and a simple majority of both chambers of Congress was rejected. In light of this history, it is interesting that the executive agreement plus joint resolution is one of the accepted treaty alternatives.

Significant events in U.S. history have occurred pursuant to these other agreements. For example, the annexation of Texas in 1845 was accomplished by executive agreement plus joint resolution. The President opted for that alternative after the Senate vote did not yield the two-thirds supermajority necessary for a constitutionally defined treaty.[18] More recently, and significant to this volume, a constitutional challenge to the validity of the North American Free Trade Agreement (NAFTA), based on its being concluded as a congressional-executive agreement, failed.[19]

Clear constitutional language on treaties notwithstanding, presidents have come to treat the formal agreements together with sole executive agreements and executive agreements plus joint resolution as interchangeable. Even the U.S. Department of State endorses these three alternative approaches to making international agreements: (1) agreements pursuant to treaty; (2) agreements pursuant to legislation; and (3) agreements pursuant to constitutional authority of the president: (a) as chief executive representing the nation in foreign affairs, (b) to receive ambassadors and other public ministers, (c) as commander in chief, and (d) to take care that the laws be faithfully executed.[20]

These trends notwithstanding, there are some subjects that warrant an agreement that follows the traditional constitutional Article II treaty process.[21] These include themes that are central to this volume: human rights, boundaries, immigration, intellectual property, taxation, the environment, and agreements to join international organizations (most but not all). On the other hand, it is advantageous to have the flexibility of utilizing different forms of international agreements as other matters key to this work are within the traditional congressional-executive realm: trade and finance, for example.

Because the U.S. Constitution gives authority in Article I, § 8, to both houses of Congress to conduct foreign commerce (another term for international trade), and to the executive branch in Article II, § 1, "to make treaties," the responsibility to negotiate trade agreements is shared and is treated specially under U.S. law. Through periodically renewed "fast-track authority" legislation, the Congress sets forth detailed U.S. trade negotiating objectives to be followed by the executive in reaching agreement on, for example, establishment or revision of World Trade Organization (WTO) Agreements or regional agreements such as the NAFTA or the U.S.-Chile Free Trade Agreement (FTA).[22]

After consulting with congressional trade committees, the executive signs the trade agreement with his counterparts, then the president formally notifies the text of the agreement to both houses of Congress for the drafting of implementing legislation that will exercise whatever discretion is given the signatories by the agreement's terms. Congress may not make revisions to the agreement at this stage, else the negotiating credibility of the United States would be destroyed. The agreement and legislation must be considered quickly (thus the legislation's nickname) and, if both houses of Congress agree, the implementing legislation will also "approve" the agreement—the final step in making it binding on the United States as a "treaty" within the meaning of the Vienna Convention, if not within the meaning of the U.S. Constitution.

Several observations regarding custom, treaties, their relationship to each other, their role as U.S. law, and some principles of U.S. law are appropriate. Article VI of the Constitution makes treaties the law of the land. Therefore, an Article II treaty has the status of domestic law in addition to being international law. Courts of the United States must give effect to international law and to international agreements. A non-self-executing agreement, however, will not be given domestic effect absent implementing legislation. An agreement is non-self-executing if by its terms the agreement evinces an intent that it is not to become domestic law absent implementing legislation or if the Senate, in giving its advice and consent, or Congress in a joint resolution, expressly notes that the treaty requires implementing legislation to become effective as domestic law. In addition, there may be instances in which implementing legislation may be constitutionally required. An international agreement cannot take effect as domestic law without implementation by Congress if the agreement would achieve what lies within the exclusive law-making power of Congress under the Constitution. For example, an international agreement creating an international crime could not become part of U.S. criminal law without the appropriate congressional enactment.[23]

As noted above, both custom and treaties are part of U.S. law as well as of international law. Custom and treaties, both primary sources of international law, are of equal authority in the international realm. Absent the expression of intention to the contrary, the later in time rule applies to resolving conflicts between custom and treaty: a rule established by treaty will displace a prior inconsistent customary norm, except if the prior custom is a peremptory norm from which no agreement can derogate. Conversely, if there is a clear intent, a later customary norm will supersede a prior inconsistent conventional obligation.[24]

Similarly, there is a later in time rule that applies in instances of inconsistency between a U.S. domestic norm and an international norm—be it customary or conventional. Under the Constitution, treaties and statutes are coequal, much like treaties and custom are coequal. Article VI of the Constitution, the Supremacy Clause, creates this relationship. Specifically, the article provides that "this Constitution, and the laws of the United States which shall be made in pursuance thereof; and all treaties made, or which shall be made, under the authority of the United States, shall be the supreme law of the land."

Thus, given their coequal status, if congressional intent is clear, a later congressional act supersedes an earlier international norm. In this regard, two observations are appropriate. One, unless there is a clear intent to the contrary, domestic rules will be interpreted as far as possible to be consonant with existing binding international norms. Consequently, the later in time rule will be applied so as not to conflict with international law. Two, even if the clear congressional intent exists to supersede the international norm, while as a matter of domestic law the new domestic norm is binding in U.S. domestic courts, the rule of international law that is superseded domestically is still binding on the state internationally and the state remains internationally obligated to obey the norm.

The later in time rule also operates when a treaty is adopted that has a provision that conflicts with existing domestic law or treaty so that the later in time prevails. In effect, a later treaty—and in the United States this includes all its functional equivalents, such as the sole executive agreement and the executive agreement plus joint resolution—can supersede domestic law so long as the subject matter lies within the constitutional authority of the body or bodies concluding the agreement. If the agreement's scope lies beyond the powers of the entity concluding the agreement, however, it will not supersede a prior norm made with full authority.[25] For example, a sole executive agreement concerning a trade embargo, which is a subject matter that constitutionally lies within the jurisdiction of Congress under the provision governing the regulation of commerce with foreign nations, will not be "later in time" so as to supersede a prior domestic law or a prior treaty.

Finally, a brief note on federalism is appropriate. Because treaties and custom are within the federal government's jurisdiction, any inconsistent state law or policy, regardless of whether it is earlier or later in time to the federal policy, will fail. Such was the fate of a Massachusetts law seeking to forbid trade with Burma because of that nation's human rights record.[26]

With these basic rules of international law and with some foundational interpretive tools for establishing the relationship between international and domestic norms, we now review the general concepts of trade (chapter 2), human rights (chapter 3), and their intersection (chapter 4). Subsequent chapters will study particular human rights in light of this extensive background.

2

Pillars and Escape Hatches
Basic Concepts of International Trade Law in the Americas

2.1   Overview of the GATT and WTO

This chapter discusses the fundamental premises and economic underpinnings of the global trading system that are necessary for the reader to appreciate the varied interactions of trade and human rights law.[1]

We described the General Introduction how trade law and human rights law developed along parallel tracks after the Second World War. The same horrors of war that inspired the founding of the United Nations and the development of modern human rights law, discussed in chapter 3, also led finance ministers of the world's leading trading nations to gather in Bretton Woods, New Hampshire, in 1947 to establish global cooperative financial and economic institutions. Such an initiative was not entirely new; states have used rules to regulate trade at least since the Middle Ages in the form of bilateral treaties of navigation and commerce. The first serious attempt to create global economic rules, however, followed formation of the United Nations. The Bretton Woods system that resulted included the International Monetary Fund (IMF) to govern exchange rate policy and the World Bank to function as the central source for reconstruction and development funds. Trade ministers later fashioned the third leg of this economic and financial stool in Havana with the drafting of rules for transborder commercial relations.

While it is not surprising that the Second World War's human atrocities led to stronger rights of the individual in the form of human rights treaties, it is not quite so intuitive that the war's nightmares also inspired economic change. The connection that world leaders perceived between the inferno that the world had just experienced and future economic policy among nation states was the severe inward turn toward protectionism

during the late-1920s Great Depression. Leaders traced protectionist policies directly to the rise of fascist regimes in nations isolated after the First
World War. The initial economic instrument, the General Agreement on
Tariffs and Trade (GATT), was seriously flawed. Critics noted aptly that it
possessed neither sheriff nor jail, yet it succeeded in bringing together in
a single document the basic rules to be applied when countries wished to
restrict the free flow of goods across borders.

The general rule was that trade was to be unrestricted, except in the
specified situations, and under the enumerated conditions, described in
the treaty. The exceptions included tariffs—border taxes—that the rules
permitted Members to charge on a product's importation. Other exceptions to unhindered trade involved the kinds of licenses with which
Members could limit imports, the technical standards to which they could
subject products, and the proper remedy for "unfairly traded" imports—
dumped and subsidized goods.

In 1995, almost half a century after the historic Bretton Woods meeting,
trade ministers created the WTO as the umbrella organization to administer the nearly two dozen agreements that became annexes to its Charter.
This marked completion of the process begun by the GATT to form both
a central organization to administer global trade rules and a dispute settlement system to interpret them. Because of the WTO, and the seven wide-
ranging rounds of multilateral GATT trade negotiations that preceded its
creation, detailed WTO Agreements now provide an elaborate set of rules
spanning a broad range of subjects to govern how Members must act in the
global marketplace. Negotiators prescribed rules for trade in agriculture and
in textiles and for national laws governing subsidies, dumping, intellectual
property rights, investment, and customs procedures applied at the border. Ministers established detailed procedures for "safeguard" actions that
Members may take temporarily to protect domestic industries from import
surges, for border protections against unsafe or unsanitary products, and a
separate agreement governing the mushrooming trade in services.

2.2   Economic Underpinnings: Comparative Advantage

(A)   Introduction

World trading rules are based on the concept of comparative advantage, described by British economist David Ricardo at a time nearly two
hundred years ago when the sun never set on the British Empire. How

does this theory help us understand why nations will export some products and import others, rather than simply producing all products domestically, which would render unnecessary any international trade?

(B)   Absolute Advantage

In 1776 in *The Wealth of Nations*, Adam Smith introduced the theory of absolute advantage that set the stage for Ricardo's brilliant and powerful further observation forty years later.[2] Adam Smith analogized an individual worker to a country: If Worker A is more skilled than Worker B at making coats, and Worker B is more skilled than Worker A at making shoes, then Worker A will sell coats to Worker B and use the proceeds to purchase shoes from Worker B, rather than making both coats and shoes. It is cheaper—that is, more economically efficient—for Worker A to do so. We may say that Worker A has an absolute advantage over Worker B in the production of coats. By the same logic, Worker B has an absolute advantage over Worker A in the production of shoes.

Analogously, if Country A's climate is ideally suited for growing grapes, but its workforce is not sufficiently trained to assemble computer chips, whereas Country B has a highly trained labor force but is located in the far North—a climate unwelcoming to grapes—we may say that Country A has an absolute advantage, in relation to Country B, in the production of wine. Country B has an absolute advantage over Country A in the production of computer chips. Therefore, Country A should not make both wine and computer chips. Country A will find that it is "cheaper" to export wine to Country B in order to earn the foreign exchange needed to buy Country B's computer chips. In this way, the income of both countries will be highest.

In transitioning to Ricardo's comparative advantage, it is important first to define "cheaper" in economic terms: Country A's "opportunity costs" are lower. Opportunity cost describes the trade-offs that a country makes in choosing to produce with its finite resources one product instead of another; we may think of them as lost opportunities. So when we say that it is "cheaper," or economically more efficient for Country A to produce wine rather than computer chips, we mean that Country A's opportunity cost for making wine is lower than its opportunity cost for making computer chips. Country A will make fewer trade-offs in the production of wine than in the production of computer chips. Country A will use fewer of its finite resources.

(C)   Comparative Advantage

To introduce David Ricardo's contribution to the economics of trade, we may begin with a famous example used by economist Paul Samuelson to help us understand the comparative aspect of the theory. Suppose that a lawyer has created a court submission that must be typed and that she is a faster typist than any secretary she could hire. To use Adam Smith's terms, she has an absolute advantage in both legal and typing work. Even though she could type the submission faster than could a secretary, the theory of comparative advantage tells us that the lawyer nonetheless should hire a secretary. Why? Because the value created by her legal services is greater than the value created by her typing services.

The opportunity cost, or trade-off, that she would make by spending an hour typing is the three hundred dollars that she could earn by performing legal work, which is greater than the opportunity cost of spending that hour on legal work (she has "lost" the lower value of secretarial earnings). Even though the attorney has an absolute advantage, then, in typing—she is faster at typing than anyone she could hire—and thus the typing will be slower, the total value created by the legal office will be greater if the lawyer sticks to her legal work. Translating this concept to international trade means that if each country produces only those goods in which it has a comparative advantage, nations together will create greater world wealth. Trade allows countries to specialize in the goods and services in which they are the most efficient producers. Such specialization will raise the gross domestic products (GDPs) of all trading partners. Consumer standards of living for this reason are higher in an atmosphere of open trade than when government measures artificially restrict trade.

Another example demonstrates that in a world of perfectly competitive markets, trade will be beneficial to countries whenever there are relative differences in costs of production. In Country A, one hour of labor produces six bushels of wheat or four bushels of corn. In Country B, that hour results in one bushel of wheat or two bushels of corn. Using only Adam Smith's observations, we would conclude that Country A has an absolute advantage as to Country B in the production both of wheat and of corn. Does this mean that trade cannot benefit Country B at all and that it should simply leave production of wheat and corn to Country A? Because of David Ricardo, we know that the answer is no, because Country A's absolute advantage in wheat production (six bushels to one) is greater than its absolute advantage in corn production (four bushels to two). In other words, Country A has a comparative advantage in wheat as compared with corn.

What may we conclude about Country B? Of course, Country B is at an absolute disadvantage as to both wheat and corn, but its labor force is one-sixth as productive as to wheat and one-half as productive as to corn. That is, Country B has a comparative advantage, in relation to Country A, in the production of corn. According to the principle of comparative advantage, both countries will benefit if Country A trades its wheat for Country B's corn.

2.3   Four Pillars of GATT

(A)   Relevance of Comparative Advantage

We learn first about comparative advantage in our exploration of the basic concepts of international trade because the drafters designed global trade rules to allow countries to make full use of their comparative advantage by removing government impediments to the free movement of goods and services. Thus, comparative advantage is a foundational theoretical assumption, a structural basis, of the trade system. Ministers provided in that first basic instrument of global trade rules, the GATT of 1947, and continued in 1995 in the WTO, that the principle of nondiscrimination should underpin trade. That is, WTO Members must treat goods from all other Members alike.

In basing global trading rules on a principle of equal treatment among all partners, trade powers left behind the mercantilist approach of the 18th century that demanded close state intervention to maintain favorable trade balances.[3] Even more significantly, states turned away from a basic principle of sovereignty: that a state is free to treat others in a discriminatory fashion if the state believes that such action serves its best interests.[4] Viewed through the lens of sovereignty, abandonment of the state's ability to choose among its trading partners the ones on which the state would bestow preferences counts as notable recognition of the political as well as economic importance of Ricardo's theory. This principle of trading relations helps remove state intervention in the trading process.

(B)   Most-favored Nation and National Treatment Clauses

The two aspects of the nondiscrimination principle are codified in the first and third articles of the GATT (see Item 7 in the online Documents

Annex); they are also the first two basic concepts of trade, or the Four Pillars of GATT—the more colorful phrase often used by GATT experts. Article I, called the Most-favored Nation Clause (MFN), explains how WTO Members must treat imported products originating in the territory of one Member in relation to imported products of other Members. Article III, called the National Treatment Clause, prescribes the manner in which Members must treat imported products in relation to domestic products.

Article I provides that if a WTO Member gives a benefit or privilege to any country, it must automatically and unconditionally grant that same benefit to every other WTO Member. The reference to most-favored, then, means that the importing Member must provide equal treatment for imports of a product from, and exports of that product to, all Members based on the treatment that it gives its most-favored trading partner with respect to that product. The United States might negotiate with Mexico a lower tariff for imports of Mexico's shrimp in return for Mexico's granting U.S. exports of computer software a lower import duty. But if a WTO Member not involved in that negotiation—for example, Japan—then exports shrimp to the United States or computer software to Mexico, the United States and Mexico must, without cost or conditions, give Japan the full benefit of the tariff reductions negotiated between Mexico and the United States, despite the fact that those reductions were based on reciprocal concessions only of Mexico and the United States. The MFN nondiscrimination principle results at once, and following but a single negotiation, in reductions in trade barriers by the United States and Mexico on two products for the 150 other WTO Members.

The National Treatment Clause has the same effect. As the name suggests, the requirement of Article III is that once foreign goods have entered the stream of commerce, Members must treat them in the same manner as Members treat "like" domestic products. "Like products" are goods similar in physical characteristics and uses to the imported goods. WTO Members must accord similar treatment only to like domestic goods. Members, for example, need not treat tractors in the same manner as they treat lawnmowers. National treatment means that the national or local government could not require that a wine from Spain, once it has satisfied tariff obligations at the border, be sold only in liquor stores, if the rules allow a like California wine to be sold in grocery stores as well. The Spanish wine also could not be subject to a California alcoholic beverages tax that did not apply equally to the California wine. Officials must regulate the Spanish wine's sale, distribution, transportation, and use in the same manner as the California wine, and must impose similar taxes on the imported wine.

(C)   Third and Fourth Pillars: Tariffs Bound and Quotas Outlawed

Article II of the GATT embodies the Third Pillar. Each WTO Member makes a commitment to charge no more than a certain tariff on a particular import. As in our Mexican shrimp example, countries will continue to negotiate these tariff reductions based on reciprocity. For example, if the United States buys most of its lumber from Canada and sells to Canada most of its computers, U.S. computer makers and Canadian lumber mills still benefit most from the lowered border taxes of lumber and computers, even though the MFN Clause will create "free riders" from other WTO countries.

Article II refers to the thousands of pages of these schedules of concessions on tariffs for hundreds of products. These tariffs are then "bound." That is, the Member can charge a lower tariff if it wishes (and often does in order to gain the advantage of a lower tariff on a product that the Member wishes to export to a particular market), but the Member cannot charge a higher tariff than that set out in its schedule of concessions.

The Fourth Pillar of the GATT, Article XI, creates a basket of disciplines to address most other barriers to the free reign of Ricardo's theory with its sweeping general prohibition of all other border restrictions on importation or exportation of products that other GATT articles do not permit. Article XI thus prohibits, for example, quotas or other restrictions on the volume of a product that can be imported or exported, as well as licensing systems that act as barriers to the exportation or importation of products.

Article XI effectively provides that there may be no restrictions on the import or export of a product except those permitted elsewhere in the WTO. Article XI itself lists two exceptions: import duties—tariffs—which of course are regulated by Article II; and taxes and other charges, regulated by Article III.

(D)   A Closer Look at National Treatment and Like Products

A fuller examination of the Third Pillar and the concept of like products will aid our understanding of the Pillars. After eight rounds of GATT negotiations on import duties and other trade barriers, tariffs—in developed countries at least—no longer constitute significant restrictions to the free movement of goods across national borders. Most disputes over the Pillars thus revolve around the complex rules requiring equal conditions of competition for imported and domestic like products. Understanding the like product concept is necessary to appreciate operation of the Pillars and most other aspects of global trade rules. The term is critical in nine articles of the GATT and three other WTO Agreements, so it comes up repeatedly in studying the relationship between trade and human rights.

The decision by the WTO Appellate Body—the Supreme Court of world trade—in the *EC-Asbestos* case offers the clearest explanation of the like product concept in a GATT Article III context that implicates human rights concerns. Canadian asbestos producers awoke one morning to find that France had shut down a major export market for their asbestos insulation through a total ban on all products containing asbestos, which it justified on human health grounds, citing evidence that asbestos is a known carcinogen. Although the ban applied both to foreign imports and to domestic production, the second article of the decree made an exception for importation and production of asbestos that had no substitutes.

Canadian producers were not amused to learn that the decree effectively banned only the type of chrysotile or white asbestos that they produced, because polyvinyl alcohol and cement-based substitutes existed for Canada's type of asbestos. French companies were the leading producers of these polyvinyl alcohol- and cement-based articles, while Canada produced virtually none. Although it made other arguments, including that the ban violated the WTO Agreement on Technical Barriers to Trade (TBT), which prevents countries from disguising trade barriers as product safety standards, Canada's most potent claim was that the French ban discriminated between imported and domestic products in violation of Article III:4 of the GATT.

Paragraph 1 of Article III sets out a general statement of policy that dispute settlement panels have held "informs" the rest of the article, including Paragraph 4, which does not even mention it. The Members recognize in Paragraph 1 that they cannot apply taxes and regulations "so as to afford protection to domestic production." That statement, incidentally, is the purpose of almost every GATT provision—to ensure that Members do not nullify or override their Article II agreement to reduce tariffs on products by imposing nontariff barriers that have the same effect of restricting trade.

Thus, when Paragraph 1 states that the purpose of Article III is to prevent Members from protecting "domestic production," the reference is not to all domestic production, but only to those products that compete with the imported product. Article III requires examination of the competitive relationship between the two products at issue. Paragraph 2 converts this general language into a specific prohibition against assessing internal taxes or other charges on imported products in excess of such charges collected on like domestic products. Paragraph 4 addresses the specific measures at issue in the *EC-Asbestos* case by imposing essentially the same obligation with respect to regulations and other requirements affecting the internal sale of imported products.[5]

The Appellate Body's report in *EC-Asbestos* points out that the initial panel had found that the asbestos products and their PVA substitutes are "like products" and that France had treated the imported asbestos products "less favorably" than their domestic substitutes by totally banning the imports. France could not have mounted a viable argument against a finding of violation of Article III:4 under these facts if it had accepted the panel's finding that the products were "like." In fact, the parties did not even bother to argue this point on appeal. France, through the European Communities (EC), did argue that the panel improperly had found that the products were "like" within the meaning of Article III:4.

If the two products were not "like," France could not have violated Article III by treating them differently. For example, if the United States tests imported beef for foot-and-mouth disease, but performs no such test on domestic chickens, it has not violated the national treatment obligation. A WTO Member need not treat chickens and cows alike, nor must it regulate baseballs similarly to computers. Therefore, if the EC could convince the Appellate Body that the two products were not "like," then it could work a narrowing of Article III's requirement to provide national treatment, with the result that a greater number of safety measures could be imposed on imports.

The initial panel analysis of the term employed the four general criteria recognized in a 1970 Working Party Report on Border Tax Adjustments: (1) the physical characteristics of the two sets of products (one deck baluster is made of wood, the other of vinyl), (2) the end uses of the products (polyurethane foam for attic insulation or for beer coolers), (3) consumer expectations (would the purchaser complain if hot-dip galvanized fasteners are substituted for the specified stainless steel fasteners), and (4) the tariff classification of the products (electric typewriters might be in one tariff group, charged a 5 percent tariff, while computer keyboards might be in another, charged 3 percent). Each of these criteria would be relevant in an examination whether two products are competing for the same buyer and no single criterion would necessarily outweigh the others.

The initial *EC-Asbestos* panel's analysis gave compelling weight to the end-use criterion. The panel reasoned that, although the asbestos products and their substitutes were not physically identical—in that they had a different chemical composition, and in fact asbestos was unique—their end uses were the same for some applications. In effect, the panel concluded that their properties were effectively equivalent under Article III:4, which aims to prevent parties from using internal measures to protect domestic industry.

The panel explicitly declined to consider the health "risk" of the product as a separate criterion, reasoning that if it did so the other criteria would become meaningless, because the health risk clearly would overshadow other physical differences, as well as the other "like product" criteria. The panel almost had it right with this comment. Tellingly for purposes of this volume, the panel also found that taking account of the health risk would make the Public Health exceptions of Article XX superfluous. The Appellate Body examined the findings of the panel regarding the carcinogenicity of asbestos, noting that the types of cancer that it caused had a 100 percent mortality rate. Its conclusion from the assessment was that the toxicity of asbestos was indeed a "defining aspect" of the product, one that hardly could be overlooked when determining whether two products had the same physical characteristics. The Appellate Body also noted that under the criterion of consumer expectations, a manufacturer choosing among alternative inputs certainly would not be indifferent to the fact that one caused cancer and the other did not.

Having found that the products were physically distinguishable, that consumer expectations were likely to be significantly different, and that the panel simply had concluded without much analysis that the end uses of the products sometimes were the same, the Appellate Body found that asbestos and its substitutes were not like products within the meaning of Article III:4. France thus had not acted inconsistently with that article. One wonders if the Appellate Body did not have in mind how useful its narrowing of Article III might be to a Member looking for other ways to protect health and the environment, and perhaps other human rights as well, without being found to have violated the WTO Agreements.

(E)   If It Quacks Like a Duck

A GATT dispute panel reminds us of another principle applicable to Article III's discipline on internal regulations and taxes. Some countries collect internal taxes or impose internal regulations—for administrative purposes—at the border, rather than waiting for the imported product to clear customs procedures by payment of the appropriate tariff and meeting other importation rules. These countries find it easier to take care of everything at once while the product is still seeking permission to enter its customs territory. The drafters of GATT Article III recognized this fact by providing in a Supplementary Note to Article III (see Item 7 in the online Documents Annex) that these charges or regulations nonetheless are "internal" and must therefore be consistent with Article III. The nature of the regulation, not its point of collection, determines whether the WTO Member must apply national treatment principles to the product.

2.4   Exceptions to the Pillars

Left alone, the Four Pillars would ensure virtually unrestricted trade, the perfect realization of Ricardo's principle. Members do not, of course, leave them alone. Members do not wish to accept imported food with unsafe ingredients, or heaters that blow up in the consumer's face, or cocaine arriving on container ships, or trade surges that bankrupt domestic industries in need of a reasonable period to become internationally competitive. Trade is never, then, completely "free." The Four Pillars of GATT are by no means without exception. The most important exception authorizes FTAs or customs unions such as NAFTA or the European Union (EU). Parties to such an agreement are permitted by the WTO to violate the Pillars by discriminating against WTO Members who are not parties to the Agreement, for example, by not granting other WTO Members the benefit of the reduced tariffs that characterize all FTAs. Because such agreements now number about three hundred and cover nearly half of all world trade, bilateral and regional economic preferences are a significant deviation from the GATT, justified on the ground that FTAs and customs unions have major multilateral wealth building effects.[6]

Notably, the WTO permits Members to erect trade barriers in their implementation of human rights law. Article XX of the GATT creates a set of General Exceptions authorizing Members to restrict trade under certain conditions in order to protect public health and welfare. We address these exceptions, and their strict conditions, in some detail in section 6.5. Paragraph (a) (public morals), Paragraph (b) (public health), and Paragraph (g) (exhaustible natural resources) provide fertile ground for affirmation of the primacy of human rights policies over economic considerations. Article XX articulates general exceptions. That is, once the conditions are met, "nothing in this Agreement shall be construed to prevent the[ir] adoption or enforcement by a Member." Scholars have emphasized the narrow and begrudging interpretations of early GATT and WTO dispute settlement panels that set unnecessary barriers in the path of human rights enforcement, particularly in the sphere of environmental protection. We prefer to herald the amazingly broad reach that the 1947 drafters gave to these powerful provisions.

In particular, consider the Public Morals Clause of Article XX(a). Members have imposed frequent trade restrictions based on the "immorality" of activities in other countries. These restrictions have ranged from prohibitions on trade with countries practicing or condoning slavery to bans on importation of child pornography. The exception is broad enough to justify trade restrictions to encourage countries to abandon denial of freedom of the press, to allow their citizens to emigrate, to forbid work by indentured children, and to provide a remedy for other human rights violations, especially when a consistent pattern of such violations by the country are evident. In Antigua's challenge to U.S. prohibition of Internet gambling, the WTO's Appellate Body—the World Trade Court[7] (WTC)—interpreted the equivalent Public Morals Clause in the General Agreement on Trade in Services (GATS), which sets rules for trade in services as opposed to the trade in goods regulated by the GATT and the other WTO Agreements. The WTC left undisturbed the broad definition of public morals advanced by the panel below: "'Public morals' denotes standards of right and wrong conduct maintained by or on behalf of a community or nation."[8] If the restrictive border measure unmistakably implements a human rights objective, our opinion is that few aspects of human rights law could not qualify as enforcing a Member's "standards of right and wrong," and thus fall, under this interpretation, within the policy addressed by the Public Morals Clause. We should think this result especially likely in view of the explicit charge by the UN Charter that Members promote human rights.

The Appellate Body explicitly noted the relevance of its analysis to the similar Public Morals Clause of GATT Article XX.[9] We detail in section 6.4 the additional conditions that a Member must meet for full exemption, but we are confident that the *U.S.-Gambling* case takes an important step toward integrating human rights policies into the economic ends of the WTO Agreements. Importantly, the WTC has situated the General Exceptions on an equal plane with the Four Pillars, requiring that panels strike a balance in interpretation so that neither cancels out the other.[10] The Court thus has effortlessly brought customary and other non-WTO international law into the room with WTO dispute panels and reminded panels that they must interpret "evolutionary" language in the 1947 treaty in light of contemporary concerns of the community of nations, taking advantage of other precepts of international law, including the opinions of the ICJ.[11]

We take considerable comfort in these interpretations of the General Exceptions, which verify the wide berth that WTO Members have given themselves to implement human rights policies and the direction that the WTC has extended to panels to find guidance in the broader precepts of international law in their analysis of claims that Members have violated the WTO Agreements.

Article VI contains another important exception that permits Members to restrict trade in unfair imports, as defined by the WTO Anti-dumping and Subsidies Agreements. These Agreements treat imports as unfair if exporters "dump" them (i.e., sell the goods at a lower price for export than they sell them in the home market, or for a price that is below their cost of production). The Agreements also identify as unfair products that benefit from targeted government subsidies, because the subsidy gives them an artificial comparative advantage in trade.

The WTO TBT Agreement and the Sanitary and Phytosanitary Measures (SPS) Agreement (treated in detail in sections 7.4 and 6.6) provide increasingly important road maps to Members that desire to restrict trade in pursuit of the protection of human life or health and the environment at the level that the Member considers appropriate. Through these and other exceptions, the apparently straightforward Pillars of the GATT become more complex than at first they seemed: (a) Article XI proscribes restrictions on imports or exports; (b) successive rounds of multilateral negotiations have substantially reduced tariffs, which Members then "bind" at the lower rate under Article II; and (c) articles I and III ensure through nondiscrimination that the benefits and privileges of local trading accords will be spread to all WTO Members, thus accelerating trading wealth across all Members. GATT's Four Pillars have spawned many exceptions, some quite logical and consistent with the Pillars themselves, others needed to carve out a place within global trading rules for a precious package of continuously developing human rights policies.

2.5 WTO Dispute Settlement

As we would expect with twenty-seven thousand pages of trade rules, Members frequently have disputes over their interpretation and compliance. The centerpiece of the WTO is its powerful dispute settlement system, with its singular international law triumph of automatic adoption of dispute panel reports. Unlike the situation during the GATT's first fifty years, the losing Member no longer may block implementation of a panel's decision. Members of course still are sovereign states and may choose not to implement a panel's "recommendations." Noncompliant Members, however, now will suffer substantial financial pain in the form of trade retaliation by the winning Member for trade lost through the violative border measure. In almost every instance during the first ten years of the WTO's operation, permission by a dispute panel to retaliate has been sufficient to convince the losing Member to bring its measure into compliance with a panel recommendation.

By contrast, during the first fifty years of trade dispute settlement, GATT parties authorized retaliation in only one instance (as it happens, against the United States for its dairy quotas), which illustrates the diplomacy-driven nature of the early years of trade dispute settlement. Virtually automatic adoption of panel reports operates by "reverse consensus." Unless a consensus exists to reject the report, WTO Members acting jointly as the Dispute Settlement Body must accept every panel report (or the Appellate Body's report after appeal, which is also an automatic right). A consensus rejection of the report must include the winning Member, because reverse consensus is defined to mean that no Member present formally objects. We are confident that Members will refuse only an egregiously ill-reasoned "outlaw" report—that is, one whose adverse impact on other programs would more than offset its favorable effects in the actions under dispute. In fact, Members have yet to reject a report, although in an instance in which both the winning and losing Members equally feared the future effects of a panel's broad opinion, disputants agreed not to appeal the decision so that future panels could more easily ignore the ruling.[12] As with all international dispute resolution, neither panel nor Appellate Body reports create binding precedent, although future panels or later Appellate Body decisions rarely disagree with Appellate Body reports.

A useful holdover from GATT dispute settlement, in which only positive consensus satisfactorily could end a formal disagreement among Members, is that the purpose of dispute settlement remains "a positive solution." While the adjudicatory systems after which its creators patterned WTO dispute settlement emphasize winners and losers, the WTO's Dispute Settlement Understanding (DSU) repeatedly facilitates crafting of a mutually agreed solution that is consistent with WTO law. This central theme explains as well the four complex stages of WTO dispute settlement (good offices, conciliation, and mediation also are available, but are not used): consultations (sixty days), panel consideration (six to nine months, longer in technical cases), appeal (if desired) of the panel's decision (sixty to ninety days), and, finally, implementation of the decision's "recommendations" through the losing Member's legislative or regulatory rescission of the offending border measure (up to fifteen months, sometimes extended). The DSU provides precious little guidance to panels beyond charging them to make "an objective assessment of the matter," which is perhaps the minimalist approach required in melding the civil and common law systems of WTO Members. In these circumstances, we should marvel that panels have achieved the high level of legal discourse that we may find in their more than two hundred opinions. This achievement is even more notable in light of the almost certainly conflicting requirement on one hand "to clarify" provisions of the WTO Agreements while adhering to the dictate, on the other, that they "cannot add to or diminish the rights and obligations provided" in those Agreements.[13]

The WTC has begun not only to create a substantial body of international trade law, but also to have impact on public international law generally. This result flows from the essentially binding nature of its decisions and the increasingly broader reach of the WTO's disciplines. Some commentators, in fact, have argued that its system of settling disputes elevates international trade law to a unique category in relation to other international law, because its rules are enforceable dictates, not aspirations, guidelines, or policies. Some analysts believe the WTO dispute settlement system to be the most sophisticated in international law and its decisions, "by almost any criteria imaginable, . . . far more important than the work of all the other" international adjudicatory bodies.[14] In any event, the automaticity of the process makes WTO dispute settlement a potent alternative in the business world to traditional arbitration or litigation in foreign courts.

2.6   *Trade in the Americas*

(A)   Commonality of Interests

Professor Hernández-Truyol has observed that the constraint of international treaties reaches beyond local laws.[15] Both global and local rules, of whatever nature, must yield to human rights law.[16] This observation not only has powerful relevance in the trade field, but we believe that it is in local and regional trade rules that negotiators may expect to make the most significant progress in crafting a purposeful intersection of these two pervasive areas of law and policy. To understand why this is so, let us first ask why Chile would be more likely to sign a free trade agreement with Peru than with Great Britain. Geographically, they are neighbors, so trade between them is inevitable; they speak the same language, so communication is easier; they share the same civil law history, so their legal systems will be similar; they are Southern Pacific Ocean nations whose citizens engage in many of the same occupations because of similar natural resources.

In other words, regional trade agreements always involve more than economics. They are about culture, foreign policy, and national security. The Declaration of Principles of the First Summit of the Americas in 1994 initiated negotiations toward a Free Trade Area of the Americas (FTAA). Among its goals is promotion of democracy as "the sole political system which guarantees respect for human rights and the rule of law." The 1994 Declaration also seeks elimination of discrimination in the Hemisphere, holding that "it is politically intolerable and morally unacceptable that some segments of our populations are marginalized and do not share fully in the benefits of growth." Finally, the Declaration aims to strengthen the role of women, stating that doing so "in all aspects of political, social, and economic life in our countries is essential to reduce poverty and social inequalities and to enhance democracy and sustainable development."[17]

(B)   North American Trade Agreements

Regional trade agreements, we have noted, reach far beyond economics. More positively, we could say that trade is an aspect of myriad other policies, and trade negotiators must not fall into the easy operational pretense that trade operates in a vacuum. FTAs identify countries that are comfortable forging closer economic, as well as social and cultural, ties. For these reasons, regional trade agreements carry the potential to resolve the human rights and trade dilemma earlier than global agreements can do so. The comfort level created by a commonality of interests leads to greater willingness to experiment. For example, Article 104 of NAFTA, among Canada, Mexico, and the United States, explicitly identifies the multilateral environmental agreements that will take priority in the event of a conflict with a NAFTA provision.[18] Because all three NAFTA parties have ratified these environmental agreements, they had no interest in allowing their regional trade obligations to interfere.

This kind of commonality—and thus solution—is virtually impossible at the WTO level of 150-plus states. Because of its reliance on nondiscrimination, trade liberalization requires breaking down access barriers to a country's market, which in turn leaves domestic actors unprotected from exporting companies with a comparative advantage in the domestically produced good. From a political standpoint, leaders far more easily may justify to their citizens according greater access to companies in neighboring countries, some of which may be joint ventures that include local businesses, as was frequently the case—for example, in the automotive industry—between Canada and the United States long before the U.S.-Canada FTA that preceded the NAFTA.

NAFTA of 1993 is in many areas a precedent-setting achievement. NAFTA was the first trade agreement to cover services such as computer software or engineering, as opposed solely to goods such as machine tools or soybeans. The services field is a critical one for the United States that accounts for close to three-quarters of its GDP.[19] NAFTA also was the first to address the intersections between trade and the environment and between trade and labor. The treaty contains the most expansive rights ever given to private investors. At Canada's insistence, the agreement also places limits on trade based on preserving a country's culture, as reflected, for example, in its magazines and films. We shall see in chapter 11 the importance of safeguarding culture in protecting the human rights of indigenous populations. Finally, NAFTA initiated unique dispute settlement systems, including one that later treaties have yet to emulate, which ceded judicial sovereignty to binational panels that act in the place of domestic courts with equal powers over administrative agencies.[20]

(C)   Caribbean and Central and South American Agreements

The move toward regional or bilateral trade agreements with neighboring states began in Latin America, as elsewhere, in the late 1950s, although those early efforts hardly were free trade models. Regional economic integration to foster economies of scale yielded in those days to the protectionist economic policies then in vogue. For regional economic integration to work, the FTA parties ultimately must test the economies of scale built through opening the larger FTA market to competition among FTA parties by lowering external barriers to bring in world competition. Only in this way may companies in the internal market, strengthened by the FTA's promotion of scale efficiencies, be tested against the world's players to make them even more efficient or, alternatively, to convince the domestic companies to pursue other interests. That second step never happened for the first forty years of Latin American economic integration. Only after Latin American governments abandoned the discredited isolationist policy in the 1990s did today's powerful models for regional integration begin to emerge. These integration agreements have created some of the world's most active and efficient companies.

Not all agree with the desirability of this growth. Critics point to these companies as behemoths of globalization that serve to enlarge the income gap not only between rich and poor people within countries but also between rich and poor states, flame the race to the bottom, and displace local businesses, including small subsistence agricultural farms. This volume seeks to find ways to retain NAFTA's benefits while ameliorating its adverse effects.

Second only to the NAFTA in economic strength in the Hemisphere is the Common Market of the South (MERCOSUR in Spanish), which initially brought together the four countries of Eastern South America—Brazil, Argentina, Paraguay, and Uruguay. Venezuela is a recent adherent, although its basis for switching from the Andean pact has more to do with populist politics than economic considerations, a motivation that also describes Bolivia's renewed attention to MERCOSUR. With the exception of certain products, in 1995 the treaty created a customs union—an FTA with a common external tariff—and the parties have made progress in harmonization of a number of further economic integration and environmental protection matters.

MERCOSUR is the earliest example of the change in economic philosophy from protectionist to free trade. Its objective was not to encourage industrial development behind high tariff walls, known as import substitution industrialization, but to promote the concept of comparative advantage by encouraging each party to specialize in—and export—those goods that it could produce most efficiently. For this reason, MERCOSUR requires that parties keep their external tariffs—duties charged to non-parties—low so that the output of MERCOSUR countries will remain internationally competitive. As a result, we could not easily name an industry in which Brazil, Argentina, and, to a lesser extent, Paraguay and Uruguay did not have one or more of the leading companies. Brazil since 1994 has been the Latin American powerhouse on the other side of the table with the United States and Mexico determining Hemispheric trade policy.

In 1992 the northwestern states of South America—Venezuela, Colombia, Ecuador, Peru, and Bolivia—formed the free trade area now known as the Andean Community of Nations (CAN in Spanish), which is well on its way to becoming a customs union. There have been some false starts, and some setbacks, most notably Peru's suspension from the pact for three years when it slid back into military rule, but the Andean Commission now is responsible for an increasing array of economic functions of the parties, including a judicial function for trade matters that has had a unifying effect. The recent bolting from the CAN of Venezuela under Hugo Chávez, and Bolivia's threats to do the same following the election of Evo Morales, initially suggested a crumbling of the bloc. Chile's quick movement to fill some of the gaps, the continuation of most business ventures that previously existed, and new trade ties with the United States by the remaining Andean states, however, support confidence in the continued strength of the CAN, even as Chávez transforms Venezuela from a democratic to an authoritarian populist state.

The Central American nations of Guatemala, Honduras, El Salvador, Nicaragua, Costa Rica, and Panama signed the treaty creating the Central American Common Market (MCCA in Spanish) in 1991. Panama has yet formally to ratify the pact, but the other MCCA parties nonetheless extend to Panama the reduced tariff benefits. The MCCA has been a model of the new economics underpinning Latin American trade agreements, because the FTA has increased significantly both trade flows among the parties and the region's exports to the rest of the world.

(D)   Regional Negotiating Blocs

Another phenomenon has multiplied the economic and political impacts of these regional trade arrangements. Once these basic FTAs were completed, the parties often negotiated as a unit in other free trade forums, both bilaterally and with other blocs, thus creating a dizzying array of interlocking economic structures, some more important than others. Mexico, Canada, and the United States, on the other hand, despite the commonality of their membership in the NAFTA, always negotiate as separate countries, never as part of a NAFTA bloc, which illustrates a major difference between the NAFTA and these other major Hemispheric agreements. The NAFTA parties seek no greater economic integration than reduction of trading barriers among themselves on all products and services. While this is an ambitious goal, to be sure, it is nonetheless substantially unlike the objective of full economic—and deeper—integration sought by the other FTAs in the Hemisphere.

For example, MCCA seeks the free movement of labor and a monetary union, both forbidden subjects in the North. Before we discuss the most ambitious regional negotiation of them all, we should examine the Hemispheric free trade loners. Chile, despite its negotiation of FTAs with the three parties to the NAFTA, did so one country at a time. Since withdrawing from the CAN in 1976, Chile has negotiated alone, despite its small size, a result of a very early opening of its markets and its reliance on trade as the engine of its impressive economic growth. Chile does not burn bridges, however, and has partially filled the chasm created by Venezuela's apparent transfer under Hugo Chávez to MERCOSUR.[21] In 2006 it accepted associate membership in the CAN, complementing its similar status in MERCOSUR that is shared by MERCOSUR's other neighbors in the CAN.

(E) Cuba, the Noncountry

Then there is Cuba. Cuba exports many products successfully, such as sugar, cigars, rum, and citrus, but because of its long reliance for subsidies first on the United States until 1959 (sugar) and then the Soviet Union until 1993 (oil) and its unwillingness to embrace democratic principles along with the rest of the Americas (see chapter 13 on democracy), it has remained isolated economically. President Nestor Kirchner's longtime relationship with Fidel Castro resulted in the signing of a modest FTA with Argentina, and Canada and Mexico have taken advantage of the vacuum created by the fifty-year economic embargo imposed by the United States (see section 14.6) by investing nearly two billion dollars there in recent years. The real story has been Venezuela's enormous economic assistance under President Hugo Chávez in the form of subsidized oil, which Cuba then can resell for foreign exchange. Cuba thus has regained the lucrative trade in oil that it lost in 1991 when the Soviet Union stopped similar shipments, except that today the price of oil has skyrocketed to record heights.[22]

The powerful economic and political influence of the United States on Cuba that began with active U.S. engagement in Cuban affairs under the Monroe Doctrine in 1823 abruptly ended with Castro's revolution in 1959. In fact, since the day in 1961 when the United States tossed the Monroe Doctrine into the Bay of Pigs, that relationship worsened with each new Castro undertaking. First, the United States eliminated Cuba's sugar quotas and Castro responded by nationalizing agricultural property in his initial land reforms. The United States then refused to refine Russian crude after Castro tightened economic ties with the Soviet Union in the 1960s. The Helms-Burton law in 1996 initiated a virtual economic war as foreign investors started to take advantage of nationalized property once owned by Americans. Five facts seem to us incontrovertible.

First, despite Venezuela's recent rescue efforts, Cuba is today in dire economic straits, and while the extent to which the U.S. embargo has contributed is unclear, we believe that normal trade relations with the United States would substantially help Cuba rebuild its economy and alleviate the suffering of its people. Second, insofar as the purpose of the embargo was to destabilize the Castro regime, it has failed. Third, its trading partners have never fully supported the tough policy of the United States toward Cuba. While the United States at one time garnered support from the Organization of American States (OAS), even that sympathetic nod ended nearly thirty years ago and for the last decade annual UN resolutions condemning the embargo have become the norm, with even the Vatican joining the chorus in 1998. Fourth, the rest of the world indeed is investing in Cuba. The total foreign direct investment anticipated as of 1997 was over $6 billion. Ironically, NAFTA partners Canada and Mexico plan the largest investments at over $1.8 billion apiece. Finally, the reasons espoused by the United States to justify the embargo gradually have lost credibility over time. Without downplaying the risk from terrorists, while the security threat of a Cuba-Soviet alliance was real, it is harder to argue today that any country should consider the debilitated Cuban government a danger. With the peaceful passing of the ruling baton in 2006 from Fidel to his brother and "enforcer," Raúl Castro, the United States has even less reason to suppose that a continued embargo will accomplish any purpose but further the suffering of the Cuban people.[23]

Even the human rights justification often given by the U.S. government has lost some of its grip on the high ground in light of U.S. support for nondemocratic and oppressive—but anticommunist—regimes throughout Latin America and Asia, not to mention the vote to admit China into the WTO and close economic ties to Jordan, Saudi Arabia, and Turkey. President Clinton's 1994 China speech, given about the same time as the Miami Summit of the Americas that initiated FTAA talks, announced that the United States best could promote democracy and human rights through engagement, not isolation. China acceded to the WTO in 2001. Cuba, which, like the United States, negotiated the Bretton Woods Conference and was a founding member of the IMF, the World Bank, and the GATT—whose terms were negotiated in its capital in 1947—remains the only Hemispheric state not involved in its largest regional integration initiative, the creation of an FTAA.

(F)   Ultimate Hemispheric Integration: FTAA

The FTAA encompasses the 850 million people of the Western Hemispheric democracies with their combined GDP of $13 trillion, thereby surpassing the EU as the world's largest trading bloc. As we have noted, the FTAA process began when leaders of the thirty-four democracies of the Hemisphere concluded the Summit of the Americas in Miami in 1994, deciding on a range of objectives, including eradication of poverty and discrimination and strengthening democracy in the Hemisphere.

The FTAA is an ambitious negotiation with nine separate negotiating groups, and committees on smaller economies and civil society covering virtually every trade topic. There is no FTAA entity examining human rights, despite the fact that Hemispheric heads of state at the Second Summit of the Americas in Santiago in 1998 embraced promotion of the Universal Declaration of Human Rights and its regional counterpart, with particular reference to women, migrant workers, and indigenous peoples.[24] We are convinced that a basic commitment to human rights will emerge as part of a completed FTAA.

After eight productive years of work, the FTAA became a casualty of its own ambition in 2003, with Brazil effectively breaking off talks when it became clear that the United States was not going to put its huge agricultural subsidies and its powerful anti-dumping law on the negotiating table. In essence, FTAA talks are on hold until trade ministers can take these two subjects to the next liberalization as part of the WTO's Doha

Round of multilateral negotiations, which also have broken off because of protectionist pull-backs in the leading developed countries.

How may we summarize the place of regional trade agreements in the Hemisphere in the human rights and trade interface? In addition to the promise that they hold as ubiquitous instruments that may more easily than the WTO begin to address the intersection purposefully, now they serve human rights by buttressing national efforts to promote the rule of law, and with it, institutions and systems that hold government accountable for the treatment of its citizens.[25]

3

Global Laws, Local Lives

*Basic Concepts and Legal Regimes of
Human Rights Law in the Americas*

3.1 Introduction

International human rights are essential predicates to life for human beings.[1] They are rooted in moral, social, religious, legal, and political concerns for respect and dignity of individuals.[2] Such rights are vital to personhood, to a human being's identity.[3] The human rights idea is a relatively recent one. There are strong disagreements regarding whether there is a single, universally applicable concept of human rights. While some insist on such universality, others urge a culturally relative view.[4]

The evolution of international rights of persons dates to the 19th and early 20th centuries. At that time, particularly with shifting national borders, states began to enter into treaties that protected the rights of minority populations within a state. Also, treaties that abolished the practice of slavery effectively were for the protection of individuals.

The watershed events for the emergence of the human rights framework followed the unparalleled Nazi atrocities of the Second World War. After Nuremberg, for the first time individuals, and not only states, were accepted as actors in the global sphere. In the post–Second World War era individuals are both objects and subjects of international law.

This narrative about the emergence of the human rights system has been critiqued as Northern and Western in perspective and scope. In response to the criticism, however, the human rights community has enabled a platform for broader participation—a platform in which the North/West domination has begun to cede to global participation. The North and South, East and West—with women at the forefront—have started efforts to work side by side to create an inclusive blueprint for the further development of human rights in the 21st century.

The consensus documents that make up this blueprint address issues ranging from the environment to education; from universality of rights to respect for cultural traditions; from population growth to economic growth and sustainable development; from gender equity and equality to the empowerment of women; from the role of the family to the role of the government; from health to migration; from equity among generations to the placing of people at the center of development; from the recognition that social development is both a national and international concern to the recognition of the need to integrate economic, cultural, and social policies to achieve desired ends; and from employment to affordable housing so that the health, education, and welfare goals of individuals, families, governments, and the global community can be met.

3.2 Theoretical Underpinnings of Human Rights Law

The origins of human rights can be traced to Greece and Rome; they have been identified with "premodern natural law doctrines of Greek Stoicism (the school of philosophy . . . which held that a universal working force pervades all creation and that human conduct therefore should be judged according to, and brought into harmony with, the law of nature)."[5] After the Middle Ages, natural law became associated with theories of natural rights, although in medieval times natural law was viewed as imposing duties on, as opposed to granting rights to, "man." The underpinnings of natural law are assumptions that there are laws existing in nature—both theological and metaphysical—that constitute a higher law identified with all humankind and that requires protections of individual rights. An underlying assumption of natural law is that there is a common human nature that presupposes the equality of all human beings.[6] Of course, it is intrinsically contradictory that the idea of human rights developed at a time during which slavery and serfdom—concepts anathema to the notion of human rights, liberty, freedom, equality, and dignity—were legally accepted.[7]

It is noteworthy that from the early days, however, the language used to analyze or discuss these rights of "man" suggested that they were inalienable. For example, Locke argued that "certain rights self-evidently pertain to individuals as human beings (because they existed in 'the state of nature' before humankind entered civil society); that chief among them are the rights to life, liberty (freedom from arbitrary rule), and property; that, upon entering civil society, pursuant to a 'social contract,' humankind surrendered to the state only the right to enforce these natural rights, not the rights themselves; and that the state's failure to secure these reserved natural rights . . . gives rise to a right to responsible, popular revolution."[8]

The writings of St. Thomas Aquinas evince the religious foundations of natural law philosophy. Aquinas posited that all human laws derive from, and are subordinate to, the law of God. He viewed the law of nature as "a body of permanent principles grounded in the Divine Order, and partly revealed in the Scripture."[9] In his 13th-century writings, Aquinas even endorsed the notion that one sovereign can interfere in the internal affairs of another when one sovereign mistreats its subjects.[10] Spanish theologians Francisco de Vitoria and Francisco Suárez carried forward the religious view of the natural law. They both recognized that beyond individual states, there existed a community of states—that is, international rules that, established "by rational derivation from basic moral principles of divine origin," governed interactions between and among states.[11]

Hugo Grotius, a key thinker in the development of the law of nations (international law), was guided by natural law. As a "rationalist who derives the principles of the law of nature from universal reason rather than from divine authority,"[12] however, his natural law concept was secular, based on a person's rationality rather than revelation and deduction of God's will.[13] Grotius recognized the notion of state sovereignty over its subjects. Like Aquinas, however, he recognized that sovereignty was not an unfettered right. Grotius wrote that "if a tyrant . . . practices atrocities towards his subjects, which no just man can approve, the right of human social connexion is not cut off in such case."[14]

Grotius provided a bridge to the positivists by distinguishing between natural law and the customary law of nations based on the conduct and will of nations. The "will of nations" was central to positivism, which relied "on the practice of states and the conduct of international relations as evidenced by customs or treaties" for the statement of the law.[15] Positivism focused on states' conduct—that is, what states did in practice rather then what occurred based on forces existing in nature. The shift to positivism corresponded to the rise of the independent and sovereign nation-state.[16]

The value of the positivists' contributions lies in their recognition of the importance of organizing rules by established processes of the states. Once states authoritatively can formulate rules, they can protect human rights. Positivism's weakness, however, lies in the fact that the values promoted as human rights become wholly dependent on the perspective of the governing elite.[17] Under a positivist model, human dignity is what a state makes it.

Some contemporary theories have affected, expanded, and transformed traditional human rights law analysis. These theories include the communications theory (viewing law as an interactive process), the legitimacy theory (concluding that states follow international law because they have a legitimizing voice in its formation), the feminist theory (asking the "woman question" and noting the exclusion of women in international processes and institutions), the Third World or development theory (critiquing the Northern/industrial bias of international law), the Asian critique (noting the Western biases in international law), and the LatCrit critique (emphasizing the Western, industrial, gender bias of law and urging a pluralistic, multidimensional approach).

3.3   Origins of International Human Rights Law: General Concepts

The Second World War was the watershed event for the change of the status of individuals in international law. Nazi atrocities resulted in the punishment of war criminals at Nuremberg and Tokyo. The interrelated desire to prevent the recurrence of such crimes against humanity resulted in the development of new standards for the protection of human rights. It is important to note, however, that the individual was recognized in the global setting prior to the Second World War. Early writers recognized the importance of individuals to the law of nations because individuals constitute "the personal basis of every State," and, consequently, international law needed to "provide certain rules regarding individuals."[18] Individuals, however, were deemed to be objects, and not subjects, of the law of nations.[19]

After the Thirty Years War in central Europe, the diversity of peoples and ideologies required orderly processes for state-to-state communications and interchanges. Indeed, in the 17th century, Grotius's visionary statement that "human rights norms must exist today in a diverse world of immensely varied ideologies and beliefs" effectively predicted the development of a sophisticated human rights system.[20]

Although in its beginnings international law applied only to states, both customary and conventional norms emerged that dealt with individuals. The individuals were those in whom the state had an interest, such as diplomatic personnel (diplomatic privileges and immunities) and nationals of foreign sovereigns. To accommodate the latter, treaties of friendship, commerce and navigation, jurisdiction, and laws of war emerged. While in these early stages of providing for individuals the obligations always remained with the state, the benefit redounded to the individual.[21] Other early instances of protections of individuals also existed (such as the 17th-century negotiation by Catholic princes to ensure appropriate treatment of Catholics by Protestant princes, and vice versa).[22]

What is presently known as human rights to life, liberty, and equality were unformulated until the last decades of the 18th century. These rights emerged in conjunction with the establishment of democratic forms of government.[23] In the 19th and early 20th centuries, states entered into an increasing number of treaties with the purpose of protecting the rights of certain classes of persons, mostly minority groups (that is, persons of a different race, religion, or language from the majority group), within a state. The origins of these treaties can be traced to the period after the First World War when changes in sovereign boundaries required the expansion of rights to minorities because of the rise of nationalistic sentiments that created a real danger of oppression of racial, ethnic, linguistic, and religious minorities. Consequently, the allied and associated powers concluded a number of treaties in which states promised to treat such minority groups justly and equally.

In 1919, states that participated in the First World War endeavored to establish an international organization, the League of Nations, which would be responsible for the maintenance of world order, resolve disputes between states, and halt aggression.[24] The League of Nations, succeeded by the United Nations in 1946, played an important role in protecting minorities after the redrawing of boundaries following the First World War.[25]

Notwithstanding their treaty obligations, states regularly breached their commitments to equal treatment of minority groups. States considered provisions imposing limitations on how they could treat persons located within their borders as intrusions into their national sovereignty. A noted scholar reported: "Before the Second World War, scholars and diplomats assumed that international law allowed each equal sovereign an equal right to be monstrous to his subjects. Summary execution, torture, conviction without due process (or any process, for that matter) were legally significant events only if the victim of such official eccentricities were the citizen of another state. In that case, international law treated him as the bearer not of personal rights but of rights belonging to his government, and ultimately to the state for which it temporarily spoke."[26] This attitude resulted in the Permanent Court of International Justice's (PCIJ) reiteration that discrimination against minorities within a state constituted a violation of obligations under the treaties protecting minority groups.[27]

In addition to these "minority treaties," other important 20th-century human rights developments included treaties aimed at abolishing slavery and the slave trade. Freedom from slavery as a customary international norm dates to 1915. This norm was reaffirmed in international conventions such as the 1926 Slavery Convention and the 1956 Supplementary Convention on the Abolition of Slavery. Subsequent treaties further prohibited the trafficking in women and children.[28]

In his early treatise, Oppenheim listed "rights of mankind" guaranteed to all individuals by their state of nationality, as well as by foreign sovereigns, pursuant to the law of nations. These included the "right of existence, the right to protection of honor, life, health, liberty, and property, the right of practicing any religion one likes, the right of emigration and the like."[29] While acknowledging that individuals cannot be subjects of law that is limited to relations between states, and recognizing the sovereignty of states, Oppenheim acknowledged the supra-sovereign nature of "human" rights: "There is no doubt that, should a State venture to treat its own subjects or a part thereof with such cruelty as would stagger humanity, public opinion of the rest of the world would call upon the Powers to exercise intervention for the purpose of compelling such State to establish a legal order of things within its boundaries sufficient to guarantee to its citizens an existence more adequate to the ideas of modern civilization."[30]

That human rights limit state sovereignty is now accepted. During the Second World War, German Nazis were punished for committing atrocities against millions of innocent civilians, including German Jews. Thus, the state was not insulated from sanctions by an international tribunal for crimes against its own nationals.[31]

The modern view of human rights, with the individual at the center, emerged in the wake of the Nuremberg and Tokyo trials. In a now oft-quoted phrase, the Nuremberg Tribunal asserted that "crimes against international law are committed by men, not by abstract entities and only by punishing individuals who commit such crimes can the provisions of international law be enforced."[32] International law moved from being a statist discipline to being one that recognizes the interests and rights of individuals.[33]

3.4 Modern Human Rights Developments

(A) The Internationalization of Human Rights Law

Since the signing of the UN Charter in 1945, states have concluded international agreements that provide comprehensive protections for individuals against various forms of injustice, regardless of whether the abuse or injustice was committed by a foreign sovereign or the individuals' own state of nationality.[34]

The UN Charter provisions address human rights. The preamble provides that Members "reaffirm [their] faith in fundamental human rights, in the dignity and worth of the human person, in the equal rights of men and women and of nations large and small," as well as the institution's goal "to promote social progress and better standards of life in larger freedom." In addition, Article 55(a) mandates that the United Nations promote "universal respect for, and observance of, human rights and fundamental freedoms for all without distinction as to race, sex, language, or religion."[35] To achieve this end, at Article 56, state Members "pledge themselves to take joint and separate action in co-operation with the Organization for the achievement of [such] purposes."

The UN Charter embraces the natural law notion of rights as "rights to which all human beings have been entitled since time immemorial and to which they will continue to be entitled as long as humanity survives."[36] These natural rights are inalienable, permanent, and universal. They are part of the UN Charter's equality goal.[37] The universality of rights is contested as founded in Western philosophy and lacking Eastern and/or Southern linkages. Instead of universal, some posit that rights are culturally contingent.

There exists an ongoing debate as to whether the human rights provisions of the UN Charter create binding legal obligations on a Member state to respect the human rights of persons located within its borders, be they nationals or nonnationals. States have reached different conclusions with respect to the nature of the Charter's human rights obligations. Some view the obligations as binding,[38] others have concluded, particularly in older writings, that they are not binding.[39] Notwithstanding such inconsistent interpretations, the International Court of Justice (ICJ) has referred to the Charter's provisions as "obligation," and to breaches thereof as "violations of the purposes and principles of the Charter."[40] The ICJ also has stated that "distinctions, exclusions, restrictions and limitations exclusively based on grounds of race, colour, descent or national or ethnic origin which

constitute a denial of fundamental human rights . . . [are] a flagrant violation of the purposes and principles of the Charter."[41] Further, many pro-
pose that the rights in the Charter, together with other documents, have
become part of the customary international law of human rights.[42]

The key documents that create human rights obligations today include
the so-called International Bill of Human Rights comprised by the Universal Declaration; the Internationan Covenant on Economic, Social, and
Cultural Rights (ICESCR); and the International Covenant on Civil and
Political Rights (ICCPR) and its two Optional Protocols. Other significant
human rights treaties include the Convention on the Elimination of All
Forms of Discrimination Against Women (CEDAW); the Convention on
the Elimination of All Forms of Racial Discrimination (CERD); the Convention on the Rights of the Child (CRC); the Convention Against Torture and Other Cruel, Inhuman, or Degrading Treatment or Punishment
(Convention Against Torture); and the Convention on the Prevention and
Punishment of the Crime of Genocide. There are also three regional human rights treaties: the African (Banjul) Charter on Human and Peoples'
Rights, the American Convention on Human Rights (ACHR), and the (European) Convention for the Protection of Human Rights and Fundamental
Freedoms. Furthermore, numerous other instruments resulting from UN
conferences also address human rights concerns relevant to this volume.[43]
Such declarations and resolutions, while not legally binding, carry moral
persuasion and reflect the trend toward customary international law status.

It is instructive to review the historical background of the first three
of these documents. In 1947, with former First Lady of the United States
Eleanor Roosevelt (the U.S. representative) as chair, the UN Commission
on Human Rights (UNCHR) commenced the drafting process for an International Bill of Human Rights as mandated by the UN Economic and
Social Council. In December of that year, at UNCHR's Second Session, it
was decided that the International Bill of Human Rights should consist of
a "declaration," a "covenant," and "measures of implementation."[44]

The Universal Declaration was unanimously adopted on November 10,
1948.[45] When the UN General Assembly adopted the Declaration, it re-
quested that priority be given to preparation of one covenant and measures of implementation that would embody the principles contained in
the Declaration.[46] Significantly, the Universal Declaration is a comprehensive document dealing not only with civil and political rights but also
with economic, social, and cultural rights. (For a discussion of the different types of rights, see section 3.5.)

While debate about the legal status of the Universal Declaration is ongoing, many scholars consider it to be legally binding as a general principle of international law; others consider it to have the status of *jus cogens*,[47] even though at the time of its adoption the U.S. representative to the UN General Assembly stated: "It is not a treaty; it is not an international agreement. It is not and does not purport to be a statement of law or of legal obligation."[48] Subsequent developments in both domestic and international law, however, generally confirm that at least some provisions of the Universal Declaration have status as customary law.[49] In fact, the *Restatement (Third) of Foreign Relations Law* provides that "almost all states would agree that some infringements of human rights enumerated in the Universal Declaration are violations of the Charter or of customary international law."[50]

The finalization of the covenant that was to follow the Universal Declaration presented significantly more difficulties than the drafting and adoption of the Declaration. From 1949 to 1954 the UNCHR devoted six sessions to preparation of the covenant.[51] The problems resulted from interrogations by so-called developed states as to whether social, economic, and cultural rights—already articulated in the Declaration—were relevant to, or appropriate as, human rights. Such states maintained that social, economic, and cultural rights were aspirational goals—the attainment of which was dependent on economic resources and economic theory and ideology. Consequently, Western states held that economic rights were inappropriate for framing as binding legal obligations. On the other hand, then-Second and -Third World states held that economic rights were the most important. The different viewpoints resulted in the drafting of two international documents—the ICCPR and the ICESCR—to be submitted simultaneously for consideration by the General Assembly. One document was to contain civil and political rights and the other social and economic and cultural rights. The General Assembly instructed that, in order to maintain uniformity, both covenants should overlap to the greatest extent possible.[52]

Finally, on December 16, 1966, the General Assembly adopted and opened for signature, ratification, and accession the ICESCR, the ICCPR, and the Optional Protocol to the ICCPR.[53] In the two covenants that emerged, the only overlapping provisions were those on nondiscrimination (including discrimination based on sex), self-determination, and sovereignty over natural resources. These two covenants, like the UN Charter, reflect the natural law origins of human rights law. For example, the

ICCPR's prohibition against the suspension of certain rights by the state, even in the event of public emergencies that threaten the life of the nation, reflect the notion of the inalienability of certain rights.[54]

(B)   The Regional Systems

The three regional human rights systems cover the European, Inter-American, and African regions; there is currently no Asian or Middle Eastern regional human rights system. Of these, the one of concern in this volume is the Inter-American system, which is composed of various documents and has two overlapping frameworks. First, the OAS Charter,[55] in Article 106, established the Inter-American Commission on Human Rights (IACHR), which was given limited power to promote the human rights embodied in the 1948 American Declaration on the Rights and Duties of Man (American Declaration). In 1970 the OAS Charter was amended by the 1967 Protocol of Buenos Aires, which strengthened the IACHR and institutionalized the implementation of the American Declaration.

Second, in 1969, states of the Inter-American region adopted the ACHR, which contains a long list of substantive rights. This framework includes the IACHR, which also is part of the OAS system. In 1979 the IACHR was charged with "develop[ing] an awareness of human rights among the peoples of America."[56] The IACHR may receive complaints of violations and issue reports on the status of human rights in the region. As established by this framework, it can receive cases only from state parties. In 1988, the Protocol of San Salvador,[57] which covers social and economic rights, was attached to the ACHR.

3.5   Classification of Specific Human Rights

United Nations documents emphasize the indivisibility and interdependence of all categories of human rights.[58] Human rights are grouped in three categories: civil and political rights (so-called first generation); social, economic, and cultural rights (so-called second generation); and solidarity rights (so-called third generation).

(A)   Civil and Political Rights: The First Generation

Civil and political rights, "the rights of Man," were at their apogee starting in the 18th century. These rights are traced to the "bourgeois" revolutions—particularly the French and American revolutions in the last quarter of the 18th century—that gave rise to the [French] Declaration on the Rights of Man and the U.S. Declaration of Independence, the foundational documents for this group of rights.[59]

Civil and political rights originally were conceived as negative rights— that is, realms that should be free from government interference.[60] Such a conception of negative rights, however, is exceedingly (and misleadingly) limiting. For example, the right to a fair trial falls into this category, yet it requires "positive" state action—the creation of a system of justice for it to be realized.

The right to nondiscrimination on the basis of race, gender, language, religion, culture, family, ethnicity, national origin, and social origin is a basic tenet of civil and political rights. Yet, notwithstanding such a foundational principle, civil and political rights are gendered and racialized. For example, women are far from enjoying equal rights to speech, participation, travel, or owning land.[61]

Rights of the first generation have been criticized because they have "meant for the majority of the working class and peoples of conquered lands the right to be exploited and colonized. They were regarded as 'formal' freedoms that neglected the material realities of social conditions."[62]

(B)   Social, Economic, and Cultural Rights: The Second Generation

Socialist states posited that the freedoms of the first-generation rights simply permitted the exploitation and subjugation of working and colonized people. The second generation, in contrast, reflects the ideals of the socialist revolutions of the first two decades of the 20th century. The "usher[ing] in [of] the second generation" was effected and underscored by the post-socialist revolution Mexican and Russian constitutions of 1917 as well as by the 1919 Constitution of the International Labour Organization (ILO).[63] Contrasted to the first generation's emphasis on protecting individual rights from governmental tyranny through participation in the political processes, the second-generation rights underscored a rejection of the exploitation of peoples and focused on the intervention of the state in order to effectuate certain claims. As distinguished from the "negative" civil and political rights, social, economic, and cultural rights are positive rights—rights that require state action. These rights emphasize the collective or group, as opposed to the individual.

This second generation includes three different types of rights. First are social rights that consist of, for example, the right to an adequate standard of living, adopting the notion that everyone should enjoy subsistence rights such as adequate food and nutrition, clothing, and housing.[64] Economic rights are also included, ranging from the right to social security to the right to work. Finally, a broad spectrum of cultural rights includes the right to take part in cultural life, the right to enjoy the benefits of scientific progress and its applications, and the right to preserve the cultural identity of minority groups.[65] Such protection of cultural traditions is significant because culture contains the basic source of identity and preservation of identity, which is important for the well-being and self-respect of a human being (rights that can be called first-generation human rights). Western states in general have resisted the notion of social and economic rights. U.S. President Franklin Delano Roosevelt, however, appears to have wholeheartedly embraced them.[66]

It is important to note before closing this section that the South's historical exclusion from enjoyment of rights is particularly true and marked when one considers social, economic, and cultural rights. Colonial regimes deprived persons of their rights to such opportunities as work and education and allowed the exclusion of women from full participation in the public and private spheres. The justification for such exclusion often was based on the pretext of tradition and cultural classifications. Thus, rather than these new rights resulting in women's equality, they allowed communities to continue their traditional practices or customs that subordinate women.

(C)   Solidarity Rights: The Third Generation

Like the first and second generations of rights, the third generation is also sourced in revolution—the anticolonialist revolutions that immediately followed the Second World War and, around 1960, resulted in the independence of many nations. Such revolutions influenced the text of human rights instruments by giving importance and context to the rights to self-determination and nondiscrimination—both of which are found in the ICCPR and the ICESCR. This movement also emphasized the rejection of foreign domination and occupation, freedom from aggression, and threats against national sovereignty. These rights, too, have been labeled as inalienable rights.[67]

Two distinctive characteristics are attendant to third-generation rights. First, solidarity rights do not belong to the individualistic tradition of the first-generation rights nor to the socialist tradition of the second-generation rights. Second, while these rights are in an early phase of legislative process, documents reveal that they were in the process of being recognized as international human rights during the 1980s. The rights falling under this generation category include the right to environment,[68] development,[69] peace,[70] democracy, as well as rights to common heritage, communication, and humanitarian assistance.[71]

The notion of interdependence and indivisibility of rights recently was reiterated in the Vienna Declaration, which plainly states that "all human rights are universal, indivisible and inter-dependent and interrelated."[72] Moreover, the generational scheme of classification of rights is questionable in light of the myriad significant documents in which the first-, second-, and third-generation rights coexist, such as in the CRC, the CEDAW, the CERD, and the African Charter.

3.6 Human Rights and Trade

In relation to trade, rights of all generations are relevant. Some rights might appear to have a closer nexus to trade than others. For example, labor rights, including the right to work, to association, to form trade unions, to safe working conditions, to fair wages, and to equality, are plainly connected to trade. The rights to liberty, personhood, and freedom from slavery are key concerns of the trafficking for labor. In addition, the right to a healthy environment is directly linked to trade. Protecting the Amazon has been one of the loudly articulated concerns. With these examples in mind, it is not surprising that labor and environment activities have been among the most vehement opponents to "free trade."

Other rights, such as the right to a fair trial, have a less direct or obvious linkage to trade, yet the linkage exists. Trade is more likely to occur in a location where investments are secure and travel is safe and, if some problem arises, there is a system of justice that will resolve it in a fair and equitable manner. Yet other rights have both direct and indirect linkages to trade. The right to property has a direct connection regarding economic development. It also has an indirect tie. For instance, foreign investor protections may decrease the enjoyment of property. The chapters in this book will explore the linkages—sometimes direct and sometimes less obvious—between trade and numerous human rights.

4

Splendid Isolation's Progeny
The Intersections of Trade and Human Rights

4.1 *Central Dilemma: Lack of Purposeful Correlation*

Having presented in the opening segments the foundational principles of international law-making and the basic concepts of both trade and human rights norms and structures, this chapter turns to an overview of the relationship between human rights and international trade. The chapter begins by exploring the philosophical differences in the approach of the two disciplines and their structural placement in public international law in order that the reader may gain a better understanding of their commonalities. In searching for resolution of conflict, the chapter next analyzes the hierarchy of these fields under international legal principles. To prepare the reader for the particular lessons of trade's intersection with the subjects of the chapters to follow, the final section firmly reminds governments that trade agreements alone cannot inculcate a human rights consciousness into their leadership.

4.2 *Philosophical and Structural Divides*

(A) Introduction

Commentators perceive a fundamental tension between international human rights law and international trade law based on their supposed commitment to different values. For example, international trade law is utilitarian—devoted to the most economically efficient outcome and to the satisfaction of market preferences—while human rights law is deontological—premised on minimum standards of treatment that recognize the moral worth of each individual.[1] For example, the WTO TRIPS Agreement employs a cost-benefit approach to balance the need to encourage invention (by giving patent holders monopolistic rights) against the conflicting need to ensure wide dissemination of technology to permit fast development in the Third World and deliver lifesaving medicines to the sick (by allowing compulsory government licensing and actions against anticompetitive practices). The WTO's SPS Agreement balances the interest in food safety against the policy of unrestricted trade by requiring solid scientific evidence to justify import restrictions.

Even so, characterizing the WTO as utilitarian and human rights law as doctrinal is far too simplistic to withstand scrutiny. Human rights law is indeed deontological, in that exploitative child labor does not become valid when the scale of economic benefits reaches a certain point—for example, by attracting foreign direct investment that otherwise would not bring its job-creating project. Torture cannot be justified under human rights treaties by the importance of the information to be obtained. But this does not mean that human rights law is immune to trade-offs, as most clearly demonstrated in the environmental protection movement. The concept of "sustainable development" itself, which is the central paradigm of the mainstream environmental protection movement, assumes that growth will continue, if for no other reason than to eliminate poverty.

One also should characterize as compromise on the part of human rights law the acceptance, and even promotion, of market systems and economic growth in democratic societies, despite the imperfections of globalization in realization of human rights goals.[2] The human rights policies given priority over trade's fundamental maxims by GATT Article XX, including health, public morals, and natural resources, put the lie to claims that trade policies cannot be normative and nonutilitarian. Hence, the purpose of this volume: to show that it is neither trade's utilitarianism nor human rights' humanitarianism that governments and civil society should pursue as if they were unrelated. Rather it is the utilitarianism and idealism of both, working with their synergies and strengths, that should be the focus of policy development. These are disciplines that, when approached together, can indeed make the world a better and more prosperous place.

(B) WTO as Separate Entity from UN Structure

One also is asked to accept that the WTO's ideological placement, spinning unfettered outside the protective galaxy of the UN system, where human rights law revolves around a unifying centrality, severely handicaps trade's ability to act with human rights motivation. To be sure, the three legs of the Bretton Woods "stool" of international economic and financial entities were established outside the firmament of the United Nations by conscious design, with the Bretton Woods entities as the private, economic arm to the public, political United Nations. Architects of post–Second World War international institutions saw great danger in the decisions by politicians following the First World War to erect high tariff barriers, manipulate exchange rates, and otherwise create the isolation that made possible the rise of demagogues amid the squalid economic conditions of the Great Depression.[3] Thus, the political institutions whose charge was to secure the peace revolved around the public United Nations, while the international economic institutions of the World Bank, the IMF, and GATT would be established as private entities with a purely economic role and run by technocrats, not diplomats.[4]

One might also identify a critical difference in the evolution of trade and human rights rules. Within a very few years after the Second World War, the modern human rights regime had mushroomed into a comprehensive, revolutionary, holistic codification of human rights that an outside observer might characterize as burdened with unrealistically high expectations. Trade rules began with humble promises and built their foundation with small steps over fifty years of nearly continuous rounds of multilateral negotiations, each proclaiming slightly more ambitious measures to counteract the natural inclination of states to protect their national industries. In addition, because the trade rules began without an institution to house them (the WTO created in 1995 is the deferred realization of the "International Trade Organization" first proposed in 1947), the institutional framework that emerged a half century later boasted an effectiveness born of five decades of experience with administering global trade rules without an infrastructure.

To be sure, this classical view of the separation of economic institutions from public international law held little promise for integration of human rights, as reflected by the Articles of Agreement of the World Bank, which provide that loans shall be used only for "economy and efficiency and without regard to political or other non-economic influences or considerations."[5] In the early days, the Bank's General Counsel went so far as to opine that the Bank was prohibited from compliance with UN decisions on human rights because the objectives of the International Bill of Human Rights were contradictory to the Bank's financial and economic mandates.[6] The IMF reached a similar conclusion.[7]

Of course, these views have dramatically changed. The World Bank's definition of poverty is evidence of the transformation (see epigraph to Chapter 12). Yet, these early traditional views are similar to those of the GATT classicists, who hold that the WTO is a self-contained entity that human rights advocates must allow to pursue its free trade mission unburdened by other public international law, including human rights claims.[8] This view was difficult to maintain even at GATT's beginning, because it was forced to coexist with the inescapable reality that GATT's drafters had accorded overriding importance to certain explicitly exempted human rights policies, such as protection of public health, prisoner rights, and the environment.[9] Nonetheless, the private, classical view received further impetus from the failure of the International Trade Organization to receive approval, which meant that until 1995, the GATT existed as a contract instead of a treaty.[10]

With this isolationist structure built into their foundations, each of the economic institutions has been forced to take sometimes wrenching measures to reverse course on the role of human rights. Even so, the World Bank and the IMF have taken notable recent steps to polish their human rights reputations.[11] As to the WTO, in its first decision, the Appellate Body of the Organization debunked the notion that trade treaties operate in a vacuum separate from other public international law by pointing out that "the GATT is not to be read in clinical isolation from public international law."[12] Like international human rights law, WTO law is a branch of public international law,[13] which is sufficient to dismiss the classical view that the WTO is a self-contained body of law that constitutionally can ignore human rights.

The origin of the WTO and the other economic institutions in a non-UN context surely has handicapped their human rights records, but only in the sense that history has delayed their recognition of the need to come to terms with the human rights consequences of their actions. The Bretton Woods entities may no longer claim a constitutional or other legal debarment from human rights concerns.

(C) Statist WTO Structure Versus Individualistic Human Rights Regime

The WTO assumes without inquiry that a state's titular leaders are the appropriate representatives for the state. WTO's rules directly impose disciplines on states, so the officials who can implement these prescriptions are accepted at the WTO. The result is that any form of political or social organization is acceptable to the WTO, as well as any treatment of a state's citizens. Many WTO Members were—and still are—communist, socialist, and even fascist. This result follows from the fact that protection of individuals is not the central focus of WTO rules, which instead regulate the conduct of states.

Human rights treaties, similarly, address actions of a state and require a state to limit its intrusion into individuals' sphere of existence (with negative rights) as well as mandate the state to take certain actions to ensure human well-being (with positive rights). Because of the supra-sovereign nature of human rights, however, the discipline also looks to what goes on inside the state vis-à-vis individuals. Thus, as human rights concerns travel across state lines, this deterritorialization of authority over human rights oversight translates to acceptance as legitimate only those state leaders whose treatment of their citizenry accords with basic human rights norms. To be sure, the UN Charter gives sovereignty to states, but on the assumption that sovereign national authority ultimately must yield to the power of the people whom state leaders purport to represent. A critical limitation on the legitimacy of state leaders is their respect for the human rights of their civil society.[14]

Yet the lines drawn are not so clear. For example, the CEDAW, which aims at women's equality, is replete with reservations—indeed, it is the most reserved-against treaty in history—that entrench women's subordinated status. The legitimacy of the reservations is rarely, if ever, questioned. Similarly, there was nary an outcry when one of the proposed constitutions for Iraq disenfranchised women, with the world, by its tacit response, ostensibly accepting institutionalizing broadly proscribed discrimination.

4.3   Legal Hierarchy of Trade and Human Rights Norms

(A)   Generally

Given the actual relationship between these fields, it is relevant to explore the legal hierarchy of human rights and trade norms in international law. That is, which should prevail in the event of conflict, which may and does occur in the cases both of silent indifference and of direct contradiction in terms? In fact, conflicts likely will intensify as the cultural heterogeneity of the WTO proceeds apace and the Third World's reliance on trade for economic progress grows.[15] Given that human rights norms are indisputably the foundational, widely shared standards of justice and right conduct, human rights norms intuitively should prevail over trade norms, which, at bottom, govern the movement of widgets across borders, not the right treatment of the individual in society.

Law is not, of course, founded on intuition. Moreover, the bases of trade laws, too, are central principles of public life, including nondiscrimination and the rule of law, that describe elemental standards of justice and underpin societal values far weightier than simple economic efficiency.[16] In large part because of their intersection with a wide range of human rights, trade rules profoundly affect almost all segments of society and find relevance in almost all other rules of international law.[17] Through their mandates to states of transparency, accountability, and due process,[18] trade rules "require governments to have a conscience and to hold a mirror to themselves" in their treatment of civil society.[19]

Nonetheless, even if we could agree that human rights law occupies the higher moral rank, we cannot for this reason alone conclude that human rights law trumps trade law from a legal perspective. As a matter of international law, neither policy presumptively prevails in the event of conflict. The lack of a formal hierarchy in international law follows from its origin in the consent of states: it is a law of coordination, not subordination, because the creation of international law relies on the explicit or implicit consent of states, which are complete equals in the creation of law.[20]

Chapter 1 explained that one type of international law—*jus cogens*—governs over any other conflicting rule of international law, whether sourced in custom or treaty. At a minimum, such practices by the state as genocide, torture, slavery, and systematic racial discrimination fall into this category. A dispute settlement panel, whether convened under authority of a trade or human rights treaty, should find that such norms "trump" any conflicting international rules of a lesser status.

(B)   Application of International Law's Hierarchy to WTO Cases

As with other international treaties, WTO rules form part of the larger body of public international law: "Each new state, and each new treaty, is automatically born into" that wider corpus of law,[21] which includes human rights law whether sourced in treaty or in custom. The WTC acknowledged in its first decision that the WTO "is not to be read in clinical isolation from public international law."[22] A WTO panel correctly has observed that custom applies generally to the economic relationship among Members unless a particular provision of a WTO Agreement contracts out of the custom.[23]

With respect to treaties, other international law norms govern the relationship among WTO Members subject to *pacta tertiis*. That is, the non-WTO treaties bind only WTO Members that are parties to them.[24] Customary international law, on the other hand, binds states regardless of whether they have given written consent. Freedom from torture is a human right so widely accepted as a legal obligation in the practice of nations that it has become customary international law. WTO Agreements thus need not explicitly provide a "torture" exception to justify a WTO Member's successfully pleading the custom before a WTO dispute settlement panel in defense of a violation of the Four Pillars. For some customs, the WTO could "contract out" of the custom by a later disavowal of the principle.[25] Nothing in the WTO Agreements suggests that the WTO has done so with respect to any fundamental human right. Moreover, a party cannot contract out of a *jus cogens* norm. In the example above, given that the prohibition against torture is *jus cogens*, regardless of whether a particular WTO Member has signed the Convention Against Torture, no WTO Member could contract out.

Putting observation to practice, a number of WTO panels have applied rules of general international law independent of interpreting a particular WTO provision, for example, in deciding the role of amicus curiae briefs, drawing adverse inferences, and deciding a panel's jurisdiction.[26] The question must be asked, however, How does the human rights norm at issue enter the field of play? One noncontroversial instance is to aid textual interpretation. A panel may examine later treaties to give present meaning to inherently dynamic treaty terms. For example, the WTC found that the term "natural resources," in GATT Article XX(g), is inherently evolutionary, citing to an ICJ decision as support for application in the WTO case of this general international law principle. The WTC proceeded to search current multilateral environmental treaties to justify its conclusion that the term includes living resources and not solely the mineral products that the GATT's drafters had in mind in 1947.[27]

For other treaties to find relevance in defining WTO terms, they must reflect the "common intentions" of the Members.[28] These other sources of international law, whether custom, general principles, or other treaties, need not explicitly bind all WTO Members to give meaning to WTO Agreement provisions, but all WTO Members must at least implicitly tolerate the other source (it must be "applicable in the relations" among WTO Members).[29] With respect to customary human rights law of a peremptory nature, WTO Members are bound; if the human rights norm is not *jus cogens*, WTO Members are bound unless a WTO Agreement has opted out of such custom—either explicitly (rare) or by adoption of a later in time, clearly conflicting provision (discussed in section 7.5(B) in respect to the Precautionary Principle).

The Vienna Convention recognizes in Article 30(3) a possible additional test to resolve conflict between two rules of international law. Because all such rules have the same status, the later in time—*lex posterior*—overrules an earlier expression of state consent. Major difficulties nonetheless exist in applying *lex posterior* to international law in general and in particular to the international human rights and trade norms addressed in this book. States periodically revise both human rights law and trade law through treaties that both confirm prior norms and either expand them or provide detail as to particular aspects.[30] In these circumstances, deciding which norm was created later in time is fraught with difficulty, making *lex posterior* an interpretive principle of lessened value. This is only problematic with respect to clearly conflicting norms, however, because another rule of interpretation urges that rules be constructed as consistent with each other whenever possible.

One final Vienna Convention rule may be relevant to resolve conflict. Even though an established custom can overcome an earlier conflicting treaty provision, or vice versa, the earlier provision still may prevail if it qualifies as *lex specialis*, a specific rule on the subject as compared with a more general norm.[31] As compared with general principles of international law, the detailed and arcane rules of the GATT/WTO may in particular circumstances qualify as *lex specialis*, although that fact certainly makes no case for the proposition that the WTO is a self-contained system outside the general corpus of public international law.

(C)   Beyond Textual Interpretation?

At the other extreme from using non-WTO law to aid textual interpretation, a WTO dispute settlement panel has no jurisdiction to entertain a claim that arises from a human rights treaty or norm, such as an EU complaint against U.S. treatment of terrorist suspects whose gravamen is the Convention on Torture.[32] The difficult remaining question is whether a panel may use the Convention Against Torture and other human rights norms only to interpret WTO provisions—for example, the Public Morals Clause of GATT's General Exceptions—or whether a country, say France, successfully could plead the Convention Against Torture as a defense, for example, to an import ban on U.S. beef. If, in applying the Vienna Convention rules for determining the hierarchy of international legal norms, the human rights law occupies the higher plane, the answer should be in the affirmative.

For the human rights addressed in this volume that intersect with trade's legal regime and trump trade law, however, the question may be unnecessary. In these cases, the breadth of the human rights policies addressed in the General Exceptions of both the GATT and the GATS, as well as in other provisions of WTO Agreements that are in the nature of exceptions,[33] human rights law is the natural and often only other international law relevant to interpretation of the noneconomic policy at issue. This fact will stand out repeatedly as this volume interrogates the intersections of human rights and trade law.

One example may be instructive. If France justifies its violation of GATT's MFN Clause based on the necessity to protect "public morals" under Article XX(a) of the GATT, a WTO dispute settlement panel should take notice of the *jus cogens* status of torture in deciding whether public morality is involved. *U.S.-Gambling* is a case involving the meaning of the Public Morals Clause in the WTO's GATS[34] where the United States had banned cross-border supply of gambling services. The WTC accepted the initial panel's definition of public morals as referring to "standards of right and wrong conduct maintained by or on behalf of a community or nation." The panel recognized that "Members should be given some scope to define and apply for themselves the concepts of 'public morals' and 'public order' in their respective territories." The panel acknowledged that Members would find interpretation of the terms to be a sensitive undertaking and that the concepts will "vary in time and space, depending upon a range of factors, including prevailing social, cultural, ethical and religious values."

Nonetheless, in deciding whether U.S. limitations on gambling fell within the range of policies protected by the Public Morals Clause, the panel turned to other international law, including treaties and the common practice of other states.[35] The panel implicitly recognized that resorting solely to the particular customs and cultures of one of the WTO's diverse 150-plus Members might create an unfettered exception to GATT's Four Pillars. The panel's search for other international rights benchmarks to corral the broad Public Morals Clause opens the dispute panel door to human rights norms to interpret a standard that inherently sounds in the rights of the individual.[36]

(D)   Does GATT Article XX Require a Trade Nexus?

An additional question is whether the WTO panel's response will depend on whether the targeted practice (routine torture of prisoners) must affect trade between the Members to justify a restrictive border measure (the ban on beef imports).[37] In most cases, banning beef imports from Country A bears a relatively distant relationship to Country A's treatment of its prisoners. The trade nexus is weaker, for example, than a ban on radios made with prison labor, a border measure expressly permitted by GATT Article XX(e). On one level, the nexus issue implicates Article XX(a)'s "Necessity Test," discussed in sections 2.4 and 6.5(B) and (C). From this perspective, the nexus/necessity question is how effective the beef ban must be in preventing torture by Country A's leaders: the WTC has found that the measure of effectiveness depends on the importance of the value that the trade measure seeks to achieve. If the value is important, the border measure need only make a contribution to achieving its end; if low in priority, its effectiveness must be closer to indispensable in preventing the targeted action.[38]

If the ban was imposed by Country A's principal importer of beef, the restriction might well meet even the strictest end of this continuum. If the measure seeks to prevent a *jus cogens* human rights violation (torture), its burden in meeting the Necessity Test should be no greater than a ban aimed at protecting against human deaths from cancer (*EC-Asbestos*).[39]

The trade nexus question also invokes the "Relationship Test," which substitutes for the Necessity Test in the GATT Article XX exceptions for products of prison labor (Paragraph (e)) and for exhaustible natural resources (Paragraph (g)). Again, the test of how close the measure's nexus/relationship to trade must be should respond to the importance of the measure's ends in a common system of values. As when one views the nexus to trade through the lens of the Necessity Test, pursuit of human rights compliance favors a less demanding standard in a relationship/nexus context than an attempt to achieve solely economic objectives. In the absence of an explicit "Trade Nexus Test" in Article XX and given the importance of human rights in a common system of values, human rights policies should fare well in the balance with GATT's Four Pillars. It ought not to matter whether a panel examines the trade nexus of a border measure undertaken for human rights purposes through the lens of the Necessity or Relationship tests.

Regional FTAs involving the United States consistently include an explicit Trade Nexus Test to introduce a human rights defense. The side agreements to the NAFTA on environment and labor rights require allegation that the violation is "trade-related" (environment) or involves sectors that produce goods or services "traded between the territories of the Parties." Explicit Trade Nexus tests for worker rights and environmental protection in U.S. FTAs continue today.[40] Despite differences in structure, the absence of an explicit Trade Nexus Test in GATT Article XX's exceptions for environmental, labor, and other human rights measures may be one factor in arguing that no trade nexus dimension exists beyond those included in the Necessity and Relationship tests.[41]

(E)   Preventing Conflict

In light of the complexity of finding a proper hierarchy among sources of international law, we may ask what positive steps states have taken in advance to avoid these conflicts. The surest way, of course, to avoid conflict, whether between provisions in a contract or norms in a treaty that are likely to intersect is to anticipate the situations that could cause conflict and describe in the contract (or legislation or treaty) which in fact will take priority.

To a limited extent, the GATT began that process in 1947 with Article XX, which provides that certain human rights objectives—those involving public health and welfare—can be accorded precedence by states over global trade rules if the state meets certain conditions. GATT's drafters did not explicitly mention "human rights," but several provisions of Article XX sound in human rights subjects, from guarding public morals, to protecting public health, to banning products of prison labor, to conserving exhaustible natural resources. States may under certain circumstances restrict importation of goods if the state acts on the basis of one of these listed purposes.

From the human rights side, Article 103 of the UN Charter gives that document primacy over any conflicting other international obligation of a UN Member. The Charter obligates Members "to take joint and separate action" in cooperation with the United Nations to promote human rights and establishes objectives that run the gamut of human rights, including higher living standards and freedom from racial and sexual discrimination. The Charter does not itself resolve the hierarchy question, however, because the Charter leaves specific rules to the Universal Declaration and to human rights treaties.

Both the United Nations and the WTO thus recognize the potential for conflict, but neither attempts specific solutions if conflict occurs. If the contract itself—here the treaty—does not clearly resolve the conflict, how should we attempt to reconcile conflicting treaties? That we are faced with an "equal legitimacy" of trade and human rights norms places a premium on purposeful coordination of both sets of norms with those of the other field.[42] The primary sources of international law are treaty and custom, the former of which binds only those who consent to be bound by signing the treaty, the latter binding on all who do not expressly contract out of the custom.

As we examine the many aspects of the human rights and trade intersection in later chapters, it will be useful to identify which human rights norms have been so generally accepted as to constitute customary international law. Some are clear: for example, genocide, slavery, systematic racial discrimination, and torture.[43] Others, such as a living wage or freedom of association, trace their source solely to human rights treaties, while political philosophy underlies some concepts. Even if the human rights norm in question clearly is customary, and thus binds all, resolution of conflicts in actual cases usually requires additional steps.

We will ask repeatedly in this volume whether the intersection between trade and human rights must, of necessity, be characterized by conflict and indifference, as well as the consequences for the success of policies in both fields if the answer is yes.

4.4 Indispensable Role of Government

As Professor Powell has observed, trade rules cannot "directly inject rules-based governance into a country." Observance of human rights for their citizens is an essential and irreplaceable role of national governments.[44] As the leading advocate of "fair trade," Oxfam, has succinctly observed, "Trade has the power to create opportunities and support livelihoods; and it has the power to destroy them."[45]

Negotiators can structure trade agreements to create the economic opportunities sought, but national governments will succeed in creating societies committed to the rule of law and human rights in general only if they are prepared to intercede in the market to shape the effects of the economic growth created by trade.[46] Trade, and capitalism in general, create the menu for improving social benefits, but both are inherently unstable and insensitive to unfairness. Without oversight and regulation, governments will squander trade's opportunities for the advancement of human rights.[47] This thesis is in tension with one of globalization's premises: diminished government presence in the daily lives of civil society through privatization of government-owned infrastructure and lessened regulation.

In all cases, the essential concern with the hierarchy is the enjoyment of trade benefits without ignoring or trumping human rights norms. In that regard, it is important to emphasize that the WTO does not come into the world in a vacuum; there are existing norms—some domestic and some international—in the world that it inhabits. Thus, the agreements made pursuant to the WTO not only have to conform with trade's premises, but also to those other domestic and international norms with which they coexist. This is not a novel concept. In *Hartford Fire Insurance Co. v. California,* the U.S. Supreme Court confronted the issue of whether, under international law, U.S. antitrust law could reach the conduct (conspiracy to set rates) of London reinsurance companies that had adverse effects in the United States. Although that case presented an issue of jurisdiction, it is instructive. The conduct in which the insurance companies engaged was legal in London, but it had effects in the United States where the same conduct would be illegal. The English norms were not in direct conflict with the U.S. norms; the insurance companies could have complied with both. They chose not to do so. Rather, they purposely opted to act the way they did, which breached U.S. antitrust law. Thus, the Court concluded, U.S. courts could, consistent with international law, exercise jurisdiction over the acts carried out in London, and the insurance companies were found liable.

This scenario is similar to the trade/human rights tension. Entities can enter into agreements pursuant to the WTO; yet they also must comply with human rights norms. If they enter into agreements that do breach those norms, then the entity that breaches the norm is held responsible to all its obligations.

5

Who Belongs, Who Rules

Citizenship—Voice and Participation in the Global Marketplace

5.1 Overview

Globalization is changing the nature of citizenship. What used to be considered a legal status now becomes more of a social bond. What used to be a particular relationship of an individual to the state may now be a relationship of an individual to multiple states. A status that once defined national belonging may now signify marginalization. Moreover, the power that individuals derived from citizenship to define the political, social, and cultural landscape now has been shifted to corporate entities whose loyalties lie in economic well-being as defined by the bottom line. This chapter will explore these new meanings, and attendant tensions, of citizenship in an era of globalization.[1]

5.2 Human Rights Framework

(A) Normative Setting

The concept of citizenship is well-grounded in the human rights documents. These documents ensure a right to a nationality,[2] the right of members of society to the realization "of the economic, social and cultural rights indispensable for his dignity and the free development of his personality,"[3] the right to participate in the cultural life of a community,[4] self-determination,[5] and a citizenship's right to participate in the government.[6]

(B) The Development of the Concept of Citizenship

Two different concepts of citizenship—the "legal status" model and the "desirable activity" model[7]—underlie general understandings of citizenship as a legal, political, and social construct that resonates and has impacts both locally and globally.[8] In seeking to identify the framework that defines and delineates citizenship and its attendant rights, privileges, and obligations, some theorists refer to its natural law foundations.[9]

A classic usage of citizenship identifies groups of persons with shared descent, language, culture, and traditions.[10] In this regard, "Citizenship . . . becomes less an entitlement than a definition . . . [for p]eople [who] want to know where they belong, and they want to belong to familiar and homogeneous groups."[11]

Contrary to such "definition" of citizenship is the view that "the true test of the strength of citizenship is heterogeneity [because] common respect for basic entitlements among people who are different in origin, culture and creed proves that combination of identity and variety which lies at the heart of civil and civilized society."[12] Significantly, some posit that "modern citizenship is inherently egalitarian."[13] A different characterization of modern citizenship is that it does not permit "arbitrary treatment . . . [yet] acknowledges individuals' abilities to make judgments about their own lives."[14] Hence citizenship is like "a series of expanding circles" that increasingly includes outsiders.[15] Consequently the very concept of citizenship incorporates the ideal of equality. Indeed, many contemporary theorists insist that the concept of citizenship must embrace differences among persons—differences of race, sex, sexuality, ethnicity, and religion, to name a few—and that a new conception of citizenship must be developed because, as "originally defined by and for white men, [it] cannot accommodate the special needs of minority groups."[16]

The 1990s experienced "an explosion of interest in the concept of citizenship."[17] Far from the early liberal understanding of citizenship as limited to political activity, which some critics presently view as translating simply into the right to pursue individual economic interests in a market,[18] contemporary citizenship theories have a broad, flexible sense of participation in public life. Some perceive citizenship as a reciprocal relation between an individual's location and his or her rights.[19]

In 1949 T. H. Marshall distinguished three types of citizenship that emerged "in such a way that each new type was standing on the shoulder of its predecessor."[20] Indeed, since Marshall's conception of "the ideal of citizenship as full participation in the community,"[21] the relational aspect of citizenship has shifted from an individual-vis-à-vis-state model to an individual-vis-à-vis-society model.[22]

5.3 Citizenship in a Globalized World

In today's globalized world, citizenship is a contested concept. The re-thinking of citizenship along critical lines is informed by the application and development of cross-fertilized ideas of rights. As such it promotes, defends, and facilitates full participation in society, in particular by those persons who live at the margins.[23]

The concept of citizenship in a globalized world is unlike the liberal idea(l) of citizenship[24] that embraces the notion that human beings are "atomistic, rational agents whose existence and interests are ontologically prior to society."[25] Feminist writers have objected to such a model as "something like equal membership in an economic and social sphere . . . dedicated to the assumption that the 'market maketh man' . . . [and] less a collective, political activity than an individual, economic activity—the right to pursue one's interests, without hindrance, in the marketplace."[26] Nor is this idea of citizenship even like Marshall's[27] broader notion of full participation in the community, as outsiders also have criticized his view for its lack of focus on or furtherance of equality and participation.

Also essential to a realistic formulation of citizenship in a globalized world is the failure of both the legal and social versions of citizenship for marginalized groups. One writer has suggested that for persons at the margins, citizenship "may not make much difference to one's life" as neither vision has enabled such persons to attain desired social justice and equality.[28] The two rationales offered to explain this failure of citizenship are significant to this analytical project of ending trade and human rights' splendid isolation. Just as trade, inconsistently in light of Article XX of the American Declaration, insists that it is a discipline separate from human rights, so too do some citizenship theorists suggest that the concept of citizenship might aspire to but cannot guarantee full participation in society. One explanation of the failure of citizenship for those at the margins suggests that because citizenship is a political category, it cannot "deal with substantial inequalities in the social and economic spheres."[29] The other posits that a notion of citizenship that focuses on "an evolving complex of civil, political and social rights" could include "even more characteristics of the dominant groups"[30] and thus reinforce marginalization.

In considering the intersection of the trade and human rights discourses especially in the context of globalization, any citizenship construct must deal with social, economic, and political inequalities as well as account for varied cultural concerns and circumstances within which real people lead their real lives. In this context, citizenship is not just about individual rights, but also about culture, community, and society. The proposed idea of citizenship incorporates and is responsive to varied cultural concerns, ideas, and traditions. It is not about individuals as "independent of any immediate social or political condition,"[31] but about individuals having and living within varied cultures and communities. Interestingly, the popular market notion of globalization itself is one that reinforces and confirms "the Western liberal commitment to the primacy of universal markets over national borders [which] necessarily undermines . . . claims of citizenship"[32] that are atomistic, individualistic, and tied to those transcended borders.

To reconceptualize citizenship, the right to participate in government must be problematized (see also chapter 13) to expose how hegemonic discourses and conceptualizations about community suppress subaltern ones. For example, the deterritorialization of states effected by globalization, along with the undoing of sovereignty effected by human rights norms, effectively have upended the notion of citizenship as a condition of membership specific to the nation-state. As persons, culture, and capital travel and become diffused and not bound to territorial borderlands, membership in more than one community—even more than one political community—becomes inevitable.

Globalization, particularly the aspect of movement of persons across myriad borders, signifies that multiple alliances will be formed. As globalization renders citizenship an increasingly deterritorialized concept, its nexus to and communion with a nation-state will continue to erode and widen.[33] The migrations and relocalizations of members of national, ethnic, religious, sexual, racial, and gender groups outside of clearly defined national territorial borders will result in inter- and transnational communities that exist without respect to nation-state boundaries. These new geographies and locations will result in changing concepts and boundaries of accountability, and an erosion and re/constitution of the citizenship model(s).

The redefined concept of citizenship in the globalization context uses as its foundation the critically re/formed, developed, expanded, and transformed international human rights vision.[34] It embraces and includes as indivisible, interdependent, and inviolable not only the non-discrimination norms and other civil and political rights (which include, for example, language that is often absent from U.S. discourses), but also social, economic, and cultural rights.[35] Certainly, this is a much broader notion of citizenship than the "legal status" that binds a person to a state—although, as the *Nottebohm Case* has taught us, even such a purportedly narrow, statist conception of citizenship has less clear boundaries than many would have us believe[36]—or even the desirable activity model that focuses on social relations, both of which have failed marginalized groups.

For individuals, citizenship, in the framework of globalization, is a paradigm based on attributes of human beings qua human beings.[37] It is centered and founded on the reality that the fulfillment of personhood is indivisibly connected to the entitlement not only to individual rights, including the amalgamation of geographies and locations of individuals' identities and conduct, but also to membership and participation in their varied and various communities, including political communities as well as economic and social locations such as the family, religious affiliations, and place(s) of employment.[38] Thus citizenship as full personhood does not view the liberal individualistic and communitarian traditions as alternative, independent, irreconcilable visions, but rather as indivisible and interdependent dimensions of human existence. Full personhood requires not only an individual freedoms and dignity component but also a relational community component.

It cannot be disputed that globalization already has dramatically transmogrified the concept of participation. With the adoption of a fitting citizenship model, the holistic construct of human rights norms, and not the narrow concept of legal, individual rights, forms the legitimate foundation on which personhood is evaluated and determined within an individual's various spaces, even within the state.[39] Personal citizenship constitutes the proverbial bundle of sticks that belong to persons *because* they are human beings. In this regard, individual and group citizenship is a concept, an exercise, an orientation with a commitment to shared responsibility within human reality that is exercised through participatory, democratic mechanisms (see also chapter 13).

5.4 Transnationalization of the Individual

Before we were able to travel with ease, people developed stronger ties to the community, communities were smaller, and the rights and obligations of the citizen were closely tied to land as well as to status. But the ease with which we can now communicate and displace ourselves has resulted in a change in the rights and obligations that attach to citizenship. It is no longer useful to think of citizenship as synonymous with one nation beyond the borders of which nationals seldom travel. Thus, what originated as a static concept of citizenship has been transmogrified into a dynamic one—one that, for instance, allows for the possibility of having social and cultural ties to one country, but economic and physical ties to another.

At the heart of the intersection between trade and human rights, particularly considering citizenship, is the exponentially rising number of people crossing national borders, particularly between South and North America. Over the last three decades, the United States has been experiencing an overwhelming increase in the number of Latin American immigrants, who have been settling throughout the nation. Although still predominantly Mexican,[40] these Latin American migrants now represent virtually every country in Central and South America. This magnitude of migration has raised critical questions about its dynamics, management, and ramifications for the U.S. economy, as well as for U.S. cultural identity.

Despite such a flow of persons from South to North, the countries of Central and South America keep losing the battle for equity, democratic participation, human security, and true development. Income distribution indicators reveal that the gaps between rich and poor are widening, and that trade is not benefitting all.

Core-periphery exploitation is not a new phenomenon, as the history of colonialism makes evident; it is a product of the globalization that has been going on in the world since at least the 17th century.[41] With the end of the Cold War and the advent of the information age, however, the relationships of dependencies and the populations that are affected have been deterritorialized and redefined by a core of unified global actors, classified in terms of capital ownership and political access. Thus, it is no longer useful to attach the description of rich and poor to countries. This overly simplified model fails to take into account the extraordinarily high living standards enjoyed by very few in the upper echelons of power in the developing world, as well as the deteriorating situation of the poor in the global North. In both locations, however, the poor lack voice, a key characteristic of citizenship (see also chapter 13).

Migration from Latin American, and the potential exploitation that it entails, is closely tied to trade. While it is not the "poorest of the poor" who migrate, those who travel northward away from their cultural roots and their families do so to satisfy the North's demands for cheap labor[42] (see section 8.7 on trade and immigration). On the other hand, globalization also has seen the embrace by the South of neoliberal economic policies. The expansion of markets in the South has also affected citizenship as it has "reconfigur[ed] . . . popular culture and . . . introduc[ed] . . . new consumption standards bearing little relation to local wage levels."[43] Ironically, while the North increasingly tries to close borders to the human migrants on whose labor it so greatly depends, it works exhaustively to facilitate the cross-border movement of goods, capital, commodities, and information—a reality incorporated in the NAFTA in 1994 and embraced by the aspiring FTAA.[44]

The migration is ultimately the result of the expansion of markets into peripheral, nonmarket, or premarket societies, and the disruptions that occur in the process.[45] The diametric opposition with which we regard the transmigration of cultures through the migration of individuals across national borders, as juxtaposed to the integration of world markets, is affecting the very right of citizenship. Indeed, with no shame, former Mexican President Vicente Fox actively encouraged emigration, and called for a fully open border within ten years to ensure a continuing flow of remittances—"the third largest source of revenue in Mexico's economy, trailing only oil and manufacturing"—a record of thirteen billion dollars in 2003.[46] Moreover, Fox also worked to change the law so that former Mexican citizens living in the United States, even if naturalized, could continue to vote in Mexican elections. This move is indicative not only of the transnationalization of citizenship but also of the impact of globalization on the very institutions of citizenship.

Fox's legal change rewards those who send remittances home and makes them feel that they still have a home—that they are still full citizens. It is significant because of another linkage with citizenship: according to one author, "Migrants remain active in their homelands because they are unable to achieve full social membership in the United States."[47] To be sure, the climate in the United States is that new migrants will seldom become completely accepted as full citizens—as "American"—because they "often experience blocked mobility, racism, and discrimination."[48] Thus, these migrants, even those who are naturalized citizens, live in two spaces and experience two partial levels of citizenship simultaneously—one in their spiritual homeland in which they no longer live and another in their migration geography where they live but do not fully belong—and constantly strive to bridge the gap between the two. Another author suggests that "persons in the sending and receiving societies become participants in a single social unit. To [engage] this [notion of citizenship], researchers must boldly sever their concept of society from their concept of national territory."[49]

One author observes that the new center and periphery of dependency in the context of globalization is not based on geography, but instead on economics and politics.[50] The core has been transnationalized through the affluent elites, regardless of geographical location. This "core-periphery conflict persists as a form of interaction, but it occurs mainly *between social sectors* within both developed and less-developed societies."[51]

In the context of both trade and human rights, the regional integration that has occurred "serves both as a mechanism to protect disparities that have arisen within the world-system, and as an ideological mask and justification for the maintenance of these disparities."[52] Thus, some claim that NAFTA, CAFTA-DR-US, GATT, and other similar integration initiatives are actually not so much about free trade as about protectionism, and not of workers so much as the profit interests of multinational industries such as the pharmaceuticals companies. They also instigate wage competition among Latin American countries, to see who would produce goods for the U.S. and Canadian consumer markets for the lowest possible wages.[53] This is a major economic component of the "race to the bottom"—the competition between states that, in order to attract investment—that is, to improve the state's competitive advantage—results in increased deregulation of, among other things, labor and the environment, which, in turn, results in lower socioeconomic conditions and erodes the social safety net.[54]

The process of integration has facilitated core-periphery exploitation and the accumulation of corporate wealth on the backs of the working class who travel North for employment opportunities.[55] Those who engage in Northern migration, the Latin American diaspora, have mainly, through the continual stream of remittances, become deterritorialized dual citizens who facilitate the core-periphery exploitation and are not full citizens in any location.

At the heart of this core-periphery, North-South relationship is the increasingly powerful corporate entity. With globalization, the transnational corporation's power has multiplied; it increasingly affects governments and governance, such as in creating the ubiquitous race to the bottom. Yet, as a private actor, its actions are not fully transparent and it is not fully accountable. The corporation's new influence over global social and political systems endows it with innovative citizenship status.

5.5 The Transnational Corporation and the Rise of Economic Citizenship

Any discourse on globalization and citizenship is incomplete without consideration of what the idea signifies for the corporation—undoubtedly a powerful and influential global actor central to the trade regime. The emergence of the corporation, and its growth as an economic superpower capable of exerting great influence on individuals, communities, and even governments and public policy, creates yet another layer of analysis with respect to the already complex concept of citizenship. Traditionally, the association of citizenship was between individuals and their country. It has been extended, however, to juridical persons. Thus now, corporate entities, with great economic power, and with their citizenship rights, can have more influence on the state than the average individual citizen. Such powerful citizenship, emerging from globalization, is having an impact on the citizenship discourse.

Saskia Sassen engages in an in-depth analysis of corporate power on the institution of citizenship.[56] After reviewing the particular "combination of conditions that had to crystallize for citizenship as we know it to emerge," she deploys the notion of economic citizenship as a construct to destabilize the "linearity" of history. As she poignantly observes: "Economic globalization has transformed the sovereignty and territoriality of the nation state." But her take has a "twist": economic globalization has eroded the environment in which the idea of citizenship evolved, particularly "social rights." Consequently, Sassen urges that there is a need to develop the idea of economic citizenship to include the "rights to economic well-being and to economic survival,"[57] which includes the right to work for a living. Sassen concludes that there "exists a *reality* today that represents an aggregation of economic rights that one could describe as a form of economic citizenship in that it empowers and can demand that governments be held accountable in economic matters."[58] The holders of such economic citizenship, however, are not individuals but "global economic 'actors.'" Thus, such economic trappings of citizenship need to be extended to individuals (see section 8.9 on corporate abuse of labor rights).

The basis for the economic citizenship demanded by Sassen is the impact of the increasingly global capital market on economic policy and hence governmental policy. The global financial markets have many new rights and huge power, giving them much economic influence over government policy and other, even noneconomic, initiatives.[59] The global economic reality translates to "a partial privatization of key components of monetary and fiscal policies" that inevitably results in the undermining of the voice of the individual citizen in the social, economic, and political system to which he or she belongs. Thus, the economic interests of the larger corporate actors trump the popular vote; the basis of public decision-making is the corporate interest rather than the desires of individual citizens as expressed at the ballot box. (See, however, section 13.4(A), examining the idea of voting.)

In sum, the new corporate actors that have emerged, as a result of existing globalization and the world economic systems, have put pressure on, if not effectively changed, the traditional concept of citizenship. Powerful private economic actors have supplanted the individual vote by gaining access to and having the ability to influence the government's decision-making. Governments thus implement policies favorable to corporate interests; hence, corporate enjoyment of a somewhat innovative citizenship status—Sassen's "twist" on the traditional notion of economic citizenship, which concerns individuals' economic rights.[60]

Globalization has centralized market economies and marginalized, indeed rendered invisible, human economies. In a peculiar turn, hegemonic globalization forces, because of their emphasis on financial markets and their marginalization of human lives, currently equate the existence of a market economy with democracy (see section 13.4 (A)), a notion that effectively excises pluralistic participation from democracy.

5.6 Final Thoughts

Bringing together the discourses on trade and human rights can offer a balance to this morphing of the citizenship idea. While trade depends on the economic actors, it also largely depends on human capabilities to realize the trade goals of economic well-being for all. Reinforcing individual citizenship in its social and economic sense—access to a job that enables human thriving; access to food, health, shelter—would enhance, not detract from global actors' economic goals. A human rights lens on globalization can recapture personhood from the edges or perimeters to the center of a globalization project. It can reconstruct the concept of citizenship as one that includes the relocalizations, multiplications, and recreations of cultures, people, communities, and languages[61]—events that occur because of the ubiquity of global actors and the opportunities created across increasingly porous borders.

As we already are seeing in the travel of goods and peoples across myriad borderlands, globalization has blurred the characteristics of citizenship. We see much exportation and importation of language, culture, dress, food, and religion. It explains the travel of music, musicians, food, and dress from Peru to Capitol Square in Madison, Wisconsin, every Sunday during the Farmers' Market. On the other hand, one travels to Peru and sees Levis and Burger King.

A human rights perspective on globalization and citizenship will return value to human economies; it will relocate people from the margins to the center.[62] This new geography, centrally mapping human rights, reconstitutes sovereignty, redefines legitimacy of states under the rule of law and the concept of territoriality, and revaluates humanity irrespective of borders or boundaries.

Such a broadened notion of citizenship marks the expansion not only of global economic entities but also of an international civil society.[63] Although at present it may be a contested space, it represents a space where subaltern communities—within and without national borderlands—can gain visibility and protections as members of a newly constituted polity. The needs of individuals and groups who find themselves in the midst of new world geographies will not be defined exclusively within nation-state borders.

Human transmigrations can constitute the basis for building bridges across communities and memberships and for enacting cross-border solidarities based on identity. As members of our own countries, our varied communities, and also of a transnational citizenry, persons—workers; women; native/first peoples; ethnic, racial, and sexual minorities; children; subaltern groups—can draw on international alliances to improve their conditions, to ensure participation, and to assure that any evolving conceptualization of citizenship includes individuals and their cultural environments and circumstances.

6

Ecosystem Degradation and Economic Growth

Trade's Unexploited Power to Improve Our Environment

6.1 Overview

Governments committed to ensuring the human right to a healthy, sustainable environment for their citizens increasingly face limitations from trade rules that dictate unconditional nondiscrimination and distinguish products based on their physical characteristics instead of whether their production or harvesting methods cause environmental damage. In this chapter, we examine trade's inflexible commitment to outdated interpretations that, in any event, GATT's actual provisions never demanded. We suggest approaches to the linkage between the environment and trade that promote sustainable development, including protection of nonrenewable resources as part of the common heritage of humankind, without sacrificing economic progress.

6.2 Human Rights Framework

When trade or environmental experts analyze trade's intersections with environmental protection, they do not treat a healthy environment as a fundamental human right.[1] Experts address protection of the environment as a discipline separate from human rights, although one that some analysts at least concede has linkages to human rights.[2] The listing of trade's collective intersections most often is styled as "trade and the environment, labor, and human rights." Other variations are "trade and noneconomic issues," "trade and social issues," or sometimes simply, as if in exasperation at the range of issues trade touches, "trade and . . . "

Yet, a healthy environment is certainly as much a human right as are prevention of torture and assurance of religious freedom. The reason that this apparently semantic difference matters is that the failure of environmental advocates to interrogate sustainable development as a human rights issue deprives the environmental protection discipline of the normative strength of the human rights *acquis*. In addition, this separation from the human rights system removes from the reach of environmental advocates the enforcement mechanisms of the human rights courts and commissions at global and regional levels. While the human rights enforcement mechanisms concededly do not have the compliance record of international trade's more developed dispute mechanisms, the human rights system at least assures that a definitive ruling will follow the filing of a complaint. In light of the weakness of dispute settlement systems under multilateral environmental agreements, the guarantee of a definitive ruling would be a material improvement over the present situation.[3] At the same time, exploring environmental protection apart from its roots in human rights deontology decreases the chances that policy-makers will approach other human rights issues with the flexibility and pragmatism that in recent years have characterized the successes of the environmental movement. At bottom, the demarcation of "human rights law" and "international environmental law" is done for teaching and research purposes, not because they are independent disciplines. Each is an aspect of international law, governed by the same general principles.[4]

The rights to life and to health and well-being articulated in articles 3 and 25 of the Universal Declaration would not be possible without clean water, clean air, and adequate food and shelter, all of which are directly dependent on a healthy environment. As Judge Weeremantry of the ICJ stated in the *Gabcíkovo-Nagymaros Case*, "The protection of the environment is . . . a vital part of contemporary human rights doctrine, for it is a *sine qua non* for numerous human rights such as the right to health and the right to life itself." The absolute identity of the right to life with a healthy environment led the UNCHR in the *Port Hope* case to decide that the right to life guaranteed by Article 6(1) of ICCPR includes protection against environmental harm. This nexus is brought into stark relief in reviewing Standard Fruit Company's 2003 spillage of fungicide into the Río Pacquare at its banana plantation in Siquirres, Costa Rica. The ecological disaster that followed—an amazing succession of dead fish, reptiles, manatees, eels, and birds—saw 80 percent of the local ecosystem destroyed, and made commercial and subsistence fishing, ecotourism, and other sources of income from the land impossible for years after the calamity, in addition to involuntarily sterilizing a thousand workers.[5]

That same merger of the right to life with environmental concerns underpins Article 11(1) of the Protocol of San Salvador. The Protocol provides that "everyone shall have the right to live in a healthy environment and to have access to basic public services."[6] The regional economic agreement between several Central American countries and the United States also recognizes this inexorable connection in its explicit provision that the agreement's general exceptions include "environmental measures necessary to protect human, animal, or plant life or health" under GATT Article XX(b).[7] As discussed in section 6.4(C), connecting public health with protection of the environment introduces a new level to the social policy exceptions of the WTO.

6.3   International Trade Framework

Troubling instances of tragic environmental consequences flowing from trade's excesses have become commonplace. For twenty years, Texaco pumped oil from the Ecuadorian Amazon after drilling three hundred wells and cutting eighteen thousand miles of trails through pristine rain forests. The company failed to follow even the most basic of industry practices—pumping waste back into the well—and filled over six hundred pits with toxic waste that leeched into the aquifer. Because of this frenzy for quick economic enrichment, at least thirty thousand people in Ecuador have suffered pulmonary and epidermal diseases that continue to this day.[8] The cost to indigenous populations, and to plant and animal species, of the loss of subsistence sources through the disappearance of habitats has not been calculated; it might well be incalculable. The environmental justice movement emerged from precisely this cohabitation of the human rights to a healthy environment and to adequate medical care.[9] The Metales y Derivados maquiladora plant in Tijuana, for example, produced refined lead from recycled wastes such as soils that contained lead, lead oxide, and discarded batteries. Before finally being shut down by the Mexican government in 1994, the factory's grossly negligent operation had exposed town residents to six thousand tons of lead slag, sulfuric acid, and arsenic, promising generations of health disasters.[10]

In countries that do not enforce other human rights, such as freedom of the press and participation in governance, devastation of the environment has been most severe, because a citizenry deprived of its ability to protest will be ineffective in articulating its concerns over environmentally unsound projects. The lure for a state of massive tax revenues or reduction in unemployment rates may be too great to resist based on protecting the environment for future generations whose voices it cannot yet hear. Thus, for example, Chile approved construction by multinational companies of a massive hydroelectric plant on the Bíobío River with devastating environmental consequences.[11]

In addition to trade's non-sustainable excesses, trade's governing principles run directly counter to the strategies chosen by governments in multilateral environmental agreements to protect the world's remaining resources. GATT's Four Pillars command unconditional nondiscrimination, while the principal enforcement tool of environmental treaties is discrimination among countries based on their environmental performance.[12] These contradictory approaches create important and unnecessary obstacles to realization of sustainable development, even though both human rights and trade law profess to share that objective.

Trade's regulatory regime also has caused a shift by developing countries from producing a wide variety of agricultural crops for domestic food consumption to reliance on more efficient production of the limited numbers of crops in which the countries hold a comparative advantage and thus profitably can export to developed country markets. With small farmers abandoning their traditionally biodiverse cultivation techniques in favor of chemical fertilizers, uniform seeds, and synthetic pesticides, trade liberalization unwittingly has decreased the genetic diversity of crops, not to mention contaminating ground waters and diverting limited water sources to agribusiness farming operations.[13]

6.4 Processes or Production Methods (PPMs)

(A)   PPM Distinction and GATT Article III's Safe Harbor

Global trading rules present the environmental community with a regulatory nightmare. If a Member can craft a border restriction to fit within the snug confines of GATT's Four Pillars, it need not seek immunity from trade retaliation by successfully navigating the narrow passage offered by GATT's General Exceptions. Yet the GATT refuses entrance to the safe harbors of the Four Pillars to border measures that distinguish among products based on the way that they are made or harvested—their processes or production methods. The environmental community universally denoucnes this approach as a devastating flaw in trading rules because PPMs are the lifeblood of environmental protection.

An environmentally friendly product is one created or harvested with minimal adverse effect on ecosystems, whether steel manufactured with low carbon and sulfur emissions, shrimp harvested without killing sea turtles, or wood cut using sustainable forestry methods. Multilateral environmental agreements commonly seek broader membership by banning imports of nonparties, while permitting import of the same product from parties. The Basel Convention permits export of hazardous waste to countries qualified to prevent dispersal of the substance, but denies export of the same product to unqualified countries. The Endangered Species Convention bans trade in the threatened population of a species (for example, one species of Algerian ostriches), but permits trade in nonthreatened populations of the same species from another country (for example, Australia). In each of these instances, the restricted products are physically identical to the unrestricted products. Without access to GATT Article III's safe harbor, environmental measures will continue to founder on the complex requirements of the General Exceptions outlined in the next section. Thus, finding an answer to the PPM conundrum is critical to solving the conflict in trade and human rights law relating to a healthy environment.

To appreciate how important the PPM distinction is to our thesis, consider the analysis in *U.S.-Tuna-Dolphin I*. The U.S. Marine Mammal Protection Act (MMPA) banned imported tuna caught by the setting of fishing nets on dolphins. Mexico complained that the U.S. blockage of its tuna exports violated GATT Article XI. Although Article XI prohibits restrictions on imports, one exception is GATT Article III, which allows an internal regulation that affects imported products if it meets three conditions. The restriction must satisfy (1) the requirement that regulations applied to imports comply with the MFN principle (Article I:1); (2) the *caveat* that such regulations may not "afford protection to domestic production" (Article III:1); and (3) the National Treatment obligation (Article III:4).

Mexico argued that Article III did not apply—the U.S. ban was simply a restriction on imports that violated Article XI. The U.S. contention was that the panel should consider the border restriction under Article III because it met all three conditions: the measure treated tuna from all countries alike; the restriction did not protect domestic industry because the same strict rules applied to U.S.-caught tuna; and the measure treated imported tuna no less favorably than tuna of domestic origin.

The panel disagreed, treating the PPM debate as a subset of GATT's "like product" concept introduced in section 2.3(D). First, it concluded that Article III could only describe internal regulations "applied to the product as such." The panel found that the purpose of the MMPA regulations was to protect dolphins and could not possibly affect tuna "as a product." A "dolphin-safe" tuna is indistinguishable from a tuna caught in a dolphin-unfriendly manner—they are "like products." For this reason, the MMPA regulations could not be considered Article III internal regulations and thus could not find refuge in the safe harbor of that article from Article XI's broad prohibitions against restrictions on imports. For the MMPA measure to prevail it would have to satisfy the far stricter discipline of GATT's General Exceptions (see section 6.5(B)).

U.S.-Tuna-Dolphin II confirmed the earlier panel's reasoning, making even clearer the connection with "like product" analysis by noting that different harvesting methods could not affect the "inherent characteristics" of tuna as a product.[14] The conclusions of the *Tuna-Dolphin* panels are clear: a WTO member cannot regulate two products differently based on the manner of their production unless that production changes the product's physical characteristics. Although neither tuna panel decision is GATT "law" because the parties did not formally adopt them, the PPM distinction that these cases invented, for reasons unrelated to the actual language of the treaty, remains viable.[15]

(B)   PPM Distinction's Avoidable Fallacy

Human rights and trade lawyers offer starkly different views of GATT's PPM distinction. The human rights analysis is that the repeated reference to "products" in Article III and throughout the GATT cited as evidence by the *Tuna* cases is proof only that the GATT is about the regulation of products, as opposed to the regulation of capital, or services, or labor. These references do not speak to whether a PPM affects a product "as a product" or whether the regulation is "applied to the product as such."[16] Article III:4 applies to "internal laws, regulations, and requirements affecting the internal sale . . . of products." One cannot doubt, this legal camp maintains, that PPMs affect the sale of products. The MMPA's burdensome requirements for the purchase of special netting and its time-consuming use at sea after extensive training certainly affected both the price and quantity of tuna sold, whether U.S. or foreign boats were catching the fish. This side observes that no evidence for this distinction may be found in GATT's drafting history and, in fact, GATT Article III itself expressly lists "regulations requiring the mixture, processing, or use of products" as within the purview of the National Treatment Clause.[17]

The rejoinder from the trade side is that the repeated reference to "products" in the GATT furnishes a basic textual justification for the distinction. The more important point, this side claims, is that abandonment of the PPM limitation on Article III's safe harbor for internal regulations leads to the notorious slippery slope.[18]

These arguments are a weak defense for the PPM distinction. The fact that the word "product" appears repeatedly throughout the GATT lends support only to an unacceptably superficial analysis. Neither do we find persuasive the admission by panels that the true reason that they have retained the distinction is not its interpretive strength, but because Members might abuse border restrictions to protect domestic industry. The WTO's drafters adorned virtually every provision with language meant to prevent just this sort of creative abuse by Members. The irony in the origin of the PPM distinction is that GATT Article III and its rich interpretive history offer stronger protection against disguised protectionism than any other WTO provision. With reduction in the importance of tariffs and other obvious trade barriers, discrimination in national treatment remains one of the few available mechanisms to favor domestic production. With increasingly creative use of internal regulations and taxes have come increasingly specific interpretations of the bounds of GATT's National Treatment Clause.

Consider a telling hypocrisy in the PPM saga. Prisoners make license plates in some countries.[19] GATT Article XX(e) exempts measures "relating to the products of prison labour." Under like product criteria, license plates made by prisoners are identical to those made by other workers. Distinguishing between two license plates on the basis of the incarceration status of the person who made them is obviously a PPM distinction, one directly authorized by Paragraph (e).

In the final analysis, the PPM distinction stands as an unspoken understanding by WTO Members and the WTC that the approach permits them to tackle the international values that justify "policy-forging" unilateralism[20] in one place: within GATT's Article XX General Exceptions— "where they belong"—rather than also within the sacrosanct walls of the Four Pillars. There is no legal impediment to the Court's disavowal of an outdated policy basis for prohibiting Members from using trade's power to protect human rights within the confines of GATT Article III's central

National Treatment Clause. Notwithstanding the point often made by WTO scholar John Jackson that the lines separating lawful from unlawful activity must be administrable to be effective, these lines need not be so simple as to "enable ordinary people to come to grips" with them, because trade negotiators and WTO panelists bring extraordinary expertise to their tasks. Even if the PPM distinction may have served as a minimally acceptable device to avoid drawing foggier lines against protectionism in an earlier time, no legal or policy basis can justify its unnecessary retention in the face of today's widespread demand for human rights support from the trade regime.

(C)   *EC-Asbestos*: Roadmap Around the PPM Distinction?

Section 2.3(D) discussed the *EC-Asbestos* case with respect to GATT's critical but undefined "like product" concept. The case also raises the question whether the WTC has signaled a way to distinguish products based on their compliance with environmental or other human rights objectives, which usually involves a PPM (for example, unsustainably produced biofuels). France treated imported asbestos products less favorably than domestic asbestos substitutes. France thus had no credible defense to Canada's claim of a violation of Article III:4 if it accepted the initial panel's finding that the products were "like." The WTC found that the carcinogenicity of the asbestos was "a defining aspect" of the product's physical characteristics and that the health risk alone of a product properly could distinguish it from another product with similar physical characteristics and uses.

Significantly, *EC-Asbestos* was not a PPM case. The imported products contained asbestos and the domestic substitutes did not. Clearly there were differences in the physical characteristics of the two products. In asking, then, whether *EC-Asbestos* opens the door to consideration of a product's environmental impacts in distinguishing it from another product, one must guard against an overoptimistic reading of the WTC's findings. Nonetheless, the initial panel in *EC-Asbestos* did not consider health risks to be relevant to the "likeness" analysis, even when faced with this very real physical distinction. In dismissing the panel's concern that taking account of health risks trumped the other like product criteria and made GATT's General Exceptions irrelevant, the WTC directed panels to adhere to the Vienna Convention's instruction to interpret treaty language in accordance with its ordinary meaning. The toxicity of asbestos is a defining aspect of its physical characteristics that panels may not ignore. The health risks relevant to an Article III:4 analysis relate to the competitive relationships of products in the marketplace, a very different analysis than that relevant under Article XX(b)'s Public Health exception.

On another level, the WTC's more nuanced test for "like products," permitting consideration of health risks, may have relevance beyond the physical characteristics criterion of the test for "likeness." For example, consumer tastes and expectations are relevant when a potential user confronts two types of tuna, one whose harvest killed dolphins, or two types of coffee, one whose production left the farmer with little to show for her labor. Of course, no single criterion is controlling, but the like product test already is subjective (consider whether a Chianti is "like" a Merlot).[21] The WTC has added a health criterion relevant to environmental protection and to human rights generally. *EC-Asbestos* furnishes a legal basis for WTO Members seeking an interpretation of GATT provisions that takes account of the measure's human rights impacts, one that is not limited to the product's health impact, but to any factor—regardless of whether within the four criteria blessed by previous cases.[22] This approach is consistent with the WTO preamble's statement that protection of the environment and raising standards of living are among the purposes of the WTO Agreements.

6.5   GATT's Public Health and Welfare Clause

(A)   General Exceptions at a Glance

Even if a Member's environmental border restriction contravenes one of the Four Pillars, GATT's Public Health and Welfare Clause—Article XX (see Item 7 in online Documents Annex)—may provide an effective defense. The first unnumbered paragraph, styled in treaty parlance as the "Chapeau," ends with the article's resounding operative language: "Nothing in this Agreement shall . . . prevent the adoption or enforcement by . . . any [WTO Member] of measures" that fall within the range of policies specified in one of the categories naming a particular social—non-trade, that is—human rights priority:

- Paragraph (a) "necessary to protect public morals";
- Paragraph (b) "necessary to protect human, animal or plant life or health";
- Paragraph (d) "necessary to secure compliance with laws or regulations which are not inconsistent with the provisions of this Agreement, including those relating to . . . prevention of deceptive practices";

- Paragraph (e) "relating to the products of prison labour";
- Paragraph (f) "imposed for the protection of national treasures";
- Paragraph (g) "relating to the conservation of exhaustible natural resources if such measures are made effective in conjunction with restrictions on domestic production or consumption."[23]

Article XX tells Members that, despite the Four Pillars and the other two dozen articles of the GATT restricting government interference with open borders, "nothing" in the Agreement will prevent a Member from taking measures that fit within the human rights policies of the listed General Exceptions.[24] How could the GATT have garnered the status of "splendid isolation" from human rights law with so clear an attempt by its mid-20th-century drafters to integrate the two disciplines?

While Article XX takes a broad approach to the balancing of trade and human rights policies, dispute settlement panels have been endlessly creative in finding reasons to deny the General Exceptions their evident reach. Initially, panels decided that they must interpret Article XX's provisions strictly and narrowly because they are "exceptions" to the elemental nondiscrimination rules of the GATT. The *Tuna-Dolphin* decisions discussed in section 6.4(A) are representative of the narrow reach accorded Article XX during most of its existence. In the *U.S.-Shrimp-Turtle I* case, the WTC discredited this view of Article XX as a provision of secondary importance. The Court reasoned that, despite the title of Article XX, the General Exceptions set forth rights and obligations of Members that have equal status with the Four Pillars. Panels should not read Article XX so expansively as to emasculate the nondiscrimination purposes of GATT's Pillars, but neither should panels deprive Members of the benefits of the General Exceptions by allowing the Four Pillars to undermine the intent of the drafters in permitting certain human rights policies to override other basic GATT principles.[25]

(B) Necessity and Extraterritoriality Tests: *Tuna-Dolphin* Cases

Despite the complete immunity from GATT's Four Pillars created by Article XX, absolution comes with a price. As substitutes for the border-opening requirements of the Four Pillars, each Paragraph of the General Exceptions lays down conditions to prevent Members from using Article XX as a disguised means of protecting their domestic industries. Toward the same end, Article XX's Chapeau tacks on three conditions that a trade measure based on any of the specific policy exceptions of the article also must meet to gain immunity from the principles of the Four Pillars. In many cases, these conditions parrot the rules they replace, further recognition that the Four Pillars are the foundation stones of the trading system. GATT and WTO dispute settlement panels until recently have brought a strict liability mindset to enforcement of these conditions, denying to human rights policies Article XX's safe harbor to an extent that its drafters cannot possibly have intended.

To begin, keep in mind the WTC's teaching as to the proper analytical order. Even though the Chapeau appears in the text before the article's lettered paragraphs, logic demands that examination begin with the language of the individual paragraph implicated by the measure at issue. A panel first should decide whether the measure falls within the range of policies identified by the particular paragraph. If so, the panel should consider whether the paragraph's specific terms are satisfied. If the measure hurdles this obstacle, only then should the panel turn to the Chapeau's general conditions and analyze whether the measure is arbitrarily or unjustifiably discriminatory or constitutes a disguised trade restriction. The Chapeau must be the final step in the analysis because the specific policy that the Member is pursuing will affect the meaning of the Chapeau's "necessarily broad" conditions.[26]

The Public Morals exception of Paragraph (a), the Public Health exception of Paragraph (b), and the Other Laws exception of Paragraph (d) require that the border restriction implemented in violation of the Four Pillars be "necessary" to accomplish its purpose. Other Paragraphs require only that the measure "relate to" the policy listed, such as Paragraph (e)'s Prison Labor exception and Paragraph (g)'s Natural Resource exception. The first interpretation of the Necessity Test to gain notoriety was that in *U.S.-Tuna-Dolphin I*, discussed in section 6.4(A) in reference to GATT's PPM distinction. This 1991 GATT panel case awakened the environmental community to the importance and extent of the disengagement of trade and environmental treaties.

After losing its contention that the MMPA ban fit within GATT Article III, the United States argued that its border restriction on tuna imports was shielded by the Public Health and Welfare policies of Paragraphs (b) and (g) of GATT Article XX. The MMPA ban both protected the lives of animals within the meaning of Paragraph (b) and conserved exhaustible natural resources within the meaning of Paragraph (g). The panel first found that, although the U.S. ban to protect animal life fell within the range of policies addressed by Paragraph (b), it failed the Necessity Test. The panel concluded from the negotiating history that the purpose of Paragraph (b) was to permit "the use of sanitary measures to safeguard life or health . . . within the jurisdiction of the importing country."[27] The panel also faulted the MMPA ban by misreading an early Necessity Test case as holding that Paragraph (b) allows Members to impose measures inconsistent with other GATT provisions only to the extent such inconsistencies are "unavoidable."[28]

The panel's third basis for finding the ban inconsistent applied also to Paragraph (g): if Article XX immunizes a Member's attempts to apply its social policies outside its borders, a Member would be empowered unilaterally to determine the life or health protection policies of other Members that wished to trade with the Member. The panel reasoned that this result would be inconsistent with the basic premise of a trade agreement that is multilateral in nature.[29]

European nations that canned tuna harvested elsewhere filed a challenge to the MMPA's secondary boycott. Although the secondary nature of the import ban is irrelevant to the Article XX analysis, *U.S.-Tuna-Dolphin II* trod new ground to the same end. In disagreeing with *U.S.-Tuna-Dolphin I* on the extraterritoriality question, the panel observed that several other provisions of Article XX, of the GATT as a whole, and of general international law anticipated impact on matters outside the importing country's jurisdiction. For example, Article XX(e)'s exemption of restrictions on imports of products made with prison labor immunizes measures whose only purpose is to change the public policies of other countries.[30]

The panel then softened *U.S.-Tuna-Dolphin I*'s reading of *Thailand-Cigarettes* by holding that the Necessity Test does not require that the measure be "unavoidable," but the least GATT-inconsistent among reasonably available measures. Despite this lower standard, the panel found that the MMPA ban could not be "necessary" by stating an obvious fact: unless countries catching tuna changed their policies, the U.S. embargo by itself could not accomplish its objective of conserving dolphins. Discarding the possibility that the large U.S. market for tuna could accomplish the result intended by the MMPA, the panel reached the same conclusion as had *U.S.-Tuna-Dolphin I*. The ban sought to force other countries to change their policies on non-trade issues. Enforcing such a ban would undermine the basic principles of the GATT, because panels must read Article XX's General Exceptions narrowly to preserve the basic principles and objectives of the GATT. In this broad interpretation of a non-articulated rationale, the panel followed its predecessor panel in making yet another reach far outside the language of Article XX to the overall purposes of the GATT to interpret a relatively straightforward word, "necessary."[31]

(C) *EC-Asbestos* Concept of Balancing Harms Weakens Necessity Test

In *EC-Asbestos* the WTC seven years later changed the nature of Article XX(b)'s Necessity Test. The Court surveyed the adopted GATT and WTO decisions on the Necessity Test, concluding that to decide whether an alternative and less GATT-inconsistent measure is "reasonably available" is a "balancing test." A pivotal aspect of that balancing is the importance of the objective that the Member is pursuing through its import restriction: France with its asbestos ban was seeking to save human life and thus second-guessing France's decision might have life-threatening consequences. The WTC found that France's ban bore the "highest degree" of value.[32]

The severity of the consequences of imposing a less restrictive import measure thus weighs heavily in deciding whether a particular measure meets Paragraph (b)'s Necessity Test. Economists would call these "error costs" and the *EC-Asbestos* decision shows the reluctance of panels to hold that a less restrictive measure would be "good enough." This exercise resembles a cost-benefit analysis, although without the use of quantifiable data. When human life is at stake, doubt as to the efficacy of alternative measures likely will result in panels finding the restrictive measure to be "necessary." These cases reveal the Necessity Test's mutation toward a more exception-friendly condition.

The strained reading of the *Tuna-Dolphin* cases—that extraterritorial effects make a measure unnecessary under Article XX—has vanished, despite the WTC's reservation of decision on the issue.[33] In addition, the "reasonably available alternative" interpretation of *Thailand-Cigarettes* has been nuanced further by the Court's "balancing" test, which tells panels to take account of "error costs." The panel must decide how high on the public policy scale the objectives that the Member is pursuing are and how much doubt exists that a less-inconsistent alternative such as labeling or controlled use will achieve the chosen level of protection. These changes bode well for human health protection, perhaps less so for protection of animal and plant resources, although animal and plant resources are necessary to human life and health.

The error-cost approach is equally relevant to food safety issues under the WTO's SPS Agreement, which covers a narrower range of health considerations than GATT Article XX(b), such as food safety, pests, and disease-causing organisms. The SPS Agreement has incorporated virtually all of Article XX(b)'s jurisprudence while adding strong reliance on science as the basis for permitting partial discrimination, as explained in *EC-Hormones* discussed in section 7.4(D).

(D) WTC's Swift Neutering of Article XX's "Relationship"
and "Domestic Restriction" Tests

Instead of a Necessity Test, Paragraph (e)'s exemption for measures addressing prison labor (see section 8.4(B)) and Paragraph (g)'s sheltering of restrictions giving refuge to exhaustible natural resources require that the measure "relate to" the human rights purpose being pursued. The Relationship Test of Article XX has experienced substantial evolution in reaching its present literal translation. Paragraph (g) adds to the Relationship Test the condition that restrictions on domestic production must have been imposed "in conjunction with" the import limitations.

Because "exhaustible natural resources" are the theme of innumerable environmental treaties, most environmental dispute settlement cases have focused on Paragraph (g), which also is the target of most of the environmental backlash against globalization and the WTO. In interpreting the Relationship Test, an early GATT Panel in the *Canada-Herring and Salmon* case found that the condition meant that the border measure must be "primarily aimed at" conserving a natural resource. Conservation could not be one of many equally important objectives; the conservation objective must be paramount.[34] Other GATT panels followed this holding, pursuing the path of strict interpretation that had claimed all aspects of the General Exceptions as victims in the early days. Taken together with the shortcuts and lack of fundamental legal logic of the *Tuna-Dolphin* Panels, the conclusion of environmentalists that the GATT simply was running as fast as it could from the potential power of Article XX to implement human rights law is logical.

In *U.S.-Gasoline*, the WTC in its first decision dealt gingerly with the finding in *Canada-Herring and Salmon* that "relating to" meant "primarily aimed at." The WTC first noted that as a judicial body it would not decide an issue on which all parties agreed. It observed that "primarily aimed at" were words found nowhere in the treaty. It concluded that U.S.

rules to force cleaner air from gasoline production met the Relationship Test because they bear "a substantial_relationship," not an "incidental or inadvertent" one, to conserving clean air.[35] A "substantial relationship" standard is far easier for a measure to meet than a requirement that the measure be "primarily aimed at" conservation. The result is that, quietly and with as little fanfare as possible, the WTC begins to make its mark on the trade and environment intersection by substantially reducing the burden of Paragraph (g)'s first condition.

By the time of the *U.S.-Shrimp-Turtle I* case two years later, the WTC had entirely discarded the "primarily aimed at" language of *Canada-Herring and Salmon*. It softened *U.S.-Gasoline's* "substantial relationship" interpretation by concluding that the "means must be reasonably related to the ends."[36] This language, borrowed from an *amicus* brief filed by a private environmental group, returns to an essentially literal reading of the actual words in Paragraph (g). The Appellate Body thus denudes the Relationship Test of the machinations in which prior panels had engaged to support a strict and narrow interpretation. Following the interpretive dictates of Article 31 of the Vienna Convention, these appellate decisions give the language its ordinary meaning, taken in context and in light of the object and purpose of the WTO Agreements.

Turning to Paragraph (g)'s Domestic Restrictions Test, that domestic restrictions must be made effective "in conjunction with" border restrictions on imports of the like product, the Court held that these words mean simply that restrictions must be placed on domestic production, not solely on imports. Identity of treatment could not be what the drafters meant, nor could they have intended no restrictions whatever on domestic production. The tribunal used strong but simple examples to demonstrate why these two extremes were illogical. First, if treatment of imports and domestic production had been identical, how could there have been a violation of Article III in the first place? Second, if there were no domestic restrictions, a panel must conclude that the measure does not relate to conservation, but instead is naked protection of domestic production.[37]

The most striking difference between the WTC's first opinion and those of most GATT Panels that had preceded it was the clear legal analysis—word by word, clause by clause, and sentence by sentence. There were leaps neither of logic nor of faith. The decision announces with authority that dispute settlement for trade rules is no longer a diplomatic process, as it had been under the GATT, but an unmistakably judicial one.

(E)   Chapeau's Nondiscrimination Tests

(1)   THEORY

Even if the border restriction is found to meet the conditions of one of Article XX's substantive Paragraphs, the measure is considered only "provisionally justified" until it passes the three tests of Article XX's introductory clause. The Member may not apply the measure in a manner that would constitute (1) "a means of arbitrary . . . discrimination between countries where the same conditions prevail"; (2) "a means of . . . unjustifiable discrimination between countries where the same conditions prevail"; or (3) "a disguised restriction on international trade."

Article XX exempts a Member from all of GATT's Pillars, including its Article I/Article III nondiscrimination foundation. In the end, however, it provides only partial exemption from this sine qua non of global trade. The Chapeau reintroduces Article I's Most-favored Nation principle, but, unlike Article I, qualifies the requirement. Under the Chapeau, discrimination in the protection, for example, of exhaustible natural resources may be practiced as long as it is not arbitrary or unjustifiable or otherwise a disguised restriction on trade. The human rights policies underlying the General Exceptions substitute for the unconditional nondiscrimination that is the hallmark of trade rules. This is a powerful statement of the primacy of the broad human rights policies listed in Article XX over trade's otherwise single-minded quest for the benefits of comparative advantage, made all the more remarkable for having been penned at the very birth of modern human rights law.

The Chapeau's third condition—no "disguised restriction on international trade"—is most reminiscent of Article III's national treatment provisions, except that Article XX is not limited to internal taxes or regulations. In fact, it would apply beyond the national treatment context of comparing how the Member treats imported products in relation to domestic products. The Chapeau's third condition thus plays a role similar to Article XI's—no quotas or other restrictions on imports or exports. It disqualifies protectionist measures hiding behind human rights labels that have not been outed by the gamut of previous conditions.

(2)   APPLICATION IN *SHRIMP-TURTLE* CASES

The *Shrimp-Turtle* cases demonstrate that meeting the Chapeau's conditions is difficult, but well within the reach of states interested in pursuing human rights compliance. As with dolphins, the United States used its lucrative import market to protect endangered sea turtles from the nets of shrimp trawlers. Shrimp were denied access to the U.S. market unless caught on a trawler using the same turtle excluder device required of U.S. trawlers. The trawler's country of registration also must have received U.S. certification that it mandated use of the device. In 1998's *U.S.-Shrimp-Turtle I,* the border measure that had passed Paragraph (g)'s conditions foundered on the Chapeau's proscription of unjustifiable discrimination.

The WTC found "unjustifiable" U.S. discrimination against trawlers whose countries may not have regulated use of turtle excluders, even when the trawler catching the imported shrimp had used the desired excluder. Because turtles are highly migratory species, the Court also found unjustifiable U.S. closure of its border without efforts to engage the complaining Members in "serious, across-the-board negotiations" to conclude treaties to protect the turtles. Without crossing the "equilibrium line" of serious diplomatic effort, U.S. border regulations would not be excepted from GATT Article XI's general prohibition of import restrictions.[38]

Three years later, Malaysia challenged U.S. compliance with the WTO decision. In *U.S.-Shrimp-Turtle II,* the WTC found that the United States had satisfied the Chapeau's conditions through further attempts to negotiate a treaty solution with the East Asian nations that had brought the original case and by interpreting its rules for turtle excluder devices more flexibly. The WTC in *U.S.-Shrimp-Turtle I* was not, as some had feared, requiring that negotiations be successful, which would have been the end of Article XX because any Member could have nullified use of Article XX as a defense simply by refusing to agree.

In *U.S.-Shrimp-Turtle I,* the WTC also had found U.S. shrimp regulations to be "arbitrary" in their discrimination, in violation of the Chapeau's second condition. In essence, the "arbitrary" analysis looked to due process and the overall fairness of the certification system. Initially, the United States provided no hearings, no transparency through notice of the reasons for denial, and no appeal of a denial. This discrimination between certified and noncertified countries logically caused the WTC to brand the certification process as arbitrary, thus equating due process with nonarbitrariness. The WTC found that the United States had cured these failures as well by the time of the second challenge.[39]

(E) Viability of GATT Article XX for Environmental Protection

The *Shrimp-Turtle* cases provide proponents of integrating environmental and other human rights comfortably within the trading system with a logical and accessible, although admittedly skeletal, legal arena in which to engage opponents in the battle. The various conditions of GATT Article XX that appeared insurmountable during the era of the *Tuna-Dolphin* cases and their progeny, from the Necessity to the Relationship to the Domestic Restrictions Tests, and the Chapeau's prohibitions of arbitrary or capricious discrimination, no longer seem out of reach.

The extraterritoriality issue, although not explicitly resolved, has retreated into the background and, as we discuss in other chapters, should be susceptible to increasingly specific statements of international human rights law. Multilateral environmental agreements and other human rights instruments that articulate global standards for health, worker rights, environmental protection, and other human rights make less relevant the issue of whether the Member's border restriction seeks to protect human rights solely within its territory. To be sure, WTO Members may yet mount difficult challenges against particular uses of trade access that harm other trading interests. The WTC has emphasized that progressive human rights enforcement on a unilateral basis raises important questions for a multilateral system that panels must carefully address. The WTC has crafted the road map, however, and affirmed that the public health and welfare interests protected by GATT Article XX reside on the same level as GATT's Four Pillars.

6.6 Harmonization of Product Standards: TBT Agreement

(A) Technical Standards at a Glance

For certain environmentally motivated restrictions, fitting within GATT Article III's safe harbor or, failing that, meeting the conditions of one of GATT Article XX's General Exceptions is not sufficient to ensure WTO compliance. Illogically inconsistent national product standards (consider the many designs of electric plugs)—even if applied in a nondiscriminatory manner—can increase substantially a company's costs in selling its product in multiple markets. To harmonize product standards affecting trade and, in so doing, reduce producer—and thus consumer—costs and the potential for abuse of standards to protect domestic industry, the WTO's drafters created through the TBT Agreement an elaboration of GATT Article III:4's disciplines on internal regulations (see section 2.3(B) and (D)).[40]

The TBT Agreement requires that a Member use benchmarks set by international standard-setting bodies, such as the International Organization for Standardization (ISO), when the Member seeks through "technical regulations" to protect human health or safety, animal or plant life or health, or the environment, to prevent deceptive practices, or to pursue other "legitimate objectives."[41] Despite the WTO's reputation for adversity toward ecological policies, the TBT Agreement explicitly recognizes environmental protection as a valid purpose for restricting imports through product standards.

"Technical regulations" (see Annex 1 of Item 10, online Documents Annex) set mandatory criteria for the physical characteristics that a product, its packaging, or its label must—or must not—contain to permit its importation. Examples are the maximum decibel level of a chain saw or the warning label required on lawn fertilizer or cigarettes. Even the total ban of a product, such as France's measure in the *EC-Asbestos* case, is a set of product characteristics that fits the TBT's definition of "technical regulation."

In addition to the requirement that a Member's technical regulations be based on extant international standards unless inappropriate or ineffective in attaining the Member's objective,[42] the TBT Agreement requires that products imported from any WTO Member be accorded MFN and national treatment, that standards be drafted in terms of performance rather than design, and that standards not create unnecessary obstacles to trade. These three conditions should present little difficulty to ecosystem-based measures: compliance with GATT Article III:4 will already mean that the measure is applied on an MFN and national treatment basis; environmental standards rarely are based either on performance or on design criteria; and the Necessity Test is the familiar standard encountered in GATT Article XX's General Exceptions—discussed in section 6.5(B)—which requires only that the Member show that no reasonable alternative that is less restrictive of trade is available to accomplish the Member's objective.

The breadth of the TBT Agreement's coverage means that most environmentally intentioned internal regulations that affect imports must comply with the TBT Agreement's harmonization procedures in addition to passing muster under Article III(4) and other relevant GATT 1994 provisions. The 2002 case of *EC-Sardines* shows the difficulty of avoiding international product standards, which for some environmentalists represent an undesirable lowest common denominator. Peru challenged an EU requirement that the only product that could be labeled as "sardines" was fish of the species *Sardinus pilchardus*. The European rule had the effect of displacing Peru as a source of EU sardine imports because the *pilchardus* species does not swim in Peruvian waters. The panel found that the EU's purposes of ensuring fairness in labeling and protecting consumers from fraudulent practices, while "legitimate objectives" under the TBT Agreement, would not be rendered "ineffective or inappropriate" by using the existing international standard. That standard allowed a product to be labeled as "sardines" even if the contents were not *pilchardus* if the geographic origin of the sardine contents was included somewhere on the label (for example, "Peruvian sardines").

Setting meaningful barriers to a Member's attempt to avoid harmonization is consistent with studies finding that product standards differing from international benchmarks often do so to protect domestic producers.[43] Moreover, Members will not be able to use GATT Article XX's Public Health and Welfare exceptions to justify noncompliance with a relevant international standard because the TBT Agreement takes precedence over the GATT in the event of conflict.[44] Claiming a GATT exception to the TBT's "ineffective or inappropriate" standard presents such a conflict. Even so, Members have three reasons to be optimistic about their own progressive environmental standard in place of a less robust international standard.

First, the WTC has held that the "ineffective or inappropriate" test is not an exception to the requirement in Article 2.4 of the TBT Agreement to use international standards. Rather, it is an autonomous right coterminous with that requirement. The complaining Member thus bears the burden of proving not only that an international standard relevant to the responding Member's objective exists (or its completion is imminent), but also that this standard is not "ineffective or inappropriate" to the objective chosen by the responding Member.[45] Second, while the question of whether an international standard is "ineffective" is relatively straightforward (the standard does not accomplish the objective), whether the standard is "appropriate" to the Member's chosen level of protection is decidedly less so. In the WTC's typically literal approach, the "inappropriate" part of the test asks whether the standard is specially suitable, fitting, or proper to accomplish the objective. Members have substantial discretion under this reading to decide that there are more desirable means than the relevant international standard to accomplish their chosen environmental objective.

The third reason for optimism is that the TBT Agreement does not specify the international standardizing bodies whose benchmarks are relevant. If an international environmental agreement such as the Montreal Protocol limits trade in products containing ozone-depleting substances, those science-based provisions may qualify as international standards.

(B)   May a Member Base Technical Regulations on PPMs?

Section 6.4(A) notes that for most human rights, the concern arises not from the product itself but from its manner of production, whether in violation of worker rights or contrary to sound environmental practices. The TBT Agreement seems to include such PPMs through its definition of "technical regulation" as reaching not only "product characteristics," but also "their related processes and production methods" (see Item 10, online Documents Annex). As discussed in section 6.4, controlling interpretations hold that GATT regulates products, not PPMs. If a product from Country A and a product from Country B would be considered "like products" under the physical characteristics, uses, consumer expectations, and tariff classification criteria, the Four Pillars would require that the two products be treated similarly. Nondiscriminatory treatment is required even if Country B's product was produced using environmentally unsound methods, such as clear-cutting a virgin tropical forest, creating pollution that increases global climate change, or overfishing a depleted stock. The products continue to be indistinguishable based on the "like product" criteria—they are identical physically and in other "likeness" respects.

On its face, the TBT Agreement's reference to "their related processes and production methods" seems to change GATT's basic approach. It appears to envision that a Member might take into account the way that a product is made when designing "technical regulations" that will determine whether the product may be marketed in the importing country. Consider two examples that demonstrate the importance of how a panel interprets these words. In one instance, a Member acts to protect air quality by prohibiting spray starch that uses as its propellant ozone-depleting chlorofluorocarbons (CFCs). Such a product standard would be permissible under the GATT's basic approach because—using "likeness" criteria—spray starch containing CFCs is physically different from spray starch not containing CFCs.

In the second situation, the Member seeks to protect air quality worldwide by banning semiconductors cleaned with a solvent containing CFCs.[46] This technical regulation is based on a PPM that does not affect the product's characteristics because the solvent evaporates during the cleaning process. Commentators disagree on whether such a measure would fall within the TBT Agreement's reference to PPMs. Some answer in the negative, arguing that the PPM language modifies the term "product characteristics," not the product in general. Under this analysis, the solvent measure would not be covered by the TBT because the PPM does not "relate to" the product's characteristics. That is, use of the solvent does not change the physical nature of the finished semiconductor,[47] just as a tuna fish caught in association with dolphins does not have different physical characteristics than dolphin-safe tuna.[48]

Others contend that interpreting the PPM language as permitting only product-related PPMs renders the language a nullity. A technical regulation requiring, for example, a minimum of 25 percent recycled content in newsprint will survive the TBT's nondiscrimination rules without need of the PPM language because the two products are physically unlike. It is a measure such as one prohibiting import of newsprint that uses pulp harvested through clear-cutting that needs the PPM language to qualify as a TBT technical regulation.[49]

(C) Ecolabels Based on PPMs

By changing consumer buying patterns, labels that reveal a product's environmental burden—ecolabels—aim to change production methods that are harmful to the ecosystem. Just as developing countries fear introduction of environmental standards in FTAs, these countries oppose use of ecolabels to shrink their comparative advantage by identifying unsound environmental practices attendant on a product's manufacture. The same interpretive debate about whether a Member may craft a "technical regulation" based on a product's PPM applies to "standards," defined as technical regulations that are voluntary.[50] Most ecolabels are voluntary appeals to green consumers, and for the most part the TBT Agreement applies to them the same rules required for mandatory labels or other technical regulations under Article 2.

Ecolabels are an effective environmental protection device. For example, although the *Tuna-Dolphin* cases are notorious, in effect the war was already over before the United States implemented its tuna ban: the U.S. tuna industry voluntarily had adopted the "dolphin-safe" label to satisfy green consumers. Tuna without this label gathered dust on grocery shelves. Most ecolabels give us PPM information: whether the tuna was harvested without harming porpoises ("dolphin safe"); how much of the earth's resources were used in a product's creation ("no animal testing"); or what level of harmful pollution was created ("organic").[51] The ongoing debate over whether PPMs unrelated to the product's characteristics are "technical regulations" is for this reason important.

Coverage under the TBT Agreement is a two-edged sword. On one hand, a covered PPM measure based on an international standard gains the presumption under Article 2.5 of compliance with that Agreement's Necessity Test, which likely will be dispositive if the Member also must defend the measure under GATT Article XX(b). If the measure also is applied on an MFN and national treatment basis, a separate challenge under the GATT likely will fail because one of GATT Article XX's General Exceptions will be met, even if the measure is found to contravene GATT Article III:4 (or the general prohibition of nonexempt import restrictions in GATT Article XI). On the other hand, if PPM measures, whether ecolabels or other import restrictions, are not covered by the TBT Agreement at all, then a Member may bring a challenge only under the GATT, where Article XX will be the only hurdle. In the latter case, however, unregulated social labeling and other PPM-based restrictions may have sufficiently adverse effects on trading patterns to arouse a backlash less favorable to the human rights movement than working within the broad confines of the TBT Agreement. Despite the fear of Emerging Market countries that PPM measures will deprive them of their comparative advantages, inclusion of non–product related PPMs within the tighter disciplines of the TBT Agreement could allay protectionist concerns.[52]

6.7   From Rio to Johannesburg: Sustainable Development Sues for Peace with Trade Rules

The effort to merge economics and ecology dates from the 1992 Earth Summit—the Rio Conference on Environment and Development, in which 178 nations adopted sustainable development as a guiding objective to be pursued by all nations. As wildlife and air and water pollution treaties proliferated in the 1970s and were overtaken in the 1980s by a second generation of more complex conventions on biological diversity, on the law of the sea, on the ozone layer, hazardous waste, and climate change, the absence of a central theme for international environmental law—the role played for trade by the GATT's nondiscrimination concept—became starkly apparent. In preparation for the Rio Summit, the United Nations challenged the prime minister of Norway, Gro Haarlem Brundtland, to lead a search for a central theme to remodel the apparent conflict between continuing development through economic growth and the limits of environmental sustainability.

"Our Common Future," the Brundtland Commission's report, brilliantly defined its response to the charge, sustainable development, as "development that meets the needs of the present without compromising the ability of future generations to meet their own needs." In this maddeningly simple but impossibly complex formula, there are four guiding precepts. As long as millions of people are hungry or without shelter or jobs, development is a fundamental assumption. A policy that simply stops using resources is unacceptable. From a purely environmental standpoint, poverty must be reduced because poverty itself causes environmental degradation through pollution and inefficient use of resources. As Indira Gandhi observed at the 1972 Stockholm Conference, "Poverty is the greatest polluter." Second, there must be limits both to the use of resources and to population growth, and these limits must protect against the ecological disaster that would follow exceeding the capacity of our natural ecosystems.

Third, change in the ecosystem from economic activity is not automatically adverse. Development needs require use of forests, fisheries, and water, and regulators must permit such use as long as it does not exceed regeneration rates. Finally, we cannot afford to let plant or animal species become extinct because the lack of biodiversity greatly limits the choices of future generations.[53] As much a statement of political as economic principles, the concept was transformed into a specific and unanimously adopted plan of action at 2002's World Summit on Sustainable Development in Johannesburg. Signatories are far from realizing its ambitious but precatory agenda, which range from cutting world poverty in half to restoring the world's fishing stocks, reducing use of ozone-depleting substances, reducing child mortality, and ensuring primary schooling for children everywhere.[54]

The Brundtland Report's identification of the ingredients of sustainable development created even greater demand for rapprochement between ecosystem preservation and its conjoined policy of transnational commerce. Attempts by environmental advocates to reach accord with trade's paradigm began in earnest with Principle 12 of the Rio Declaration, which declares, in language conspicuously identical to GATT Article XX's Chapeau, that "trade policy measures for environmental purposes should not constitute a means of arbitrary or unjustifiable discrimination or a disguised restriction on international trade." By acknowledging that nations may abuse environmental regulation to protect not nature but their own industries, Principle 21 at once distanced itself from such tactics while recording formally the conviction that genuine border restrictions to protect the environment should be protected from WTO/GATT sanction by GATT's General Exceptions.

Ecolabeling has in particular drawn commentators to search for a harmonious formula because of the effectiveness of ecolabels to the environmental movement, as shown in section 6.6, paired with the minimal disruption that ecolabels cause to trade flows, at least as compared with outright bans.[55] If the WTO abandons its PPM distinction,[56] consumers will gain substantial information about the environmental burden of the available choices at minimal cost to trade flows. Short of that momentous step,[57] harmonization by international standard-setting bodies of environmental labels will bring data on environmental burdens to consumers in a manner wholly consistent with the TBT Agreement, because that treaty encourages use of international standards by blessing them with Agreement consistency.[58]

6.8 Natural Capitalism and the Equator Principles

(A) Natural Capitalism

Led by Professor Daniel Esty, environmental experts for more than a decade have documented the urgent need for environmental modernization of international trading rules, a "greening of the GATT" through addition of an environmental exception to GATT Article XX or a separate WTO environmental agreement. Either of these steps would unburden from the tight disciplines imposed by global trading rules escalating governmental efforts to protect our biosphere.[59] Beyond corporate appeals to "green consumers" discussed in section 6.6, two whole-system approaches to the interface between free movement of traded goods and sustainable development—natural capitalism and the Equator Principles—have gained ground.

Advocates of an approach to production based on natural capitalism begin by noting that economic and ecological health are inseparable because living resources are an integral input into production, as necessary as human and financial assets. The dangerous shortages in living resources thus threaten our present economic livelihood unless production systems adapt to this new reality.[60] Pointing out to the business world that the actual value of the biological resources it now consumes approximates the gross world product, natural capitalism posits four central strategies that attribute proper value to this irreplaceable production factor. Businesses must radically increase the productivity of the living resources that they consume, toward the end not only of drastically reducing production costs, but also to stop the present degradation of the biosphere. Through "biomimicry," industry would enable the constant reuse of materials in a closed cycle that not only eliminates waste, but also would usually eliminate toxic pollution that has been so often the byproduct of our industrial society. Attainment of a "service and flow economy" requires a change in the value that consumers attribute to biological services so that sellers will price and assess acquired goods based on how well they achieve biomimicry and a substantial increase in the productivity of resources. Adhering to natural capitalism's principles, companies will not only meet their corporate social responsibilities, but will also see an increase in profits, employee productivity, and customer satisfaction.

While this new paradigm entails substantial investment in sustaining and restoring stocks of natural capital,[61] corporate cost savings can be substantial. A typical example is an Amsterdam bank whose innovative design of its headquarters saved the company nearly three million dollars a year in energy costs.[62] A switch from ordinary lighting ballasts to electronic ballasts that automatically dim the lights to match available daylight, and from ordinary motors to highly efficient ones, have eighteen separate benefits for a company, only one of which is cutting energy costs in half. Workers would see better and be less disturbed by noise, and thus be more comfortable, with proportional increases in both productivity and quality. The change in corporate mindset required will not come easily. With resources provided by the World Bank and the IMF, an international group must educate businesses about the benefits of natural capitalism. The UN Principles for Responsible Investment, together with education on John Elkington's "triple bottom line" of people, planet, and profits, can convince transnational companies in particular that they are no longer simply money-making machines, but leading agents of the new economic order that must also be good global citizens.

(B)   Equator Principles

A related movement, one underpinned by the strong commitment to sustainable development of the World Bank and its private sector arm, the International Finance Corporation, finds 80 percent of global project lending now covered by the voluntary guidelines for managing environmental and social risk called the Equator Principles.[63] Borrowers must prepare a social and environmental assessment, accompanied by proposed mitigation measures, to qualify for financing. Uniform industry-specific guidelines militate toward harmonized environmental protection, and assessments must include consultation with communities that the project is likely to affect.[64] Expansion of both the Equator Principles beyond the forty-one transnational banking groups that have adopted them, as well as incorporation of the fundamental principles of natural capitalism into production engineering, portend well for increased environmental sensitivity in the business community and an end to unsustainable production methods.[65]

6.9   Final Thoughts

Just as international trade law was born into the existing sphere of public international law, so too are nations beginning their own industrialization revolutions bound by present customary and treaty law governing the human rights of their citizens. It is unacceptable that simply because the First World two centuries ago used resources in an unsustainable manner, created unhealthy levels of air and water pollution, employed slave labor to reduce production costs, or maintained unsafe places of work, developing nations should be permitted—as a matter of equity—to employ unsustainable production methods and abuse their workforce to ensure their own economic development.

The fact that slavery contributed substantially to the development of the First World would never justify a return to human servitude in order to promote faster industrialization of the developing world. Neither would this proposal justify violation of other human rights that nations have proclaimed since the Second World War. Our planet's ecosystem, because of greenhouse gases and centuries of overused resources, cannot withstand another round of the damage wrought by the First World's industrial revolutions. Just as they must accept today's moral standards, developing nations must take modern ecosystems as they find them. In any event, developing nations will be the first to suffer from further degradation of our atmosphere—in the form of droughts, deforestation, floods, rising sea levels, forest fires, and loss of biodiversity.[66]

Aggressive implementation of the WTO's human rights policies can lead to purposeful integration of environmental protection into the WTO system. No legal or policy reason exists why WTO bodies, including dispute panels, cannot use WTO rules to enforce customary norms prescribing minimal standards of environmental protection. These bodies also must recognize—and end—the early GATT insertion of a product/process distinction in the nondiscrimination principles of GATT articles I and III. The PPM distinction is legally unnecessary, unhelpful as a policy matter to WTO objectives, and severely damaging to goals of multilateral environmental agreements whose enforcement is completely consistent with the ultimate purpose of trade agreements.

The WTC must also take the next logical step in interpretation of GATT's vital General Exceptions. We laud its view that GATT Article XX's human rights policies reside on the same plane as GATT's Four Pillars. We find great promise in the Court's charge to panels to find equilibrium between a WTO Member's exercise of its rights under the Pillars and its rights under the Exceptions. What remains is finding, as it has done for the SPS and TBT Agreements through interpretation of similar language,[67] that the General Exceptions are autonomous rights that shift the burden of proof to the Member challenging their exercise. The minor differences in language among these WTO provisions cannot justify the Court's reluctance to deliver to the human rights community this decisive insight.

7

Not Just a Question of Capital
Health and Human Well-Being

7.1 Overview

International trade and other manifestations of globalization have un-matched potential to spread the benefits of the transnational interchange of goods, services, and knowledge. In fact, the link between personal wealth—a factor strongly influenced by trade—and health is indisput-able: trade creates wealth and wealth produces health.[1] Concerns about international trade's adverse effects on health, however, particularly in the poorest nations and as to food safety, environmental toxins, and access to lifesaving medicines, have fed doubts about the value of globalization.[2]

Chapter 6 showed that WTO Members have used the General Excep-tions of GATT's Article XX effectively to immunize from WTO sanction border restrictions taken to protect the environment, even though such restrictions otherwise would have been subject to sanction for violating the foundational principles of GATT's Four Pillars. This chapter considers what ends Members concerned with human rights that sound in health or related aspects of human well-being may pursue with assistance from the GATT's General Exceptions or from other WTO provisions, in particular the TRIPS and SPS Agreements.

With Brazil's AIDS crisis close in mind, we examine whether trade agreements have done enough to satisfy world health concerns and pro-pose ways to deploy the rules to benefit the human right to health.

7.2 Human Rights Framework

Measures to protect health implicate a number of human rights, begin-ning with the elemental right to life. Another important human right that fits within the policies protected by GATT's Public Health and Welfare

Clause is the right to reasonable limitations on working hours, given that over-arduous labor has negative health effects. Human rights conventions ensure a standard of living adequate for a worker's own and his or her family's health and well-being, a standard that anticipates medical care and security in the event of sickness as well as special care and assistance for motherhood and childhood.[3] The UNCHR has gone farther in resolving that UN signatories should in particular recognize as a human right access to AIDS drugs for those stricken with the disease.[4] The Universal Declaration also identifies in Article 24 the human right to rest and leisure. Like reasonable limitations on working hours, time to engage in nonwork avocations is a health-related human right.

The American Declaration proclaims in Article VII that women, during pregnancy and nursing, and all children have the right to special protection.[5] The Protocol of San Salvador proclaims in Article 12 the right to adequate nutrition, in Article 11 the right to a healthy environment, and in Article 10 the right to health, "understood to mean the enjoyment of the highest level of physical, mental and social well-being."[6] Thirteen of the thirty-four OAS Members have ratified the Protocol of San Salvador. The United States and Canada are not parties, a continuation of their opposition to economic, social, and cultural rights treaties, which resulted in exclusion of these rights from the ACHR.[7]

7.3   International Trade Framework

A healthy population literally depends on effective delivery of essential medicines. Trade rules have made such delivery less reliable with respect to diseases that have reached epidemic proportions (or worse). This fact is crucial in the Americas where Brazil is the epicenter of the HIV/AIDS epidemic and accounts for 57 percent of all AIDS cases in Latin America and the Caribbean. About 640,000 Brazilians live with HIV/AIDS,[8] resulting in an adult prevalence approaching 1 percent. Countries across Latin America and the Caribbean, especially Belize, Honduras, and Guatemala, contain similar numbers of AIDS cases proportional to their populations.

AIDS is not just a health crisis in some parts of the world. To use the language of international trade, the epidemic is nondiscriminatory. This mortal, modern-day plague does not spare its victims based on origin, sex, race, or sexual orientation, nor does it shun babies, children, or geriatrics;[9] it is causing the wholesale collapse of Africa. More than 20 percent of people in many sub-Saharan African nations have the virus. A fifteen-year-old in South Africa has a better than even chance of dying of AIDS.[10] Experts worry that in a decade or two, this disease will be having effects the likes of which we cannot even comprehend now. The world has never yet seen a continent virtually die because its people are poor. We may yet see that result from HIV/AIDS.

AIDS is a manageable disease for people in the First World and the rich. Triple-cocktail drug therapy has caused AIDS death rates to plummet in places where people have access to medicines. The corporations that make those medications, however, charge between ten thousand and fifteen thousand dollars a year per person. While the United States can afford to make them available to its people, no Emerging Market nation can. Leaving aside research and development costs, the pills cost pennies actually to produce. Any developing country could manufacture these drugs and treat AIDS. Nevertheless, pharmaceutical corporations—the most profitable industry in the world—depend on patent laws to make billions of dollars in profit and prevent others from producing the pills. World trade rules in the form of the TRIPS Agreement make those patent rules effectively enforceable on a global scale.

Fears of mad cow and hoof and mouth diseases from beef, E. coli and other bacterial infections from animal and vegetable products (seen in the recent pet food problems), and uncertain health concerns from genetically modified foods have focused global attention on the food safety rules of the WTO. The SPS Agreement added substantial scientific risk assessment requirements for governments wishing to protect their citizens from health concerns. Critics ask whether the desire to keep borders open to trade have forced governments to subordinate critical health considerations that traditionally resided within national discretion.

7.4   SPS Agreement

(A)   Negotiating Background

During six rounds of multilateral negotiations since GATT's creation in 1947, trade ministers successively eliminated or substantially reduced the traditional ways that countries restricted imports to protect domestic industries. They reduced the high tariff walls that made imports non-competitive, and they simplified complex licensing systems whose administrative requirements were impossible for importers to penetrate. They imposed controls on export subsidies, which make unsubsidized exports from other countries noncompetitive in third-country markets.

After the Tokyo Round in the 1970s, which saw membership in the GATT nearly double to 102 in ten years, countries again put on their protectionist thinking caps to devise ways to deal with the political realities that surface when imports start putting domestic producers out of business. One very effective hidden trade barrier was in the area of product standards, the physical characteristics that determine whether a particular import is permitted. Japan, for example, had come up with the condition, supposedly to protect against unsafe softball bats, that each bat be individually x-rayed. In the late 1980s, EU Member states were considering banning for health reasons beef from cows fed growth hormones.

With these new trade-restricting measures in mind, negotiators in the Uruguay Round that began in Punta Del Este in 1986 created two new agreements to regulate these types of nontariff barriers: the TBT Agreement and a fresh SPS Agreement, excerpted in Item 8 of the online Documents Annex.

(B)   Overview of the SPS Agreement

Section 6.6 explained that the TBT Agreement principally governs product standards that set out the physical characteristics, quality benchmarks, or labeling that determine whether a particular product may be imported. Under the SPS Agreement, a WTO Member may protect human, animal, or plant life or health from a wide variety of ills, such as pests (bugs and weeds), disease-carrying or disease-causing organisms (such as citrus canker), and contaminants or toxins in food (such as trace pesticides). Footnote 4 to the Agreement's Annex A defines "veterinary residues" as a "contaminant," reflecting that negotiators had in mind the growth hormones issue. There are still open questions about the extent of the Agreement's reach. For example, experts disagree about whether regulation of genetically modified organisms is subject to SPS review. The first WTO panel to examine the issue, *EC-Biotech Products*, answered resoundingly in the affirmative, as discussed in section 7.5(C). Even so, the Agreement covers most measures that a country could take to protect human, animal, or plant life or health. In fact, at one point, the top five U.S. agricultural exports (beef, poultry, soybeans, corn, and pork) could not be exported to EU Member states because of SPS barriers.[11]

Protection of the human right to health and well-being may require measures to guard the food supply, whether plant or animal. Those aspects of the SPS Agreement, as well as GATT Article XX(b), that address animal or plant life or health, therefore, are important toward enforcement of human rights relating to the physical and mental health of civil society. The SPS preamble makes an explicit connection with GATT Article XX(b) by enunciating that among its purposes is the desire "to elaborate rules for the application . . . of GATT provisions which relate to [SPS] measures, in particular the provisions of Article XX(b)."

Article 2.4 of the SPS Agreement provides that SPS measures that conform to the SPS Agreement are presumed to satisfy the conditions of GATT Article XX(b). The converse is not true. The General Interpretative Note to Annex 1A of the Marrakesh Agreement Establishing the WTO provides that, in the event of conflict between the GATT and another WTO Agreement, the other WTO Agreement prevails. This means that because the SPS Agreement contains the elaboration of public health measures that will be consistent with the WTO/GATT system, if the Member's health measure is covered by but not consistent with the SPS Agreement, the Member has no ability to claim that the measure is nonetheless consistent with GATT Article XX(b). GATT Article XX(b) continues to have vitality, but only with respect to measures "necessary to protect human, animal or plant life or health" that are not regulated by the SPS Agreement. An important example is the *EC-Asbestos* decision that we studied in section 6.5(D) in regard to GATT's PPM distinction. France's purpose in banning asbestos insulation certainly was to protect the health of its citizenry. The French ban, however, did not fit within one of the definitional categories of the SPS Agreement Annex A—pests, disease-causing organisms, and food toxins—and thus France could use GATT Article XX(b) in its defense.

(C) Primary Conditions of the SPS Agreement

The dispute settlement cases analyzed in the next subsection teach that the SPS Agreement's discipline of government regulation rests on five basic requirements. The first is that any border restriction undertaken for food safety or other Agreement reasons must be based on "sufficient scientific evidence." Before applying the border measure, the Member must also have performed a risk assessment—that is, an evaluation of the likelihood and consequences of a foreign pest or disease. In pursuit of the harmonization of food safety measures globally, Members must base their SPS measures on international standards, although Members may apply a higher level of protection if they can show a scientific justification for doing so.

The last two requirements reintroduce conditions from GATT Article XX(b), which the SPS Agreement partially replaces. Members may not apply SPS measures that are more trade-restrictive than required to achieve their chosen level of protection, which is, of course, the GATT Necessity Test. Finally, reflecting the GATT Article XX Chapeau, SPS measures may not arbitrarily or unjustifiably discriminate and they may not be applied in a way that constitutes a disguised restriction on trade.

Notably for human health rights, the Agreement gives Members an exemption from the "sufficient scientific evidence" requirement by permitting temporary measures based on incomplete evidence if the Member continues to seek a more objective assessment of the risk within a reasonable period of time. This version of the precautionary principle is a significant basis for protecting public health from dangers that require long-term study or whose effects are difficult to gauge. The WTC has elaborated on these bare-bones requirements in a series of important cases.

(D) The Dispute Settlement Cases

In addition to the *EC-Biotech Products* case discussed in section 7.5(C), three dispute settlement cases decided under the SPS Agreement provide clear guidance to WTO Members interested in protecting the human right to health of their citizens. Each addresses protection of a separate recipient of the health benefit: human, animal, or plant. The phytosanitary (plant health) case, decided in 1999, was a challenge to Japan's method of dealing with potential infestation of its fruit crops with the codling moth, which could be contained in certain imported fruit. Japan long had banned the importation of apples, cherries, nectarines, and walnuts that could potentially be affected with codling moth. Finally Japan lifted the outright ban in favor of a fumigation requirement and a quarantine period. A solid risk assessment supported this approach.[12] Japan went further, however, and required that each variety of fruit be individually tested. For each product, the agriculture ministry granted exemptions from the import ban on a variety-by-variety basis. In other words, to obtain an exemption, the applicant had to seek a permit for a specific variety of a product listed. Obtaining a permit for one variety of a product did not entitle a company to import other varieties. Granting permits on a varietal basis added huge time and financial burdens to the process of exporting fruit to Japan, given the dozens—even hundreds—of varieties of apples, cherries, nectarines, and walnuts covered by the measure. In response to a complaint by the United States, the WTC found that the "science" requirement of Article 2.2 called for an "objective relationship" between the SPS measure and the scientific evidence underpinning it. The Appellate Body found that although the evidence supported fumigation and quarantine to guard against this pest, there was no evidence at all that a separate test for each variety of fruit would add anything to the protection that Japan purportedly sought.[13]

The second case involves animal protection, the *Aust.-Salmon* case decided in 1998. Canada complained about Australia's ban on the importation of fresh, chilled, or frozen salmon. Australia's stated purpose was to prevent domestic salmon from being exposed to exotic pathogens not present in Australian waters. Smoked salmon that had been heat-treated could be imported, but Australian authorities had not specified any means for other salmon to be qualified as pathogen-free and thus escape the ban.

The WTC first addressed whether the study on which Australia based its measure qualified as a "risk assessment," defined in relevant part to mean "evaluation of the likelihood of entry . . . or spread of a pest or disease within the territory of an importing Member . . . and of the associated potential biological and economic consequences" with and without the proposed SPS measure.

Noting that the study by Australia was rife with "general and vague statements of mere possibility of adverse effects . . . with neither quantitative nor qualitative assessment of probability," the WTC concluded that the study did not qualify as an evaluation either of the likelihood that pathogens in imported salmon would result in spread of disease, or the likelihood that available sanitary measures would prevent that spread. The risk, it said, must be "ascertainable," and although a risk assessment can be acceptable even if it finds but an "extremely small risk," a measure may not be based solely on the theoretical risk that underlies all scientific inquiry.[14]

The Appellate Body found another problem that it called a "warning signal" that the salmon measure was a disguised restriction on trade: the scientific study relied on by Australia found the same potential problem for herring as for salmon, but herring were not—unlike salmon—a major aquaculture industry in Australia. Instead, herring were imported for bait or as ornamental finfish. In fact, the study actually had found a greater risk from herring imports because of the use to which they were put. That is, they would often come into close contact with other fish, which would not be true of a chilled salmon eaten in a restaurant. The WTC found that the discrimination between salmon and herring suggested that Australia's motive was less to protect domestic fish than to protect domestic producers.[15] In other words, despite the allowance under the SPS Agreement of some discrimination, when the restrictive border measure is not based on the scientific evidence, it is nothing more than a disguised trade restriction.

The first case decided by the WTO under the SPS Agreement is the most interesting. The *EC-Hormones* case, noted in section 7.4(A) as unfolding in the background of Uruguay Round negotiations, is the human health case. The EC prohibited importation of meat or meat products from cattle that had received one of six growth hormones on grounds that these hormones might be carcinogenic. The United States and Canada complained to the WTO and the two dispute settlement panels established in response both found against the EC. The case that we have excerpted as Item 9 in the online Documents Annex is the Appellate Body's review of these two panel decisions.

As the WTC notes, and we will explore in greater detail in section 8.2(C), Article 3 of the SPS Agreement attempts to harmonize global SPS measures by providing in Paragraph 2 that if the measure conforms to an international guideline, the Member employing the measure benefits from a rebuttable presumption that its border restriction is consistent with the Agreement (and with any other relevant WTO provisions). In an important concession to the skepticism of human rights groups about the scientific neutrality of international standard-setting bodies, Members may decide to accord a higher level of health protection for its citizens than an existing international benchmark. For food safety, the designated standard-setting body is the Codex Alimentarius Commission (Codex). For animal health, the Agreement looks to the International Office of Epizootics. For plant health, the SPS Agreement assigns jurisdiction to develop global standards to the International Plant Protection Convention.

Some NGOs believe that these bodies are controlled by large transnational corporations and thus are not reliable as true indicators of health concerns. Article 3, therefore, permits Members to impose measures different than those considered adequate by an international guideline. Importantly, however, the Member may do so only if the Member is able to establish a scientific justification for the higher level of protection. If a country chooses to go beyond the protection given by the international standard, no presumption of compliance will follow. Thus, if the EU sets the goal of 0 percent chance of harm from growth hormones, it needs a scientific basis and must perform a risk assessment under Article 5.

As the Appellate Body later was to affirm in the *Japan-Agricultural Products* case, the requirement of a risk assessment is, ultimately, that the results must reasonably support the chosen SPS measure. That is, the importing Member must show a rational relationship between the measure and the risk assessment. The WTC did not find that it was necessary that the measure be based on the majority scientific view, so long as a qualified minority points to an "identifiable risk."[16]

The initial panel had concluded that the dozen studies relied on by the EC all had found that growth hormones posed no safety risk to humans, as long as the drugs were administered in accordance with "good veterinary practice," such as correct dosages. The EC argued that its ban was based on the risk that enforcement of good practices would be inadequate, but the panel below noted that none of the studies cited by the EC even considered the risk of abuse of hormones. In conclusion, the WTO dispute process found that the EC had the right to insist on a higher level of protection than the Codex standard, but that the EC simply had not followed the scientific disciplines required by Article 3 to justify the trade restrictions that resulted from its acting on that higher standard of health protection.

(E)   A Human Rights Criticism of the SPS Agreement

Human rights advocates mount two principal criticisms of SPS Agreement standards. First, they regret that by adopting the GATT Article XX(b) language regarding the protection of human, animal, or plant life or health, drafters set into concrete the Article XX(b) requirement that such measures be "necessary" to the ends sought. Article 5.6 of the Agreement provides that SPS measures may not be "more trade-restrictive than required to achieve their appropriate level of protection." The concern is that this condition requires balancing a human rights initiative relating to food safety against its trade impacts and, in doing so, gives primacy not to the human rights concern, but to trade impacts. By making the "least-restrictive" standard part of the explicit terms of the Agreement, negotiators displayed indifference to the urgent need to account for the greater reliance by human rights policies today on trade measures.

The second criticism is that risk assessment under the SPS Agreement must take account of a cost-benefit analysis. The requirement of an economic analysis is objectionable, even in an economic agreement, because trade negotiators have permitted economic factors to override human rights concerns. The legal aspects of this criticism warrant further study. While there are passing references to "economic feasibility" and "economic consequences" in relation to risk assessment, the principal provision mandating that economic factors be taken into account applies only to the assessment of risk to animal or plant life or health and would not as a consequence seem a direct barrier to most human rights initiatives.

There is a third area of concern not addressed in the human rights literature. As discussed in section 7.5(B), drafters of the WTO Agreements, especially the SPS Agreement, certainly could have given greater weight to the Precautionary Principle. From the standpoint of a human rights advocate, permitting governments greater leverage in their SPS measures by requiring less reliance on hard science would result in greater trade protection to human rights measures.

7.5   Cartagena Protocol on Biosafety

(A)   An Environmental and Health Agreement

In the strictest sense of the word, the SPS Agreement is not a health agreement. The SPS Agreement is a trade agreement that disciplines border regulations taken for health reasons to ensure they are not disguised means to protect domestic industry. Therefore, even though the Agreement supplies governments with a road map for how to protect the health of their citizens without running afoul of trade rules, the Agreement's primary purpose is to ensure that WTO Members do not thwart Ricardo's concept of comparative advantage without scientific evidence.

There is a new player on the health scene since the SPS Agreement entered into force, one that clearly is an environmental treaty, and in some respects also a health agreement. As such, this later covenant is of particular relevance to enforcement of human rights in the context of trade. The Cartagena Protocol on Biosafety, agreed in the context of the Convention on Biological Diversity (CBD), intends, as the name suggests, to protect the environment from hazards to the diversity of plant and animal species. The United States is not a party, although its trade officials were deeply involved in negotiating the Protocol because of its potential impact on producers of genetically modified products. Almost 80 percent of genetically modified commodity exports originate in the United States— mostly soybeans and corn—and about 65 percent of the products found in the typical U.S. grocery store contain genetically modified products. One could say without exaggeration that the U.S. population is involved in a massive scientific study of the long-term impact of genetically modified foods.

The Biosafety Protocol regulates the transfer of genetically modified organisms (GMOs), which it styles "living modified organisms" (LMOs) to avoid the plethora of unsavory history brought to mind by the other term. If an LMO is to be "introduced into the environment"—that is, consists of seeds that are to be planted to produce genetically modified (GM) crops or animals to be bred—the exporting nation must furnish advance notice of such activity to the importing country. The importing country may limit the proposed transfer after conducting a risk assessment.

If the exported GM product is meant for direct consumption by humans or animals, the exporting country need not provide advance notice, a major concession secured by U.S. trade negotiators for U.S. producers of GM commodities such as soybeans and corn. The importing country may nonetheless conduct a risk assessment and ban or otherwise limit entry of the GM commodity, although the importing country would not have benefit of notice to trigger its action.

(B)   The Dueling Precautionary Principles of the Biosafety Protocol and the SPS Agreement

A key provision of the Protocol is that risk assessments need not be based on undisputed or complete scientific data: "Lack of scientific certainty due to insufficient relevant scientific information and knowledge regarding the extent of the potential adverse effects of a living modified organism on the conservation and sustainable use of biological diversity in the Party of import, taking also into account risks to human health, shall not prevent that Party from taking a decision, as appropriate, with regard to the import of the living modified organism in question . . . in order to avoid or minimize such potential adverse effects."[17] This is an exposition of the Precautionary Principle, which posits that "where there are threats of serious or irreversible damage, lack of full scientific certainty shall not be used as a reason for postponing cost-effective measures to prevent environmental degradation."[18] The SPS Agreement is not unfamiliar with the concept. Article 5.7 of that Agreement permits Members provisionally to impose SPS measures in situations in which scientific evidence is incomplete.

We may ask whether the Precautionary Principle finds true reflection in SPS Agreement Article 5.7 or whether the SPS Agreement's version causes more harm than good. This issue of course is part of the much larger one of whether the SPS Agreement, in tightening disciplines on border restrictions that governments may employ to protect health and safety, has made a bad situation worse for the enforcement of human rights. In the *Japan-Agricultural Products* case, the Appellate Body laid out the four requirements of SPS Article 5.7: (1) relevant scientific information is insufficient; (2) the measure is adopted on the basis of available pertinent information; (3) the Member seeks to obtain the additional information necessary for a more objective assessment of risk; and (4) the Member reviews the measure within a reasonable period of time.

There are differences and similarities between Article 5.7 of the SPS Agreement and Principle 15 of the 1992 Rio Declaration. Perhaps the most striking is a difference in presumption or approach. The SPS version requires a Member to use science to justify a border measure (if not based on an international standard), while the Rio Declaration declares that a country must not postpone taking action to protect the environment solely because the scientific data are as yet incomplete.

Environmental advocates often cite this difference in attitude as a major defect of the SPS, because it gives free trade priority over protecting the environment. This difference is not surprising, given that the primary purpose of WTO agreements is to prevent Members from circumscribing open markets. Another difference seems to give the environmental edge to the SPS Agreement's definition. Rio Declaration Principle 15 requires that "serious or irreversible" environmental damage be on the horizon to justify abandonment of full science, whereas the SPS Agreement allows Members to choose their own level of protection, whatever the nature of the harm anticipated, although as noted in section 6.5(D), WTO panels display greater deference to national discretion as the health risk rises. The Rio Declaration may also be less friendly to environmental causes in its requirement for a cost-benefit analysis. Cost effectiveness is not a central requirement of SPS Agreement Article 5.7, although it is listed as one factor in risk assessment.

The most frequently criticized aspect of Article 5.7 is its provisional nature. Members must seek out full scientific evidence within a reasonable period of time. The Biosafety Protocol arguably allows a signatory permanently to base its risk assessment on a precautionary approach. The criticism of Article 5.7 as a temporary permission to use incomplete evidence may not be appropriate. Members who have lost on this basis, such as Japan in the *Agricultural Products* case, had completely stopped gathering evidence. WTO dispute panels have not been asked to rule as to what period of time may be "reasonable" when scientific evidence in a particular situation is difficult to obtain, or when a proper study requires long periods of time, which may be the case for GM foods. Similarly, would a Biosafety Protocol Member that chooses to ignore continuing scientific evidence relevant to its measure be acting consistently with the Protocol, despite its apparent lack of a time limitation on the use of incomplete evidence? The better interpretation is that both versions of the Precautionary Principle authorize only temporary deviations from "sound science." Scientific inquiry into issues of great importance simply does not stop at some artificial point.[19]

How will WTO dispute settlement panels address a measure banning a GM product based on a risk assessment consistent with the Biosafety Protocol? Near universal acceptance of the Protocol's procedure justifies panels in treating that procedure as a relevant international standard, even though the SPS Agreement does not identify the Biosafety Protocol as an international standardizing body for human health. The following section notes that the first WTO panel to address this question chose not to take advantage of its opportunity to bring the SPS Agreement into alliance with the Biosafety Protocol toward the common goal of improving global health conditions.

(C)   The *EC-Biotech* Products Case

In a case that had been germinating even while the SPS Agreement was in negotiation, the United States, Canada, and Argentina filed WTO complaints against European bans on importation of various corn and wheat crops that had been genetically modified. In a decision that is disappointing from a human rights standpoint, the panel first brushed aside claims that the Biosafety Protocol had any relevance to the complaint. Noting that the Vienna Convention provides for consideration of those rules of international law applicable in the relations between all parties to the treaty being interpreted, the panel observed that the United States had signed but not ratified the CBD and that the United States, Argentina, and

Canada had not ratified the CBD's Biosafety Protocol.[20] Thus, not even all parties to the dispute, much less all parties to the WTO, were bound. This approach was a lost opportunity because the provision cited deals only with conflicting provisions in two treaties. There is no conflict presented if the panel had treated the Biosafety Protocol's approach to GMOs as an international standard applicable to the trade in these products. The panel also was convinced that it need not apply the Precautionary Principle as customary international law. The panel found no evidence in the intervening eight years to question the Appellate Body's finding in the 1998 *EC-Hormones* case that "there has, to date, been no authoritative decision by an international court or tribunal which recognizes the precautionary principle as a principle of general or customary international law."[21]

The EC fared no better with respect to the SPS Agreement itself. In an effusive reading of the Agreement's reach, the panel found first that EC regulations on GM products fall within each of the Annex A definitions of an SPS measure. Officials intended the regulations to protect against "disease-causing or disease-carrying organisms" within the meaning of Annex A(1)(a). As to Annex A(1)(b)'s inclusion of measures to protect human or animal health from additives, contaminants, toxins, or disease-causing organisms in food, beverages, or feedstuffs, the panel found the EC's rules to be aimed at each of these categories as well. The EC's intent went beyond food safety in attempting to protect against allergen-inducing effects on human health, which the panel viewed as prevention of establishment or spread of "pests" within the meaning of Annex A(1)(c). Finally, in the panel's view, the EC's purpose to protect the environment from harm through the spread of weeds affected by genetically modified seeds implicated Annex A(1)(d)'s concern with "other damage" from pests.

The EC argued that Member state import bans were justified under Article 5.7 of the SPS Agreement, which provides that "in cases where relevant scientific evidence is insufficient, a Member may provisionally adopt sanitary or phytosanitary measures on the basis of available pertinent information," provided that "Members shall seek to obtain the additional information necessary for a more objective assessment of risk and review the sanitary or phytosanitary measure accordingly within a reasonable period of time." The panel found that none of the sanitary measures at issue was based on a full risk assessment that would be required for permanent import restrictions under Article 5.1 of the SPS Agreement because the scientific studies proffered by the EC found no valid basis for the import bans. Noting that the first requirement of SPS Agreement Article 5.7 is that the relevant scientific evidence must be "insufficient," the Panel rejected EC Member State reliance on the precautionary approach of Article 5.7. The risk assessments in existence, cited by the EC in support of Member state SPS measures, the Panel noted, were more than sufficient to conclude that the sanitary actions were scientifically ill-advised.[22] Given the tight conditions of the Agreement's version of the Precautionary Principle and the WTC's continuing refusal to find that the Principle is customary international law, this technical resolution of the first biotechnology case to be addressed by the WTO's dispute settlement system, while disappointing in its timidity, is not surprising.

Even if we concede that current data do not support a ban on importation, information about a food's biogenetic content could aid the consumer in purchase decisions. The United States has not been forthcoming in this respect. The U.S. Food and Drug Administration (FDA) does not agree that consumers need information on genetic modification. In fact, the agency's view is that including information on the GM content of foods would only clutter food labels with confusing messages and decrease the effectiveness of labeling.[23] As we saw in section 6.6, certain labels may constitute trade barriers under provisions of the TBT Agreement. In Europe, for example, a food product carrying the label, "Contains GMOs," likely will be considered inedible by many consumers. Perhaps we are being overly kind in suggesting that the FDA's refusal to require informational labeling on GM content anticipates the possible WTO inconsistency of such a rule.

(D)   A Compromised Attempt to Avoid Indifference

The Biosafety Protocol contains ammunition for those who claim that the pact is consistent with the SPS Agreement and for those who hold precisely the opposite view. In one paragraph of the preamble, the Protocol maintains that it does not intend to affect rights under other treaties, presumably including the WTO's SPS Agreement. In the next paragraph, the Protocol's preamble suggests that the Biosafety Protocol indeed overrides other provisions that might apply to GMOs. This embarrassing response to the natural question of what hierarchy negotiators intended between the Protocol and existing WTO Agreements that also address food safety and environmental protection reflects the tortuous negotiations between proponents of GM crops—primarily Canada and the United States—and countries reluctant to foist these products on their consumers without further research, represented most vehemently by the EU.

The lesson we may take from this botched effort to assign priorities to two important conflicting policies reflects the broader problem of the splendid isolation of human rights law and international trade law. We may be certain in this case, however, that the U.S. and Canadian negotiators who insisted on leaving unresolved the legal hierarchy realized that the result would be dominance of the issue by the WTO's SPS Agreement, whose provisions—unlike those of the Biosafety Protocol—are enforceable through a robust dispute settlement system. A party to the CBD may pursue settlement of a dispute only through a conciliation panel, whose proposals must be considered in good faith by the losing party, unless both parties agree to arbitration or submission of the conflict to the ICJ. Even so-called binding arbitration under the Convention envisions no penalties for failure of the losing party to implement the arbitration tribunal's decisions.[24] The predictable result has indeed come to pass in the WTO's first case to address a ban on GMO foods, the *EC-Biotech Products* case, discussed in section 7.5(C), which was forced to search more deeply within Article 30 of the Vienna Convention with respect to the application of later treaties because the Protocol's parties were unable to specify clearly which treaty should prevail in the event of conflict.

7.6   *Using the WTO and Biosafty Protocol's Health Provisions for Human Rights Ends*

One observer argues that the human right to health has become a de facto interpretive principle that informs a wide range of WTO disputes, even though the WTO Agreements are silent on the existence of such a standard.[25] For example, in *EC-Hormones*, the Appellate Body broadly confirmed that the SPS Agreement effectively relegates to Member state discretion determination of the health protection level for its citizens. While most WTO provisions aim for consistently applied rules among all Members, the SPS Agreement takes a different approach by not mandating particular standards for specific sanitary threats. Article 3 encourages harmonization by granting the Member that adopts an international standard applicable to that threat a presumption of compliance with the Agreement. Nonetheless, a Member is free to seek a higher level of protection—even a zero tolerance level—for the threat in question so long as the Member readies "a scientific justification." Whatever the breadth of the SPS Agreement's version of the Precautionary Principle in Article 5.7, the ability to select ab initio whatever protection level the Member desires constitutes an extraordinary degree of deference to the culturally divergent membership of the WTO. The WTC's cursory review of Member action in the public health arena contrasts starkly with its painstaking deconstruction of Member measures in the so-called trade remedy area of anti-dumping, subsidies, and safeguards.[26]

The WTC has in addition narrowed the ability of complaining Members to tangle a Member's health measure in difficult searches for less trade-restrictive alternatives by recognizing that choosing the level of health protection also means that the Member must be given wide latitude to choose the means to effectuate that level. In *EC-Asbestos*, the WTC tossed aside complaints by Canada that France could have protected the health of its citizens through strict controls of asbestos use, rather than an outright ban on importation and sale. The WTC's reasoning was that only a full ban allowed France to reach its chosen objective of zero tolerance, a potent linkage of Article XX(b)'s Necessity Test with the newfound principle of national discretion to choose the level of health protection.[27]

As further support for a WTO interpretive principle of the human right to health, we note that the only amendment to date of a WTO Agreement involved granting substantial discretion to Members to decide when a public health emergency relating to AIDS, malaria, tuberculosis, or other epidemics justifies compulsory licensing of essential medicines, thereby overcoming otherwise protective patents as well as reversing the thrust of a provision of the TRIPS Agreement that previously had severely limited government action in this respect. The Amendment, discussed in the next section, is further support for the proposition that the WTO "has recognized a soft, non-justiciable right to health in all but name."[28] That is, these powerful instruments of control over a Member's health protection also stand ready to increase Member compliance with its human rights obligations with respect to citizen health.

7.7   Health in the Americas and WTO's TRIPS Agreement

(A)   Brazil's AIDS Crisis

Section 7.3 explained that Brazil's AIDS crisis is greater than that of other countries in the Americas. In part, this head start of the disease over serious public health treatment efforts resulted from the initial view that

AIDS was *doenca de rico*, a disease of the rich. With the press coverage focused primarily on high-profile Brazilian citizens with the disease, the government's lack of attention to the problem was excused. By the time that popular opinion recognized the universal scourge of the disease, AIDS outbreaks had occurred throughout the poorest parts of Brazil and the decaying public health system was unable to meet the level of the crisis.[29]

The government's reaction was all the more effective when finally it came. By 1991 Brazil began providing free and universal access for all Brazilian citizens to antiretroviral therapy and combined treatment with a comprehensive educational program to raise awareness of the disease and the methods of its transmission.[30]

(B)   Essential Medicines and the TRIPS Agreement

Because of the prohibitive cost of newly patented medicines, over one-third of the world's population lacks access to medicines essential to their health.[31] The WTO's TRIPS Agreement presents the stark reality of conflict between trade rules and human rights. On one hand, global trade rules assume that strong protection of intellectual property rights (IPRs) is the premise to protecting investments and encouraging innovation. On the other, national authorities seek to provide access to essential medicines at affordable prices.[32] This is not to say that low-priced antiretroviral drugs alone will ensure treatment success. The virus associated with AIDS constantly mutates, which dictates highly individualized drug treatment and therapy. Countries that would succeed in reducing the plague of AIDS need appropriate technology, education, and treatment resources, including laboratories and assistance of experts.[33]

Nonetheless, low-priced drugs must be the starting point. The WTO cemented the current Western approach to patent law into place by creating a global IPR regime that requires WTO Members to provide minimal levels of protection for IPR owners. Mandates of the TRIPS Agreement are enforceable under the virtually binding WTO dispute settlement system, which added unprecedented weight to the existing treaties of the World Intellectual Property Organization. Because developing nations could not afford to give up the increased access to First World markets provided by the WTO, these countries accepted the TRIPS Agreement as part of the WTO's "single undertaking," despite studies showing that justification for the Western-style patent system not only did not exist for them, but was in fact disadvantageous to their economies.[34]

Thirteen million people, mostly in Emerging Market countries, die annually of infectious diseases. The general perception is that drug companies spend little to find cures for most of these diseases because the market for such medicines would not be lucrative. The list of such Emerging Market diseases is long: dengue fever, African sleeping sickness, malaria, and elephantiasis are among them.[35] The failure of drug companies to search meaningfully for cures or treatment for such diseases calls into question the very reason why IPR systems afford monopoly protection to medical patents, that is, to encourage continued research for the public benefit.[36]

Notably, Brazil meets 100 percent of its need for antiretroviral drugs through aggressive price negotiations with drug companies. In the rare instances in which companies refuse to lower prices, Brazil issues compulsory licenses for their patented drugs to Brazilian generic pharmaceutical manufacturers.[37] For example, when Merck offered only a 30 percent discount on Efavirenz, Brazil issued a compulsory license in 2007 that saved its public health network $237 million annually on distribution of the antiretroviral drug to seventy-five thousand HIV-infected patients.[38] By contrast, governments have reached far smaller percentages of patient needs in Mexico (50 percent) and Peru (19 percent),[39] in part because their efforts were chilled by pressure from the United States, and in Peru also because of the absence of generic drug producers.

WTO trade ministers now expressly recognize compulsory patent licensing under these circumstances, in which the Member provides "adequate remuneration" to the patent owner, as consistent with the TRIPS Agreement. The solution ultimately found by WTO negotiators, memorialized in a Ministerial Declaration and ultimately in an amendment to TRIPS[40]—the first amendment of a core WTO Agreement—should alert us to a potential model for resolving conflicts between trade rules and human rights policies. The resulting revision to the Agreement's Article 31 was reached without weakening the fundamental principles of either human rights law or international trade law. It grants an exception to the requirement that patents may not be overridden except to meet a health emergency in the country producing the drug by allowing export of generic medicines to Members without generic drug industries. The amendment has been criticized by groups such as Doctors Without Borders for its burdensome drug-by-drug and country-by-country nature that prevents the lowering of prices from economies of scale provided by competition among several manufacturers.[41] Recent regional trade agreements, such as that between the United States and several Central American countries and the Dominican Republic, known as the CAFTA-DR-US, may be another barrier in its "TRIPS-Plus" approach to protecting pharmaceutical test data.[42] In-country experts have opined that no Latin American country will issue a compulsory license because of pressure from both governments and transnational companies of the First World.[43] In a hopeful sign, the Bush administration and the Democratic majority in the Congress agreed in 2007 to lessen the negative human rights impact of IPR provisions in the U.S. FTAs with Peru, Colombia, and Panama by removing the TRIPS-Plus provisions that extended patent periods and complicated production of generic medicines.[44]

Despite the admitted weaknesses of the WTO solution, we favor a more positive critique because of the sacrosanct IPR protection regime that Members were required to overcome toward its culmination. Argentina, Costa Rica, and Uruguay have moved toward the Brazilian model's provision of 100 percent of the antiretroviral needs of their populations through similar tactics. The Amendment overcame, albeit with burdensome eligibility conditions, the original Article 31's worthlessness to Members without the technical or industrial capacity to manufacture their own pharmaceutical goods. The Amendment should thus be viewed as a significant new Public Health exception to the Agreement, a reversal, in fact, of the paradigm of unbalanced protection of intellectual property memorialized by adoption of the TRIPS Agreement during the Uruguay Round. The change represents an important swing of the pendulum toward restoration of the balance of IPR protection with the need to transfer technology to those in greatest need. The Amendment is an unusually strong WTO recognition of the human right to health. More must be done, because only 1 percent of the new drugs approved in the last quarter of the 20th century are aimed at the tropical diseases that ravage the developing world.[45]

7.8 Colorism and Health in the Americas

One can readily appreciate that women of the developing world face substantially higher health risks from such global plagues as HIV/AIDS because of physiological differences that make them twice as likely as men to contract the disease from an infected partner, as well as their lack of control over whether their partners wear condoms.[46] One may be less aware that the color of one's skin on a spectrum of light to dark also figures prominently in delivery of adequate health services. Experts recognize "colorism" as an oft-employed method of discrimination both more subtle than racism and quite distinct from racial or nationality biases, one that finds its own category of unlawful discrimination in U.S. law and that can be categorized as unconscious racism.[47] In the color caste cultures in particular of Brazil, the Caribbean, and the United States, a "beauty hierarchy" reminiscent of Enlightenment justifications for colonialism and slavery[48] silently walks the halls of government health agencies and hospitals, and strongly influences the action of medical personnel and other deliverers of health care.

The significance of skin color to socioeconomic status among Mexican Americans[49] and wages of Latinos/as in the northeast United States[50] connotes that colorism among health care providers affects both the extent and the nature of health services delivered. Substantial evidence establishes that economic and social status play greater roles in a population's health status than actual medical care.[51] When designing trade measures to promote health, officials need to appreciate the effect of colorism on the efficacy of these measures, and even on their own understanding of the nature of the health problem that they face. This shows a more indirect trade-human rights link, with trade norms affecting the rights to health and nondiscrimination. Failure of trade rules to accommodate and address health concerns results in a disproportionately negative health impact on unprotected classes.

7.9   *GATT's General Exceptions and the Right to Health*

The discussion of the SPS Agreement in section 7.4(B) showed that the Public Health exception of GATT Article XX(b) has continued vitality for trade-related health concerns that do not fit the food safety and agricultural definitions of a sanitary or phytosanitary measure. The carcinogenic properties of asbestos implicated in the *EC-Asbestos* case call to mind other health issues to which Article XX(b)'s immunity would be crucial, such as trade limitations that WTO Members have imposed to thwart SARS disease from China, Ebola fever originating in the Congo, and avian flu outbreaks from Indonesia. Despite conditions that Members must anticipate before undertaking trade measures to promote public health, included in section 6.4(A) and (B), GATT Article XX(b) remains an able ally in the advancement of the human right to health.

7.10 Final Thoughts

Because the Biosafety Protocol has not been ratified by all WTO Members, or even by all Members likely to be involved in challenges such as those represented by the *EC-Biotech Products* dispute, WTO dispute panels will not have the opportunity to explore a harmonious reading of the SPS Agreement and the Biosafety Protocol to the CBD. With dissembling language in the Protocol's preamble, a WTO panel will be justified in taking an aggressive approach to the intent of the Protocol's drafters. This day of opportunity will not come until the United States abandons its policy of bullying disengagement with respect to resolution of contentious international human rights issues, from climate change to war crimes to law of the sea to economic and social rights to genetically modified foods. We believe and hope that that day will soon come.

8

Exploitation or Progress?

Terms and Conditions of Labor

8.1 Overview

After centering the debate by inquiring into the problematic question of how to identify the labor rights that trade should use its power to advance, we examine in this chapter which labor standards qualify as fundamental human rights and the extent to which workers and labor organizations successfully use existing trade agreements to protect core labor rights. In particular, we will evaluate the potential for advocates of worker rights to use GATT Article XX's exceptions for public morals and health and welfare. We also will examine the labor side agreement of the NAFTA and the labor chapters of the U.S.-Chile FTA and CAFTA-DR-US as possible models for addressing the role of labor rights in future trade pacts.

We will assess concerns of less-developed countries (LDCs) that conditioning trade access on worker treatment robs poorer countries of their comparative advantage and permits developed countries too easily to abuse such conditions as yet another means of disguised protectionism. Conversely, we will explore the degree to which globalization can erode labor standards and reward inconsistent values. The chapter will ask why trade agreements inevitably avoid confronting the immigration effects that they cause and whether worker rights advocates may take comfort in negotiations to expand protection for the movement of natural persons in the WTO's GATS.

8.2 Human Rights Framework

(A) Who Determines the Labor Rights That Trade Should Protect?

We find instructive in confronting the many intersections of international trade with labor to ask at the start whose conception of human rights should be posited as that which trade rules should use their enormous power to protect. We may believe that the answer is obvious: the rights of the underpaid worker, the exploited child laborer, the woman suffering under sweatshop conditions, and the employee fired for attempting to organize a union. Accepting this uncomplicated response, however, leads to certain troubling consequences.

First, it requires that we reject the universal opposition of developing country governments to any linkage of trade concessions to labor standards.[1] Leaders of LDCs argue convincingly that requiring payment of higher wages, enforcing restrictions against child labor, and insisting on collective bargaining rights in their factories has the inevitable consequence of reducing the comparative advantage of poorer countries in the global market. If developed countries deny access to goods from LDCs based on noncompliance with labor standards, the LDC governments argue, companies in such nations never will gain the economic strength needed to raise the wages of their workers and otherwise to match the labor standards of the markets to which they seek access. They accurately draw attention to the fact that one could find fault with the same developed nations now insisting on global observance of labor standards, because these nations failed to protect the rights of workers before their own industrial revolutions made attention to labor standards compelling. (Industrialization is, of course, no guarantor of a government's sensitivity to human rights, as the situations in China and Nicaragua attest.)

Governments of LDCs fear also that the motivation of developed countries in their attempts to link trade access with labor rights is less the protection of LDC worker rights than yet another disguised means of protection for domestic industries in developed countries. Virtually every provision in the nearly two dozen agreements of the WTO is drafted with a view to guarding against such hidden protection of domestic industry in contravention of the GATT's Four Pillars. As chapter 2 presented, WTO Members have been creative indeed in sculpting border restrictions— purportedly aimed at food safety, protection of the environment, or ensuring against consumer fraud—that favor their own producers. Examples that later were overturned include China's banning of Florida grapefruit for phytosanitary reasons, Australia's restrictions on imports of salmon to protect against exotic pathogens, and the EU's denial of trade in genetically modified organisms on health grounds. Less-developed nations also find support for their skepticism in the insistence by powerful labor unions in the United States that labor standards be included in FTAs with LDCs.[2]

Governments, however, do not always have the human rights of their citizens first in mind. Individuals possess human rights not as a function of their governments, but in recognition of their personhood. Individuals possess these rights in spite of the action—or inaction—of the state's leadership. Nonetheless, the question of whose rights trade rules should protect is complex. One should not accept the willingness of a ten-year-old boy to engage in grueling work in an Ecuadorean banana field to earn money for his impoverished family as the measure of whether the hacienda owner is committing a human rights violation. Anecdotal evidence suggests, however, that many workers agree with their governments at least as to the general outlines of the comparative advantage and protectionism contentions. Consider the example of a woman supporting her family on two dollars per day in a Haitian garment sweatshop. She is unlikely to believe that trade rules improve her situation if the factory owner, now required to pay a higher minimum wage under a FTA with the EU, eliminates her job because company income will not support current employment levels at the increased wage rates.

Pursuit of a "human rights perspective" for trade requires that we "consult the affected individual to ascertain what that person considers to be harm, to be a violation of human rights."[3] The Western/Northern conception of core labor standards does not necessarily reflect the minimal acceptable standards of the typical worker on the coffee plantations of Guatemala or the textile mills of India.

(B)   Which Labor Rights Should Trade Rules Protect?

It would be helpful if there existed a set of universally acknowledged minimum labor standards that trade rules should help to enforce. Despite continued urging by the United States and other developed nations,[4] the WTO unambiguously has ceded all matters relating to labor standards to the ILO. In its definitive 1996 Singapore Declaration, trade ministers, while affirming their nonbinding commitment to observance of "internationally recognized core labor standards," pointed to the ILO as the "competent body to set and deal with these standards," albeit with the continuing "collaboration" of the WTO Secretariat.

Trade and labor experts credit the WTO's 1996 commitment to "internationally recognized core labor standards" as the telling impetus that led directly to ILO consensus two years later in resolving the long-contentious issue of exactly which are the "core" labor standards in the context of trade agreements.[5] The ILO's Declaration on Fundamental Principles and Rights at Work (ILO Work Declaration) concludes in its preamble that the ILO must adopt these principles in furtherance of its pledge to maintain tight linkages between economic growth and social progress. The ILO Work Declaration establishes that the policies that nations must adopt to ensure that workers have equal opportunity to share in the wealth that they helped to generate are those contained in the adopted ILO Conventions.[6] The ILO Work Declaration groups these core labor standards into four categories: (1) freedom of association and the right to collective bargaining; (2) the elimination of forced or compulsory labor; (3) the effective abolition of child labor; and (4) elimination of discrimination in the workplace.[7] Each of these standards is expressly identified as a human right by UN human rights conventions.

Adopted by consensus, the ILO Work Declaration provides that ILO Members have an "obligation arising from the very fact of membership in the Organization, to respect, to promote, and to realize" these principles even if they have not ratified the Conventions from which they are drawn. The ILO Work Declaration also lends credence to the concerns of LDC representatives[8] with language overtly imported from the WTO Singapore Declaration—that the WTO Ministers "reject the use of labour standards for protectionist purposes, and agree that the comparative advantage of countries, particularly low-wage developing countries, must in no way be put into question."[9] This provision has the evident purpose of smoothing the path toward adoption in trade agreements of compulsory compliance with core labor standards. This intent notwithstanding, one can see the potential for inherent contradiction in a declaration that identifies the "fundamental rights" of workers while simultaneously recognizing that, for certain countries, the very ability to participate in the global market relies on not fully granting these rights to their citizens. For example, the ILO's Minimum Age Convention prohibits employment of children less than fifteen years of age. For nations whose economy and educational facilities are insufficiently developed, however, the minimum age drops to fourteen years.[10] Does the need for education to meet a child's present and future human rights depend on the economic development of the country in which the child happens to reside? Despite progress in reducing the worst forms of violence against child laborers— what one U.S. politician called "the underbelly of globalization"[11]—we must be sobered by the knowledge that millions of child laborers and legally employed adolescents face systemic violence at their places of work, ranging from physical or verbal abuse to sexual harassment, rape, and even murder.

Juxtaposed with these internally confused principles is an argument against attempting to force a single global cookie-cutter model on all states without accounting for their level of economic development. In this view, treatment of workers that would be considered a human rights violation in one country should pass muster as a fair labor standard in another, at least until the latter country's development reaches some minimum level. The hidden danger in this view is the assumption that economic growth alone is the guarantor of worker rights. Profits are not wrenched from companies in favor of workers solely because those profits are higher in a given year. In developed countries, advances in worker rights take place because workers and their supporters insist on these rights, using the weapon of nonperformance to enforce their entreaties. In LDCs, human rights for workers rely not on company largesse but on committed and informed governments.

Accordingly, the ILO Work Declaration makes clear that these rights are universal and that they apply to all people in all states, regardless of the level of economic development. The ILO Work Declaration singles out groups with special needs, including the unemployed and migrant workers. It recognizes that economic growth alone is insufficient to ensure equity and social progress, or to eradicate poverty.[12]

Article 2 substantially narrows the universe of labor rights considered fundamental or "core" human rights. In its recognition that membership in the ILO alone provides endorsement of its basic principles, which "have been recognized as fundamental both inside and outside the Organization," Article 1 makes denial that these are indeed core labor standards difficult, even by non-signatories to one or more of the ILO Conventions.[13] On the other hand, the ILO Work Declaration enables LDCs with greater force to oppose additional labor standards that developed countries attempt to link with trade concessions or sanctions, on the ground that such further labor requirements are not considered fundamental by the international body identified by WTO Members to have sole competence in the field of "the internationally recognized core labor standards." The United States often includes substantive labor standards, such as a particular minimum level of wages or certain health and safety standards at work, in its labor conditionality requests of LDCs.

Perhaps the ILO Work Declaration is not the most basic of international instruments that addresses the rights of workers. To begin, Article 2 of each of the three most important human rights documents—those composing the "International Bill of Human Rights"—uniformly condemns discrimination in all its forms. Racial and gender discrimination are common in the workplaces of virtually every WTO Member, and their elimination has been promised through treaties signed by each of those Members. Labor rights are treated in some detail in the ICESCR, adding substance to similar guarantees in the Universal Declaration. Article 6 recognizes the right to perform the work of each citizen's choosing. Article 7 protects "just and favorable conditions of work," in particular equal pay for equal work (especially for women), a decent living for themselves and their families, safe and healthy working conditions, and reasonable limitations on work hours. Article 8 guarantees the right to form unions and to strike.

Because more than 30 of the WTO's 150-plus Members, including the United States, have failed to ratify the ICESCR, it is important to look more closely at the so-called first-generation rights inscribed in the IC-CPR to which most of these Members do subscribe. Article 8 duplicates the ILO Work Declaration's prohibition against forced or compulsory labor. Article 22 provides rights of association similar to those ensured by the ILO Work Declaration. Article 24 protects the child in accordance with the child's status as a minor, a requirement on the state that surely includes prohibition of the worst forms of child labor. We have noted that Article 2 of the ICCPR seeks, as does the ILO Work Declaration, elimination of all forms of discrimination, which must indeed include that "in respect of employment and occupation." We could note that Article 1's right of self-determination would be impossible without the ability to earn a living wage in a safe working environment, free of discrimination and mindful of just and favorable conditions of work.

This simple exercise in demonstrating the inevitable overlap of human rights is part of the strategy described elsewhere by Professor Hernández-Truyol as "centering personhood"—that is, embracing the ideal of the indivisibility and interdependence of rights. Whether a country chooses to sign only one of the basic human rights conventions, the fact is that each of these rights is inseparable from the others. Even the categorization of rights either as civil/political or as economic/social/cultural is an artificial distinction that cannot withstand even minimal examination of the constructs of these entitlements.[14] As Albie Sachs has cogently observed, the so-called choice between bread and freedom is an invidious one.

For these reasons, we do not believe that the ILO's adoption of a set of core labor standards should determine the outer parameters of the trade and labor linkage. To be sure, such a result would leave unanswered a variety of critical social, economic, and cultural human rights. On the other hand, in light of the wide opposition by LDCs to compulsory labor clauses in the WTO or free trade agreements, the ILO baseline holds promise as at least the starting point for cementing the natural linkage of labor with trading rules.

The ACHR adopted in 1969 and now ratified by twenty-five of the thirty-four OAS Members (Canada and the United States are the only large non-signatories) builds on the UN human rights treaties protecting civil and political rights. Nineteen OAS Members have in addition ratified the 1988 Protocol of San Salvador's guarantee of economic, social, and cultural rights. Like its UN counterpart, the Protocol promises fair pay, safe and sanitary job sites, adequate rest and leisure, and that education will take priority over work for children.

Unfortunately, these seemingly solid rights for workers constitute but soft law. With one-fourth of its membership from industry,[15] the ILO's 185 Conventions contain no meaningful dispute settlement system and its only effective tool for bringing signatory nations into compliance is public disapprobation.[16] For this reason, we explore whether the powerful dispute settlement systems of global and regional economic treaties can lend a "helping hand."[17]

8.3   *International Trade Framework*

The persistent position of the WTO is that, as stated by the chair at the final session of the 1996 Singapore Ministerial Conference, "the Declaration does not put labour on the WTO's agenda."[18] Indeed, the organization has no committees or working groups addressing labor rights. The indisputable evidence is that the link between trade and worker rights is among the strongest of trade's intersections with human right law. When Europe opens its market to increased banana imports, thousands of workers, including children, in Ecuador and other banana-exporting countries in Latin America feel the effects through additional backbreaking and dangerous work in the plantations.

When the United States increases the textile imports available under its Caribbean Basin Initiative, garment workers in Haiti can expect harsher treatment to ensure increased output. Canada's elimination in 2000 of its tariff on sugar and the 2007 agreement between Brazil and the United States to increase trade in ethanol bring at once to mind the treacherous nature of growing sugarcane, scarring the bodies and burning the feet of nine-year-old boys using *chumpas*—small knives—to cut just-burned cane stalks to make ethanol to put in U.S. cars and to make sugar to put in the tea of Canadians.

New jobs created by additional export and investment opportunities may provide only the most begrudging of wages, insufficient to support a family but impossible to refuse in the face of total unemployment. These jobs may also subject workers to wholesale denial of their basic rights as workers to freedom from discrimination, of association, and against slave-like conditions, including for children.

Trade's denial of its inevitable linkage with worker rights and, worse, trade's refusal to use its economic power to ensure compliance with human rights treaties guaranteeing basic labor rights springs not from the absence of treaty language justifying the linkage, but the outdated and dangerous belief that human rights have no place in the trade firmament.

8.4 How May GATT's General Exceptions Heighten Labor Rights Compliance?

(A) In General

Despite the WTO's "benevolent disregard"[19] of a critical human rights problem, the Public Health and Welfare exceptions of GATT's Article XX, examined in general in chapter 2 and in chapter 6 with respect to protection of the environment, may have unanticipated relevance to the protection of labor rights. GATT Article XX's General Exceptions (see Item 7 in online Documents Annex) announce ten purposes that will shield a border protective measure from sanction for violation of the nondiscrimination or other prescriptions of the Four Pillars. These include measures

- Paragraph (a) "necessary to protect public morals";
- Paragraph (b) "necessary to protect human, animal or plant life or health";
- Paragraph (e) "relating to the products of prison labour."

As we explore existing precedent on these policy exceptions, we look beyond their 1947 usage to imagine their potential benefit to modern human rights law.

(B)   Products of Prison Labor

The provision that seems at first glance most relevant to furtherance of core labor rights is Paragraph (e). A WTO Member could justify a prohibition of importation, for example, of goods produced by prisoners from another WTO Member whose requirements for labor by its incarcerated citizens are excessive by human rights standards.[20] In fact, an importing WTO Member can meet the conditions of Paragraph (e) even without a human rights motivation. As explained in Chapter 6, the WTO Appellate Body has held that a proper Article XX analysis must begin with a finding that the purpose of the border measure is among the policies protected by the particular paragraph claimed by the importing Member. In this instance, the conditions of Paragraph (e) are easily met, requiring only that the import restriction be one "relating to" prison labor products.

Although no Member has challenged a border measure imposed under Paragraph (e), the WTC has interpreted the identically worded Relationship Test in Paragraph (g) as requiring only that the purpose of the measure bear a reasonable relationship to the measure applied to accomplish this purpose.[21] The Appellate Body in the *U.S.-Gasoline* case quietly overturned a line of GATT case law that had in effect equated the Relationship Test with the substantially more rigorous Necessity Test of other Article XX paragraphs mandating that the border measure be "necessary" to accomplish the intended objective.[22] As worded, a WTO Member may comply with Paragraph (e)'s Relationship Test merely by ensuring that its border measure is reasonably related to goods produced by prisoners. This language does not even require proof that the exporting WTO Member violated the labor rights of its imprisoned populace in the production of the goods in question. If the goods were produced by prison labor, they may be restricted without further justification. The drafting history of Paragraph (e) explains why the Member that bans products of prison labor need possess no broader motivation. The concern that gave rise to inclusion of the exception was not that prisoners might be mistreated by their governments, but that a country might gain an artificial comparative advantage by forcing prisoners to make products for export for little or no compensation.[23] Despite its trade-oriented motivation, Paragraph (e) will in the event immunize border measures taken to advocate against mistreatment of prisoners from a labor rights perspective.

GATT Article XX (e) may have far broader relevance to modern human rights law than prohibiting importation of prison-made merchandise.

May a Member use Paragraph (e) to defend a border restriction on the products of forced laborers who are not incarcerated? In 1999 the U.S. Business Roundtable suggested that the WTO clarify this ambiguity by affirming that governments may ban products made using forced labor.[24] We discuss in section 6.4(c) one basis for doing so. Although drafted in 1947, the term "prisoner" appears to meet the standard adopted by the Appellate Body in the *U.S.-Shrimp-Turtle* I decision for an "inherently dynamic" term that may, under standards set by the International Court of Justice, be interpreted in a modern context.[25] If a WTO dispute settlement panel looked to the plethora of post–Second World War treaties prohibiting labor servitude, we believe that it could support the finding that modern interpretation of the term extends beyond workers who are officially incarcerated.

(C)   Worker Health

Another Article XX exception might benefit a Member seeking to advance labor rights. Section 8.2(B) notes that labor rights often find reflection in concerns for the health of workers. Abolition of child labor, in particular, aims to protect the physical and mental health of underage workers.[26] Other labor standards seek to ensure safe working conditions[27] and to protect against an unhealthy work environment, such as by the improvement of industrial hygiene and prevention of occupational disease.[28]

Paragraph (b) permits a Member to protect human life or health through border restrictions that otherwise would risk sanction for violation of the Four Pillars. From the perspective of human rights, one of the most noteworthy WTO cases, the Appellate Body's *EC-Asbestos* decision, arose under Paragraph (b). We noted in section 6.5(A) that France in this case successfully defended a challenge by Canada against its ban on importation of asbestos insulation on the ground that such insulation is carcinogenic and thus unhealthy for its workers and other consumers of the product: "This carcinogenicity, or toxicity, constitutes, as we [the Appellate Body] see it, a defining aspect of the physical properties of chrysotile asbestos fibres."[29] If a Member is permitted to distinguish two products based on their health risks, the GATT Article III National Treatment safe harbor widens by sheltering from WTO sanction the Member's discrimination against an import based on the well-being of its workers.

EC-Asbestos is not a PPM case—the health risk was inherent in the product itself, not solely in its production—but the holding nonetheless increases Member discretion to protect a wider variety of worker rights, such as protection from an inadequately shielded chemical product, even when doing so constitutes discrimination against the product by comparison with another product whose only physical difference is that it does not present a health risk to workers who will handle the product. The WTC in *EC-Asbestos* also eased considerably the burden of proving under GATT Article XX(b) that the border restriction met Paragraph (b)'s Necessity Test by holding that the Member need not quantify the level of health risk that the border measure was designed to avoid. A Member is entitled to determine the level of health protection that it deems desirable for its citizens and to select the severity of the border measure to achieve that level unless there is available to the Member "an alternative measure which it could reasonably be expected to employ and which is not inconsistent with other GATT provisions."[30]

(D)   Public Morals Clause

Exploitation of children in a Member's labor force unquestionably implicates moralistic concerns. Forced or compulsory labor, regardless of whether children are involved, raises issues of public decency, particularly in light of the *jus cogens* nature of the prohibition against slavery. Article XX(a) also seems appropriate to immunize Member action against the worst forms of unsafe working conditions.

Interpreting the Public Morals Clause in Article XIV(a) of the WTO's GATS, the panel in the *U.S.-Gambling* case recognized the necessarily disparate foundations of 150-plus WTO Members by stating that the meaning of "societal concepts" such as public morality "can vary depending upon prevailing social, cultural, ethical, and religious values." The panel found that prior WTC rulings that Members have the right to determine their own level of protection for "similar societal values" such as public health suggest that "Members should be given some scope to define and apply for themselves" the concept of public morality and good order.[31] Western Hemispheric nations now routinely include protections for workers in their FTAs. Although the "level of protection" varies in these pacts, the widespread linkage of trade with labor rights strongly suggests that the WTO's Public Morals Clause will reach the range of protections inherent in realization of the human rights of workers.

The Public Morals exception from the GATT rules can be found in GATT Article XX(a), which states that "subject to the requirement that such measures are not applied in a manner which would constitute a means of arbitrary or unjustifiable discrimination between countries where the same conditions prevail, or a disguised restriction on international trade, nothing in this Agreement shall be construed to prevent the adoption or enforcement by any contracting part of measures: (a) necessary to protect public morals."

One central issue that arises from the Public Morals Clause is whose morality is relevant. May the moral basis for trade measures differ from country to country or must the Member adhere to a universal standard?[32] The Public Morals Clause appears to be written quite broadly indeed. Although Members often base trade restrictions on morality grounds, the first WTO challenge to its use did not come until 2005 in the case of *U.S.- Gambling*.[33] *U.S.-Gambling* was decided under the Public Morals Clause in GATS Article XIV(a), which is similar to GATT Article XX(a).[34] In *U.S.- Gambling*, the WTC held that gambling was an issue of public morality based on evidence external to the state whose regulation was in question, the United States. For instance, the panel examined the domestic regulations of other states, regional practice, and historical evidence regarding treatment of gambling by the League of Nations. Thus, the *U.S.-Gambling* holding answered the issue of whose morality is relevant by analyzing how the community of nations had approached the issue, although the panel did not address whether an international perspective would be needed when moral issues other than gambling were in play.

A number of perspectives can inform the issue of whose morality is relevant. One perspective is originalism, which examines what "public morals" meant when trade officials first applied it to international trade law in 1947. The major criticism of this perspective is that the plain meaning of "public morals" involves contemporary beliefs and norms. Another perspective is universalism, which examines what "public morals" are common to other Member nations. It is when opinions are diverse, however, that Members most need the public morals exception. On the other end of the spectrum is unilateralism, which allows nations to define morality unilaterally. Under this approach, nations easily could disguise protectionist trade measures using the cover of morality. Thus, the question of whose morality is relevant can have different answers depending on the perspective applied.

Another issue is whose morals a Member may protect. Unquestionably, a Member may use trade measures to protect the morals of its own citizens. May a Member apply a public morals trade measure extraterritorially—that is, to promote moral values in another country? The *U.S.-Tuna-Dolphin I* case first introduced the concept of extraterritoriality. The panel found that GATT Article XX did not shield the U.S. ban on tuna caught in association with dolphins because its purpose was to protect dolphins beyond U.S. waters, an objective that the drafting history of Article XX would not support. The panel in *U.S.-Tuna-Dolphin II* found no such limitation in the language of the exception, but reached the same result by opining illogically that the extraterritorial reach of the tuna import ban meant that its purpose could not be to conserve natural resources.[35]

Although the *Tuna-Dolphin* cases analyzed GATT Article XX(b) and (g), they suggest how an Article XX(a) defense of an extraterritorial import ban might be analyzed. If a WTO panel was persuaded by *U.S.-Tuna-Dolphin I*, it would conclude that Article XX(a) applies only to domestic morality and cannot be used to promote moral values in another country. On the other hand, under *U.S.-Tuna-Dolphin II* a panel would find that Article XX(a) has extraterritorial reach, but that the Clause does not by that attribute confer on a Member the right to impose a higher moral standard on other nations.[36]

GATT Article XX(e), which permits trade restrictions relating to prison labor, contains the only explicit reference to labor in the WTO agreements. In *U.S.-Shrimp-Turtle I*, the WTC applied the ICJ's evolution principle to find that the WTO exception relating to the environment, "in light of contemporary concerns of the community of nations," includes live animals "even if it did not encompass living species at the time of drafting." WTO panels likewise should interpret the Public Morals Clause broadly to include core labor standards stated in the ILO as "contemporary concerns of the community of nations."[37]

The final step in any Article XX analysis is the Chapeau Test, which requires that trade measures not be applied in a manner that would constitute (1) a means of arbitrary or unjustifiable discrimination between two countries where the same conditions prevail or (2) a disguised restriction on international trade. In *U.S.—Shrimp-Turtle I*, the Appellate Body held that the Chapeau Test requires a balancing between the right of a Member to invoke an exception under Article XX, such as the Public Morals Clause, and the duty of the Member to respect the rights of the other Members under GATT's Four Pillars.[38] Plainly, the severity of the deprivation of worker rights at issue will determine the outcome of that balancing test.

We understand that the realistic assessment is that a WTO panel might attempt to limit the reach of Article XX(a) because, as noted earlier, conferring complete discretion on a Member to control its borders through its own concept of morality effectively gives the Member an unlimited veto over imports. For this reason, the moral purpose of a Member's border limitation must be measured against universal or international moral standards contained in widely accepted human rights treaties. We can think of no more perfect blending of international trade law and international human rights law than by elevating generally accepted moral standards over trade's economic imperatives.

8.5 Relevance of the TBT Agreement

The WTO TBT Agreement (Item 10, online Documents Annex), discussed in section 6.6 with respect to the human right to a healthy environment, lists protection of human health among the legitimate objectives that a Member may pursue through technical regulations—that is, product characteristics that the Member requires as a condition of importation. May a Member base a technical regulation on protection of worker rights? We have repeatedly noted in this chapter that a healthy working environment is a central labor right. In this view, a technical regulation that imposes as a condition of importation of a product that its manufacture or harvest must take place within a healthy working environment seems consistent with the TBT Agreement's terms.

We also believe that a Member's enforcement of a product characteristic of this nature would be consistent with the unconditional MFN and National Treatment clauses of the TBT Agreement's Article 2.1, so long as the requirement is uniformly applied, including with respect to FTA partners. While GATT Article XXIV exempts FTAs and customs unions from the nondiscrimination clauses in GATT Articles I and III, application of the technical regulation to products of FTA partners is necessary because of the primacy over the GATT of other WTO Agreements in the event of conflict.[39] Interestingly, such technical regulations could be used to buttress labor rights protections in the many FTAs among Western Hemisphere nations discussed in section 2.6.

The list of legitimate objectives in Article 2.2 of the TBT Agreement is not exclusive. There is no reason why a WTO dispute panel should not find "legitimate" other objectives, such as protection of a worker's right to a living wage or the freedom to form a union, even if not explicitly listed.

The measure would not in that case benefit from Article 2.5's presumption of compliance with the obligation in Article 2.2 that technical regulations must not create unnecessary obstacles to trade. Nonetheless, compliance with this iteration of the Necessity Test discussed in section 6.4(B) and (D) as to GATT Article XX requires only that other approaches reasonably available to the Member would not accomplish the Member's chosen objective. For example, the Member must consider whether the worker right that the Member is pursuing may be secured with a less restrictive border measure, such as a technical regulation requiring that the product's label identify the failure of the manufacturer to furnish a safe working place. Our discussion of ecolabels in section 6.6 illustrated the powerful effect of supplying human rights information to the consumer. The United States no doubt could have accomplished its purpose of protecting dolphins through a technical regulation requiring that "dolphin-unsafe" tuna be labeled as such. The marketplace would have taken care of the rest.

The balancing of a violation of GATT's Four Pillars through a discriminatory border restriction with the policy expressed by a legitimate objective under the TBT Agreement should be subject to the same weighting process applied by the WTC to GATT Article XX's Necessity Tests. While there are no WTO dispute cases addressing Article 2.1 of the TBT Agreement, the Court in the *Korea-Beef* decision noted that "the more vital or important [the] common interests or values pursued, the easier it would be to accept as 'necessary' measures designed to achieve those ends."[40] Compliance with the human rights of workers, while lower on the list of vital interests than the 100 percent risk of cancer implicated in the *EC-Asbestos* case, occupies a high enough rung on that ladder to justify substantial interference with unfettered border trade.

8.6   Trade and Labor in the Americas

(A)   North American Agreement on Labor Cooperation

An executive agreement rather than a trade treaty (which would have required approval of both houses of the U.S. Congress), the North American Agreement on Labor Cooperation (NAALC) does not appear in the text of the NAFTA and was not submitted for legislative consideration. The Republican president (Bush) had already signed the Agreement and submitted it for approval of the Congress when a Democratic president

(Clinton) who had made campaign promises to labor unions took office. The new administration's desire to meet these promises without opening the Agreement to a complex rebalancing of carefully negotiated rights and obligations in dozens of sectors led to the crafting of the NAALC.[41] While its ingenuity lay in avoiding the impossible task of reworking the thousands of compromises reflected in the body of the FTA, this creative solution also meant that the parties needed to find all bargaining chips within the four corners of the NAALC itself: the U.S. goal of greater protection of labor rights could not be traded, for example, for Mexico's increased access to the U.S. sugar market or by increased protection of Canada's cultural rights.

Unlike most subjects of trade agreements, the NAALC's purpose was not to harmonize the labor laws of the three parties, although it does require that each Party "ensure that its labor laws . . . provide for high labor standards." The primary method by which the NAALC addresses labor rights is through the requirement in Article 3 that each party enforce its own labor laws. To narrow even further its scope, actionable violations are limited to three areas: minimum wage, child labor, and job safety and health. Within this narrow jurisdiction, the NAALC authorizes dispute settlement only when a party has engaged in a "persistent pattern of failure to enforce" its laws.

Completing a dispute settlement case involving non-compliance with the NAALC can take up to four years, as contrasted with the one- or two-year timetable contemplated for violations of the textual provisions.[42] In addition, the primary remedy is a monetary fine, although trade sanctions are authorized if the party does not pay the fine.[43] Although weak, these provisions have prevented Mexico from looking the other way on enforcement of its strong worker protections, many of constitutional stature, in order to gain a competitive advantage in trade or to attract foreign investment.

(B)   U.S-Jordan FTA

Two important aspects of the 2001 FTA between the United States and Jordan demonstrate improvement in the approach of the United States toward use of regional economic arrangements to protect the rights of workers. Jordan's is the first trade agreement to include labor rights in its text, as contrasted with NAFTA's side agreement approach. The ostensible consequence is that the Agreement's standard dispute settlement provisions apply to alleged violations. The U.S.-Jordan FTA encountered the same kind of implementation problem as had the NAFTA, however, except that this time a pro-labor Democratic administration was succeeded by a pro-business Republican administration determined to placate Republican opponents of using trade sanctions to enforce FTA labor and environment provisions. In this case, trade ministers exchanged unofficial letters anticipating that dispute settlement procedures based on the labor chapter would not be used "to block trade."

The second improvement over the NAFTA is that, in addition to NAFTA's requirement that each party enforce its own labor laws, parties agree in Article 6.1 of the U.S.-Jordan FTA to "strive to ensure" that five "internationally recognized labor rights" (listed in Paragraph 4) are protected by domestic law. The provision puts an affirmative obligation on the parties to have at least minimally harmonized labor laws, a notably more specific aspiration than the NAALC's requirement "to provide for high labor standards."

(C) U.S.-Chile FTA

Between the 2001 agreement between the United States and Jordan and Chile's 2003 agreement with the United States, representatives of pro-labor and pro-business interests in the U.S. Congress found harmonizing voice with respect to the proper linkage of trade and labor in 2002's Bipartisan Trade Promotion Authority Act.[44] The Act's extension of presidential authority to continue the trade liberalization process by negotiating additional economic agreements contained the first articulation of the labor protections that the executive branch must seek in such pacts. The Act's more tightly drawn "principal objectives" borrow generously from the NAFTA and the U.S.-Jordan FTA framework that seek effective enforcement of each state's own labor laws. Somewhat dissonantly, these higher priorities on one hand recognize the right of states to exercise discretion in the enforcement of labor protections while, on the other, calling for betterment of the capacity of states to pursue "core" labor standards.[45] In a show of disapproval of separate sanction systems for labor rights violations (as in the NAFTA side agreement), the principal objectives call for "parity of enforcement" with other principal negotiating objectives.[46] The more flexible "overall" labor rights objectives of the 2002 Trade Act sound a more aspirational note by reference to ILO core labor standards—including ratification of the Convention for the Elimination of the Worst

Forms of Child Labor (CEWFCL)—and restrictions on relaxation of the nation's domestic labor laws.[47]

In some ways, the 2003 U.S.-Chile FTA improves both on the NAFTA and on the primary U.S. negotiating objectives by explicit recognition of the ILO core labor standards, the ILO Work Declaration. Each party reaffirms its obligations to these principles as members of the ILO. With respect to enforceable obligations in this respect, the Agreement sets down two conditions. First, the parties agree only to "strive to ensure" that their labor standards are consistent with core rights, and they dismiss ILO jurisprudence by separately stating these standards in the Agreement, rather than by reference to the ILO Work Declaration itself.[48] The import of the precatory language with regard to core labor standards demonstrates the small steps through which labor protection in trade agreements progresses. As to the attempt to distance the "obligation" from extant public international law, it will by definition fail, for this treaty, as we noted in section 4.4(B), like all others, is born into the corpus of such law and will be controlled by its custom and general principles.

In arguable departure from the "parity of enforcement" stricture of the U.S. 2002 Trade Act, which was made a "principal," thus less discretionary objective, the Chile Agreement permits fines up to fifteen million dollars to be substituted for traditional trade sanctions—that is, prohibitive tariffs on an imported product of the violating country that will encourage bringing of the violating condition into compliance. This alternative remedy at first reading seems a backward step from the U.S.-Jordan FTA, which anticipated, at least in the Agreement itself, if not in the side letter exchanged by the parties, that traditional trade sanctions would be available for labor rights violations. Moreover, one doubts that fines, particularly of such small limits, would pass the test of "parity of enforcement" with trade retaliation limited only by the size of the harm inflicted by the infraction.[49]

(D)   Post-Chile Agreements

In 2004, the United States continued its policy of "competitive liberalization"[50] by concluding a trade pact with five Central American states and the Dominican Republic.[51] One could at least argue that Mexico, Jordan, and Chile had strong labor protections on the books, albeit far weaker than those in Canada and the United States, and those envisioned in widely ratified ILO treaties. That contention becomes hollow in the case of the broad challenges facing labor groups included in this treaty, which have made credible claims of ongoing abuses of internationally recognized labor rights.[52] As in the case of the U.S.-Chile FTA, state parties "strive to ensure" that their labor laws are consistent with ILO core labor standards, as defined without reference to ILO treaties.[53] CAFTA-DR-US is for these reasons stronger than FTAs with Chile and Jordan in its solicitation of ILO assistance in drafting needed legislative changes, in its anticipation of increased funding of labor ministries, and in its initiation of international programs to train government officials.[54]

The labor chapters in later FTAs between the United States and Peru (2006), Colombia (2006), and Panama (2007) initially followed the limited protections once viewed as templates of the U.S.-Chile FTA. Despite continuing reports of unchecked violence against union organizers in Colombia, labor protection in these newer FTA states is, in general, more secure than in the Latin partners of the CAFTA-DR-US. In Peru's case, as a result of reforms undertaken following restrictions enacted during the Fujimori presidency, Peru has ratified seventy-one ILO Conventions, including all eight of the core treaties, and has enacted significant enhancements for workers, among them elimination of limitations on union rights and of restrictions on the right to strike.[55]

During its last years, the Bush administration was content to mimic worker protections for these three FTAs to the labor provisions negotiated in its early days. The Democratic majority that assumed control of the U.S. Congress in 2006, however, was not so inclined. An accord between the Congress and the administration discussed in section 7.7(A) (as to IPR) resulted in renegotiation of all three agreements to include stronger worker protections. The new language, enforceable through regular dispute settlement proceedings, commits parties to "adopt, maintain and enforce" in their laws and practice the ILO core standards.[56] If these labor chapters are enforced—and Peru and Colombia seem committed to them because they agreed to the changes even after formal ratification of the FTAs—they will serve as best practices models of worker protections in future FTAs.

(E) MERCOSUR

In 2002, parties to the Southern Cone Common Market signed a protocol whose goal is to make movement of workers among Members easier, including qualifying for citizenship in the new nation of work. By reducing the problem of undocumented workers driving down wages for all those seeking employment, the pact seeks to raise the standard of living for workers and their families. With this step toward the free movement of labor, a necessity for truly "free trade," MERCOSUR moves beyond an economic arrangement and decidedly in the direction of the combined economic and social arrangement that is the EU.[57]

(F) FTAA

Labor is not among the nine negotiating groups that the thirty-four states have created to conduct the detailed discussions needed to draft specific rights and obligations as to the major areas of contention.[58] Unless pro-business interests in the United States gain significant ground, however, the complete absence of labor protections in an FTAA would seem incompatible with the detailed objectives of the 2002 U.S. trade law that enables negotiation of the FTAA.[59] The sheer economic and political diversity of the thirty-four participating nations predicts a race to the bottom rather than meaningful improvement of the bilateral—or small regional—pacts that have tacked successive gains onto the basic labor rights model negotiated in the NAFTA. Given the consistent model being followed in the FTAs with Chile and CAFTA-DR-US, a major change of paradigms will be necessary for the FTAA to break new ground in the protection of Hemispheric worker rights.[60] The populist nature of the new administrations taking power throughout the Hemisphere suggest that they may be willing to listen to arguments such as those of the United States as to why trade rules must contribute to enforcement of worker rights. One may wonder whether the FTAA will be the vehicle for realization of these goals, because some of these citizen-oriented leaders would condemn the FTAA to its final resting place once and for all, in favor of what Venezuela's Hugo Chávez styles the Bolivarian Alternative, which foresees regional integration with the goal of fighting poverty and social exclusion.[61]

With this background, one may ask what would be a model trade agreement that does all that can be expected to increase the power of workers. First, would it limit itself to core labor standards so as not to chase off potential signatories? Would it be satisfied with monetary fines for enforcement purposes? How much less effective, if any, are monetary fines from traditional trade sanctions in the form of economic retaliation, such as 100 percent tariffs on the products most successfully exported to the prevailing nation? Should the ILO be the primary forum for use of trade sanctions? Does it have the expertise to do so? This approach would encounter the same problem as in asking WTO trade experts to learn the language, objectives, and history of human rights law.

Borrowing a note from the U.S. model for labor protections in the Hemisphere, why could we not demand that companies seeking the benefits of the market access granted by lowered tariffs and nontariff barriers, as well as expanded investor protections, be required to prove that they are at least following the labor laws of the country in which they are doing business? Such a provision could be enforced through the FTA's dispute settlement system, by challenging the government of the nonconforming company for the company's violation of the agreement. This approach would take the burden from the often-inadequate enforcement mechanisms of the LDC and place it in the hands of the entities that benefit from the trade agreement—and their governments. By this means, corporate actors would share responsibility for the human rights of workers their activities affect.

8.7   Trade and Immigration

(A)   North-South Divide Revisited

The reduction of tariff and nontariff barriers through regional trade arrangements between developed and developing countries inevitably has led to increases in both legal and undocumented immigration among the regional trading partners. From an economic perspective, these effects are the natural result of "market clearing," with unskilled workers, particularly farmers in developing countries (Mexico in the case of the NAFTA), leaving the agricultural sector because of overpowering competition from developed-country fruit-and-vegetable conglomerates (in the case of the NAFTA, firms like ADM and Cargill located in Canada and the United States) to move to the cities, then to the border areas, and ultimately to the developed country. Economic theory predicts that in the long run these outward migration effects will be reversed as they cause wages to increase in the developing country and decline in the developed country and as foreign investors make job-creating investments in the developing country.[62]

Long-run economic effects are cold comfort to the Mexican families split by the overwhelming preference of managers in the maquiladoras for women workers.[63] With the post-NAFTA growth in Mexico's maquiladoras driving toward 1.25 million employees,[64] large numbers of unemployed Mexican men found that their only viable employment prospects lay in the United States, resulting in a "migration hump" that saw the number of unauthorized Mexicans in the United States more than quadruple during the NAFTA's first decade.[65] Many migrants thus are women and children joining their husbands and fathers who emigrated previously for better wages.[66] As trade agreements clear the path for unfettered operation of Mr. Ricardo's comparative advantage, the industries responsible for the products and services that each country can most efficiently provide will draw workers away from work that has no export value, so that the pattern of separated families is repeated time after time, and is felt with particular force in countries with marginalized workers.

Moreover, the predicted market clearing rarely occurs because governments restrict immigration—the cross-border flow of people—even as they free up the cross-border flow of goods. The price of labor services, like other services, is equally as subject to comparative advantage principles as the price of goods, and the WTO recognized this truth in the 1994 creation of the GATS.[67] The GATS applies GATT's fundamental principles to services trade, with variations that recognize the different ways that services are provided as compared with goods.

Even so, the developed-country partners to such arrangements resist addressing what they style "immigration policy" in trade agreements, usually for two reasons. The first is that a nation's treatment of immigration relies on a plethora of policies unrelated to trade. Foreign policy, education, national security, and the financial ability—and willingness—of local governments and private corporations such as hospitals to provide basic health care also are implicated. Trade agreements, according to this position, are ill suited to resolve these policy considerations because their constituencies and the necessary government expertise do not belong to trade advisory groups or take part in trade delegations. Second, immigration concessions are difficult to measure with the normal economic models employed by trade negotiators. How does one calculate in trade terms the value of increasing an immigration quota by ten thousand people per year? A third reason, compelling in itself, is that trade negotiators would need to face directly the human rights concerns created by the agreement on the table, which negotiators have so far been unwilling to do.

(B)　Immigration Policy Through the Back Door:
　　　Delivery Mode 4 in the WTO's GATS

The presence of natural persons, known as Mode 4, is one of the four possible forms of providing a service under the GATS.[68] Mode 4 is found under GATS Article 1(2), which states that GATS applies to measures by Members affecting "the supply of a service . . . by a service supplier of one Member, through presence of natural persons of a Member in the territory of any other Member." Therefore, GATS Mode 4 concerns the temporary movement of natural persons to another country to provide a service and was included in the GATS as the result of developing-country demands to take account of the actual effects of liberalized trade. Industrialized WTO Members contend that opening developing country markets to products, services, and investments from more developed Members will reduce, not increase, the pressure for emigration of workers to larger countries. As noted in section 6.7(A), developing countries know that this economic maxim is far from realistic because competition from more efficient producers creates—at least in the "short term"—unemployment in agricultural and other developing country sectors that is not met by increased employment in other sectors for which these unemployed workers may be qualified. As a result, many of these jobless workers will emigrate to larger nearby markets with larger labor forces.

Despite its origins, GATS Mode 4 does not guarantee service suppliers access to another country. As with the GATS in general, access is determined by the specific commitments granted by each Member's schedule to the GATS, which are given both by industry and by mode of supply. Developed countries have not opened their service sectors to foreign workers who would supply such services by immigrating into the developed country—that is, through GATS Mode 4. Further, the GATS Annex on the Movement of Natural Persons places two important limitations on Mode 4. First, the GATS does not cover natural persons seeking access to the employment market nor measures regarding citizenship, residence, or employment on a permanent basis. Therefore, this mode relates only to the temporary admission of foreign nationals or foreign permanent residents as service providers.[69] The GATS does not specify the length of stay allowed. Members determine the maximum length of stay in their individual schedules, and the length varies depending on the underlying purpose. For example, business visitors are generally allowed to stay up to ninety days, while intra-corporate transferees tend to be limited to periods between two and five years.[70] The GATS also does not prevent governments from regulating the entry or temporary stay of natural persons, if such measures do not nullify or impair the benefits under a specific commitment. Footnote 1 of the Annex states that differential visa requirements are not to be regarded as nullifying or impairing benefits under a specific commitment.

Developing countries want to use Mode 4 to aid their professionals in securing lucrative positions abroad. Developed countries, however, especially the United States after the terrorist attacks of September 11, 2001, are weary of Mode 4 because of the political issue of immigration controls.[71] Some members of the U.S. Congress are concerned that Mode 4 will undermine their control over immigration policy.[72] The U.S. Trade Representative (USTR), who is responsible for developing and coordinating U.S. international trade policy and overseeing trade negotiations, is constrained in her ability to negotiate concessions on Mode 4 as a result of objections by the House and Senate judiciary committees.[73] In a 2005 letter to the USTR, House Judiciary Committee Chairman Sensenbrenner indicated that Congress's main concerns with including immigration policy in trade agreements is that it limits Congress's ability to debate, amend, and later modify the immigration provisions to take account of changing policy decisions.[74]

WTO members can use Mode 4, however, to liberalize immigration policy in developed countries. Currently U.S. Mode 4 policy limits most temporary entry rights to executives, managers, or employees of a foreign company that has a physical presence in the United States in the form of a branch, subsidiary, or affiliate.[75] In contrast, the EU's 2005 proposal expanded temporary entry rights by removing such barriers as an economic means test and also by increasing the right to stay from three months to six months.[76] Business groups in the United States are applying pressure to the USTR to offer to expand Mode 4 in order to obtain concessions regarding the agriculture and industrial goods trade.[77] Groups such as the Coalition of Service Industries have developed proposals demonstrating that Mode 4 access will benefit the U.S. economy and assure improved market access offers from other WTO Members.[78] In addition, the House Judiciary Committee has expressed interest in the creation of a temporary entry visa to respond to needs for employment and desires for emigration.[79] Developing countries have submitted proposals asking for expanded Mode 4 concessions, and U.S. officials have suggested that there is hope for some concessions from the First World.[80]

The current political environment in the United States has complicated the use of Mode 4 to expand immigration policy in developed countries. Even if developed countries wanted to use Mode 4 to provide global distributive justice—that is, to ensure that the countries most in need of work permits would find them available—the MFN provisions of the GATS, as with WTO nondiscrimination provisions in general, militate against this kind of discrimination among WTO Members.[81] The GATS does not include the GATT's provisions permitting preference for developing countries. Nonetheless, the device of GATS Mode 4 remains in place and with a change in the political environment can well serve to liberalize the movement of natural persons and immigration policy of developed countries, so that developed nations finally may directly address the multifaceted effects of trade agreements on immigration.

8.8 Colorism and Labor Rights

(A) Introduction

The ILO identifies freedom from racial discrimination in the workplace as one of the four fundamental worker rights. As Professor Hernández-Truyol has demonstrated, Latinas/os face discrimination beyond simple racial stereotyping. Differential treatment can be based on their language, surname, national origin, and color.[82] Discrimination on the basis of the shade of a person's skin color has become the new face of racism in the labor field, crafting an economic hierarchy that finds lighter-skinned individuals of whatever "race" at the top of both pay scales and job tiers. Colorism is distinct from "racism," although inextricably linked with it. Prejudice based on the relative lightness of skin color is so widespread that it deserves its own category as a type of discrimination. We explore in this section the extent and effects of colorism, conscious or not, in the realization of labor rights in the Americas.

(B) Colorism and Income/Professionalism Levels

In the United States, dark-skinned blacks earn seventy cents for every dollar that a light-skinned black worker earns.[83] Light-skinned blacks hold nearly twice the managerial and professional jobs occupied by black Americans with dark skin. This more hidden form of discrimination is self-perpetuating, because professionals and managers with lighter skin determine who will be promoted or successfully fulfill educational prerequisites.[84]

Discrimination based on skin color also is deeply rooted in Latin American society. Darker-complected, Indian-looking Mexican Americans reported more discrimination than lighter-complected, European-looking Mexican Americans, including by other Latinas/os[85]: "In Brazil, as people climb the class ladder by educational and economic success, their racial designations often change," reflecting the higher status associated with lighter skin tones.[86] Social and economic status strongly correlates with skin color.[87] Black-skinned Cubans are subject to discrimination not encountered by their lighter-skinned compatriots:[88] "Colorism exists throughout Latin America and is reflected in Spanish language media, through standards of beauty and images of what a Latina looks like."[89]

The Spanish language itself reveals the importance of distinctions based on skin color, with many categories to describe this physical characteristic, from *blanco* to *trigeño* to *claro* to *moreno* to *negro*. These classifications largely parallel the now-discredited racial categories of the old American South, based on the number of drops of "colored" blood, during the apogee of the "one drop" rule, which provided that one drop of black blood rendered a person black. The Latina/o equivalent means that one drop of white blood starts one toward whiteness. In fact, Brazil, with the largest black population outside Africa, has managed to create over three hundred terms to designate skin color, aiding the exclusion of dark-skinned Brazilians from the spoils of that country's strong economic growth.[90]

Reflecting this hidden preference system, displays in Latin American countries advertising cosmetics and other beauty products consistently show white-skinned models, however dark the skin tones of the local community. Carl Degler describes what the authors have witnessed in a color caste system in Brazil with dark-skinned blacks at the bottom.[91] Despite the large demographic proportion of blacks in Cuba, jobs in the most dynamic sector of the Cuban economy, the tourist industry, are reserved for persons *de buena apariencia* (which literally means "good looking" but is commonly understood as limited to white Cubans). The tourist sector not only promises well-paying jobs, but also access to valuable foreign currency and scarce foods and consumer goods (like soap) that are extremely difficult to locate within the strained government rationing system.[92] The ability to earn extra income with foreign currency tips from tourists enables these lucky Cubans to shop for scarce foods and consumer goods within the U.S. dollar–only shops and restaurants. Therefore, being excluded from employment in the tourist sector restricts Afro-Cubans to job positions in which they are paid in the undervalued domestic currency of the peso.[93]

Contemporary Latin America, in short, maintains the racial hierarchy based on colorism that began in its own slavery period, a colorism hierarchy that excludes dark-skinned blacks and indigenous populations from the better jobs, as well as to educational opportunities that could change that result.[94] "Racial" discrimination must be understood as a blended preference for or aversion to a host of physical and behavioral character- istics, including ethnicity and skin tone. Because dark skin is not con- sidered desirable by any culture—not white, not Latin, not black (except, ironically, in the case of suntans), we must guard against the belief that even partial liberation from the black/white paradigm lessens the crisis nature of "racial" discrimination. Unless states begin to address the dark/ light paradigm that has become racial discrimination's formidable proxy, they risk condemning dark-skinned Latinos/as to "the bottom of society's barrel,"[95] including in the realization of labor rights.

8.9   *Role of Corporate Governance*

(A)   Introduction

In 1996 the reputation of U.S. television star Kathy Lee Gifford was sul- lied by reports that her clothing line for Wal-Mart was produced by un- derage workers whom she was paying thirty-one cents an hour to work in Honduran sweatshops.[96] Many similar accounts soon followed of corpo- rate abuse of labor rights in foreign production facilities chosen because of the availability of low-cost workers. Escalating consumer sensitivity to the ethics of transnational corporations (TNCs) with respect to worker rights finally has validated assertions of human rights advocates that cor- porations have responsibilities not only to their shareholders but also to the communities in which they operate.

Firms that own, manage, and control income generating assets in more than one country in effect constitute some of the world's largest economies and exert the influence that accompanies control of great financial assets, including outsized effects on the host country's employment rates, tax rev- enues, and credit standing.[97] Large transnational conglomerates developed in the second half of the 19th century as corporations, led by those from the United States, spread their manufacturing and distribution networks throughout the world in search of new customers and lower production costs. By the early 1990s, some forty thousand companies controlled one- fourth of the world's assets. As an example, resources of General Motors exceeded the national economies of all but seven countries: the United States, Italy, Germany, the United Kingdom, France, Japan, and the Neth- erlands.[98] Fifteen of the largest firms have total revenues greater than all but thirteen nations.[99] With these greater revenues comes greater power than many national governments possess.

Typically, these exceptionally efficient economic entities outperform smaller, more nationally oriented businesses and exploit their ability to trade and invest as well as coordinate their operations internationally to generate high returns on their investments. They operate on the assumption that corporations are in business solely to make maximum profits for their shareholders.[100]

Forcing TNCs to take responsibility for their actions is difficult given their power in relation to the national governments whose citizens are affected by these actions. Great corporate economic power brings with it substantial political influence over national governments responsible in theory for regulating issues ranging from international patent protection to trade. Governments often defer to foreign corporate interests because big firms employ large numbers of employees who can vote and hire political action committees that lobby governments at all levels. Multinational companies have often used their tremendous power to influence naive and divided governments abroad.

Given the power of large firms compared to national governments, and their operation beyond territorial reach of corporate headquarters, what entity effectively can assume responsibility for ensuring that corporations act with respect for human rights? Moreover, precisely what are the duties of a TNC to its workers and to the communities in which they live? As the power and wealth of corporations has grown, so too has the concern over their negative social impact, which has given birth to theories of corporate social responsibility—that is, the expectation that corporate operations and strategies will be conducted in ways that respect people, communities, and the environment. The protection and promotion of labor rights represents the heart of corporate social responsibility.[101]

(B) Corporate Codes of Conduct

In response to mounting consumer and shareholder demands, inspired in part by scandals involving the defense industry and companies manipulating the U.S. stock market in the 1980s, transnational corporations have developed their own codes of conduct in recent years, both to forestall government regulatory efforts and to increase profits. Corporations viewed business ethics as a way to police industry action and deter government intervention and regulation. Global corporate actors found it cheaper to develop their own "regulations," which of course allowed them to dictate the content.[102] External pressure from Western consumers also spurred corporate self regulation, including anti-sweatshop campaigns.[103] Media reporting of labor rights abuses in foreign countries has resulted in costly negative corporate images, affecting consumer purchasing decisions in corporate target markets.[104] Corporations increasingly also have come to the belief that better labor standards are more profitable, even though they may seem more expensive in the short term. The benefits from labor standards that are sensitive to the worker's human rights include better employee morale, lower employee turnovers, fewer accidents and sick leave, and better-quality products.[105]

Corporate social responsibility, once seen as a form of philanthropy, increasingly is being viewed as complementary with profitable operation. Far from being solely profit-making machines, global companies are leading agents of the new economic order and must be good global citizens sensitive to the "triple bottom line" of people, planet, and profits. Corporate social responsibility is the modern corporation's new way of thinking about doing business, the new social contract between the corporation and society. A great corporation today is one that not only offers excellent products and services, but one that also works to make the world a better place.[106]

Corporate codes of conduct are voluntary policy statements that define ethical standards for company conduct and can take any number of formats and address any number of issues, although in almost all cases, implementation is left solely to the company's discretion. Forms of private regulation, these codes of conduct often are based on core conventions of the ILO.[107] Members of other international organizations also have articulated soft-law codes that address both civil and political protection of workers, as well as economic, social, and cultural guarantees. For example, the Organisation for Economic Cooperation and Development (OECD) adopted its Guidelines for Multinational Enterprises in 1976. One year later, the ILO approved a Declaration of Principles Concerning Multinational Enterprises and Social Policy.[108] TNCs and their governments promise through these codes to act responsibly in protecting and guaranteeing working conditions and other labor rights. The codes often also address protection of the environment and similar human rights sensitive to corporate activity. They require corporations to ensure by contract that manufacturers, subcontractors, and suppliers abide by these standards as well.[109]

(C)   Problems with Accountability

Many TNCs have developed codes of conduct. Time and again, however, studies have demonstrated that the codes are for the most part window dressing because they are neither monitored nor enforced. An OECD study showed that corporations rarely dealt with enforcement issues and those that did stated that someone in-house monitored compliance.[110]

One way to increase accountability is to have inspections of the facilities. The U.S. Department of Labor survey discussed above found that all the plants that exported garments to the United States that were visited by that agency confirmed that they are visited regularly by their U.S. customers or agents. Whether these monitored visits are announced or unannounced varied. The Department of Labor suggested that the visits were not to monitor compliance with the labor provisions of the codes of conduct, however, but rather to monitor production quality and schedules.[111]

Even a field inspection would entail difficulties in determining whether child labor is being used. The inspector could only note whether the workers look young. In addition, the inspector could not easily establish whether reasonable working hours are being followed unless workers consistently appear highly fatigued. Working hours could only be discerned through auditing the records of the company and plant records, if any; such an investigation undoubtedly would confirm that all workers were of age and working reasonable hours. Therefore, field inspections contribute little to human rights enforcement when the inspector cannot confirm compliance visually.

Even if we could accept the sufficiency of corporate conduct codes, in light of obvious compliance deficiencies, we may ask who should be responsible for enforcing code compliance. By developing voluntary codes of conduct, TNCs have of course shifted to the private sector the power of regulation normally resident in government. If the companies themselves cannot be trusted to comply with their own conduct codes, perhaps not only compliance but the nature of the corporate conduct must revert to the state. Taxation, securities regulation, safety standards, and a host of other routine areas of government regulation of businesses must balance the particular public concern at issue with the necessity that companies make a profit if they are to remain viable. The corporation clearly has certain fiduciary duties to its shareholders. But accepting the proposition that corporations breach this fiduciary duty by putting some other interest before operating in a profitable manner does not mean that a company owes nothing to the community in which it is located, the workers it employs, or the environment which it affects.

Just as trade's enormous power and ubiquity inexorably bring human rights responsibilities, so do these same traits of TNCs. We suggest that global corporations must obey and through their actions encourage and effect compliance with the core labor standards of the ILO, specifically those human rights identified in the ILO Work Declaration. As noted in section 8.2(B), Member states of the ILO, prodded by the WTO, have singled out these four basic rights as necessary accompaniments of international trade: freedom of association and the right to collective bargaining; the elimination of forced or compulsory labor; the abolition of child labor; and elimination of discrimination in the workplace. These are not the only labor rights deserving of attention; they are the fundamental worker rights requiring immediate compliance by all means available to ILO Members.

(D) Making Corporations Accountable for
      Human Rights Compliance

In order to increase accountability of TNCs to human rights, national governments must assume a greater role. Corporate codes of conduct are a good first attempt by global corporations to regulate their behavior. Because of conflicts of interest, however, governmental regulatory activity must accompany corporate self-regulation. Even here, conflicts of interest will surface. Many developing countries consider lower production costs associated with low wages and marginal working conditions part of the comparative advantage that attracts job-creating investment from transnational companies. The developed country that usually is the headquarters of the multinational firm may be reluctant to hamstring the profitability of its own companies. These South-North differences condemn to failure global agreement on trade rules regulating corporate social responsibility. Regional trade agreements are the natural venues for finding in a smaller and more comfortable forum the proper balance among these conflicting interests.

Endless dialogue occurs over the nature of the problem, hamstringing solid progress on corporate social responsibility. Should the mandate be to pay a living wage in the country of investment, to contribute to infrastructure development in that country, to reduce the government corruption documented by the World Bank as having a direct correlation to a nation's economic performance? Each is a laudable goal, but they also are objectives that states are not yet prepared to reach. In the meantime, requiring that corporations that benefit from the investment, transparency, predictability, and due process protections of the FTA comply with the ILO-decreed fundamental principles for workers is a necessary provision of future regional economic agreements.

8.10 *Soft Landings: Retraining Assistance*

Economists admit that the economic growth triggered by trade is accompanied by sea changes in employment patterns within the affected countries. When a developed and a developing country eliminate trade barriers, the products of small agricultural farms in the LDC normally cannot compete with huge agricultural combines found in developed states. Newly unemployed farmers will migrate to the city (or to other countries; see section 8.7) in pursuit of the new jobs created by the economies of scale made possible by lowered tariffs and the state's advantaged resources.

It is important to retrain farmers so that they can work in the sector that offers employment, be it learning to assemble computer chips or keeping an automated Volkswagen assembly line in operation. The United States uses the trade adjustment assistance program to cushion for workers the negative blows struck by the shifting efficiencies of trade and to maintain support among its civil society for trade liberalization, a necessity if its legislature is to continue approval of new trade treaties.[112] Cushioning the negative effects of free trade is both a necessary function of government and a necessary predicate for continued support of free trade. For more than two decades, the trade adjustment assistance program has provided technical assistance and cash benefits to farmers, fishermen, plant workers, firms, and communities adversely affected by changes wrought by international trade and investment.[113]

For example, a farmer experiencing low prices as a result of increased imports would be eligible for financial compensation, for training in growing alternative crops, and for assistance on progressive marketing techniques.[114] A firm that has lost orders from import competition can have the program match its expenditures aimed at improving the company's competitive position.[115] A factory worker whose job has moved to a country with lower labor costs can receive training, job search and relocation allowances, income support, health insurance tax credits, and other reemployment services.[116] The program uses existing resources of a number of federal agencies and, particularly with respect to retraining programs, of all U.S. state governments.[117] The program was substantially expanded with approval of the NAFTA and again in 2002 as a result of the raft of free trade agreements negotiated by the United States. Among other improvements, the 2002 amendments created an alternative program for older displaced workers, for whom retraining may not be appropriate, to accept reemployment at a lower wage and receive a wage subsidy.[118]

This type of soft landing is possible in LDCs as well, with minimal financial outlays of the increased revenues from investments and the expansion of domestic industries formed to respond to the nation's comparative advantage and global demand. Peru and other countries have begun to experiment with trade adjustment assistance laws.[119] With such programs, trade agreements can, with the initiative of the government signatories, begin to address core labor standards.

Although globalization and trade have yet to create the large middle class to which economically disadvantaged members of society aspire, the only way to reach this objective is through additional trade.[120] The marginalized members of society will not reap trade's gains overnight. Increasing the educational and skill levels of workers is necessary to create better paying jobs. Wise government decisions will be needed over the next generation to push the additional state wealth that will follow from FTAs with developed countries and other trade liberalization downward to the workers while not impeding active capitalists from also benefiting from their risk-taking in the global market. As the respected Washington think tank the Institute for International Economics put it in a recent report, "Distribution has often been wrongly derided, but nonetheless it remains true that one needs to have a lot of output before one can worry about how to distribute it. All the evidence suggests that one needs a thriving private sector nurtured by a competitive market economy for rapid and sustained increase in output. Yet this view is not dominant in Latin America. That is a threat to the future."[121]

8.11 Final Thoughts

The LDCs' argument (section 8.2(A)) that the same developed nations now insisting that developing economies adhere to ILO standards failed to observe such standards before their own industrial revolutions holds little sway with the four-year-old boy crushing rocks in the quarries of

Zambia to make the construction gravel that may help his family survive. It is promising that Latin America and the Caribbean have, as their economies have prospered, decreased by twelve million the numbers of children under fourteen active in the labor market. Only in Africa is child labor growing.[122]

Neither a legal nor policy basis exists to permit the developing world to use 19th-century human rights standards to justify presently unacceptable labor practices on the ground that they may result in lower production costs. Workers simply cannot be asked to support a country's comparative advantage in the global market by forfeiting their human rights to freedom of association, protection from child and forced labor, and elimination of workplace discrimination. Worker rights identified by ILO Members as essential to human dignity in the workplace must be the nonnegotiable opening position guaranteed by trade agreements. In any event, a safe and sanitary workplace in a job that ensures a fair wage that enables the worker to feed, clothe, shelter, and provide health care to a family promises a far greater increase in profits from more efficient production than any comparative advantage that may follow from denial of worker rights.

9

Human Bondage

Trafficking

9.1 Overview

In this chapter, we will look at a different type of trade—the trade in persons. Some of such "trade" inextricably is linked to trade regimes, bolstered by their demand for cheap labor. With the objective of convincing officials to make necessary changes, we examine the way that trade rules have heedlessly promoted a modern form of slavery.

9.2 Human Rights Framework

The modern-day prohibition against trafficking is couched in explicit international human rights documents protecting freedom and personhood. The Universal Declaration and ICCPR prohibit servitude, slavery, and the slave trade in all its forms (art. 4 and art. 8(1) and (2), respectively). The ICCPR goes further to provide that "no one shall be required to perform forced or compulsory labor" (art. 8(3)(a)). The ICESCR and CERD not only provide for the rights to work and to fair and healthy working conditions, they also recognize the right of workers to organize to attain these rights (arts. 6–8 and art. 5, respectively).

Other general human rights treaties address trafficking directly. CEDAW specifically mandates that state parties "take all appropriate measures, including legislation, to suppress all forms of traffic in women and exploitation of prostitution of women" (art. 6). Similarly, the CRC protects children against sexual exploitation and sexual abuse (arts. 19 and 34), and charges state parties to "take all appropriate . . . measures to prevent the abduction of, the sale of or traffic in children for any purpose or in any form" (art. 35). It also specifically protects the child against "economic exploitation and from performing any work that is likely to be hazardous or . . . to be harmful to the child's health, or physical, mental, spiritual, moral or social development" (art. 32(1)).[1] In the Americas region, ACHR prohibits slavery, involuntary servitude, the slave trade, and traffic in women (art. 6(1)). It clearly provides that "no one shall be required to perform forced or compulsory labor" (art. 6(2)).

Beyond these general covenants and conventions that address trafficking, there are relevant international conventions that focus specifically on the problem of trafficking in persons, including two instruments concerning the trade in women that were created early in the 20th century. The 1904 International Agreement for the Suppression of the White Slave Traffic prohibited the trafficking of women and girls without their consent for the purposes of prostitution. The 1910 International Convention for the Suppression of the White Slave Traffic imposed obligations on state parties to punish anyone who recruited into prostitution a woman who had not reached the age of majority, notwithstanding her consent. It underscored racial hierarchies and the relegation of racial and ethnic minorities to subordinated "otherness."

The agreements exclusively addressing trafficking include two conventions adopted by the League of Nations dealing with traffic in women and children and prohibiting traffic in women even if they were adults and consented to the practice: the International Convention for the Suppression of the Traffic in Women and Children and the International Convention for the Suppression of the Traffic in Women of Full Age. In 1949 the United Nations adopted the Convention for the Suppression of the Traffic in Persons and of the Exploitation of the Prostitution of Others, which combined and superseded the earlier agreements. Other pertinent documents are the UN Protocol to Prevent, Suppress, and Punish Trafficking in Persons, Especially Women and Children (Palermo Protocol); Optional Protocol to the Convention on the Rights of the Child on the sale of children, child prostitution, and child pornography; Optional Protocol to the Convention on the Rights of the Child on the involvement of children in armed conflict; International Labour Organization (ILO) Convention concerning Forced or Compulsory Labour (ILO Convention 29); ILO Convention concerning the Abolition of Forced Labour (ILO Convention 105); and CEWFCL (ILO Convention 182).[2]

The Palermo Protocol, at Article 3(a), defines trafficking as "the recruitment, transportation, transfer, harbouring or receipt of persons, by means of the threat or use of force or other forms of coercion, of abduction, of fraud, of deception, of the abuse of power or of a position of vulnerability, or of the giving or receiving of payments or benefits to achieve the consent of a person having control over another person, for the purpose of exploitation." Exploitation includes "at a minimum, the exploitation of the prostitution of others or other forms of sexual exploitation, forced labour or services, slavery or practices similar to slavery, servitude or the removal of organs" (art. 3(a)). If the consent of the trafficked person is obtained by means listed in the trafficking definition, then consent is deemed to be irrelevant (art. 3(b)).

The ILO defines forced labor as "all work or service which is exacted from any person under the menace of any penalty and for which the said person has not offered himself[/herself] voluntarily."[3] In contrast, trafficking is regarded as "the movement of individuals, most often across borders but sometimes within a country, a state, or even a local jurisdiction, for purposes of forced labor, sexual exploitation or other forms of indentured servitude."[4] Regardless of any distinction, it should be noted that once an individual is trafficked or subject to forced labor, slave-like working conditions are indistinguishable and those driven to commercial exploitation are escaping the same conditions as those labeled as trafficked. In fact, the Palermo Protocol includes a provision that condemns "the abuse of power or of a position of vulnerability or of the giving or receiving of payments or benefits to achieve the consent of a person having control over another person" (art. 3(a)). The Palermo Protocol also renders the consent of a victim irrelevant (art. 3(b)). Some argue that narrower definitions put traffickers outside the reach of local law and further increase the number of individuals trafficked under the guise of smuggling.[5] One concrete example of how the two terms become indistinguishable is in circumstances where trafficked individuals have been coerced into leaving their homes and, in another instance, victims are deceived about the nature or the conditions of their perspective employment.[6] In either situation, the end result can become an endless cycle of involuntary servitude.

Beyond the direct prohibitions against trafficking, slavery, and slave-like practices, trafficking in persons is an affront to human rights in a broader way. Victims of human trafficking suffer physical, psychological, and emotional harm. Trafficking deprives victims of other protected human rights such as the rights to life, liberty, freedom, family life, dignity, free movement, and fair pay for work, among other things.

In addition, in today's slavery work, often the victims are sold and bought numerous times. At every junction and with every transaction, victims of sex trafficking are exposed to myriad health problems beyond the psychologically traumatizing experience of prostitution itself. For example, prostituted women are often raped, physically abused, at risk for HIV/AIDS, and exposed to numerous sexually transmitted diseases and infections.

9.3 International Trade Framework

(A) Generally

The linkage with and concern regarding trade and trafficking includes trafficking for sexual exploitation but focuses on the trafficking of people for slave or slave-like labor. Estimates of the number of persons, including children, worldwide in bonded or forced labor or sexual servitude vary widely.[7]

Although trafficking in human beings has always existed, the last part of the 20th century showed an immense growth in the deplorable practice. Indeed, it is a multibillion-dollar industry run by individuals, groups, and organized crime networks. The rise in trafficking results from a complex web of social, economic, and cultural conditions that generate push, pull, and facilitating factors. The push factors—those factors that push people out of their home state or location within the home state to other parts of the home state or to other states—include increased civil strife, women's subordinated status, and, most significantly for trade, uneven economic growth across the world. Both gender subordination and economic deprivation play a role in the large problem of poverty (see chapter 10). On the one hand, many try to escape poverty by migrating. On the other hand, consequences of violence and women's inequality translate to their disproportionate share of poverty and consequent disproportionate numbers in migration statistics from poor countries and areas in strife.

Conversely, pull factors—those conditions that attract people to particular states—include the economic growth in industrialized and industrializing states, which creates a demand for unskilled or low-skilled work that pays low wages and that prosperous citizens refuse to perform. For economic, social, and cultural reasons (see section 10.3), there is often a great demand for women's labor because they are deemed to be more reliable, more detail-oriented, and more submissive than men. These factors all relate to cultural perceptions of gender and allocation of gender roles. Because of these perceived cultural gender tropes, women are viewed as less likely to complain about or rebel against poor working conditions that they experience in servitude or forced labor.[8]

(B)   Globalization and Trafficking

At least part of the increase in trafficking is related to globalization—the increased flow of goods and capital that has hugely enriched some while coexisting with high levels of poverty in significant parts of the world. The deep privation, the gap in wealth, and the exposure to goods and affluent lifestyles result in people wanting to better their lives. Such disparate socioeconomics become factors in trafficking.

International trade has created a large demand for unskilled and low-skilled labor in construction, manufacturing, agriculture, and domestic work, for which the supply comes from migration—documented and undocumented alike. The trafficking consequent to the labor demands, as well as the exploitation and servitude that follows, may take many forms. This may include one domestic servant in servitude, or hundreds of workers in farms or factories in servitude.

NAFTA offers one example of the patterns of labor migration. Some economists posit that NAFTA has created a push for people to move north from Central America and Mexico where they ultimately become employed in slave-like conditions. For example, with NAFTA, cheap corn from the United States is imported into Mexico with the consequence of effectively shutting down peasant corn farmers who move off and lose their land. Some estimate that for every ton of corn Mexico imports, two Mexican persons migrate to the United States.[9] The result is that in Mexico over 40 percent of the population lives in poverty—an economic reality that makes persons vulnerable to traffickers.[10]

Another example of the impact of globalization is its attendant pressures to remain competitive, which have fueled the increase of manufacturers in the free trade zones. For example, since the implementation of NAFTA, the maquiladoras have experienced robust production and growth.[11] They have become a concrete example of how global or regional economic growth can contribute to the problem of forced labor. The maquiladoras employ more than one million workers in over 3,500 plants located along the U.S.-Mexico border.[12] They generate approximately $12.9 million in foreign exchange. In 2000, maquiladoras represented 54 percent of Mexico's manufacturing exports (a 24 percent increase over the previous year).[13] Their success, of course, is good news—one of trade's positive outcomes.

One problem with maquiladoras is that multinational companies invest minimal capital while maximizing profits. The lack of capital sets the stage for the maquiladoras' exploitation of cheap labor, which includes horrid working conditions that are often dangerous to workers.[14] There are other labor problems as well. For example, workers are not compensated adequately for their labor, and frequently are fired for their attempts to unionize.[15] Labor unions are not allowed to operate unless they are government approved. Union contracts frequently expire without timely extensions. Sexual harassment and other forms of sexual discrimination in the workplace are commonplace (see section 10.3). Maquiladoras also pollute the environment and pose environmental hazards to the people who live in surrounding areas.[16] An additional problem is the lack of choice for individuals working in the free trade zones. Without major reforms in Mexican labor law, exploitation, sometimes under slave-like conditions, of the unskilled and semiskilled will continue.

Significantly, foreign workers who are laboring in conditions of servitude often pay fees to smugglers to take them across borders before they obtain their jobs.[17] The fees generally are paid by the worker in the range of four thousand to eleven thousand dollars and are illegal under source-country laws and banned by international covenant.[18] Indeed, there is no reasoned idea why unskilled workers should be paying fees for work.

ILO Conventions 29, 105, and 182 reflect the conventional approaches to dealing with the problems of forced or bonded labor (see section 9.2). The goal is to have industries follow the established regulatory frameworks that prohibit exploitative labor.

9.4 The Reality of Trafficking

(A) Generally

Trafficking victims can be from any nation. Some persons move from developing countries to pursue low-skilled jobs in industrialized states; others find themselves in bonded labor in their own country. The ILO "estimates that there are 12.3 million people in forced labor, bonded labor, forced child labor, and sexual servitude at any given time; other estimates range from 4 million to 27 million."[19]

Current research on the United States suggests that "at any given time, ten thousand or more men, women and children are laboring against their will as prostitutes, farm and sweatshop laborers, and domestic workers."[20] Other studies imply that forced labor in the United States is much higher, yet some others give a more conservative estimate.[21] For the most part, all studies agree that women constitute the majority of victims involved in forced labor.[22] The second most victimized are children, most often girls, between the ages of five and seventeen. Men follow as a distant third.[23] It is very difficult to ascertain any reliable information, however, concerning either trafficking or forced labor.[24]

Most victims remain invisible to the public and law enforcement.[25] Coercion, fear, and intimidation prevent many victims from ever reporting their condition[26]: "Victims are often physically and emotionally abused into submission through horrific beatings, gang rapes, starvation, violent threats, forced drug use, and/or confinement."[27] After extended exposure to such abuse, some victims become active participants and even traffickers themselves.

As discussed in the prior section, the increased exchange in goods and capital has yielded enormous net gains for myriad entrepreneurs and has created an unprecedented demand for cheap labor, which has triggered the trafficking in persons.[28] Thus, trafficking also relates to economic liberalization and multinational corporations' search for increased profits.[29] Additionally, socioeconomic inequalities—in some countries poverty levels are as high as 40 percent—are also major contributors to the increase in trafficking of persons.[30]

Another factor may lie in globalization and the changes that it effects in local markets that are partly attributable to collapses of infrastructure.[31] Market privatization, market liberalization, and the spread of foreign investment add to economic instability and have led to local market collapses. As a result, there is increased migration to zones where commercial production exists—migration that often results in increased trafficking.[32]

(B)   Debt Bondage

A common contemporary example of involuntary servitude is debt bondage, in which a victim typically works to pay an employer for costs related to various expenditures, ranging from smuggling to everyday living expenses including food and lodging. Most victims live in deplorable squalor but pay exorbitant rent for small spaces shared with fellow workers; they also pay exorbitant prices for items that should be nominally priced.[33]

According to a recent study, forced labor is most prominent in the Americas due to U.S. demand for cheap labor.[34] Drawn by hopes of prosperity and livable wages, undocumented workers are vulnerable to exploitative employers and hired middlemen—known as coyotes.[35] Immigration laws, language barriers, and negative experiences with law enforcement, in their former or present country, serve as tools of coercion and deception.[36] Quite often undocumented workers are afraid to approach local law enforcement because they are always in fear of deportation.[37] Lack of legal documentation and alleged debt accumulation increase the numbers of undocumented individuals subjected to contemporary forms of indentured servitude and in some cases outright slavery.[38] Trapped in a cycle of debt and intimidation, many are subject to substandard living conditions, deplorable minimum wages, and hazardous working conditions.

Further, such conditions are reinforced by extraordinary sociopsychological dimensions. Most victims despise the conditions to which they are subject but, in some cases, become active participants in their exploitation and the conformity of others.[39] Exposed to individuals with a great amount of authority, victims succumb to rules used to obtain individual and group conformity. Methods such as isolation, favoritism—i.e. special treatment—individual antagonism, and offers of additional privileges are means utilized to maintain control over workers. During such group dynamics, one's sense of "personhood" is robbed and replaced with "feelings of hopelessness, helplessness, and a loss of will."[40] Consistent exposures to possible physical harm also result in workers' inability to escape forced labor conditions. Dehumanizing conditions result in victims violating the very personal morals and values that serve as a basis for their sense of humanity. Moreover, actively participating in the violation of others results in self-deprecation and thus creates an environment that falls outside conventional social mores.

Consistently, forced labor persists in business sectors where low wages, minimal regulation and monitoring of working conditions, and high demand for cheap labor is the industry norm.[41] Just to name a few, industries such as manufacturing, food service, hotel accommodations, and farming are common examples of businesses that thrive on workers exposed to adverse working conditions. Similar to the circumstances summarized above, ascribed conditions enable employers and criminal networks to retain control over their victims.[42]

(C) Trafficking and Children

Many experts believe that the number of children working worldwide as forced laborers is on the decline; such assertions could be questioned, however because of the rise of forced child labor in regions like sub-

Saharan Africa.[43] For example, in some countries, the ratio of children involved in forced labor is as high as one in four. Most of the children are under age fourteen, and many are involved in either full-time or part-time employment.[44]

When focusing on the Americas, it very difficult to ascertain the level of forced child labor, but some experts assert that the numbers are as high as 17.4 percent in Latin America.[45] It is difficult accurately to estimate the number of children subjected to forced labor in the United States; the United Farm Workers' Union estimates, however, that the number could be as high as eight hundred thousand (about 1.5 percent).[46] Although the number also includes children who work on family-owned farms, most child labor takes place with children hired as paid laborers. It is often common to find children as young as age four working in fields alongside their parents.

Authors of a recent report state that child labor usually begins around the age thirteen and most fulltime employment occurs during a child's seasonal vacation from school; some children, however, work year-round.[47] Laboring children can work anywhere from twelve to eighteen hours a day and usually are not paid overtime. Current law does not require overtime benefits; thus employers do not pay overtime wages.

The majority of child labor in the United States occurs in states such as California, Florida, Texas, Arizona, and Washington—otherwise known as "source states."[48] Nonetheless, child labor has been known to happen in the Midwest, on the eastern seaboard, and in upstate New York. Unfortunately, there are no states known to be free of child labor.

Child labor can, in part, be explained by societal standards and prevailing poverty.[49] In some countries, child labor is woven into social existence and is part of the norm; children are expected to work hard.[50] As noted above, many children work alongside their parents in an effort financially to support the family. In regions where prosperity is almost unreachable, the incidence of child labor is much higher than would be found in "developed" countries.[51] Many of the young victims found laboring on farms originate from "developing" countries; their parents commonly migrate from such countries.

Faced with abject poverty, some families even resort to selling their children as a means of survival. Not given choices normally seen in most Western societies, trafficking has become a normative means to an economic end.[52] Conditions such as civil unrest and governmental instability also contribute to the number of children in forced labor. In some instances, many children enter forced labor relationships voluntarily, which is quite understandable when the culture sees hard work as obligatory and norma-tive.[53] Promises of better living conditions, education, and better treatment often persuade parents to give their children up to work.[54]

Other circumstances related to forced child labor include sex trafficking and domestic work. It is estimated that 90 percent of the children prosti-tuted in Mexico are female.[55] Often marginalized, vulnerable, and deval-ued, women and girls are easily marked as "expendable," thus becoming easy prey for potential buyers or kidnappers.[56] Much of the gender-neu-tral statistics fail to reveal the male-driven demand for young women and girls.[57]

(D)   Trafficking in Women and Girls: Sex and Domestic Work

Trafficking of women and girls most often involves men, but in some instances includes women as well. There are accounts of women acting as principals—madams in charge of the care, custody, and indoctrination of victims.[58] During the indoctrination process, principals rely on beat-ings and rape, committed by male group members, to gain control and subsequent victim submission. Sexual trafficking is usually carried out by complex networks of organized families or individuals who sometimes threaten the girl's family members to prevent a victim from speaking out or escaping.

Trafficking victims also comprise those who work as domestic ser-vants.[59] Brought into the United States by foreign nationals and U.S. cit-izens alike, the number of domestic servants working and living in the United States can number in the thousands at any given time.[60] Many of the legally trafficked individuals are subject to coercion, intimidation, and physical as well as sexual abuse.[61] Quite often such activities take place behind closed doors.

Domestic workers often are underpaid. In some cases, they are not paid at all.[62] According to the ILO, domestic work is the highest source of employment for girls under sixteen.[63] Quite often women and girls em-ployed as domestics are privately employed and remain outside the pur-view of common labor statistics.[64] Unfortunately, current research lacks data concerning individuals who work in such conditions, so accurate assessments regarding this concern remain elusive. As indicated above, however, most incidents of domestic servitude occur in the United States and other wealthy nations.[65]

Further, "the burgeoning demand for cheap, docile, exploitable household labor" has contributed to the second highest incidence of forced labor in the United States, in large part with the assistance of U.S. immigration law and labor law.[66] For example, U.S. labor law does not classify domestic workers as "employees," which denies such workers national protection regarding work conditions and fair wages.[67] Another factor is an immigration policy requiring that domestic employees remain with their original employer to retain their visas.[68] Fearing for their well-being and afraid of legal authority, domestic servants become invisible in a form of captivity.

9.5   *The Ubiquity of Trafficking*

(A)   Generally

In the United States, the Victims of Trafficking and Violence Protection Act[69] (VTVPA) seeks to create protections for victims of trafficking. It defines "severe forms of trafficking in persons" as "the recruitment, harboring, transportation, provision, or obtaining of a person for labor or services, through the use of force, fraud, or coercion for the purpose of subjection to involuntary servitude, peonage, debt bondage, or slavery."[70] Since 2000, under VTVPA, efforts to curb trafficking in the United States have been increasing. In 2005, 116 individuals were charged with human trafficking and 45 were convicted, of whom 35 were implicated in sexual exploitation.[71] As of May 22, 2006, the Department of Health and Human Services (DHHS) had certified one thousand victims of human trafficking since VTVPA was signed into law in October of 2000, including victims from Bolivia, Colombia, Ecuador, El Salvador, Guatemala, Honduras, Jamaica, and Paraguay.[72]

U.S. government data suggest that "of the estimated 600,000 to 800,000 men, women, and children trafficked across international borders each year, approximately 80 percent are women and girls, and up to 50 percent are minors."[73] The majority of victims are trafficked for the purposes of sexual exploitation.

The U.S. State Department's *2006 Trafficking in Persons Report* identifies countries in various trafficking-risk tiers.[74] The evaluation depends on three factors: (a) whether the country is significant as a country of origin, transit, or destination for severe forms of trafficking; (b) whether the government complies with VTVPA's minimum standards; and (c) whether government resources are available to combat serious forms of trafficking. Tier One countries are those whose governments comply with VTVPA's minimum standards.[75] FTAA countries in this tier include Canada and Colombia.[76]

Tier Two countries are those whose governments are making efforts to comply with the established standards, although they do not fully meet them.[77] FTAA countries in this category include Chile, Costa Rica, the Dominican Republic, Ecuador, El Salvador, Guatemala, Guyana, Honduras, Nicaragua, Panama, Paraguay, and Uruguay.[78]

The next category is a Tier Two Special Watch List, which includes states that are not in full compliance with the minimum standards but are making significant efforts to come into compliance.[79] Additionally, these states either have a significant number of victims of severe forms of trafficking or fail to provide evidence of increasing efforts to combat such trafficking. States also can be placed in this category if their attempts to ensure compliance are dependent on commitments to take additional steps in the future. The Tier Two Watch List States of FTAA include Argentina, Bolivia, Brazil, Jamaica, Mexico, and Peru.

Finally Tier Three states are those whose governments do not comply with the minimum standards and are not making significant efforts to do so.[80] FTAA countries on this tier are Belize and Venezuela.[81] The State Department also places Cuba, a state geographically in the Americas region but politically excluded from participation, in this tier.

FTAA states also include some special cases: the Bahamas and Haiti. In the Bahamas,[82] trafficking is unmonitored and undocumented. Although reliable data is lacking, it appears that the Bahamas may be a state of destination for men and women trafficked for labor exploitation. For example, the approximately 25 percent of the state's population that is Haitian, most of whom are undocumented, is employed in domestic work, gardening, construction, and agriculture. The labor exploitation of Haitians may be great with undocumented workers—much as is the plight of undocumented workers around the world—laboring long hours for no or significantly below minimum wage pay. The threat of arrest and deportation and the withholding of documents contributes to the conditions. Such workers could be subjected to conditions of involuntary servitude, which would constitute a severe form of trafficking in persons.

Haiti[83] is a source, transit, and destination state for men, women, and children trafficked for the purpose of sexual exploitation and forced labor. Most of the trafficking in Haiti involves *restaveks*—the practice of poor mothers giving custody of their children to affluent families, hoping that the children will receive an education and educational opportunities. This fairly common practice generally involves sexual exploitation, physical abuse, and conditions of involuntary servitude. There also exists cross-border human trafficking between Haiti and the Dominican Republic for sexual exploitation and forced labor in the sugarcane fields where they live in shantytowns—referred to as *bateys*, in which the conditions are substandard and where guards keep workers' clothes and documents to prevent them from leaving.[84]

(B)   FTAA Countries and Trafficking

Because of the nature of trafficking, there are no facts and figures that accurately provide information on the practice in the Americas in general or within specific countries in particular.[85] The available information, however, is daunting and shows that there are trafficking concerns in at least twenty-six of the countries in the Americas—and these range across the U.S. State Department tiers[86] (see table 9.2, FTAA Countries' Trafficking Activities). Most of the countries are source, transit, and destination countries for both sex and labor exploitation. The majority are involved in international flows of persons. There are some states, however, such as Bolivia, Ecuador, and Uruguay, where the trafficking is mostly internal.

Some countries, such as Brazil, Cuba, and Paraguay, are source and destination countries but are not transit points. Colombia, Nicaragua, Jamaica, Peru, and Uruguay are source countries, with Colombia being a major source of women and girls who are trafficked for the purpose of sex. One figure suggests that between forty-five thousand and fifty thousand women and girls from Colombia are trafficked internationally every year.[87]

Interestingly, there is a gender divide in the trafficking world. Women and children, mostly girl children, are the majority of those who are trafficked for the purpose of sexual exploitation. On the other hand, men make up a larger number of those who are trafficked for labor exploitation. The sex exploitation occurs not only as sex tourism, but also related to labor flows as the demand for sexual services is often created by male migrants either as they travel through transit points or reach their destination without their families. For example, one source suggests that the existing demand for sexual services by migrant male workers and international truckers "supports a reported 60-70 establishments offering sexual services in Tecún Umán, alone."[88] With respect to labor, women and girls form the majority of those trafficked for domestic servitude. Men, however, make a larger number of those who are trafficked for work in agriculture, fishing, and timber camps. For example, Brazilian slave gangs work the Amazon rain forest, cutting down trees in order to make charcoal for the steel industry.[89]

9.6   The Faces of Trafficking

This section will present examples of trafficking in three states of the Americas. It expands and elucidates on both the realities and ubiquities of trafficking.

(A)   Guatemala

Tecún Umán is a small town in Guatemala on the bank of a river where migrants from Central America converge to cross Mexico's border on the way north.[90] Persons with documents cross a bridge over the river to Mexico; those without documents pay to be taken across the river on homemade rafts. Most migrants arrive in the town without money and fall prey to, among others, coyotes—people smugglers who make their living by exploiting the poor, uninformed, and needy whose impoverishment drives their migration. Because of the intervention of smugglers, these migrants owe a debt for the transportation so that they end up in debt bondage, often being sold many times. Some fortunate ones end up in safe houses, like Casa del Migrante, where they learn about the dangers of migration and about the unscrupulous bosses who will even take documents from those who have them and force them into slavery on remote plantations. Women at Casa del Migrante are also warned about brothels where many will be forced into prostitution, often when they think they are going to work at a restaurant or as a domestic.

(B)   Mexico

Mattel has a factory in Tijuana along the U.S.-Mexico border.[91] Mattel is a company that tries to police factories in order to ensure that the working conditions are up to standards, which include a set of rules about working hours, wages, factory conditions, and age requirements. These standards focus on issues of health and safety, and establish a good standard for accountability. Mattel not only scrutinizes its vendors' plants in the developing world, but it has built first-rate facilities, which include comfortable living quarters for its workforce.

In Tijuana, as per Mattel standards, the plant is clean and well-maintained, and the company enforces work-hour rules.[92] Outside of the parameters of the factory, however, the workers live in squalor, in dwellings made of sheet scrap metal and prefabricated wooden walls, which usually are nothing other than discarded garage doors. The homes have earth floors, few have running water, and most bathrooms consist of nothing but buckets. The company, invoking the public/private divide, asserts that it is not responsible for paying a living wage; rather, it contends (appropriately) that to establish such a wage is the responsibility of the state. Significantly, one statistic suggests that in order to have just the most basic amenities—sanitary drinking water, indoor plumbing—the 150,000 maquiladora workers would need their pay doubled.[93] It is unlikely that Mexico will establish norms that would bring wages to that level because it is continuously concerned about the companies fleeing to China. As far as the state is concerned, its main goal is to keep the companies in Mexico so that there can be employment.

Mexico is the largest source of undocumented migrants to the United States and a major transit point for third-country migration, particularly from Central America, which is now the second largest source of U.S. migration.[94] The movement of persons between Mexico and the United States has focused on two aspects of the migration: illegal immigration and people smuggling. Human trafficking, however, is different from the smuggling of persons because it involves, as the definition provides, the deception and coercion of another for the purpose of labor, sexual, or other forms of exploitation.

(C)   The United States

As one of the most profitable segments in the U.S. economy, agricultural producers hire more than 1.5 million migrant workers per year.[95] Some of the larger growers use third parties such as labor contractors to hire seasonal workers. Contributing to the trafficking dilemma, weak regulatory agencies lack adequate resources to enforce existing law, which requires employers to pay workers a minimum wage regardless of immigration status.[96] Outside the reach of federal and state labor standards, some employers in the agricultural industry fail to comply with the Fair Labor

Standards Act[97] or Occupational Safety and Health Act.[98] For example, workers are often exposed to toxic pesticides and work without breaks from sunrise to sunset.[99] It could even be argued that the U.S Congress is also a co-collaborator in the exploitation of non-documented individuals when current U.S. law enables the agricultural industry to operate outside the legal confines of national labor and public health regulation[100]: "In the fields, the United States is like a developing country."[101]

The United States, while having many laws against trafficking and slavery, still is the site of many people in servitude and forced labor. In Immokalee, Florida,[102] one finds farm workers who labor in Florida's plantations picking fruit and vegetables—products consumed throughout the United States. Many of these workers have left their homes in South and Central America because they cannot feed their family. Numbers cross the border without necessary papers. At the border, coyotes promise jobs for a price—a high one that the workers pay over time.

Picking fruit and vegetables is backbreaking and ill-paid work. Workers usually are paid on a weekly basis. From their meager earnings, first they have to pay for rent and food. The living conditions—camps in the plantations—are squalid, crowded, and unsanitary. Workers seeking to flee these conditions are stopped violently.

One specific and poignant example of these conditions can be found in Immokalee. Recently, two brothers and a cousin running such an operation were charged with trafficking in slaves, extortion, and possession of firearms, and were convicted on all counts, receiving prison sentences totaling over thirty-four years.[103] The usual population of Immokalee is twenty thousand. In the growing season, between November and May, however, it almost doubles.[104] The town is a major source of winter produce sold in the United States. Reports suggest that during growing season Immokalee looks more like a work camp than an American town.

The migrant workforce during the growing season is largely Mexican and Central American migrants, 90 percent of whom are men.[105] These men are citrus and tomato workers—often called "pickers"—who often are paid as little as forty cents per bucket of tomatoes. A full bucket weighs thirty-two pounds, so in order to earn fifty dollars per day a worker has to harvest two tons of tomatoes or one hundred twenty-five buckets. While orange and grapefruit picking pays slightly better, the hours are longer. Workers seldom discuss the harsh working conditions for fear of losing their jobs, and supervisors and labor contractors use this threat to keep them in line. Another reality is that the laborers are happy to get the jobs because farm work in Mexico pays about five dollars to six dollars a day when it is available. The availability is low because open borders have translated to importation of cheaper agricultural goods from abroad and the consequent closing of much Mexican agricultural production.

Of the over one million migrant workers living in the United States, half are undocumented.[106] They plant, tend, and harvest most agricultural commodities, including oranges, grapefruits, cherries, peaches, apples, watermelons, tomatoes, onions, eggplant, peppers, squash, cucumbers, mushrooms, cotton, tobacco, and Christmas trees. With globalization, the production and distribution sectors in the food economy have become very concentrated, with a few private firms being the suppliers. Ownership and distribution is tightly controlled in the citrus industry. According to records of the U.S. Department of Labor, between 1989 and 1998, farm worker wages declined; the average income for Immokalee farm workers is $6,574—lower than the median annual income for all farm workers, which is $7,500.[107]

But beyond plantations, slavery and slave trafficking in the United States are alive today. Indeed, such working conditions exist in all aspects of the economy that require cheap labor, such as manufacturing clothes or selling ice cream. One estimate is that there are between 100,000 and 150,000 persons working in slavery or slave-like conditions in the United States at present.[108] The U.S. State Department puts the number of people trafficked into the United States at approximately 20,000, with many ending up as sex workers, farm laborers, or domestic workers.[109]

9.7   Final Thoughts

Significantly, and of particular importance to this volume's goal of showing the positive and desirable nature and consequences of intersecting and coexisting human rights and trade discourses, the *2006 Trafficking in Persons Report* lists some FTAA countries as engaging in "international best practices" concerning trafficking.[110] These approaches may serve as a model to show how the private sector, government, and civil society can work together to pursue both human rights and trade goals.

For example, most victims returning to Brazil from foreign states enter at Sao Paulo's international airport where the state of San Paulo, working in partnership with an NGO, has established a support center near the airport so that returning victims can receive prompt help.[111] Colombia and Ecuador have used popular culture to educate the public about the problems of trafficking. For example, in Colombia, the UN Office of Drugs and Crime worked with the producer of a popular soap opera to incorporate into the plot a character who represented the plight of trafficking victims.[112] The "*novela*," which was broadcast throughout Colombia as well as exported to Venezuela, Ecuador, and the United States, reached large audiences and served an educational function and assisted victims to understand their status. In Ecuador, volunteer workers at the National Institute for Children and Family worked with entertainers to present an anti-trafficking message that reached the attendees of their concerts.[113] And in Guayaquil, Ecuador, a taxi driver's association worked with an NGO to place stickers with anti-trafficking messages inside local taxis with the purpose and intent of educating persons and disseminating information about trafficking and the plight of victims.

These cases, as well as the Mattel case discussed in section 9.6(B), show the fine line between complicity and cooperation, exploitation and comparative advantage, survival and competitiveness. The examples underscore the need to have holistic conversations that engage both human rights and trade.

The best practices examples provide a model for private sector, government, and civil society cooperation. The goal is dual: the enjoyment of the benefits of trade and the preservation of personhood. The Mattel example shows the successes and foibles of the current paradigm. A caring company sets out standards for acceptable and proper working conditions. With a focus on health and safety, the company established minimum requirements for age, hours, and working and factory conditions. Recognizing the complexity of well-being, the company even provides some of its workers comfortable living quarters. Yet privation persists outside the company walls. Only a government–private party collaboration can resolve this. As Mattel aptly states, it is not the role of corporations to establish minimum or living wages. Yet it is appropriate for the corporation to consider paying a wage that allows its workers to live in at least minimally sanitary conditions without the threat of moving its jobs where there is cheaper labor. Conversations that include the voices of the employer, the state, and the employees would provide a starting point for ascertaining a balance where the promise of trade can be a reality for all participants.

Given that this chapter vividly demonstrates the sharp intersection of trade and trafficking, especially given the push and pull factors that it generates, it is imperative to interrogate how the trade regime can act to cease "heedlessly promoting a modern form of slavery." At a minimum, it appears appropriate for trade agreements to include some protections against promoting such activity.

One possibility is for agreements to include a "best practices" clause that imposes a requirement for a partnership between governments and the private sector or investors to create and fund an agency to enforce trafficking laws in affected sectors. Such an entity would permit the filing of claims by either the victim or advocacy groups, such as NGOs, alleging that a party has failed to enforce its own domestic and international obligations on trafficking in a manner involving trade between or among the parties. A special panel would conduct the investigation on compliance with the trafficking prohibitions and issue a report, which could form the basis for a domestic complaint by a party or the basis of a petition to be filed before the Inter-American Commission or the Inter-American Court depending on the specific violation.

A different, but not mutually exclusive, "best practices" clause could require the payment of a living wage in labor-intensive industries most plagued by trafficking. Radical as this may sound, it ultimately would likely be cost-effective as the living wage rate would be tied to local economies, and developed-country investors would still obtain the comparative advantage of a developing country's economy. Moreover, it would save the cost of enforcement of the laws for the violation of which there would no longer be an incentive.

Another initiative could be the requirement of an annual report by the parties on the progress in reducing trade-related trafficking. The FTA Commission would have the right to request the data and engage the parties in relevant processes to eradicate the undesirable and illegal actions.

9.1
Relevant International Conventions

COUNTRY	Protocol to Prevent, Suppress, and Punish Trafficking in Persons		Optional Protocol to the Convention on the Rights of the Child on the Sale of Children, Child Prostitution, and Child Pornography		Optional Protocol to the Convention on the Rights of the Child in Armed Conflict		ILO Convention 29, Forced Labour	ILO Convention 105, Abolition of Forced Labour	ILO Convention 182, Elimination of Worst Forms of Child Labor
	SIGNED	RATIFIED, ACCESSED (a)	SIGNED	RATIFIED, ACCESSED (a)	SIGNED	RATIFIED, ACCESSED (a)	RATIFIED	RATIFIED	RATIFIED
Argentina	X	X	X	X	X	X	X	X	X
Bahamas	X						X	X	X
Belize		X(a)	X	X	X	X(a)	X	X	X
Bolivia	X		X	X		X(a)	X	X	X
Brazil	X	X	X	X	X	X	X	X	X
Canada	X	X	X	X	X	X		X	X
Chile	X	X	X	X	X	X	X	X	X
Colombia	X	X	X	X	X	X	X	X	X
Costa Rica	X	X	X	X	X	X	X	X	X
Dominican Republic	X				X		X	X	X
Ecuador	X	X	X	X	X	X	X	X	X
El Salvador	X	X	X	X	X	X	X	X	X
Guatemala		X(a)	X	X	X	X	X	X	X
Guyana		X(a)					X	X	X
Haiti	X		X		X		X	X	
Honduras				X(a)		X(a)	X	X	X
Jamaica	X	X	X		X	X	X	X	X
Mexico	X	X	X	X	X	X	X	X	X
Nicaragua		X(a)		X(a)		X(a)	X	X	X
Panama	X	X	X	X	X	X	X	X	X
Paraguay	X	X	X	X	X	X	X	X	X
Peru	X	X	X	X	X	X	X	X	X
Suriname			X		X		X	X	
United States	X	X	X	X	X	X		X	X
Uruguay	X	X	X	X	X	X	X	X	X
Venezuela	X	X	X	X	X	X	X	X	X

Source: Office of the Under Secretary for Global Affairs (OUSGA), U.S. Department of State, *Trafficking in Persons Report: June 2006*, DOS Publ. No. 11335 (Washington: OUSGA, rev. June 2006), 284-87 (selected countries only).

Country	Tier	Activity			Purpose
		Source	Transit	Destination	
Argentina	2 SWL	X	X	X	women and children for sexual and labor exploitation; most trafficked internally for prostitution
Bahamas	(SC)				(trafficking is unmonitored and undocumented; large numbers of illegal migrants internally raise concerns)
Belize	3	X	X	X	women and children for labor and sexual exploitation; children from Guatemala, Honduras, and Mexico for labor exploitation
Bolivia	2	X	X		men, women, and children for labor and sexual exploitation; most trafficked internally; minors internally for sexual exploitation, forced mining, and agricultural labor
Brazil	2 SWL	X		X	women and children for sexual exploitation; men for forced labor, esp. agricultural
Canada	1	X	X	X	men, women, and children for labor and sexual exploitation; most trafficked for sexual exploitation, many fewer for forced labor
Chile	2	X	X	X	women and children for sexual exploitation; mostly minors trafficked internally for sexual exploitation; destination for domestic servitude
Colombia	1	X (major)			women and girls for sexual exploitation, estimated at 45,000–50,000; internally, women and children for sexual exploitation, and some men for forced labor
Costa Rica	2	X	X	X	women and children for sexual exploitation; child sex tourism is serious problem; men, women, and children internally for forced labor as domestic servants, and in agriculture and fishing work
Cuba	3	X		X	women and children for sexual exploitation and forced child labor; major destination for sex tourism
Dominican Republic	2	X	X	X	men, women, and children for sexual exploitation and forced labor, estimated at 30,000–50,000; significant internal trafficking of women and children; destination for Haitians to work in sugarcane industry in shantytowns
Ecuador	2	X	X	X	sexual and labor exploitation, mainly internally; child sex tourism is problem
El Salvador	2	X	X	X	women and children for sexual exploitation; source for forced labor
Guatemala	2	X	X	X	women and children for sexual exploitation
Guyana	2	X	X	X	young women and children for sexual and labor exploitation; most cases are internal trafficking of adolescent girls; young men for forced labor in timber camps

Country	Tier	Activity			Purpose
		Source	Transit	Destination	
Haiti	(sc)				(trafficking unaddressed due to widespread violence and political instab ility since Feb. 2004)
Honduras	2	X	X	X	women and children for sexual exploitation; reports of debt bondage for illegal migration from outside region and China
Jamaica	2	X			men, women, and children for sexual
	SWL				exploitation and labor; women and children internally for sexual exploitation; some trafficking for domestic servitude and forced labor
Mexico	2	X	X	X	sexual exploitation and labor; women and
	SWL				children internally for sexual exploitation; child sex tourism remains problem
Nicaragua	2	X			women and children for sexual exploitation; internally, most prevalent is minors for prostitution; source for young men to Costa Rica for labor exploitation
Panama	2	X	X	X	women and children for sexual and labor exploitation; internal trafficking primarily for prostitution; child domestic laborers trafficked internally
Paraguay	2	X		X	women and children for sexual exploitation and forced labor; internally, poor children for sexual exploitation and involuntary domestic servitude
Peru	2	X			women and children internally for sexual
	WL				exploitation and forced domestic labor
Suriname	2	X	X	X	source for children trafficked internally for sexual exploitation; transit and destination for women and children for sexual exploitation; risk of debt bondage to migrant smugglers; Haitians for forced labor
Uruguay	2	X			women and children, internally and esp. to bordering states, for sexual exploitation; child sex tourism; poor children for involuntary servitude in domestic service and agricultural labor
Venezuela	3	X	X	X	women and children for sexual exploitation and forced labor ·

Source: OUSGA, U.S. Department of State, Trafficking in Persons Report: June 2006, DOS Publ. No. 11335 (Washington: OUSGA, rev. June 2006), 60–269 (selected countries only).

Key: For "Tier" column: 1—government fully complies with minimum standards; 2—government does not fully comply but is making "significant efforts"; 2 SWL (Special Watch List)—same as for Tier 2 and (a) absolute number of victims of severe forms of trafficking is very significant or significantly increasing; (b) there is a failure to provide evidence of increasing efforts; or (c) is making significant efforts based on commitments to take additional future steps over the next year; 3—government does not fully comply and is not making significant efforts to do so; and sc—"Special Case" country for which trafficking information was not available, but does exhibit indications of trafficking. Id. at 29 (box) and 29–30. For "Activity" column: a country is "'a country of origin [i.e., source], transit, or destination for a significant number of victims of severe forms of trafficking,' generally on the order of 100 or more victims." Id. at 29.

10

Bebel Redux

The Woman Question

10.1 Overview

In 1910, Bebel first asked "the woman question."[1] He examined the social location and role of women with the aim of maximizing women's participation in and contributions to society, especially in the political and economic spheres. The mere asking of the question, however, underscores the reality of the ubiquity of gender gaps. Indeed, at times women are simply invisible. As an example, in 1993, at the World Conference on Human Rights in Vienna,[2] women were not even on the agenda. At the conference, women's NGOs from all locations, representing women from Asian, Arab, Northern, Southern, African, and Latin American states, managed to form an impressive coalition and came together to condemn violence against women—a topic that affects all women—regardless of their geography, socioeconomic status, religion, race, or culture.

The United Nations itself has acknowledged that nowhere in the world are women socially or politically, let alone economically, equal to men. Nowhere do women enjoy the same levels of education, health, or respect that men do. In the trade context, the woman question raises the issue of what, if any, relation trade has to these gender gaps. As written, trade laws do not mention gender/sex. Insofar as they effect migrations from rural to urban areas in the search for labor, however, they destroy familial structures and exacerbate existing pressures on close-knit groups. In addition, trade laws result in the creation of jobs that both empower and endanger women, many of which are low-paying jobs without benefits. This chapter explores the impact of the trade regime on women, especially in the context of labor, the gendered issues raised by the terms and conditions of work, and the cultural implications and transformations that may result from women joining the workforce in positions and structures generated by responsiveness to the trade regime.

10.2 *Human Rights Framework*

Article 2 of the Universal Declaration, ICCPR,[3] and ICESCR all prohibit discrimination based on sex. The prohibition against discrimination is the only human right included in each treaty of the UN's so-called International Bill of Human Rights.

Although the general human rights documents all prohibit discrimination against women, the 1979 CEDAW in its entirety is dedicated to non-discrimination against women. It elaborates, in some thirty articles, precisely what actions constitute such discrimination. CEDAW reaches both public and private spheres, and forbids discrimination in education, in employment, in health care, in political life, in the family, before the law, as to financial credit, in participation in sports, and in preservation of nationality, as well as with respect to culture and cultural traditions. CEDAW specifically recognizes that there are some cultural tropes that might be harmful to women and requires that state parties eliminate such cultural tropes.[4] Significantly, this is not a hegemonic attack on culture. Indeed, the ICCPR protects cultural traditions (art. 1(1)). CEDAW simply clarifies that human rights norms are not to be used as a sword to eviscerate cultural differences, however, but neither should culture be deployed as a shield to perpetuate practices that discriminate against women. This prohibition notwithstanding, cultural pretexts are often used to veil sexual discrimination.

The preamble explains why CEDAW is necessary. Although on paper the general conventions promote equality and the resolutions, declarations, and recommendations follow suit, in reality discrimination against women persists. Such enduring inequality violates principles of nondiscrimination and "respect for human dignity."[5] Examples of persistent sex-based discrimination that readily surface involve killing or lack of care for female babies, genital cuttings, rape, denial of the right to vote or own property, sexual harassment at work or denial of certain jobs, and even denial of personhood separate from their husbands.

Beyond the detailed substantive provisions, CEDAW also itemizes a program of action to accomplish the treaty's purpose of eliminating all forms of sexual discrimination, including legislative, judicial, administrative, or other measures. Thus, no question at all can remain that discrimination against women in any aspect of life is a violation of fundamental human rights.

Having said that it is undeniable that sex discrimination is globally rejected, two realities weaken that statement. One, the United States, the self-proclaimed global leader in human rights protections, has failed to ratify CEDAW. Second, substantial reservations, often interposed in the context of culture, history, and/or religion, detract from the credibility of CEDAW as an instrument of equality.

In addition to these international instruments, regional documents specific to the Americas provide additional sources of protection for women. In Article 3(1), the OAS Charter reaffirms the principle that the American states embrace "the fundamental rights of the individual without distinction as to race, nationality, creed, or sex." Moreover, the Member states expressly embrace the principle that "all human beings, without distinction as to race, sex, nationality, creed, or social condition, have a right to material well-being and to their spiritual development, under circumstances of liberty, dignity, equality of opportunity, and economic security" (art. 45(a)). In addition, Article II of the American Declaration provides that "all persons are equal before the law and have the rights and duties established in this Declaration, without distinction as to race, sex, language, creed or any other factor." Other articles also provide specific protections that are especially relevant to women. For example, Article VI protects the right to establish a family, which is recognized as the basic unit of a society; Article VII protects women, during pregnancy and nursing, and children; Article IX protects the right to health and well-being; Article XIV protects the right to work and fair pay; and Article XXIII protects the right to property.

Finally, in Article 1(1) of ACHR, state parties commit to respect the rights and freedoms articulated in the Convention in a nondiscriminatory manner. Article 17 recognizes the rights of the family and provides that the family is "the natural and fundamental group unit of society"; recognizes the right of men and women of marriageable age to marry; and provides that "no marriage shall be entered into without the free and full consent of the intending spouses." Last, Article 3 of the Protocol of San Salvador reiterates state parties' obligation not to discriminate on the same grounds listed in Article 1 of ACHR.

10.3 *International Trade Framework*

(A) Generally

The question is why the makers of trade and other economic policy should take responsibility for any part of this dreadful record of discrimination, and worse, against women. To understand, additional facts are instructive. First, take note of the "amazing 70 percent factors." Women constitute about 70 percent of the world's poor.[6] Women perform about 70 percent of the world's work, but earn only about 10 percent of the world's income.[7] Women's wages are about 70 percent of those of men for comparable manufacturing labor.[8] In addition, because of gender differences—real or imposed—women hold a majority of the jobs that are especially sensitive to outsourcing and other changes brought on by the trade agreements, market forces, and other realities of globalization, such as low-paying, no-benefit jobs in apparel, small-item assembly, and services.

For example, 90 percent of the jobs in export processing zones (EPZs) worldwide, such as the maquiladoras in Mexico, are held by women.[9] Women's views also generally are not as well represented in economic policy-making as those of men. The intersection between trade and women lies, therefore, in addition to the evident relationship with trafficking in women treated in chapter 9, in the outsized negative consequences trade policy necessarily will work on women. We should look at these premises more closely.

(B)   The WTO and Women

The WTO is alone among intergovernmental organizations in failing explicitly to recognize a gender dimension to its policies. The WTO's avoidance of the woman question is difficult to understand in light of the fact that women, for reasons outlined in this chapter, "bear the brunt of economic and financial transition and crisis caused by market forces and globalization."[10] Just as the human rights concern with the woman question spans all special interest groups, so too does the potential solution.

The proposed agenda for the WTO set by the Women's Economic and Development Organization (WEDO) proceeds in this direction.[11] Although written as a "gender agenda," its four points sound in the broader issues that underpin conflict between trade and human rights. Women, WEDO first suggests, should be involved more directly in policy- and decision-making at the WTO, including on the roster of eligible trade experts for service on dispute settlement panels. Including greater numbers of women in the decisional structure will ensure better understanding of the complex interplay of factors that make the issue so elusive of resolution.

When trade negotiators consider changes to the rules, WEDO next suggests, they should be careful not to disturb the very aspects of the trading system that have brought actual benefit to women.[12] Government employment or the supply of government procurement needs and work in the agricultural sector are two such aspects. In the Doha Development Round of trade negotiations, agricultural subsidies have been targeted for elimination or reduction and efforts will be made to reduce the number of sectors of government procurement exempt from the nondiscrimination principles of the WTO.

WEDO next argues for retention of control by women over their own and their families' health and safety. National environmental, health, and safety standards and international agreements that support the Precautionary Principle[13] protect the health of women and their families. The Earth Summit's Agenda 21, the CBD, and the Beijing Declaration all expressly adopt this concept.[14]

In trade, the intervening problem regarding women's ability to retain control over their and their families' health is the WTO's SPS Agreement that we addressed in chapter 7. The view is that Codex, an independent body of government-appointed experts, which is designated by the SPS Agreement as the food safety standard-setting body, may be insensitive to the potential dangers of certain foods, in particular GM crops or those produced with growth hormones.[15] Significantly, national health and safety standards that are inconsistent with Codex's framework are deemed to be nontariff trade barriers and the state is left with the obligation to show, with scientific proof, that the product in question is unsafe and the regulations are necessary. As the EC argued in the *EC-Hormones* case (discussed in section 7.4(D)), with respect to GMOs, in the United States and around the world the scientific jury is still out. Indeed, determining the impact of GMOs may require many more years of scientific study to determine if they are harmful to human and animal health as well as to biodiversity. Codex has now established a scientific protocol for conducting risk assessment for GMOs or hormone derivatives. Questions remain about whether governments may even label foods and note that they contain GMOs if such labeling inhibits trade (see section 7.5(C)).

Because of experience in the trade field that indicates that trade rules can trump national health legislation,[16] WEDO suggests the following:

- Amend the SPS Agreement and Codex Alimentarius to ensure that standards and testing reviews include a gender-assessment component.

- There should be agreement on standard nutrition and GMO labeling of all food products based on consumer rights and protection. These standards should be developed in a participatory process that includes local citizens, independent scientists, and NGOs.
- The WTO and its surrogates are not the appropriate body for setting health, environment, and consumer standards. Trade rules should not be used to challenge laws that are designed to promote and protect health and the environment.
- WEDO supports the development of a consumer protection body that is separate and apart from the WTO.[17]

Finally, WEDO worries that the WTO's TRIPS Agreement is inconsistent with the CBD[18] (see also the discussion in section 7.6). The area of greatest danger is identified as the preservation of indigenous knowledge, most of which is protected by women. While WEDO's agenda may be unrealistic as it requires a complete reworking of the trade system, it is our view that in light of the data showing a gender connection to trade, a gender agenda is appropriate to incorporate. The Secretariat should be required to examine the gender effect of the WTO Agreements and highlight actions that can be taken by members to eliminate those effects. One must address these issues in order to interrogate the category of woman in the context of women and trade.

(C)   Women and NAFTA

It is interesting to review the data of studies that have analyzed the impact of NAFTA on Mexico.[19] These studies mostly looked at the processes of trade liberalization and the structural implementation of economic policies, and the impact these had on the labor force, including the female labor force. The results reveal that due to changes in both economic and social conditions, women entered the labor force at a pace greater than men (see section 10.5 for a discussion of some of the social conditions). Notwithstanding an increased rate of participation, however, women tended to be concentrated in the lower-paying jobs and in the informal-sector jobs (that is, street vendors and other employment not formally recognized through contracts, fixed hours, taxation, or employment benefits).[20] Consequently, although women have started to participate in the labor force at a higher rate, it does not translate to an improved standard of living. Specifically, studies show that women find increased employment in agriculture, and particularly in the vegetable and fruit export fields, where they also find longer working hours and piecework, which effectively result in the worsening of their working conditions.

Women's employment in the maquiladoras is an example of the double-edged sword of women's increased participation in the labor force in light of its structural gender biases that go unchallenged in a world that fails to contest the trade regime's claim that it operates in a gender-neutral fashion. First, women were the most desired workers in the maquiladoras. This was because the jobs were low-paying and low-skill. To be sure, even in the beginning, there were gender disparities in maquiladora employment because while the majority of the workers were women, inevitably the managers were men. Women's employment grew in absolute terms, however, but decreased in relative terms. This change was due to two main factors: there was a scarcity of all jobs and the maquiladora employers began placing a premium on higher skills in the workers.

Since 2000, the maquiladoras have lost almost a quarter of a million jobs, with women losing their jobs at a faster rate than men. The jobs have been lost to even cheaper labor in Asia. In addition, the goods being assembled have shifted from textile to electronics and transportation equipment—fields in which there is a larger proportion of males hired. As the maquiladora jobs were lost and more women than men were displaced, women sought the work available, which was in the informal sector—a sector in which they occupy more than 50 percent of the jobs. As noted above, as a result of these factors, women's labor conditions worsened.

Thus, since NAFTA, women are in poverty in larger numbers. They also are at a higher risk of violence, often based on employment conditions at the maquiladoras where they have to submit, against local law, to pregnancy tests, endure sexual harassment, and face higher crime. Evidently, trade consequences are not gender-neutral.

10.4 The Woman Question

First, it is important to note that "women" are not a unified group and are not easily characterized or classified. Rather, women are multidimensional beings. In fact, even attempting to treat women as a special interest group is objectionable, because it suggests that the woman question is a single issue that can neatly be packaged for solution along with other complex issues such as the poor, indigenous populations, plague-ravaged states, or a healthy environment.

Next, it is incontrovertible that women do not benefit to the same degree from development efforts, such as credit or low-income housing and, by extension, from trade benefits, such as new job prospects, because they have less time and flexibility to take advantage of the opportunities as the result of child-care responsibilities. They also face greater discrimination from project administrators and hiring officials.[21]

In order to address the traditional invisibility of women in multiple sectors of life, including government and work, as well as in other sectors of civil society, the UN adopted the concept of "gender mainstreaming": "Gender mainstreaming is a globally accepted strategy for promoting gender equality . . . [that] involves ensuring that gender perspectives and attention to the goal of gender equality are central to all activities—policy development, research, advocacy/dialogue, legislation, resource allocation, and planning, implementation and monitoring of programmes and projects."[22] Gender mainstreaming teaches that officials must address the woman question as part of the solution to every human rights concern. As an obvious point of reference, women constitute at least half of every special interest group, and they have been leaders in finding solutions to each of these human rights challenges. Women organizing around the problem of violence at the 1995 World Conference on Human Rights[23] is an example. Another is the success in Argentina of the *Abuelas de Plaza de Mayo*[24] with respect to the disappeared.

Women are a heterogeneous group, differing in class, religion, age, race, sexuality, and family structure. Women also have several things in common:

- Much of their work—reproductive and domestic—including work on the farm and in home-based production, is invisible, either not counted at all or seriously underestimated in national accounts.
- Their child-care responsibilities leave them with less time and flexibility than men. Inability to find affordable day care significantly limits the ability of women to take advantage of work or educational opportunities.
- Time is a precious resource because of women's "reproductive" work, which includes not only bearing and raising children, but also all domestic work (washing, cleaning, shopping, cooking), and care for the elderly.
- If a woman works outside the home as well, her workweek often is over ninety hours!
- In addition, women have reduced access to education, partly for the time and flexibility reasons that we mentioned, partly because of cultural preferences for educating male children.

- Gender-based violence is a major issue. The unending stream of violent crimes in the Americas, from murder to rape to sexual abuse to battery to trafficking in women not only is reprehensible in its own right, but it also contributes to reduced capacity for women to engage in economic activities (fear, medical costs, loss of self-esteem).
- Physical factors also exclude women from jobs that require heavy manual labor or that subject women to a greater risk of sexual assault.
- Women have greater difficulty than men in accessing services and credit.
- A woman's domestic responsibilities necessarily affect her choice of paid work.[25]

We can see from this brief analysis that the greatest myth regarding the human rights of women is that policy and law are gender-neutral. Because of gender differences, laws and policies plainly have different effects on women than on men.[26] For these reasons, development planning, as well as trade and other economic policy-making, must account for gender differences if they are to be effective and to avoid unwittingly discriminating based on sex.

10.5 Women and Culture in the Americas

> Like just about all peoples Mexicans consider woman as an instrument—an instrument of men's desires, of the roles assigned by law, society, and morality. These are roles for which her consent has never been sought and in the realization of which she participates only passively as the depository of certain values. Prostitute, goddess, lady, lover, woman. Woman transmits or preserves, but never creates the values and energies that are offered to her by nature or society. In the world created in the image of man, woman is only a reflection of men. Passive she becomes a goddess, a person who embodies the stable ancient elements of the universe, earth, mother, and virgin. Active she is always only a vessel, a means, a conduit. Femininity is never an end in itself as is manhood.[27]

We mentioned that women differ based on religion, class, family structure, and other factors. In parts of Latin America, we must take account also of the *marianista/machista* culture. Under this framework that informs all aspects of a woman's life, the model is the Virgin Mary: long-suffering, strong, invisible, and marked by sacrifice, the foundation of the family, subservient to men—in sum, subjugated both to their *marianista* role and to the *machista* male. Although around for a long time, the term "marianismo" first became commonplace in popular culture in 1997: "Marianismo is about sacred duty, self-sacrifice, and chastity. About dispensing care and pleasure, not receiving them. About living in the shadows, literally and figuratively[,] of your men—father, boyfriend, husband, son—your kids, and your family."[28] In the cultura Latina, sex role stereotypes are a reality of life: "The stereotypes of the domineering Latino and the domineered Latina must be understood in relationship to each other. *Machismo* is a term used to express that a Latino's strength and capability as a partner and father are demonstrated by an external appearance of control over his family and his display of sexual virility. Under this paradigm, the Latino controls the family's public reputation, and the Latina serves the family's private reputation by singly managing all practical responsibilities of the family and home."[29]

When designing solutions to address the woman question in Latin America, policy officials must confront the realities of the *marianista/machista* culture. For example, 85 percent of maquiladora workers in Juarez are women, employed in industries such as apparel and semiconductor assemblage that involve working with small pieces or parts that require delicate handiwork.[30] Women seek maquiladora jobs because of the need to support their families in the face of under- or unemployment by male family members. The result often is the rending of families as the women move to the environs of the maquiladoras, and the men, looking for the only work available—given that maquiladora jobs in effect are closed to them—emigrate illegally to the United States for employment in low-paying jobs shunned by the local citizenry.

10.6 Women and Work

The history of the sex-based segregation of labor dates to the industrial era, after industrialization and the emergence of wage labor. Up until then with the existing agrarian societies, there was much less role differentiation with respect to or on the basis of sex. That was a time when everyone in the family contributed to perform the necessary work. The marked role differentiation occurred post–industrial revolution. To be sure, historically the philosophers and the great thinkers were the public personalities, as were the doctors, lawyers, and business persons; the private persona was female. From a trade standpoint, women's childbearing responsibilities have enormous implications for the kind of work that a woman can perform, the time that she has, the flexibility that she has, and the educational levels that she's able to pursue. Hence, the WTO claim of the gender neutrality of trade is, at best, a sham.

As an example of the gendered inequality of the labor world one can take a look at U.S. law. Title VII of the Civil Rights Act of 1964[31] provides that discrimination on the basis of sex is prohibited. Yet, as a matter of law there is an exception to the prohibition in the case of sex if it is a bona-fide occupational qualification (BFOQ)—a requirement reasonably necessary to perform a particular job. Pursuant to this exception, women have been excluded from myriad jobs. BFOQs illustrate the point that merely having legal prohibitions against sex discrimination is insufficient to eradicate such bias. Yet although laws will often have exceptions for equality where there is a so-called BFOQ, it is difficult to understand "what could possibly constitute a BFOQ other than tasks that require different biological functions such as sperm donation, egg donation, wet nursing, or surrogate motherhood. Outside of these sex-specific 'real' limitations, any BFOQ exception simply permits the continuation and perpetuation of the hetero-patriarchal status quo—the masculinist false universe. . . . The BFOQ defense, therefore, [simply] justifies disparities based on stereotypes and traditional gender roles and grants gender discrimination a patina of legality and legitimacy."[32]

Other places in the Americas provide further examples of gendered realities.[33] There are restrictions on the exercise of a profession or work by women, insofar as the authorization of the husband is required, in Bolivia, Guatemala, Panama, Peru, and the Dominican Republic. There is differentiation between men and women with respect to the authorization to contract marriage (Bolivia and Brazil) or to remarry (Mexico and Costa Rica). Inequalities exist between men and women with respect to acquiring, administering, and disposing of assets of the conjugal union. For example, Argentina gives husbands a preference over assets whose origins cannot be determined; in certain cases, Chile grants the husband the right to administer the assets of the conjugal union as well as those of the wife; and Brazil does not recognize a married woman's equal capacity with her husband to administer certain assets. Differences also exist between men and women with respect to parental authority. In Chile, the father exercises parental authority, which is conferred on the mother only in the father's absence. Bolivia, Costa Rica, Ecuador, and Guatemala classify women with minors in labor legislation. There also exist restrictions on women's right to property. For instance, the constitution of the Dominican Republic restricts *campesinas* (rural women) from owning plots of land. There even is gender inequality with respect to treatment regarding certain criminal offenses. El Salvador and Venezuela treat men and women differently regarding adultery. Beyond de jure inequalities, de facto inequalities also persist: "In Costa Rica, . . . [as of] 1990 the average monthly salary of women was 82% of that of men. In rural areas, 60% of women earn less than the minimum wage and 34% just one half that amount. In Brazil, income earned by women is equivalent to 54% of that received by men. In Uruguay [as in the United States], women earn 75% of the income received by men."[34]

Passing, and even enforcing, laws is insufficient to attain equality, especially when laws routinely incorporate male biases. Human rights norms, therefore, cannot be the only catalyst for change:

> Women's position at the margins of employment [in the Americas and] around the world is a result of formal state, private, and cultural tropes that have created and legitimized separate spheres for women's and men's existences. In addition to the formal development of law, it is important (1) to develop an informal, parallel track to facilitate and enhance women's voices globally and locally; (2) to add to their visibility and provide access to their work and resources; and (3) to develop a formidable and impressive network of data, information, and support. Such an informal system could initiate the reconstitution of the rights essential to meet women's needs, effect their self-determination, and ensure their participation in the global and local spheres.[35]

It would also serve to debunk the myth that trade is a gender-neutral field.

10.7 Final Thoughts

As this chapter has demonstrated, trade is anything but gender-neutral. It affects women in myriad ways—some more directly than others. Directly it can have an impact on employment opportunities, especially when hiring takes place in free trade or economic development zones. Thus, there are direct consequences of trade to women in employment, including pay and other working conditions. Indirectly, it can affect women's health, safety, nutrition, family, and economic survival.

The United Nations has adopted a principle of "gender mainstreaming" that, at every point in policy development, poses the woman question: what gender impact will the particular policy have? We propose that such gender mainstreaming be integrated into trade talks so that the promise of equality and nondiscrimination—interestingly the gravamen of both trade and human rights law—can be a reality.

To be sure, trade agreements need to respect sovereignty and the internal gauge of nations to determine the best path to attain economic growth and social and economic development as well as to provide the requisite social safety net appropriate to enable both human well-being and economic development. That sovereign right is bound, however, to nondiscrimination principles that protect, oftentimes against the prevalent cultural environment, women's equality. In addition, the privatization that comes with neoliberal economic policies must be evaluated with such social needs in mind so that services necessary for social production and reproduction are not relegated to entities whose sole concern is a financially overflowing bottom line. Thus for every trade agreement there needs to be an analysis of the gender impact of the agreement and accommodation to resolve any such negative impact. In this regard, it is also important to underscore that women are a heterogeneous group and that other considerations intersect with the processing of the woman question, such as the need to protect indigenous knowledges as well as the rights of local communities.

One necessary step is for women to be participants in the trade negotiations, and all involved in the negotiations must be apprised of and educated in the potential gender impacts of the policies being instituted. In this fashion, the policies can be modified and recrafted to promote trade's promise of economic well-being for all while ensuring that women are not unwittingly excluded from such protections. Methodologicallly this process of analysis and inclusion ensures that strategies developed are both pro-development and pro-woman.

On a smaller scale, it is important that women's productive and reproductive roles both be respected and protected. Women engage in much subsistence agriculture, producing food to feed their families. With a gender mainstreaming strategy in place, trade rules that address agriculture would be sensitive to the need to ensure food security. Related to this notion, trade officials must apply gender mainstreaming to foreign investment rules so that they are socially responsible and play a positive role in the universal compact to eradicate poverty rather than contribute to its enhancement.

Gender mainstreaming includes measures to ensure improvements in living standards for women and equality of social and economic opportunities for women and men, as well as the need to establish regulations on gender and the fulfillment of international commitments, particularly CEDAW and the Beijing Declaration. This is particularly important because the costs of trade liberalization and the application and deepening of WTO rules have created serious problems of inequality in women's productive and reproductive employment, as well as lack of access to basic services for women and men, with particular repercussions on poor women. Through this process, trade agreements will be frameworks for environmental, social, and gender sustainability.

11

First Peoples First
Indigenous Populations

11.1 Overview

Globalization has exacted massive and lopsided economic and cultural costs from indigenous populations.[1] In rewarding work that is inconsistent with the nature-sensitive ways of subsistence lifestyles, by promoting unsustainable resource use, and through diversion of governments from long-range infrastructural priorities with the promise of quick riches, international trade has despoiled and degraded indigenous cultures and robbed native populations of their ability to hand down adequate resources for survival of future generations. Because trade rules give teeth to intellectual property protections, multinational companies have expropriated to great profit traditional knowledge essential to indigenous culture. These same trade rules, however, deny communal inventions any share of the royalties earned by their use. This chapter explores the nature of trade's intersections with indigenous populations and evaluates policies that governments should adopt to nurture trade while reversing its destruction both of indigenous knowledge and of the biodiversity that depends on its tribal owners.

11.2 Human Rights Framework

(A) Defining Our Terms

The ILO's Convention concerning Indigenous and Tribal Peoples in Independent Countries defines "indigenous people" as those who inhabited a country or area within a country at the time of conquest, colonization, or establishment of the present state boundaries and who, irrespective of their legal status, retain some or all of their own social, economic, cultural, and political institutions.[2] In virtually all cases, such populations represent a minority group within the state boundaries that they inhabit and usually live under economic conditions vastly lower than the majority groups within the states constructed around them.[3] As but one example, the Mayan Indians of Guatemala constitute an informal economy of nearly half the nation's population isolated in the Cuchumatanes mountain range and the virgin rain forest known as Petén. Preserving their languages and cultural uniqueness, the Mayans are economically distinct from the Ladinos of the coastal plains both geographically and economically.[4] Unemployment figures and GDP take no account of the Mayan population.

Indigenous groups often share characteristics that magnify trade's effects on their lifestyles. For example, indigenous peoples typically have little access to formal education, which usually means that they have no gauge of the value to a "developed" society of their traditional knowledge, such as the use of cat's claw by the Ashaninka Indian tribe in central Peru to bolster the immune system[5] or quinine extracted by Peru's Quechua Indians from the bark of the rain forest's cinchona tree to cure malaria or the diabetic-safe sugar of the yacón plant harvested from the cloud forests of the Andes.[6] Their lands are targeted by trade interests because of their profit potential, but only a handful of states recognize tribal sovereignty over these lands. They also have little or no access to the state's social safety net to ameliorate trade's impacts on their lives and livelihood.

(B)   Historical Treatment under International Law

From the 15th to the 18th centuries, indigenous populations had dominion over their lands, with the result that just cause was necessary to dispossess them. In fact, international law also followed Francisco Vittoria's approach. For example, treaties that decided borders, thereby defining ownership, recognized the international personality of indigenous peoples.[7]

By the 19th century, the Christian European states had worked a shift in international law that again pushed indigenous peoples to the sidelines of international law with the refusal to recognize that indigenous peoples were sovereign or, for that matter, even civilized. This second-class status went unchanged until the advent of modern human rights law in the middle of the 20th century.[8]

(C)   Human Rights Specific to Indigenous Peoples

In light of the clash between intellectual property protection rules and indigenous rights, some may find it ironic that modern society's first effort to delineate human rights makes no mention of indigenous peoples yet explicitly recognizes intellectual property rights. Article 27(2) of the Universal Declaration provides that "everyone has the right to the protection of the moral and material interests resulting from any scientific, literary or artistic production of which he is the author."

Article 2 of the Universal Declaration, ICCPR, and ICESCR each prohibits discrimination of any kind based on race, color, religion, language, social origin, or other status. Each of these characteristics, and usually more than one, serves as the basis for distinguishing and identifying an indigenous population from the nonindigenous peoples that usually inhabit the same state territorial limits. A principle of nondiscrimination can thus be a powerful protector of indigenous rights, even when that standard is general and does not expressly address the discrimination faced by indigenous or local communities. In fact, violations against the human rights of indigenous peoples represent, as in the case of women, one of those unusual varieties of discrimination that permeates every society in the world.

The Universal Declaration's identification in Article 17 of the human right to own property includes intellectual property, and thus traditional knowledge, whether reflected in folk literature, the usage of genetic resources for curative purposes, dance and music, or handicrafts. The "traditional knowledge" that struggles in the trade intersection is the historical use by indigenous peoples of herbs and other biological resources for curative and agricultural purposes that have existed for hundreds of years; these developments, however, lack the written documentation expected of patentable ideas by Western intellectual property law, including the TRIPS Agreement. Protection of traditional knowledge from biopiracy and development of rules that provide economic rewards for the knowledge is an important aspect of trade's effect on indigenous populations, as discussed in section 11.4.

The United Nations continued in Article 15.1(c) of ICESCR the recognition of the human rights of inventors contained in Article 27(2) of the Universal Declaration, with the same counterbalance for indigenous groups provided in the right of every person to own property. ICCPR, by contrast, takes a substantial step toward recognition of the particular human rights of indigenous peoples. Article 27 of ICCPR acknowledges the human right of minorities to preserve linguistic and religious cultures, and to do so "in community with other members of their group." This language would prevent states from taking actions inconsistent with minority cultural practices, which brings indigenous populations into close perspective. A Japanese district court in the *Nibutani Dam* litigation found that Article 27 technically protects "minorities," not indigenous peoples per se, but then continued with the observation that an indigenous population whose lands were taken against its will would thereby become an "indigenous minority."[9] In effect, ICCPR Article 27 supplies the details missing from Article 2 (as well as Article 2 of the ICESCR and the Universal Declaration) as to specific discrimination that would be considered a violation of human rights with regard to indigenous populations.

Article 1 of both the ICCPR and the ICESCR confirm the human right to self-determination, which includes the right freely to pursue economic, social, and cultural development. Self-determination requires nondiscrimination, respect for cultural integrity, control over lands and resources, social welfare and development, and self-government.[10] In light of our definition and description in section 11.2 of indigenous populations, these assurances have high relevance to issues facing indigenous populations, including, as explicitly recognized in Article 1 of both covenants, the prohibition by states of interfering with a population's "own means of subsistence"—a caution that trade negotiators must consider in planning for the economic development of a country.

The United Nations initially assigned to its first specialized agency, the ILO, the task of addressing the economic and social plight of indigenous peoples. Because this first international effort viewed the difficulties faced by indigenous peoples as a labor rights issue, it is not surprising that the ILO's 1957 treaty was flawed by its premise that the problems of first peoples gradually would disappear as native populations were integrated into majority societies. ILO's revised 1989 Convention Concerning Indigenous and Tribal Peoples in Independent Countries humbly corrected this mistaken assumption. The present treaty urges governments to respect and protect indigenous identities and cultures. In what we now see as a reference to the traditional knowledge of indigenous tribes, the 1989 Convention urges governments to honor the collective relationships inherent in these groups, a recognition of community intellectual property.

The most direct attempt to delimit the human rights of indigenous populations came about when the United Nations reassigned the task to a Working Group on Indigenous Populations. The Draft Declaration on the Rights of Indigenous Peoples remains soft law because the broader membership of the United Nations has not adopted it. Article 4 of the Draft Declaration identifies the right of indigenous peoples "to maintain their distinct political, social, and cultural characteristics while retaining the right to participate fully, if they choose to, in the political, legal life of the State." Article 7 affirms that indigenous peoples have the collective and individual right not to be subjected to "ethnocide and cultural genocide." The strength of the language is an indication of the importance to local communities of preserving their ethnic and cultural identity if they are to continue at all as distinct indigenous peoples.

Article 30 of the Draft Declaration reaches far by confirming the right of indigenous peoples, in the exercise of their right to self-determination, to control the "development or use of their lands, territories, and other resources," including minerals and water. In addition, indigenous populations, have the right to require that states obtain their "free and informed consent" before the state approves a project that would affect their lands or resources. As the discussion in section 11.3 indicates, approval by states of resource extraction projects to advance the economic development of the majority, in the form of investment contracts with multinational corporations, without the knowledge or against the wishes of tribal populations, has caused irreversible hardships to native communities whose future generations rely on the sustainable use of the natural resources located on indigenous land.

Two years earlier, CBD, discussed in section 11.6, had vested in national governments ownership of the IPR of indigenous peoples over their traditional knowledge. Article 29 of the Draft Declaration effectively would reverse CBD's approach: "Indigenous peoples are entitled to the recognition of the full ownership, control, and protection of their cultural and intellectual property." This avowal acknowledges the necessary correlatives to the human right of self-determination, involving nondiscrimination, respect for cultural integrity, control over lands and resources, social welfare and development, and self-government.[11]

In 1997 the IACHR approved the Proposed American Declaration on the Rights of Indigenous Peoples. In an attempt to avoid the disagreements that continue to plague the UN Draft Declaration, the American Declaration does not proclaim an explicit right of self-determination, although the document does guarantee rights of indigenous populations to determine their own social, economic, and cultural development.[12] In the sections that follow, we track these recognized human rights in the context of the international trade regime in the Americas.

11.3 International Trade Framework

Globalization in general and international trade in particular, through sea changes that promote comparative advantage, have inspired nations to covet trade's economic rewards. These changes often involve driving those industries within a country that cannot compete internationally into other nations where the industry can enjoy that combination of natural, human, and capital resources that enables survival in the global economy. Globalization of production may not directly affect an indigenous group's ability to engage in subsistence farming, hunting, fishing, or other activities that carry traditional, cultural value to the group, or that simply may be the only occupations that the group has ever known. The economic growth that trade brings has more subtle, yet equally insidious, effects on indigenous populations.

Most visibly, trade's promise of economic growth creates pressure from within and outside the native group to use ancestral lands for purposes that deliver maximum financial rewards. To that end, investors might wish to convert the land to manufacture the goods whose factors of production yield to the nation a comparative advantage over its competitors; entrepreneurs could envision a higher use for the land for shopping centers and housing developments demanded by an economically flourishing majority population. In addition, a nation that assigns value to the economic growth brought by trade may accord lesser value to lifestyles and occupations that fail to make the maximum economic contribution to that growth. For example, a state whose workforce has proven itself capable of rapid training in the assembly of picture tubes, system boards, and cabinets into television sets that the producer profitably can export may place little value on subsistence farming, and even less on preservation of a dialect known only to the three hundred members of a minority group whose refusal to learn the majority tongue frustrates national training goals.

Recognition that state—that is, majority—interests do not always or even often coincide with the interests that indigenous groups wish to protect raises the issue of informed consent. For example, the fact that the 185 speakers of Karatiana in Brazil will find no textbooks in that language is a matter of some concern to educational authorities of the state. Perhaps this example is too facile, because the tribe has in fact adopted a compromise by learning Portuguese as a second language.[13] Yet that decision, while perhaps practically necessary for the group to function within the larger society, in the end may sound the death knell for the Karatiana language. The cost of loss of a language is difficult economically to admeasure. As a matter of culture and cultural preservation, however, it arguably translates to prohibited ethnocide. Nonetheless, we must not accept obvious solutions, such as preserving all features of the indigenous culture at all cost, when the answer may lie in directions that are less familiar. In this regard, it is imperative to listen to those whose rights we would protect.

We must also recognize that majority interests may not always properly yield to indigenous ways. With respect to international actions, in particular those implicating the national security of the majority, arguments for self-determination by tribal interests are weaker. Recognition of the right of internal self-determination would protect indigenous culture without requiring the governing majority to yield to conflicts that put the rights of indigenous peoples ahead of those of the state's other citizens. Sometimes the exercise of "internal" self-determination unavoidably affects the majority, as in the example of the Ralco Dam on Chile's BioBío River. The dam was a necessity to continued economic growth of the Chilean majority, but its completion would put an end to the seminomadic lifestyle of the Pehuenche people.[14] In that instance, the Chilean government, after first denying liability in a suit before IACHR, agreed to a settlement involving rights to alternate lands, educational scholarships, agricultural assistance, and monetary reparations. Acceptable resolution of this difficult but increasingly common conflict between economic growth and indigenous self-determination would not have been possible without the leverage of IACHR to enforce preservation of the Pehuenche way of life. Even so, the settlement required substantial concessions on the part of the indigenous populations.

Should we carve out an exception for poor governments without sufficient revenues to maintain multiple cultures? By way of example, providing facilities for the hearing impaired that both honor their desire for cultural distinctness as well as participation in the majority culture has been a costly and intransigent goal, including in the United States. In Canada, translating each government document into French or English consumes enormous human and financial resources. Does the human right in the Universal Declaration's Article 27 to participate in the cultural life of the community carry with it the condition that an individual may do so only if she speaks a majority language and wishes to engage in the same activities valued by the majority? Article 27 of ICCPR answers in the negative when it demands that, whatever a person's language or customs, the state should take no action to deny minorities the right to enjoy these cultural differences. For states that have not ratified ICCPR, we nonetheless read the Universal Declaration's nondiscrimination demands in Article 2 as protecting the rights of linguistic, religious, and political minorities against majority override.

11.4 Enter WTO's TRIPS Agreement: From Bad to Worse?

(A) Origin of the Conflict

Human rights advocates single out the TRIPS Agreement as actually causing a deterioration of the admittedly weak linkages between trade and human rights that existed under the GATT. The Agreement was negotiated in the early 1990s, a time when one would think that the sensitivity among trade officials to human rights needs would have been sharp—or at least sharper than in 1947 when the GATT was created. Instead, as further proof of the "splendid isolation" between trade and human rights about which we spoke in chapter 4, some experts believe that the TRIPS Agreement exacerbated the struggle to make human rights enforceable through trade rules, or at the least to prevent the international trade regime from working against human rights objectives. No LDC could afford to pass up the opportunities presented by the market access provisions of the WTO's many Agreements. These benefits, however, were part of a "single package" of twenty-seven thousand pages that necessarily included the TRIPS Agreement.[15] LDCs were required to buy into Western standards for both determining and protecting IPRs, which ultimately created the cruel irony that to protect their traditional knowledge, communities would have to adjust their cultures away from a traditional way of life.[16]

This criticism will sound familiar if we recall the similar frustration voiced by the human rights community with the SPS Agreement, discussed in section 7.5.[17] The concern is that simply by requiring observation of the provisions of other treaties, the TRIPS Agreement had two potent effects, as we detail in section 11.4(C). First, there are 150-plus Members of the WTO and the many WTO Agreements offer the promise of trade benefits that are virtually impossible for any development-needy country to resist. In one sweeping brushstroke, the various World Intellectual

Property Organization (WIPO) treaties became much broader in reach. The TRIPS Agreement had effectively harmonized the protection of intellectually property globally.

Second, the WIPO Conventions suddenly became much more powerful because they were now enforceable under the automatic dispute settlement procedures of the WTO. Students of the ICJ familiarly call it the World Court and expect the Court to lead creation of public international law. The Appellate Body of the WTO, the "Supreme Court of world trade," however, has in little more than ten years made significant contributions to interpretation of a wide array of international law subjects during a time when the strategic importance for state relations and economic development of international trade outweighs many of the matters taken up by the ICJ in this time.

(B)   Importance to Trade of IPR Protection

Technology advances complicate participation in the global market by industries whose success relies on the creativity of their offerings, rather than on their ability to supply the product at lower capital, labor, or resource input costs. More than half the value of U.S. exports includes some form of intellectual property, some new idea or invention protected by IPR treaties.[18] This innovative content ranges from the patent on Pfizer's newest drug for high blood pressure, to the trademark crown on a Cadillac hood, to the copyright on the latest John Grisham novel, to the mask work protection on Intel's newest computer chip. A large part—in some cases by far the largest—of the value of these products resides in their intellectual property component, and these creations often are quite easy to copy. As but two examples, copyright pirates may easily burn a compact disc of the latest pop album, and trademark thieves may imprint with minimal tooling the Armani Exchange logo on leather apparel. For these reasons, idea-dependent companies for many years have lamented the weak enforcement provided by existing IPR conventions.

The WIPO, although it supervises implementation of dozens of IPR treaties, has no independent dispute settlement structure, although its Secretariat will assist countries in attempting to resolve disputes. In addition, the enforcement methods of WIPO's component treaties, normally by suit in national courts, have not resulted in adequate enforcement. An additional shortcoming is that many developing countries chose not to ratify the WIPO Conventions because they saw themselves, inaccurately, primarily as users of intellectual property, rather than as creators of new patentable or copyrightable products. In any event, nonenforcement of the theft of intellectual property was resulting in the loss of billions of dollars in sales by multinational companies that instead were going to purveyors of counterfeit goods produced with no thought of a royalty payment to the owner of the intellectual property.

(C)   Basics of the TRIPS Agreement

When it became clear that the new WTO would have a meaningful dispute settlement system, proponents of tighter controls over intellectual property, nearly all of them in the industrialized countries, worked successfully to convert a subject whose trade aspects traditionally had been viewed as incidental to trade into a WTO Agreement, the TRIPS Agreement. The reference in the title to the "trade-related aspects" highlights that IPR is not simply a trade subject, such as customs procedures or anti-dumping or tariffs. Indeed, the TRIPS Agreement is quite different from other WTO Agreements in its imposition of affirmative obligations on Members, as opposed to taking the traditional and less intrusive GATT approach—in pursuit of unregulated borders—of instructing governments as to what actions they may not lawfully take.

For example, as Steve Charnovitz reminds us, a WTO Member cannot violate the SPS Agreement by failing to protect the health of its citizens: a Member can do so only by protecting citizen health by a border restriction that is without documented scientific basis. A WTO Member cannot violate the WTO Anti-dumping Agreement by failing to protect its industries from unfairly traded imports: the Member may do so only by protecting domestic companies from such goods by an offsetting border charge that the Member calculated without adherence to the procedures of the Anti-dumping Agreement. The TRIPS Agreement, however, requires that Members take positive steps to enact and enforce laws to facilitate trade by protecting the rights of intellectual property owners.

For the most part, the TRIPS Agreement acts by requiring that Members comply with the provisions of existing IPR treaties. Members must adhere to the copyright protections of the Berne Convention, to the patent and trademark protections of the Paris Convention, and to the protection of integrated circuits dictated by the Washington Chip Treaty.[19] In a surprising show of success by multinational companies whose profits rely on the inviolability of the intellectual property in their products, however, the TRIPS Agreement did not stop with the incorporation of existing IPR agreements; in fact, it went beyond WIPO pacts in a number of important ways.

In the area of trademarks, the TRIPS Agreement eliminates many disputes by presuming that use of the same mark on the same good creates confusion among the buying public and is thus a violation. If a company in Argentina puts the mark "GE" on a refrigerator not made by General Electric Company, the mark likely will mislead the public.[20] The Agreement also improves on the Paris Convention by allowing a company to receive trademark protection even if it does not use the mark within a certain period.[21] Companies developing a drug or new software often want to protect the novel name or symbol of the good before it enters the marketplace and the TRIPS Agreement now makes such identity protection more likely. For patents, the TRIPS Agreement standardizes the term of patent protection to twenty years, as compared with the previous term of seventeen years in the United States[22] and far shorter terms in other countries.[23]

The Agreement also provides that pharmaceuticals and chemicals may not be excluded from patentability,[24] an important benefit for the pharmaceutical industry because many countries did not provide patent protection for pharmaceutical processes or for chemical mixtures before the TRIPS Agreement, including—for one or both of these processes—Norway, Mexico, India, Brazil, Argentina, and Japan. In the area of copyrights, the TRIPS Agreement now explicitly includes computer programs as literary works under the Berne Convention.[25] It also assures authors and performers fifty years for protection of their works.[26] As to semiconductor mask work—the way that engineers have designed the circuits—the Agreement extends protection to ten years and requires royalty payments from innocent infringers.[27] For example, a computer store discovered in possession of pirated Intel chips must compensate the rights holder, even if authorities have no proof that the owner knew that the chips were counterfeit—previously a virtually insurmountable enforcement hurdle.

11.5   Role of TRIPS in the Abuse of Traditional Knowledge

(A)   Western Intellectual Property Norms Codified

The WTO's TRIPS Agreement, following the lead of Western intellectual property law, grants exclusive, time-limited rights to inventors in order to encourage innovation. In return for the profits from such monopoly grants, the inventor must fully describe the invention so that it will be available to others willing to pay a royalty for its use. Let us explore the connection between indigenous rights and this approach to protecting intellectual property.

As noted by the Center for International Environmental Law (CIEL), "Intellectual property rules fundamentally affect sustainable development. IPR, as temporary privileges over the products of intellectual activity, determine who controls information and technology."[28] From this, one readily may identify the potential intersection between traditional knowledge, passed orally from generation to generation, and modern Western rules—culminating in the WTO's TRIPS Agreement—for the use of patentable ideas. To find the appropriate balance between protecting the owners of ideas and the owners of a cultural identity, it is important to unveil those IPR rules that serve as potential obstacles to sustainable development, or to the rights of indigenous populations to continue to use their traditional resources, or—for that matter—to legitimate trade itself.[29]

As the Northern biotechnology industry has flourished, the demand for Southern genetic resources—tropical rain forests that are home to more than half the species of plants and animals on earth[30]—to feed its supply chain has increased rapidly, a pattern that calls to mind the history of Northern exploitation of Southern natural resources during the industrial revolutions of the 19th century. Examples abound in which multinational pharmaceutical and chemical companies have obtained patents over uses of plants employed by indigenous cultures for centuries. Quinine, the well-known cure for malaria, originates in the bark of the Peruvian cinchona tree, and Andean indigenous populations long have used the substance as a cure for fevers.[31] Through centuries of breeding and cultivation, Latin American indigenous populations developed naturally colored cotton, economically significant to clothing manufacturers. A California scientist patented this cultivation process, yielding none of the royalties to its true inventors.[32] The University of Florida patented a fungus lethal to fire ants that damage U.S. crops. The patent application made no mention of the Brazilian communities that had discovered the idea, much less spoke of compensating its inventors. The U.S. Patent Office cancelled, at the request of nine indigenous Amazon tribes, the patent obtained by a U.S. citizen for the ayahuasca vine, which thousands of indigenous peoples use in sacred religious and healing ceremonies.[33] Eli Lilly earned millions of dollars from its patent on a cancer cure derived from the rosy periwinkle plant that long had been used for medicinal purposes by indigenous tribes in Madagascar; these groups received almost nothing for their traditional knowledge. Chemical giant W. R. Grace obtained a patent for an insecticide that uses an active ingredient from the leaf of the neem tree, whose leaves and seeds indigenous farmers in India have used for thousands of years as a natural insecticide and to treat various skin conditions. Asked why the company had decided not to compensate the indigenous farmers who had developed and protected this use for millennia, a Grace vice president dismissed their efforts as "folk medicine." The University of California and the Japanese company Lucky Biotech patented proteins in two African plants long used by indigenous tribes for their sweetening properties, with no return to the African communities. Not only have the indigenous inventors and their communities failed to benefit from the grant of these monopoly rights, but some of the companies, incredibly, have attempted to secure royalties for continuation by the tribe of the now-patented traditional use.

Using traditional knowledge to search for patent medicines has great value to the pharmaceutical industry. Indigenous populations use as many as 7,500 plant species in traditional medicines.[34] By seeking out these uses, TNCs increase the efficiency of screening plants for medicinal properties by more than 400 percent, making indigenous resources and knowledge critical to drug research.[35] Western corporations justify their appropriation of traditional knowledge by explaining that medical advances emerge only from laboratory "discovery" of their benefits.[36] Failure of developed-country entities to engage indigenous peoples in this bioprospecting/biopiracy of their cultural heritage is a shameless continuing violation of human rights treaties. In light of the contribution of traditional knowledge to the success of patented medicines, embracing participation by the protectors of this biodiversity treasure would be completely consistent with providing incentives to pharmaceutical giants to find cures for major illnesses.

(B)   Dissimilar Languages of Traditional Knowledge
and Western IPR Law

The TRIPS Agreement casts in concrete the basic IPR protection systems of modern industrialized nations. Article 27(1) makes patent protection available only to inventions or ideas that are new, nonobvious, and useful. These conditions systematically exclude traditional knowledge from patentability. These requirements also presuppose a recognizable creator who can describe the new idea by a physical manifestation—a drawing or writing. Indigenous practitioners normally do not reduce plant usages to written form, but instead pass them from generation to generation through oral histories.[37] Traditional knowledge is, by definition, the product of collective experimentation, which makes impossible associating a resource use with one individual, a recognizable creator who would apply for protection. The TRIPS Agreement protects only private rights, not the communal innovations that typify traditional knowledge. Critically, Western standards rarely will view traditional knowledge as original or new, because indigenous medicine doctors acquired their familiarity with the beneficial usage over the course of generations, thus making it, in the eyes of Western IPR law, part of the public domain.[38] Finally, even if the traditional knowledge were to meet the originality test, the protection of the TRIPS Agreement applies only to knowledge and innovation that yields profit and is capable of "industrial application." Indigenous traditional knowledge and resources, again by their very nature, do not fit this mold.

If negotiators could overcome these legal hurdles, a financial one remains—obtaining the sophisticated legal and medical expertise to satisfy the difficult conditions of Western patent offices. For example, a patent in the United States costs at least $4,000. Challenging W. R. Grace's neem-based patents cost hundreds of thousands of dollars.

A further disconnection between Western IPR law and traditional knowledge is the dynamic nature of indigenous knowledge and of history itself. Western IPR law takes as given the creation of a known, unchanging invention or idea. In fact, indigenous peoples often reinvent traditional knowledge through the interaction of the indigenous community with its surrounding natural resources or to achieve political goals, such as the elevation or demotion of past rulers.[39] The dynamic nature of traditional knowledge complicates the search for common language and suitable paradigms.

(C) Biopiracy or Bioprospecting?

How should we attribute value to and otherwise accommodate the scientific and medical breakthroughs sparked by stripping indigenous populations of their traditional knowledge? Communities have the undeniable right to protect their culture, but society in general cannot easily be denied the benefit of scientific progress. It is not clear that indigenous populations will consent to the technological use of their traditional knowledge for nontraditional purposes—that is, to allowing chemical or pharmaceutical exploitation of the genetic resource.

Of course, the solution must include adequate compensation of the indigenous communities that have safeguarded and developed these genetic uses over the centuries. What can constitute compensation, however, is contested terrain. If the knowledge is religious or sacred, to the first peoples there may be no economic measure of its value. Beyond that, under what circumstances should international law permit the ruling majority to capitalize on—to nationalize, if you will—traditional knowledge in the interest of the greater number of members of the public if the local community is unwilling to share its genetic bounty? Recognition by Article 15 of the ICESCR to the right to take part in cultural life includes the right to benefit from material interests resulting from any scientific production which the person authors. Perhaps it is important to strike a balance between those who consider biopiracy of traditional knowledge as vital acts of scientific innovation that benefit society as a whole and those who find such actions to have catastrophic effects on the indigenous world. In this process it is imperative that the taking of first peoples' knowledge not be just the next act of colonization by the West. As Western corporations and universities are enriched by marketing of the knowledge of indigenous communities, indigenous resources are depleted, thereby threatening loss of livelihood, cultural erosion, and, even more, certain status as subaltern members of society.

11.6 Convention on Biological Diversity to the Rescue

Even as appreciation by the industrialized world for genetic diversity expands, genetic resources rapidly are vanishing. Ninety-seven percent of the vegetable species that seed companies sold at the beginning of the 20th century are now extinct.

When we hear of extinction, most of us think of the plight of the rhino, tiger, panda, or blue whale. But these sad sagas are only small pieces of the extinction puzzle. The overall numbers are terrifying. Of the 40,168 species that the 10,000 scientists in the World Conservation Union have assessed, one in four mammals, one in eight birds, one in three amphibians, and one in three conifers and other gymnosperms are at risk of extinction. The peril faced by other classes of organisms is less thoroughly analyzed, but fully 40 percent of the examined species of planet earth are in danger, including up to 51 percent of reptiles, 52 percent of insects, and 73 percent of flowering plants.

By the most conservative measure—based on the last century's recorded extinctions—the current rate of extinction is one hundred times the background rate (one species per million goes extinct and is replaced each year). But eminent Harvard biologist Edward O. Wilson and other scientists estimate that the true rate is more like one thousand to ten thousand times the background rate. The actual annual sum is only an educated guess, because no scientist believes that the tally of life ends at the 1.5 million species already discovered; estimates range as high as 100 million species on earth, with 10 million as the median guess. Bracketed between best- and worst-case scenarios, somewhere between 2.7 and 270 species are erased from existence every day. We now understand that the majority of life on earth has never been—and will never be—known to us. In a staggering forecast, Wilson predicts that our present course will lead to the extinction of half of all plant and animal species by the year 2100.[40]

From this vantage point, we can appreciate the magnitude of the eye-opening reality that indigenous communities in the South have become the guardians of most of the world's remaining genetic resources. Traditional knowledge and biodiversity compose an indivisible symbiotic relationship. Protection of biological diversity enriches indigenous populations, while proper care of traditional knowledge increases biological diversity.

Loss at this pace of plant and animal species, along with their ecosystems, can have only negative consequences for scientific discovery. This is true whether or not we subscribe to an anthropomorphic view of the premises of environmental protection, which envisions a medicine cabinet theory as the principal justification for preserving plant and animal species whose place in the cosmos we have not yet discovered.[41] The solution does not lie in treating either traditional knowledge or biodiversity as static concepts. Instead, the two fields are interrelated, dynamic, and continually evolving processes of interaction between human beings and local ecologies. Human communities created biodiversity through their interaction of with local ecosystems. For this nexus, the CBD seeks sanctuary not for some sterile petri dish of scientific understanding that may exist at one point in time. Preserving traditional knowledge to protect biodiversity serves, then, as a primary incentive. Other reasons demand that we find answers to ensure that traditional knowledge continues to exist at healthy levels. For example, access to traditional knowledge by indigenous populations protects the livelihood of the poor. The world's poor rely on biological products from local sources for 85 percent of their needs, including satisfying basic demands for food, fuel, shelter, and medicine.

With this grim forecast of future biodiversity loss in mind, government leaders, urged on by environmental, development, and other human rights groups, negotiated in 1992 the CBD. Over 180 nations have ratified the treaty, a formidable group that does not technically include the United States, although one would not learn this fact from the hectic pace of U.S. participation. CBD uniquely recognizes the interdependence of biodiversity, traditional knowledge, and sustainable development, requiring signatories to preserve the knowledge of indigenous communities whose traditional lifestyles are important to the sustainable use of biological diversity.[42]

Whereas the TRIPS Agreement finds no place for the protection of traditional knowledge, CBD recognizes the crucial role of indigenous groups in preserving much of the world's remaining biodiversity by striking a historic bargain between the industrial world and indigenous groups. Southern nations will grant the North access to genetic resources in return for the transfer of biotechnology and payment of funds that recognize—for the first time—the value of traditional knowledge.[43] The only means by which negotiators could conceive to implement such a bargain was by vesting ownership of natural resources in the states in which they are located,[44] an approach that is entirely consistent with international law,[45] but which will complicate realization of CBD's benefits by indigenous communities.

For example, the treaty requires prior informed consent before a corporation may have access to genetic resources. Prospective resource users, however, must seek this consent not from the indigenous population that is protecting and developing the resource, but from the signatory government.[46] This provision seeks engagement with the keepers of the world's biodiversity—indigenous delegates—in CBD decision-making, a vital first step. In short, CBD attempts to give voice to the undeniable linkage among indigenous populations, traditional knowledge, and preservation of biological diversity.[47] Biological diversity actually increases when law supports traditional knowledge.

If we recognize and respect the cultural differences in indigenous communities, perhaps we can expect that indigenous peoples will recognize and respect the cultural differences of the majority population and the pressures born of globalization. As to what "compensation" to an indigenous population would recognize the importance of their traditional knowledge in medical and agricultural discoveries, we must understand that a particular indigenous population may have no desire or need for "modern" conveniences such as stoves and refrigerators, or even electricity. Compensation inevitably will change the cultural traditions that the population is attempting to protect, just as careless bioprospecting itself can do. In this regard it is of paramount importance to give voice to the indigenous groups to ascertain what, if any, compensation they deem to be adequate. The North has to be prepared to function within a different paradigm if there is to be a true partnership and not just another cycle of colonization. What seems to us critical is to inform the community directly affected by investment projects from a trade agreement about the benefits and costs, and to let the community participate in negotiations and decide how best to protect its interests.

This approach, of course, assumes that the majority also recognizes and respects the right of the indigenous community to its ancestral lands, to which the community has a connection that cannot be broken without destroying the community itself. Our best service to indigenous populations affected by globalization is to ensure the transparency of the decision process and their full participation and voice in that process. Failure to do so can be destructive of both majority and minority interests. For example, in order to attract foreign investment, the Mexican government revised the constitution to allow private investment on Mexican lands. The result was rebellion by the Zapatistas, who faced upheaval of their traditional lifestyles, and years of increasingly violent disputes between indigenous populations and the Mexican government.[48]

11.7 Trade Causes Overuse of Resources on Which Indigenous Peoples Rely

Trade has affected resources that are vital for the survival of indigenous peoples' way of life. Trade interests that have caused the destruction of such resources include oil development, logging, and dams. Oil development interests have detrimentally affected indigenous tribes in Ecuador's Amazon rain forest. The five indigenous tribes affected by the oil development in the Amazon rain forest are the Cofán, Huaorani, Kichwa, Secoya, and Siona.[49] Oil development by Texaco and its successor ChevronTexaco had two main detrimental effects: oil spillage and the development of the Amazon rain forest.

First, oil development caused spills estimated at 19.23 million gallons (by comparison, the infamous Exxon Valdez oil spill in Alaskan waters amounted to 10.8 million gallons) for which Texaco neither paid compensation nor cleaned up.[50] Second, oil development caused dispossession of indigenous territories.[51] Although Brazil recently has reversed its approach, a government plan to develop the Amazon encouraged colonists to turn the Amazon rain forest into ranches and farms by using Texaco's newly built roads.[52]

Another major result of oil development is destruction of plant and animal life. For example, animals affected were the crocodiles, water birds, fish, boar, turkeys, monkeys, and rodents.[53] Another effect of the oil development is the extinction of the Tetetes indigenous people, who fled their homelands as the boomtown of Lago Agrio sprang up near Texaco's first commercial field.[54] The remaining indigenous peoples also claim other effects of the contamination, such as unusually high rates of cancer, birth defects, skin diseases, and other health problems.[55] Ecuador's indigenous people sued in the United States in the case of *Aguinda v. Texaco, Inc.,* in an effort to secure compensation from Texaco for a thorough cleanup and for medical care. The U.S. court, however, dismissed the action based on the doctrine of *forum non conveniens*—that is, hearing the case in the United States would create hardships and the suit would more properly be brought in Ecuador.[56] Two new suits in Ecuador are presently underway.[57]

Moreover, the indigenous people in the Amazon rain forest in Brazil are also under attack by logging companies.[58] The logging companies want timber for mahogany coffins and furniture to sell in developed nations.[59] Furthermore, Asian logging companies have bought controlling interests in local logging companies and are purchasing rights to cut down rain forest lands for as little as three dollars per acre.[60] Logging companies create the problem of deforestation; in areas such as the Brazilian Amazon, deforestation may have an impact on overall global stability because of the biodiversity that is sustained in the rain forest.[61] The indigenous Yanomami tribe, the largest indigenous population in the Americas to retain its traditional way of life, is located in the Brazilian Amazon rain forest.[62] The Yanomami tribe's survival is dependent on rain forest resources. Further, the indigenous tribe would likely not be able to relocate, as their knowledge of the rain forest areas is vital to their survival.[63] If logging of the Brazilian Amazon continues, the way of life of the Yanomami people is at an end. To be sure, there is no economic measurement for the loss of a peoples.

In addition, economic development has also caused the relocation of indigenous people such as the Pehuenche tribe of Chile. The Pangue/Ralco hydroelectric dam project in Chile on the BioBío River caused this relocation. The hydroelectric project will provide more energy to drive further economic development for Chile. The price paid for this economic development, however, is the destruction of the indigenous Pehuenche tribe's territory because the project will flood their ancestral lands.[64] The flooding of the lands will destroy the mountain ecosystem and modify the seminomadic way of life of the Pehuenche tribe.[65]

The hydroelectric project supporters are the Chilean government, the privatized Spanish-owned electric firm of Endesa, and the World Bank's International Finance Corporation (IFC).[66] The Pehuenche tribe filed a claim against the Chilean government with the IACHR. The Chilean government and the Pehuenche tribe reached a settlement, however, and the Pehuenche tribe of Chile received rights over lands, technical assistance to develop the land, educational scholarships, and three hundred thousand dollars per family. In return, the Pehuenche tribe is abandoning the lawsuit and transferring all its legal rights to the land.[67]

In conclusion, international trade's goal of economic development is threatening the way of life of indigenous people. The effects of the destruction of the natural resources of indigenous people can lead to their relocation, integration, or extinction.

11.8 Modernization: Not Always the Best Approach

Trade often rewards the types of work that are inconsistent with indigenous, nature-sensitive lifestyles. In its quest for comparative advantage, trade economics teaches, inaccurately,[68] that wealth maximization is the end. Underutilized land, primitive instruments, and basic infrastructure—the unremarkable benchmarks of many indigenous cultures—are anathema to the most trade-efficient exploitation of property. Instead, trade teaches that farmers should use the most modern equipment feasible to grow commodity crops with the highest export value. Comparative advantage holds that these lands should attract investment in assembly or manufacture of goods in high global demand whose production best meets the human and natural resources of the region. We may question whether members of the tribal population are culturally, emotionally, or even financially more secure in accepting backbreaking jobs for little pay to grow export-worthy crops or work in factories to make goods whose profitability relies on the comparative advantage of below-subsistence wages. Even if one were to believe that this stage is necessary to beneficial modernization of the indigenous culture, we must recognize that in leaving behind the tribal heritage, the indigenous population inevitably sacrifices its stewardship of the genetic resources that may be tomorrow's pharmaceutical breakthrough.

The indigenous peoples of the region rarely are the beneficiaries of the rush to wealth maximization. As noted in section 11.3(C), biodiversity disappears as modern investment and production marginalize its protectors. As the younger tribal generations are seduced by the financial benefits offered by globalization and are drawn to Western lifestyles, tribal healers or shamans lose their appeal, with the result that the most endangered species in the rain forest are the tribal elders who use plants for healing.[69] The most telling irony in this development is that shamanic knowledge has often found the precise cures for disease that the Northern bioprospectors seek.[70]

11.9 Efforts to Bridge the Divide

(A) Traditional Knowledge Database

Criticism of CBD centers on its failure to create an infrastructure that protects indigenous knowledge along with the biological resources to which it applies. The Convention focuses instead on how to use biological resources without damaging them. Moreover, it does not adequately protect indigenous community resources, because it does not expressly address protection of IPR. CBD negotiators permitted the WTO system to retain jurisdiction over such issues, an approach that avoids direct conflict, but passes up the opportunity to bridge the divides between the Western intellectual property principles of the WTO's TRIPS Agreement and the Southern biodiversity principles with which IPR protection is so inextricably intertwined.

One approach that offers hope is creation of a database of traditional knowledge that will satisfy Western IPR requirements for a physical manifestation, while at the same time defeating competing attempts to patent the knowledge by establishing through this "prior art" that the idea is not original. Because indigenous populations of India were among the earliest exploited by pharmaceutical bioprospecting,[71] this country has seen establishment of the first such database.[72] Sacred or ritualistic information are not appropriate for such a registry, thus depriving these data of protection from exploitation. In addition, a registry may protect the traditional knowledge from exploitation, but it continues to exclude the knowledge from the benefits of the IPR system. In fact, pharmaceutical companies may actually gain knowledge from the registry that they could improve sufficiently to qualify as innovative under Western patent law.[73]

Another approach is to record the different medicinal plants used by indigenous people in their own language. Mark Plotkin, who works with indigenous people in the Amazon, created, translated, and handed over to the indigenous Tirio tribe a handbook on its medicinal plants. Before Plotkin's handbook, the tribe only had one book translated into their language, the Bible.[74] A handbook in indigenous people's own language will satisfy Western IPR requirements for a physical manifestation and defeat competing attempts to patent the knowledge by establishing that the idea is not original. Moreover, a handbook of medicinal plants in the indigenous people's language, together with teaching indigenous people about patent law, may result in pharmaceutical companies asking permission to use the handbook and paying royalties to the indigenous people. Although, as noted in section 11.9(B), the type of royalty payment helpful to indigenous people may vary from Western benchmarks, this approach would allow both indigenous people and pharmaceutical companies to gain from traditional knowledge.

(B)   Modification of the Existing IPR System

WTO negotiators are considering ways to recognize and protect traditional knowledge within the TRIPS system. These proposals would allow patents for collective knowledge and for ideas that indigenous peoples have not reduced to precise laboratory terms. The pharmaceutical industry will oppose these changes because of their large financial stake in preserving the status quo. Plant extracts account for at least half the drugs most frequently prescribed and for at least forty billion dollars in annual sales.[75]

Another approach would be to redirect the CBD's requirement of prior informed consent to the indigenous peoples themselves, rather than to their governments. As we noted earlier, while such a requirement would—if it is enforced diligently—protect the indigenous populations from exploitation, the question remains of who will protect the general interests of global society in finding elusive cures for chronic disease. What does "informed" consent entail? And even if an objective standard could be devised, would the promise of modern "riches" overcome some communities' desire to preserve their time-honored way of life? Assuming that we can find answers to these questions, we must consider that indigenous populations may not agree to or desire Western forms of compensation, such as royalty payments and profit sharing. Indigenous peoples may place greater value on nonmonetary compensation, including infrastructure development and training.[76]

(C) Sui Generis Systems of IPR

While the earliest human rights documents protect the rights of authors and inventors, neither the TRIPS Agreement nor earlier IPR treaties even mention human rights, a reflection of the placement of IPR among the law of private contracts and not within the *acquis* of public international law.[77] From this anomaly have emerged proposals to address the multifaceted clash between protection of traditional knowledge and Western concepts of IPR safeguards by creating an entirely different approach to the needs of indigenous populations, particularly because of the symbiotic link of these needs with preserving biodiversity.

A *sui generis* system would, of course, overcome the divide between traditional knowledge and the reigning IPR system. In addition to creation of the global database discussed in section 11.9(A), such a system would address the different criteria (overcoming problems with novelty, nonobviousness, and usefulness), purposes (emphasizing protection of cultural and other human rights of indigenous peoples), and rights owners (the community instead of an individual).

Powerful owners of intellectual property, having succeeded beyond their fondest hopes in gaining the broad IPR protections of the TRIPS Agreement and even more extensive TRIPS-plus provisions in a series of FTAs negotiated with developing countries by the European Commission and the United States, simply will be obstructionist and not permit adoption of an effective alternative to TRIPS to address traditional knowledge. Indigenous nurturing of the genetic resources that will crowd the pharmacy shelves of the future is precisely the position that the pharmaceutical and chemical giants prefer. No sui generis system holds a remote chance of adoption in any form that will trump the TRIPS Agreement. This is a question of power, not of the right thing to do.

11.10 Final Thoughts

(A)   Excluding Immoral Biopirated Patents

Attempting to overturn the basic principles of Western IPR protection law through amending the TRIPS Agreement (for example, by requiring disclosure of the origin of a patent application based on genetic resources) will not succeed in the face of strong and organized opposition by developed country TNCs whose IPR carries great value to them. The same is true of developing an alternate sui generis system to bring equity to the treatment of traditional knowledge. We prefer to use the system's own tools to accomplish the purpose. The same provision that guarantees the patentability of medicines, even those essential to government control of epidemics such as HIV/AIDS, permits WTO Members to deny patents to inventions when prevention of commercial exploitation within their territory "is necessary to protect *ordre public* or morality, including to protect human, animal or plant life or health or to avoid serious prejudice to the environment."[78]

Methods employed by TNCs to gain large commercial advantage from biopiracy of long-protected traditional knowledge of indigenous communities offend morality on multiple grounds, including religious and cultural. We should not facilely dismiss the chance that a WTO dispute settlement panel will be responsive to a public morality defense. Even the staunchest defender of IPR, the United States, recently proposed denying trademarks that would have sacrilegious effect for Indian tribes (such as the National Football League's Washington "Redskins"), based on the trademark's "immorality."[79] The fact that Western IPR law itself flounders in endeavoring to balance the strictures of protecting IPR against the need to satisfy other public policy demands should offer comfort to proponents of a morality defense. Denial of a patent for a medicine or other chemical use of a genetic resource obtained by bioprospectors without concern for the human rights of its traditional owners seems by no means beyond the reach of the TRIPS Agreement and implementing Western IPR law. We do not pretend that representatives of indigenous communities can utilize the morality exclusion without significant effort. For a start, the TRIPS Agreement permits, but does not require, that a Member include a morality clause in its implementing laws. Nonetheless, although couched in terms of ethics rather than morality, the sensitive issue of the patentability of DNA, and generally of plants and animals, for health care purposes raises the same considerations attendant in the biopiracy situation.

Another factor in the TRIPS Agreement's morality clause is protection of the environment. In light of CBD's strong linkage of protection of traditional knowledge with preservation of biodiversity, the morality clause has application through another policy portal that finds purchase in the debates taking place within the WTO and the CBD.

The patent-busting threats of Canada and the United States following the terrorist acts of September 11, 2001, when the immediate availability of an anthrax vaccine seemed in doubt because of patent protections, also reflect an undeniable morality component, even though that term is absent from Western patent laws. We view this challenge as one that may more acceptably be couched in equitable terms, but that will reach the same objective without casting at the windmills of stark renewal of the hard-fought TRIPS Agreement negotiations.

(B)   Landed Gentry

The right to property has special relevance to indigenous populations, bespeaking an intimate connection with *pacha mama,* mother earth. Their connection to the land goes beyond possession into a spiritual state whose enjoyment is prerequisite to preserving the tribe's cultural legacy.[80] As the "first peoples" in the nation-states that formed around them, tribal groups often clash with modern property ownership rules in efforts to retain rights over ancestral lands on which their subsistence and culture depend, but which may now be available only to the duly registered property "owner."[81] The result is an inevitable dispossession by trade's avatars in the form of cattle ranches, miners, lumber mills, and oil wells, which have destroyed hundreds of millions of acres of rain forest and other lands inhabited by indigenous peoples.[82]

We cannot hope to preserve either traditional knowledge or the culture of indigenous populations unless these populations, in addition to recognition by trade rules of the ownership by tribal groups of IPR in genetic resources, hold title to lands that they have traditionally inhabited. Some groups, such as the Kuguigi and Arahuaco tribes in the Sierra Nevada de Santa Marta in Colombia, have managed to raise sufficient funds to purchase tribal lands outright.[83] Few groups possess either the political awareness or the generous benefactors to accomplish this objective on their own; most are unaware they even face the issue until it is too late. This task must reside with alert governments and nongovernment organizations.

12

From Excess to Despair
The Persistence of Poverty

Poverty is pronounced deprivation in well-being. But what precisely is deprivation? The voices of poor people bear eloquent testimony to its meaning. . . . To be poor is to be hungry, to lack shelter and clothing, to be sick and not cared for, to be illiterate and not schooled. But for poor people, living in poverty is more than this. Poor people are particularly vulnerable to adverse events outside their control. They are often treated badly by the institutions of state and society and excluded from voice and power in those institutions.

12.1 Overview

Part of the promise of a trade system was the spread of capitalism and capital to effect an improvement in the standard of living of persons worldwide. Yet it is unclear whether indeed such an improvement in wealth has arrived. Current figures on the wage gap show increasing distances between the rich and the poor, as well as growing income and purchasing power disparities. While the poor of the world may starve or die from curable illnesses, the rich spend millions on cosmetics and pet food. This chapter explores whether the trade regime as it has evolved has in fact has met its promise or instead merely perpetuated poverty.

12.2 Human Rights Framework

(A) Normative Standards

Human rights documents recognize a number of rights that relate to the topic of poverty. They ensure the rights of "member[s] of society . . . to social security and . . . to [the] realization . . . of the economic, social, and cultural rights indispensable for his[/her] dignity and the free development of his[/her] personality."[1] Moreover, also related to poverty, the Universal Declaration and the ICESCR grant the rights to work, to just and favorable conditions of work, to a healthy working environment, to protection from unemployment, to just and fair remuneration, and to social security to ensure an existence worthy of human dignity including through old age.[2] The ICESCR, in Article 11(2), recognizes "the fundamental right of everyone to be free from hunger" and thus charges state parties to

> take, individually and through international co-operation, the measures, including specific programmes, which are needed:
> (a) to improve methods of production, conservation and distribution of food by making full use of technical and scientific knowledge, by disseminating knowledge of the principles of nutrition and by developing or reforming agrarian systems in such a way as to achieve the most efficient development and utilization of national resources;
> (b) taking into account the problems of both food-importing and food-exporting countries, to ensure an equitable distribution of food supplies in relation to need.

In this Hemisphere, the American Declaration (arts. XIV and XVI) and the Protocol of San Salvador (arts. 6, 7, and 9) similarly provide for the rights to work and to receive remuneration that ensures a suitable standard of living, as well as the right to social security. The Protocol of San Salvador at Article 12 also establishes that everyone has the right to adequate nutrition. The American Declaration states that "every person has a right to own such private property as meets the essential needs of decent living and helps to maintain the dignity of the individual and of the home" (art. XXIII). Significantly, ACHR, while recognizing the rights of everyone to use and enjoy property, also accepts that the law may "subordinate such use and enjoyment to the interest of society" (art. 21(1)).

The OAS Charter, another significant document in the Hemisphere, includes as one of its "essential purposes" the "eradicat[ion of] extreme poverty, which constitutes an obstacle to the full democratic development of all the peoples of the hemisphere" (art. 2(g)). In its statement of principles, the Charter reiterates that the "elimination of extreme poverty is an essential part of the promotion and consolidation of representative democracy and is the common and shared responsibility of the American

States" (art. 3(f)). In addition, it links "social justice and social security" to "lasting peace" (art. 3(j)).

Further, in Article 34, the Charter states that "the Member States agree that equality of opportunity, the elimination of extreme poverty, equitable distribution of wealth and income and the full participation of their peoples in decisions relating to their own development are, among others, basic objectives of integral development." Among the "basic goals" articulated to effect those ends are the "modernization of rural life and reforms leading to equitable and efficient land-tenure systems, increased agricultural productivity, expanded use of land, diversification of production and improved processing and marketing systems for agricultural products; . . . fair wages, . . . acceptable working conditions; . . . proper nutrition; . . . [and] adequate housing" (art. 34(d), (g), (j), and (k)). In that regard, the Member states agree that work is not only a "right" but also "a social duty [that] gives dignity to the one who performs it" throughout their "working years and in their old age" (art. 45(b)). The Charter also directs the Member states to develop an efficient "social security policy" (art. 45(h)). Thus, as the international and regional treaties' provisions on work and social security attest, the eradication of poverty has emerged as a collective global commitment.

(B) Antipoverty Initiatives

The eradication of poverty is a cornerstone of the UN comprehensive development agenda that emerged from the major UN conferences and summits since the 1990s. Governments and organizations around the world are taking steps necessary to ensure progress in the reduction and eradication of poverty. Indeed, at the World Summit for Social Development[3] governments committed themselves to the eradication of poverty as an ethical, social, political, and economic imperative of humankind. The Copenhagen Declaration on Social Development and the Programme of Action of the Summit[4] shifted the development paradigm from one centered on pure economics to one centered on human beings and acknowledged the intrinsic link among poverty, unemployment, and social integration.

The Millennium Development Declaration[5] asks governments to make poverty eradication a central focus of economic and social development and to build a consensus with all relevant actors and policies and strategies to reduce the proportion of people living in extreme poverty—that is, on less than one dollar per day—by one-half by the year 2015. Significantly, the Declaration also emphasizes the need for comprehensive national strategies for poverty eradication that are integrated into policies at all levels, including economic and fiscal policies; capacity-building and institution-building; and giving priority to investments in education and health, social protection, and basic social services. The Declaration encourages governments also to develop and implement sustainable pro-poor economic growth strategies that enhance the potential and ability of poor people by empowering them, providing access to productive resources and active employment, encouraging small- and medium-size enterprises, and stimulating agriculture and rural development.

Thereafter, the Commission for Social Development adopted a declaration recognizing that the implementation of the Copenhagen commitments and the attainment of the Millennium Development Goals were mutually reinforcing.[6] The recent 2005 World Summit Outcome,[7] while reaffirming the commitment to eradicate poverty and promote sustained economic growth, sustainable development, and global prosperity for all, expressed concern over the slow and uneven progress toward poverty eradication and the realization of other development goals in some regions. A comprehensive analysis of world poverty, however, shows that current global integration efforts alone are insufficient to eradicate privation.

12.3 International Trade Framework

One former vice president of the World Bank stated succinctly that "to address poverty, economic growth is not an option: it is an imperative."[8] "The belief that economic growth is a key to meeting most important human needs, including alleviating poverty," is deeply embedded.[9] That foundational belief persists and coexists with the following reality: during the last half of the 20th century the world saw a fivefold increase in global output, but the percentage of people living in extreme poverty remained stable.[10] Although specific figures differ, all agree that extreme poverty is an immense problem in the world.[11]

Poverty is arguably the most palpable link between trade and human rights. A popular belief is that "trade can play an important part in reducing poverty, because it boosts economic growth and the poor tend to benefit from that faster growth."[12] Although the closest connection between trade and poverty arguably is the labor market,[13] the foundational free market idea of the trade regime is important to engage. For one, the reform of trade can both "create and destroy markets. Extreme adverse poverty shocks are often associated with the disappearance of a market, while strong poverty alleviation can arise when markets are introduced for previously un-traded or unavailable goods."[14]

From a moral standpoint, no person should be deprived of the basic necessities for existence; there is no justification for starvation. From an economic perspective, the ideas of crop specialization and free markets naturally result in overall economic prosperity. Consequently, open world markets should be more able to yield circumstances by which there would be food for the hungry. Synergistic effects of current economic and human rights policies should result in an affluent world with enough resources to enable all human beings to have access to at least minimal necessary levels for a dignified existence, including remuneration, safe work, food, shelter, health, and an education. In reality, little progress has been made toward the eradication of poverty, particularly in the Americas, where migration to the North—voluntary, involuntary, documented, undocumented, and a consequence of the same trade growth that is intended to reduce poverty—is at an all-time high (see section 9.3(B)).

A WTO study found that while living standards in developing countries are not closing the gap with the standards in developed states, some developing countries are catching up and the difference in their progress lies with the countries' openness to trade.[15] The study showed that poor people within a particular state benefit from trade liberalization and concluded that trade is an important factor in poverty eradication. Significantly, the study recognized that not all persons are winners in the trade liberalization game and suggested that states be responsible for this shortfall by creating social safety nets and job retraining. Trade is never viewed by trade officials as a negative factor.[16]

12.4 The Reality of Poverty

(A) Data

The poverty data are clear. Between 1987 and 1998, the percentage of the world's poor living on less than one dollar per day fell from 28.3 percent to 24 percent.[17] Because of population growth, however, the absolute number of poor has remained unchanged. According to the WTO's own statistical data for a slightly different time period (1992–2002), the percentage of people living on less than one dollar per day in Latin America dropped by a mere 3 percent. Similarly, the data showed that the percentage of people suffering from nutritional insufficiency, which is an indicator of well-being, experienced a very minimal reduction.

Hunger, another one of the measures of poverty, was uneven in Latin America. In the 1990s, the proportion of hungry people almost tripled in Cuba from 5 percent to 13 percent, while Peru had the region's biggest reduction, from 40 percent to 11 percent. Under-five mortality rates fell in Bolivia (from 12 percent to 8 percent) and Ecuador (6 percent to 3 percent), while Barbados, Jamaica, and St. Vincent and the Grenadines experienced almost no improvement.[18]

Moreover, the projections are not optimistic. Whether the poverty benchmark is one dollar per day or two dollars per day, World Bank projections suggest that the number of persons in extreme poverty will remain stable through 2008. A more optimistic approach to economic growth would see only five hundred million people brought out of extreme poverty by 2008. Yet, even under the optimistic scenario, Latin America and the Caribbean would not benefit.

(B)   The Complexity of Poverty

It is important to recognize that poverty is a complex phenomenon; it has many interacting root causes,[19] all of which are particularly acute for women as well as for other subordinated groups. Two significant links to poverty are land distribution and gender roles.[20] Myriad other variables connected to poverty include lack of education, poor health and nutrition, low potential for earning a good income, unequal distribution of methods of production, imbalance between urban and rural communities, and lack of access to and the consequent lack of influence on decision- and policy-makers to convince them to address issues of concern. The World Bank embraces the complexity of poverty and defines it as encompassing "not only low income and consumption but also low achievement in education, health, nutrition, and other areas of human development . . . [and based on the definition of poverty given by the poor and of poverty by the poor, it includes] powerlessness and voicelessness, and vulnerability and fear."[21] In this context, the following indisputable realities are significant:

- Every second child—amounting to 1 billion children—lives in poverty. One in three, or 640 million children, in developing countries lives without adequate shelter. One in five children—400 million—has no access to safe water. One in seven children, or 270 million, has no access to health services. One in seven children—10.6 million—died in 2003 before reaching the age of five, translating to about 29,000 children dying daily.[22]

- "The top fifth of the world's people in the richest countries enjoy 82% of the expanding export trade and 68% of foreign direct investment—the bottom fifth, barely more than 1%."[23]
- "In 1960 the 20% of the world's people in the richest countries had 30 times the income of the poorest 20%—in 1997, 74 times as much."[24]
- In 1998, the forty-eight least developed countries accounted for less than 0.4 percent of global exports.[25]
- In 2001, almost 43 percent of the Latin American population was living in poverty, with 18.6 percent living in extreme poverty.[26]

The *Human Development Report 2003* notes that for many "the 1990s were a decade of despair"[27:]

- in 21 countries, the human development index fell;[28]
- "poverty rates increased in 37 of 67 countries with data";
- "in 19 countries more than one person in four is going hungry";
- "in 21 countries the hunger rate has increased";
- in 54 countries (6 from Latin America and the Caribbean) income fell;
- "in 14 countries under-5 mortality rates increased, and in 7 countries almost one in four children will not [live until] their fifth birthdays";
- "in 9 countries more than one person in four does not have access to safe water"; and
- "in 15 countries more than one person in four does not have access to adequate sanitation."[29]

To be sure, there has been some progress. In the last four decades of the 20th century life expectancy in the developing world increased by twenty years on average, infant mortality fell by more than half, fertility rates declined by almost half, and in the last two decades net primary school enrollment increased by 13 percent. Yet in the beginning of the 21st century, poverty remains a global problem. And many posit that trade has, at least in part, contributed as its neoliberal policies, which include a push for privatization that has eroded social safety nets, deprive the poor of the ability to engage in activities that might improve their well-being.

Moreover, in recent decades the income gap between the rich and the poor states has increased.[30] One study concludes that while there are some countries whose incomes gap are converging, with reports suggesting that the common thread among those is trade liberalization, "income gaps between the majority of countries appear to be growing over time."[31]

(C)   Measuring Poverty

One of the large debates with respect to poverty is the lack of agreement on the best way to measure it. The World Bank itself, while apparently understanding the complexity of poverty, still uses an econometric approach. In its Millennium Development Goals, the World Bank uses extreme poverty as the main indicator that measures the proportion of a population surviving on less than a specific amount of income per day. That specific amount is a poverty line that constitutes the most debated issue because, some argue, any minimal change in the international poverty line—change by just a few cents—can have a dramatic impact in altering world poverty estimates and literally "'moving' millions of individuals in or out of poverty."[32]

National poverty lines are useful in capturing the poverty picture within a country over time. This measure generally is grounded on what is needed for an individual within a particular country to live decently. That figure varies dramatically between and among countries. Indeed, "the concepts and criteria used to define poverty lines also differ across countries, making national poverty lines problematic when the analytical purpose is to make international poverty comparisons—as with the monitoring of regional and global progress towards the Millennium Development Goal for poverty."[33]

Because of the different conditions within and across countries, an international guide is necessary to compare poverty across states. The World Bank uses the extreme poverty line of one dollar per day. "The $1 a day line was chosen as representative of poverty lines in a sample of low-income countries"[34] and was subsequently adjusted to $1.08 in 1993 prices. There is no explanation of the origins of the measure.[35] The way that this method of measurement works is to convert one U.S. dollar into a country's local currency through purchasing power parity (PPP) exchange rates in the hope of reflecting a standard poverty rate throughout the world. In any case, in the 1990s in Latin America and the Caribbean the number of people surviving on less than one dollar per day increased.[36] The measure assumes that "after adjusting for cost of living differences, $1 a day is the average minimum consumption required for subsistence in the developing world."[37] This approach has been widely criticized as inaccurate and insufficient to reflect subsistence levels in developing states.

For example, the World Bank's one dollar per day extreme poverty measure depends on income and budget surveys that provide information on distribution and level of income or consumption. Some feel that the surveys underestimate the incomes of very rich people in poor countries and suggest that it would be more accurate to set poverty rates based on national accounts. National accounts, however, include data on goods and other expenditures that people do not consume. Thus, a focus solely on income inequality does not reflect real deprivation and human capability.

(D) The Trade and Human Rights Approaches

Poverty is one of those themes that the trade world and the human rights world approach in dramatically different ways. The trade world, influenced by neoliberal economic policy, uses the econometric approach to poverty favored by the World Bank—a one dollar per day line. This simplistic quantitative approach toward the complex problem of poverty nevertheless profoundly affects policy choices in designing poverty reduction strategies. There are three problems with a money-metric definition or measurement of poverty. The first is that such measures analyze poverty by an external and perhaps arbitrarily selected "objective" standard, such as a poverty line, rather than by how the poor themselves define their access to basic life necessities.[38] This is problematic not only for methodological and structural reasons but for ethical ones as well. The second problem is that an income poverty measure is a unidimensional approach to a complex, multidimensional problem. Poverty indicia can range from basic needs to political rights, from work to education, from land ownership to gender. The third problem with using a poverty line is that, given the differences in income between, among, and within countries, variations in the poverty line fail to take into account the context of vastly different societies and cultures.[39] For example, an econometric approach that focuses on household income fails to account for different societies' view of what constitutes a household, or for conditions that may exist within a household based on cultural tropes, such as gender subordination, which may determine who has access to and control over household resources, including money.[40] Thus, a "social welfare" index that includes, but is not limited to, money might be more useful as a measure for absolute poverty analysis as well as result in a better comparative tool.[41]

There also are strategic political consequences to using money-metric approaches. For example, a 1999 WTO report suggests that the one dollar per day idea of extreme poverty is limited to developing states.[42] This excludes the poor of rich countries as well as anyone within poor countries that makes over one dollar per day. Such an approach fails to account for a sizable portion of the global population—1.2 billion according to the World Bank, about 20 percent of the population of the world—living below this line.[43]

The human rights world, on the other hand, utilizes a more holistic social/society-based lens through which to analyze the theme. Significantly, although the World Bank embraces such a holistic approach to poverty, it continues to use the one dollar per day measure. Notwithstanding the divergent trade and human rights approaches, they share the same goal: to eradicate at least extreme poverty.

To be sure, rich countries have committed to increase assistance for poor countries that demonstrate good faith efforts to mobilize domestic resources, undertake policy reforms, strengthen institutions, and tackle corruption and other aspects of weak governance.[44] Among the agreements of the rich countries is to remove agricultural export subsidies, introduce protection and remuneration of traditional knowledge in the TRIPS Agreement, and determine what countries without sufficient manufacturing capacity can do to protect public health under the TRIPS Agreement[45] (see also section 7.7(B) on essential medicines). The poor countries' exports, however, continue to be blocked or to lose value on world markets because of developed-state protectionism.[46]

(E)   The Realities Under NAFTA

NAFTA has been in effect since 1994; rather than rejoicing in prosperity, the realities of life after free trade remain bleak. Data for Mexico ten years after NAFTA show the following:

- quality of living has dropped
- from 1990–2000, there was a 50 percent decline in basic goods that Mexicans can afford to buy
- GDP per capita has grown at the lowest rate in history
- seventy million of one hundred million live in poverty

- forty million live in extreme poverty
- the degree of socioeconomic inequality is one of the highest in the world
- from 1993 to mid-2000, over six million jobs were created while the working population grew by over ten million, representing a 40 percent job deficit
- sustained high unemployment under NAFTA persists because foreign investment is not largely directed to new productive activity
- rising demand for cheap food imports has shrunk the market for locally grown food, and farmers have lost their jobs
- cutbacks to social programs and privatization of public services and utilities have reduced public employees and benefits
- the informal sector, with less-secure and lower-paying jobs, has grown
- 9 million live in the United States, of which 3.5 million are undocumented
- over six million workers do not make minimum wage
- two-thirds of the working population lack job benefits, including, in 2002, one-third of workers in the formal sector
- maquiladora employment is unstable and results in family displacement and unemployment when a cheaper source of labor (Asia) is found
- indigenous populations are not protected and their knowledge is exploited or simply appropriated (see section 11.4 on biopiracy)
- women are in poverty in larger numbers and face risk of violence, sometimes based on employment conditions at maquiladoras.[47]

These data, which largely consist of poverty-related factors, suggest that it is appropriate to scrutinize trade policies to harmonize them with human rights goals.

12.5 Agricultural Reform Integral to Reducing Poverty

Throughout the Americas, fifty-four million people suffer from malnutrition (11 percent of the total population), most of whom are women and children.[48] This reality is partly blamed on trade liberalization that requires developing states to open their markets but permits developed states to subsidize their agricultural sectors. In the Latin American and Caribbean area, 25 percent of the total population lives in rural areas and depends directly or indirectly on agriculture; 63.7 percent, or seventy-seven million, live in poverty and forty-seven million in extreme poverty.[49]

One of the areas of focus for ending the poverty trap requires that small, poor farmers' productivity be enhanced. This can be done by introducing improved technologies, including better seeds, tillage and crop rotation systems, and pest and soil management. It can also be done by improving infrastructure in rural areas such as irrigation systems, storage and transport facilities, and roads connecting villages to larger markets. In addition, landholding by farmers must be secure.[50]

(A) A Plea for Food Security

The 1996 World Food Summit found that food security "exists when all people, at all times, have physical and economic access to sufficient, safe and nutritious food to meet their dietary needs and food preferences for an active and healthy life."[51] Agriculture has a key role to play in reducing poverty and providing food security in emerging markets. About 75 percent of the world's poor live in rural areas and most are dependent on agriculture.[52] A basic premise of the WTO's Agreement on Agriculture is that liberalized agricultural markets would permit surpluses in world food output to satisfy the demand of food-insecure nations. The rub is that agriculture continues to be the most protected industry sector in developed countries. As far back as Ricardo's shattering insight as to comparative advantage in 1817, agriculture has enjoyed special favor in trade.[53] The unique place of farming was so well established by the time that the 1947 GATT was negotiated that GATT's tight disciplines on government interference with free trade not only exempted government protections to growers, but in fact were drafted to be fully consistent with the agricultural policies of the major signatories.[54]

While it would be an exaggeration to argue that GATT's first half-century was without impact on agricultural benefits, the sector at any rate took center stage during negotiations to create the WTO, because by the time these talks began in 1986 subsidy-induced overproduction had led to widespread displacement of efficient producers from their traditional markets.[55] As a result, countries that once exported food have become increasingly dependent on cheap food imports,[56] as we saw was the case in Mexico. Many felt that this result was far from realization of Ricardo's compelling economic case for the smallest possible government intervention.[57]

(B)   The WTO Agreement on Agriculture: To the Rescue?

While widely hailed for bringing agriculture at last under the GATT/ WTO umbrella, 1995's Agriculture Agreement more than lived up to the promise of Article 20 that "substantial . . . reductions in support and protection resulting in fundamental reform is an ongoing process." Both as to export subsidies—those contingent on export performance and thus with the most direct impact on export prices and trade—and the remaining domestic subsidies, the Agriculture Agreement's ambitions are so modest that many experts believed its generous exemptions and undefined terms rarely would permit successful reining in by dispute settlement panels of the nearly one billion dollars a day that developed nations provide to their farmers.[58]

The Agriculture Agreement categorizes agricultural supports according to their putative effect on trade. Thus, green box programs, which must have "no, or at most, minimal trade-distorting effects or effects on production," are not subject to reduction commitments and may grow in subsequent years without affecting the Member's overall reduction commitment. An example would be crop-disaster assistance. Blue box subsidies are payments tied to output, acreage, or animal numbers that also require output limits, such as production quotas or land set-asides. For example, paying a rancher ten dollars for every head of cattle not raised would be a classic blue box subsidy. Like green box payments, blue box programs are entirely exempt from reduction commitments, although no claim is made that such subsidies are without trade-distorting effects. Any subsidy that does not fit into the green or blue boxes automatically becomes an "amber" subsidy, such as price-support payments. Amber box payments are subject to reduction commitments. In addition, the Agreement prohibits export subsidies that are not explicitly listed in the Member's negotiated schedule of export subsidies, a modest first step toward eliminating these most distorting of subsidies.

Europe's subsidies have led to most world agricultural trade distortions, holding EU prices high while world prices plummet. The United States and Japan must share in the dreadful conundrum that these circumstances present to emerging market countries. While the Agriculture Agreement required that average tariffs be lowered to 36 percent, the Agreement permitted countries the flexibility to make smaller reductions on trade-sensitive products and larger ones on imports that had no domestic competition. The products of greatest interest to developing countries—milk, cotton, sugar, tobacco, meat, rice, and cereals—survived the Agreement with high tariffs. Escalating tariffs on progressively more processed commodities also limited opportunities for diversification by developing countries of their valued-added production.[59]

(C) What Must Be Done?

Many OECD countries offer nonreciprocal trade preferences, including preferential access through tariff rate quotas, to developing countries. A number of OECD countries use nonreciprocal preferential trade arrangements as a development policy by targeting those preferences to the least developed countries. This is the rationale behind schemes such as the EU's Everything But Arms and the Africa Growth and Opportunity Act in the United States. Evidence suggests that these programs have minimal value to developing countries because they leave standing the trade-debilitating agricultural supports in developed countries.

The proposal in the WTO Doha Round that developed countries should agree to provide duty-free and quota-free access to all imports from the least developed countries, including agricultural imports, reflects a non-reciprocated approach. Some argue that sufficiently generous preferential access arrangements for developing countries would provide these countries with the advantages of multilateral trade liberalization as well as a margin of preference against non-preferential suppliers.[60] The fact that this approach emanates from the subsidy-rich EU should lead us to be skeptical of its actual benefit to emerging markets. Developing countries have countered with their own non-reciprocated proposals for special and differential treatment. Some suggest the creation of a development or food security "box," like the Agriculture Agreement's green and blue boxes, which are sheltered from reduction commitments because of their lessened or negligible trade distortion.

This approach would turn tariff flexibility and protected subsidies to the advantage of poorer farmers in smaller countries, exempting "food security" crops from reduction commitments and allowing developing countries to subsidize diversification both of crops chosen for production and export and of their economies in general, including development of nonagricultural industries whose production would be higher valued and less dependent on wild swings in world pricing. We question whether the answer to distorted trade caused by protective tariffs and government subsidies rests in immunizing further tariff protection and subsidy schemes, even if the shoe would now be on poor farmers' feet. China's powerful agricultural market in an economy ballooning ahead at a 9 percent growth rate is relatively free of distortive tariffs and government subsidies.[61]

The developed world is in a position to provide, through investment and other trade programs, the improvements to the weak infrastructure and poor business environments that would deliver long-run benefits. In fact, these actions would be much more effective than simply opening its own markets and ending its distorting farm subsidies, which it must do anyway. By encouraging World Bank projects to improve transportation infrastructure, access to credit, and agricultural technology in lesser-developed nations, richer nations can better ensure that the benefits of more open markets will be available to all developing countries, not only those countries with an existing production capacity, such as Brazil.

"Aid for Trade" projects within the WTO are essential to tackle poverty in the extreme situations that we find in Bolivia, Ecuador, Guatemala, and other Latin American countries. Under this approach, in return for greater access to less-developed country markets, developed countries would provide financial assistance to help developing countries boost their export competitiveness with new ports and better communications infrastructure. Market access alone serves only as an open door; it cannot avail countries whose infrastructure is ill positioned to step inside—often as a result of developed nation subsidies and tariff protection in agriculture, textiles, and apparel.

The WTO's Members can unblock the infrastructural barriers to full participation by emerging markets in the growth potential of the global market. Its July 2006 task force recommended action in five discrete areas: training trade officials on how to implement trade agreements and comply with trade rules and standards; promoting underwriting of business activities and investment; conducting market analyses to aid trade growth; building roads and ports; improving productive capacity for goods and services; and providing financial assistance to meet the adjustment costs of trade policy liberalization, including balance of payment problems resulting from lost tariff revenues or from the erosion of preferential market access.[62] We would add to the latter category the absolute need to support the social safety net of trade adjustment assistance to help workers displaced by trade's inevitable rebalancing of production priorities.

The rationale behind nonreciprocal trade preferences, mentioned at the start of this subsection, is to spur development, as are the Doha Round proposals for "duty-free, quota-free" access to developed country markets for imports from the WTO's thirty least-developed Members. Each of these programs includes the agricultural exports most critical to economic growth in these countries. Unless weak infrastructures and poor business environments also are addressed, however, none of these efforts is likely to accomplish substantially increased trade with these Members. Those who truly would help the poor must address the business-impeding bureaucracy and anachronistic judicial systems entrenched in a number of Latin American countries that stand as barriers to private enterprise.[63]

While elimination of agricultural subsidies in developed countries is necessary to open those markets to the developing world, drafters of the Agriculture Agreement also recognized that food security in emerging markets could be threatened by imports from more efficient agricultural producers in the developed world and a general rise in world food prices. We need look no farther than the effects on Mexico's corn farmers when the final tariffs on farm imports from the United States were eliminated in January 2007. For this reason, when the WTO was established, Ministers promised to provide technical and financial assistance to improve agricultural productivity and infrastructure in countries dependent on food imports.[64] No WTO Member has provided such assistance, in part because of complex requirements to prove a causal link between agricultural subsidy reforms and food security problems. Any reasonable amendment to the Agreement on Agriculture must make these promises specific and enforceable under the WTO DSU.

(D)   Beyond Subsidies

Other trade related issues, such as terminator seed technology—seeds that self-destruct after one season so that farmers must purchase new seed every year—"threaten . . . the food security of over one billion poor farmers in third world countries."[65] Thus food security—access to safe, healthy, nutritious food on a regular basis—is intimately related to poverty, especially as "the vast majority of the world's people—70 percent—earn their livelihood by producing food."[66] One activist has observed that "by wasting resources through one-dimensional monocultures maintained with intensive external inputs [fertilizers and pesticides], the new biotechnologies create food insecurity and starvation."[67] Thus, if we look at poverty not only in terms of income but also in terms of access to resources, food insecurity—exacerbated by trade—also is poverty.

The United States has generous subsidies for agribusiness, although these benefits do not reach small North American producers. Sixty percent of the direct payments go to 10 percent of the producers; 50 percent of farmers receive little or no government support. These subsidies hurt Latin America. For example, Brazil is believed to lose one billion per year in orange juice sales to the United States because of U.S. protectionist measures.[68]

One of the key causes of poverty in rural areas is dumping by transnational companies—that is, the exporting of products below production costs. Because of these artificially depressed prices, local farmers lose their own domestic market, often resulting in poverty. When such dumping harms U.S. farmers, "US anti-dumping laws ha[ve] been used against Chilean mushrooms and salmon, . . . fresh flowers from Colombia, Chile, Ecuador, and Mexico, tomatoes from Mexico, and honey from Argentina."[69]

Poverty will only be alleviated if the loss of labor and subsistence agriculture allows the workers remaining in that sector to increase their wages.[70] Small farms are more productive than large farms per unit of land. Therefore, more equitable land distribution helps agricultural efficiency and output. For example, "In Piaui, Brazil, farm yields increased 10-40% on non-irrigated and 30-70% on irrigated fields after land was distributed to small farmers. Equitably distributed land also reduces poverty and improves the distribution of income. For example, in El Salvador, "a 10% increase in land ownership among cultivators raised per capita income by 4%."[71]

12.6 Poverty and Immigration

Over the past several decades, South-North immigration in the Americas has been on the rise, and lack of economic opportunity in one's home country is the principal reason. People migrate to escape poverty; today, millions of people have taken great risks to reach the United States with the hope of obtaining employment in search of economic prosperity through hard work and dedication.

The unspoken assumption that is never questioned is that a "sustainable income is hard to come by in small-town Mexico,"[72] that wages in the United States are consistently "10 times the rate for the same work [in Mexico],"[73] that "the jobs in Mexico don't pay anything,"[74] and that in order to be able to afford the construction of a house in Mexico, one should probably pay for it in remitted U.S. dollars.[75] As noted in section 5.4, former Mexican President Fox took steps to support the emigration that resulted in the much-needed remittances.[76]

U.S. remittances to Mexico and Latin America tell an eloquent story. As the Inter-American Development Bank (IDB) and the Multilateral Investment Fund (MIF) state in their May 2004 study, *Sending Money Home: Remittances to Latin America and the Caribbean*, the region "is both the fastest growing and highest volume remittance market in the world. This is no cause for celebration, however. It means that the Region is not producing enough employment to meet the needs of its population."[77] Between 2002 and 2003, remittance flows increased throughout the entire region: by 11.9 percent in Central America, by 18.3 percent in the Andean countries, and by 7.5 percent in the Caribbean.[78]

It is estimated that more than $30 billion was sent to Latin America and the Caribbean in 2003: $13.3 billion to Mexico (an increase of 35 percent over the previous year), $5.2 billion to Brazil, $3.1 billion to Colombia, $2.3 billion to El Salvador, $2.2 billion to the Dominican Republic, $2.1 billion to Guatemala, $1.7 billion to Ecuador, and $1.2 billion to Peru and Cuba.[79] "In 2003, remittance flows exceeded all combined Foreign Direct Investment and Official Development Assistance to the region. And the volume continues to rise."[80]

Some reports in fact claim that "Remittances Rescue Millions from Poverty."[81] Yet, following the praise for the "estimated 2.5 million people in the region [that] have been able to escape poverty," a conflicting reality arises: "Remittances do little to reduce poverty for the population at large." A 2004 OAS report provides that, far from being a solution to poverty, remittances are just a temporary fix.[82] The Band-Aid nature of remittances is a self-perpetuating cycle. One commentator has noted that remittances are evidence of brain drain; moreover, while remittances create a flow of money, they do not create jobs, effectively "show[ing] that migration does not solve migration."[83]

12.7 Final Thoughts: Changing Paradigms

As this chapter has shown, trade liberalization is not producing its intended results: eradication of poverty, increased productivity, increased development, and an enhanced overall quality of life. It is not even producing more jobs. Thus, the current econometric model must be revisited and redefined to incorporate a human rights ideal that shares with trade the goal of prosperity. Persistent poverty worldwide is resulting in rapidly increasing marginalization of a large proportion of the population.

The motive behind the current global economic paradigm is increased production for enhanced prosperity. Yet as currently deployed, the model measures poverty purely in economic terms and does not account for any of the other dimensions of poverty. Thus, as chapter 5 on trade and citizenship urges that we reconceptualize the idea of citizenship, so too this chapter urges a reconceptualization of the measure of poverty that dovetails with the accepted idea that poverty is a complex, multidimensional phenomenon. Just as citizenship should not be defined in solely political and/or social terms, poverty should not be defined in solely economic terms. Both citizenship and poverty have political, social, cultural, and economic components. Trade and human rights share the goal of poverty eradication.

Section 10.4 recommended that policy officials engage in gender mainstreaming to ensure that decision-makers ask and answer the woman question in each of the myriad human rights contexts in which it arises. Our reconceptualization of poverty requires the WTO and other trade entities to take responsibility not only for trade's effects on poverty's economic face, but also for such defining elements as living in a state of constant fear, disenfranchisement from political life, separation from occupations of the formal economy, vulnerability, and helplessness. This chapter demonstrates that trade rules without a doubt make a substantial, if unwitting, contribution to these unstated dimensions of poverty. Armed with this new poverty paradigm, trade officials will be equipped to "mainstream" the poverty question, identifying courses of action that seek out its multiple causes and effects, including employment, education, nutrition, discrimination, and health.

As long as states continue to connect trade solely to poverty's economic side, they will waste trade's ability—properly engaged—to find holistic solutions to this living condemnation of the nonpoor that has shown itself robustly resistant to purely economic approaches. Trade officials will not come willingly to this table, citing the responsibility of the United Nations and other international organizations. As the preceding chapters explained, however, unless we hold trade rules primarily responsible for using their incalculable power to accomplish the human rights policies that they profess to embrace, other international organizations will struggle unnecessarily with duller blades. The appalling state of world poverty cannot await second-best solutions.

13

Freedom from Famine and Fear

Democracy

13.1 Overview

The emerging right to democratic governance is closely linked to economic rights. As Nobel Prize–winning economist Amartya Sen observed, "Famines have never afflicted any country that is independent, that goes to elections regularly, that has opposition parties to voice criticism, that permits newspapers to report freely and to question the wisdom of government policies without extensive censorship."[1]

There is ongoing debate about whether trade promotes or inhibits democracy. One side cites provisions in trade agreements that allow suits by private investors that invade regulatory arenas, which are traditionally within the sole national discretion of governments—such as labor, health, and the environment—to argue that trade erodes democracy. This side also notes that trade's neoliberal economic policies result in spending cuts that shrink the social safety net. On the other hand, supporters of free trade contend that trade promotes civil and political rights by opening societies to democratic ideas, and points to the correlation between countries' economic openness and their political openness.

This chapter explores whether trade is globalizing democracy or weakening the authority of the state and undermining the ability of governments to care for their citizens. It also explores the important role of "failed states" in deterring human rights progress, as well as how the "splendid isolation" of trade and human rights mimics the larger paradox—especially in today's United States—of the West's commitment in the private sphere to reveling in the spoils of unbridled capitalism while the public sector embarks on a quasi-religious crusade to spread democracy and other human rights to every single person on the face of the earth.

13.2 Human Rights Framework

(A) Democracy as an Emerging Right

There is increasing acceptance in the human rights community that democratic governance constitutes an emerging human right. Thomas Franck has argued that a "democratic entitlement . . . [is moving] from moral prescription to international legal obligation."[2] Support for this claim rests in established international normative standards, principally as set forth in detail below, in the rights to self-determination contained in the UN Charter, ICCPR, and ICESCR, as well as citizens' rights to participate in their government. Indeed, since 1988 the UN General Assembly has adopted resolutions on the desirability of periodic and open elections, and has called for states to "consolidate democracy" by strengthening human rights and fundamental freedoms.[3] In addition, scholars cite the related right to freedom of expression as instrumental to effecting the right to democratic governance.[4]

Historians, lawyers and legal scholars, and economists link this emerging right to other precious rights, including economic rights. For example, as former Assistant Secretary of State and current Dean of Yale Law School Harold Koh observed, "Democracy and genuine respect for human rights remain the best paths for sustainable economic growth."[5] Some historians claim that free-market democracies are prone to peace.[6] Similarly, Sen's observation that famines have never existed in democracies that respect a free press[7] suggests the empowerment that people experience with democracy. When persons are informed, and they have a voice in the ballot box, they can rid themselves of potentially tyrannical rulers.

(B) The Normative Setting

Many human rights documents lay the foundation for the claim to the existence of this right to democracy. In Article 21(1), the Universal Declaration provides that "everyone has the right to take part in the government of his[/her] country, [either] directly or through freely chosen representatives." In addition, it provides that "the will of the people shall be the basis of the authority of government; this will shall be expressed in periodic and genuine elections which shall be by universal and equal suffrage and shall be held by secret vote or by equivalent free voting procedures" (art. 21(3)). Similarly, ICCPR provides that citizens have the right to participate in the public affairs of the country either directly or through elected representatives, as well as have the right "to vote and to be elected at genuine periodic elections which shall be by universal and equal suffrage and shall be held by secret ballot, guaranteeing the free expression of the will of the electors" (art. 25(b)).

In addition to the right to take part in the government, Article 1(1) of both the ICCPR and ICESCR ensures everyone's right to self-determination, which enables persons to "freely determine their political status." The right to self-determination together with the right to participate in government further supports the idea of a right to democracy.

Moreover, regional documents not only ensure rights related to democratic governance, but they also directly address the role of democracy in the region. For example, the American Declaration provides that every individual has a right to "participate in the government of his[/her] country" (art. XX); the provision even creates a duty to vote in popular elections (art. XXXII). ACHR, in its preamble language, centers democratic institutions in the framework being established. At Article 23(1)(b), ACHR establishes the citizen's right to participate in government, and expressly includes the right to vote.

This regional commitment to democracy is patent in and central to the goals of the OAS Charter. The preamble expressly provides that "representative democracy is an indispensable condition for the stability, peace and development of the region." Thus, one of the Charter's essential purposes is "to promote and consolidate representative democracy" (art. 2(b)) with a goal of the region being to "require the political organization of . . . [Member] States on the basis of the effective exercise of representative democracy" (art. 3(d)). Indeed, democracy is so central to the OAS Charter that Article 9 specifically provides that a member may be suspended from its right to participate if its democratically constituted government has been overthrown by force. In fact, this clause was invoked in the 1960s because of the communist nature of Castro's government and formed the basis of Cuba's suspension from the OAS (see Chapter 14 on economic sanctions).

In addition to the direct right of participation, other rights related to democracy are fully protected. These include the protection of freedom of the press,[8] education,[9] assembly,[10] religion,[11] thought,[12] and opinion[13]— all rights that define the environmental context of the participation. Koh observed that "the right to democratic governance is both a means and an end in the struggle for human rights. Where democratic rights are guaranteed, freedom of conscience, expression, religion, and association are all bolstered. In genuine democracies, rights to a fair trial and to personal security are enhanced. Elected leaders gain legitimacy through the democratic process, allowing them to build popular support, even for economic and political reforms that may entail temporary hardships for their people."[14]

13.3 International Trade Framework

On June 2, 2002, the presentation of the U.S. delegation to a meeting of the OAS General Assembly in Barbados, titled *The OAS, Democracy, and Trade*,[15] provided insights into the trade and democracy connection. In support of the FTAA, the United States noted that such an agreement "will fortify a community in the Americas committed to democracy, the rule of law, and market-led, broad-based economic growth. As a precondition for building modern economies and forging 21st-century trade relations, the countries of the Americas have committed themselves to the fundamental freedoms that form the foundation of both democracy and prosperity." Indeed, the United States viewed "representative democracy and the rule of law . . . [as] indispensable to building modern economies, because they promote accountability, transparency, and stability and they spread economic opportunity without favor. . . . Democracy is essential to any global development strategy and trade arrangement, because it empowers the individual to share the costs and the blessings of prosperity." Consequently, it was the position of the United States that "trade furthers freedom by empowering the development of a vital private sector, encouraging the rule of law, spurring economic liberty, and increasing the freedom of choice among persons from all walks of life." The exercise of democracy, the delegation confirmed, included the participation of civil society in the negotiations leading to the crafting of trade agreements.[16]

The agenda of the Summit of the Americas was intended to promote free trade as the essential strategy for making the lives of every person as well as condition of every nation more prosperous. Free trade helps this prosperity because it can create jobs. And democracy, free of corruption, is imperative for prosperity at all levels. As the U.S. delegation stated, "In the simplest terms, while states need markets to function, markets cannot function without effective, legitimate, and law-abiding states. . . . Societies that are open to commerce across their borders are more open to democracy within their borders."[17] Significantly, it appears that the U.S.

delegation accepted the concept of an expansive notion of democracy. The delegation expressly recognized that education—a basic human right[18]—is an essential tool for being able to obtain both democracy and economic progress through trade.[19] Indeed, in this Hemisphere, the OAS embraces the complex nature of the idea of democracy. As articulated in its Charter, among its essential purposes the OAS expressly seeks "to promote and consolidate representative democracy" (art. 2(b)) and "to eradicate extreme poverty which constitutes an obstacle to the full democratic development of the peoples of the hemisphere" (art. 2(g)). Thus the trade and democracy connection is as deep as the human rights and democracy link.

13.4 Democracy, Trade, and Human Rights

(A) The Elements of Democracy

During the Reagan era, the United States actually embraced the view of democracy that equates it to the voting booth. During that time, trade and economic engagement with states was grounded on democracy. Hence the trade, democracy, and human rights link emerged.

Yet, as the discussion below will elucidate, the Reagan approach was a rather superficial idea of democracy. At that cold war–driven, politically charged time, if you had a ballot box and you elected an authoritarian leader, that was considered acceptable. In the Reagan era, flowing from the cold war idea, authoritarianism was preferable to totalitarianism—and both were preferable to communism and socialism. That idea, however, is starting to show signs of serious erosion with the Hamas elections in Palestine and the Chávez and Morales elections in Venezuela and Bolivia, respectively, as we noted in section 2.6(C).

Consequently, the very meaning of democracy must be problematized. One issue is the awkward phrase in Article 21(3) of the Universal Declaration—"or by equivalent free voting procedures"—which raises the question of what might constitute such procedures. Though this phrase is not replicated in the ICCPR, it, too, reinforces the murkiness of the concept of democracy because, at Article 25(b), it provides for "genuine" elections with "genuine" being nowhere defined. The lack of clarity in the concepts has contributed to the contestation of the meaning of democracy. It is thus important to explore what characteristics, other than the existence of popular elections, define the concept of democracy. For example, in our view democracy also must embrace the idea of the voice of the people in the workings of government, including the protection of those who are least able to protect themselves, of the rule of law, of transparency, of a free press.

If human rights standards make "genuine" elections the way for persons to engage in political participation, what constitutes such a "genuine" election must be analyzed. For example, can one consider genuine the 1985 elections in El Salvador? In those elections, all citizens were required to vote.[20] Failure to vote, including a vote of abstention, was viewed as a sign of disloyalty. While these parameters coexisted with a relatively open and national contest, the principal leftist party was excluded by law. The lack of freedom to choose to vote, the monitoring of the votes, and the exclusion of a party from the "elections" at least raise the specter of lack of genuineness in these elections, notwithstanding the existence of the ballot box.

A different and poignant interrogation of the meaning of democracy results when one considers the elections that placed the Nazi Party in power in Germany.[21] Ostensibly, these were free and fair elections. Yet they did not guarantee democracy; rather, they placed in power a most anti-democratic party. Today, some, particularly many in the business community who are experiencing nationalization of private property instead of privatization of government services, might question whether Chávez's ascent to power in Venezuela by way of "free and fair" elections is such an event.

These examples suggest that it is inappropriate—indeed flawed—to equate the right to political participation with elections alone—be they "genuine" or an "equivalent." Rather, it appears that the whole concept of human rights—focusing on rights of individuals qua individuals—needs to be connected to the idea of political participation in a more significant way. In this regard, the concept of elections becomes a proxy for the ability of persons to empower themselves by creating or having a voice in the environment in which they live so that they can fulfill their personhood. It is significant, then, that the idea of the right to participation in government, which dates to the French Revolution, has expanded beyond its original reach. Recall that at the time of the French Revolution slavery existed and around the world women were considered chattel. Thus, in the beginning, the whole concept of democracy and voting was rather un-democratic as far as equal participation. Today, the right to participation forbids restrictions based on personal status such as social or economic status (propertied), cultural background, race, sex, or alphabetism. Indeed, the human rights documents all forbid any such discrimination.

The recognition by the United States of the connection between trade and human rights is paradoxical in light of the splendid isolation in which trade and human rights have existed, which simply mimics the larger paradox articulated in the overview above. Since the George W. Bush administration took office in January 2001, Ukraine, Afghanistan, Iraq, and the Palestinian Authority have, as the result of varying levels of U.S. pressure, elected new, more democratically oriented governments. Similar influence is being applied to Iran, Syria, Egypt, and other autocratic rulers. The Bush administration points to the September 11, 2001, terrorist attacks on the United States as the primary reason for its aggressiveness in spreading democracy, although prior administrations have been equally fervent, without such particular cause, in attempting to reverse military or other dictatorial governance in Haiti, Chile, Nicaragua, and other Latin American nations.

Under the Bush administration, the United States has become a nation obsessed with the undemocratic goal of constructing a *pax Americana* global order enforced through unilateral military power, unencumbered by international law.[22] Yet President Bush also believes that "the case for trade is not just monetary, but moral." In commenting on China's continuing record of human rights violations, he observed that "economic freedom creates habits of liberty. And habits of liberty create expectations of democracy."[23]

This unflagging push for democracy has, of course, its low-road aspects, most visibly the interest in making the world safe for U.S. businesses that flourish in an environment of transparent government regulation, accessible court systems, and an equality of opportunity to prosper. One observer believes that the FTAs that have resulted from the U.S. crusade for global democracy thus are better understood not as instruments of economic integration, but as business contracts building a common legal base to be used by the FTA business partners.[24] As we will often have occasion to observe, pecuniary motivation does not necessarily mean that the result will bring fewer gains to civil society. Democratic governance is a sine qua non of a flourishing market. The business premise does mean that trade negotiators must be vigilant to ensure successful human rights as well as contractual outcomes (see section 13.3).

Nonetheless, the very idea of democracy is anathema to a number of cultures whose populations would benefit greatly if the push was less for a certain kind of governance than for establishment of a tradition of compliance with human rights.

On the other hand, the West's commitment in the private sphere to reveling in the spoils of unbridled capitalism is not sustainable. To be sure, there are those who indict any challenge to capitalism as an ideological opposition to economic liberty and a free market. Mario Vargas Llosa articulately points to the value of a free market: it is responsible for "the extraordinary advances that liberty has made in the long course of human civilization."[25] The list of claimed advances and successes of capitalism and the free market is long, including immeasurable gains in standard of living and quality of life. Included in the praises are the reality that over the last hundred years, notwithstanding two world wars, the world economy has expanded hugely, mostly due to liberal economic policies and a free market in which competition reigns. This front blames government regulation and control for economic crises.

Yet the extent of the reach of the claimed benefits is at best uneven, at worst fanciful. It is true that as economies became more robust, workers earned more. For a century, the common worker's share of national income was constant. Yet in the last twenty years, this has not held true; the workers are losing ground while the rich are getting richer. As Harvard economist Kenneth Rogoff states, "Those at the lower end aren't moving ahead as quickly as the capitalists."[26] He fears that this widespread reality may result in social tensions around the world, and while "conservatives like to say that a rising tide lifts all boats, the New Orleans disaster made it painfully clear what happens to people in deep poverty: they don't even have a boat. . . . This unbridled capitalism in the United States can't be sustained socially." He offers the example of unbridled capitalism's failure by pointing to an all too prevalent practice: with corporate mergers and takeovers, the chief executive obtains multimillion-dollar settlements while thousands of workers simply lose their jobs. Many of these workers cannot find "jobs that provide them with dignity and decent social status."

In an interesting twist, even some who support capitalism and free markets decry the "ethical imperialism" of the West. In this version, "political and cultural social engineers . . . wish to impose their own standards of conduct and institutional reform on the developing countries of the world."[27] This appears to be a direct challenge to the Reagan to Bush policies on democracy.

(B)   The Relation of Trade to Democracy

We mentioned the ongoing debate today about whether trade promotes or inhibits democracy—with interesting and credible social scientific as well as econometric data providing support for both sides. To be sure, there are a number of studies that show direct links between trade and democracy. Those who claim that trade promotes democracy generally cite research showing that increased trade promotes human rights by giving a society access to technology, communications, and the experience with a discussion of democratic ideas. Thus, free trade and its private impetus balance against government power as it creates space for civil societies' participation in enterprise. One author concludes that "the most economically open countries today are more than three times as likely to enjoy full political and civil freedoms as those that are relatively closed."[28] The author suggests that "governments that grant their citizens a large measure of freedom to engage in international commerce find it dauntingly difficult to simultaneously deprive them of political and civil liberties."[29] One study shows that democracy is "significantly related to trade between . . . two states . . . indicating that the more democratic the [state] is, the greater is trade between them likely to be."[30] Thus, the conclusion is that by liberalizing trade not only is prosperity abroad assured, but also a more democratic world. Other authors link democracy and trade by noting that both democracies and economically interdependent states are less likely to engage in militarized disputes with each other.[31]

Those who believe that trade promotes democracy also note that increased trade promotes civil and political rights by opening societies to communications and technologies that disseminate democratic ideas and ideals.[32] Moreover, by promoting growth, and the concomitant emergence of a middle class that is secure and independent, trade provides a counterbalance to excessively authoritarian governmental power. This side cites the high positive correlation between countries' economic openness and their political openness as proof that trade promotes democracy. In all cases, the erosion of national boundaries by globalization, rather than being a negative loss of sovereignty, is a positive consequence that allows individuals to form cross-border alliances to promote their interests.

On the other hand, some argue that trade does not always produce mutual benefits.[33] While the support for the coexistence of trade and democracy rests on studies that assume variables such as perfect competition and certain existing technology, those assumptions do not reflect the reality of trade. Rather, states seek to control trading patterns on behalf of private interests, as well as national interests, thus making regulation of markets a political venture that does not necessarily correlate to democracy and well-being for all.

Indeed, some even posit that trade inhibits democracy—an argument closely linked to the corporate citizenship concerns discussed in chapter 5. Those who side with this argument cite the growing power of a few multinational corporations—noting that of the one hundred largest economies in the world today, fifty-one are global corporations and only forty-nine are states; 70 percent of global trade is controlled by only five hundred companies[34]—and their deleterious impact on sovereignty. Specifically, this side cites the existence of provisions in trade agreements that allow private suits by investors against the state for discriminatory treatment where the state, seeking to protect its citizens, exercises its regulatory power in areas such as labor, health, and the environment.[35] Moreover, trade's neoliberal economic policies such as privatization, liberalization, and deregulation result in cuts in social spending, thus eliminating the social safety net and resulting in great privation, especially for those who already are needy (see chapter 12 on poverty).

This side also claims that rising inequalities—both between states and, as suggested above, between individuals within states—are the result of market forces that allow the rich to get richer and the poor to become poorer. They cite evidence such as the reality that, contrary to the experience in the European Union, where the "poor four" have experienced some convergence with their richer partners, NAFTA's "poor partner"— Mexico—has gone in the opposite direction, with the gap actually widening.[36] In 1982 at the beginning of Mexico's free market reforms, Mexico's per capita income was 40 percent of the North American average; by 2001 it had dropped to 30 percent of the regional average.[37] As the poverty figures in chapter 12 show, the well-being of Mexican civil society has not improved with free trade. If anything their voices' power has been diluted and their socioeconomic status has eroded.

13.5 Final Thoughts

One way to analyze this dilemma of the ostensibly coexisting convergence and divergence of trade with democracy is by parsing out the benefits in light of the "generation" of rights involved. It appears from empirical work that trade and democracy are indeed linked if one takes a narrow view of the connection of trade with civil and political rights, such as the existence of genuine elections.

An analysis of the impact of trade to other rights attached to human well-being, however, can support the view that trade effects an erosion of democratically linked freedoms for individuals. One author points to CAFTA-DR-US[38] as just such an example, a document whose negotiations were "anything but transparent."[39] Without knowledge of the text, which should be available under the right to receive information—one of the rights supposedly attendant to democracy—open debate about its desirability and impact are impossible. Moreover, if one looks not at corporations' right to profit, but at individuals' economic right to work and workers' right to free association—the right to organize—CAFTA-DR-US, like NAFTA, may be a roadblock to, not promoter of, such democracy-associated freedoms.[40]

One example of a potentially negative impact of trade on the right to equality is found in the maquiladoras, where, fueled by promotion of EPZs, the right to sex equality is trammeled. Human Rights Watch (HRW) reports that in Mexico and Guatemala, maquiladoras required women to take pregnancy tests, provided limited or conditional maternity benefits, denied reproductive health care, and even fired some women for being pregnant.[41]

One can conclude, then, that there are links between the human right to democracy and trade. Some are positive, such as the ties that studies show between trade and peace, democracy and increased economic activity—ranging from investment to jobs, democracy, and lack of famine and fear. Yet, at the individual level, trade also detracts from freedoms such as the right to association, to be free from hunger, and to be free of fear (see also chapter 5 on citizenship and chapter 12 on poverty). This volume's linkage of trade and human rights can be the beginning of the discourses that unveil ways to retain trade's benefits in promoting democracy while working to eliminate its erosions of democracy-linked freedoms.

14

Imperial Rules
Economic Sanctions

14.1 Overview

Much of our discussion in previous chapters centered on the ability of states to avoid WTO sanctions for border measures taken in support of human rights principles. Now we address the normative justification and viability of such measures beyond the context of their GATT consistency. Just as international trade laws are a subset of a state's foreign policy, so too are economic sanctions[1]—that is, actions taken by a government that directly restrict the transnational flow of goods, services, or capital. By raising the cost of commercial activities by a foreign government, or its businesses or citizens, an economic sanction registers displeasure with a policy or action of another country, with the ultimate goal of altering the foreign state's behavior.[2] The principal motivations for a state's imposition of economic sanctions are perceived threats to its national security or economic well-being.

Economic sanctions take two principal forms. Financial sanctions involve interruption of development assistance or other foreign aid benefits to the target country and, in the extreme, the freezing of financial assets within control of the country imposing the sanctions. A country executes trade sanctions by interrupting exports of goods and services to the target country or by imposing embargoes or lesser limitations on imports of goods and services from the target country.[3] We will confine our analysis in this volume to the human rights aspects of trade sanctions.

Economic sanctions have two types of human rights effects. First, states have used economic sanctions to discourage human rights violations, as in the case of the U.S. ban of South African gold Krugerrands in 1985 to protest apartheid, the blockage of Nicaraguan imports to deter terrorist acts of the Sandinista regime,[4] prohibiting in 1996 foreign aid to oppose the ruling regime's use of forced labor in Burma,[5] foreign aid denials to five South and Central American countries to protest human rights violations,[6] and the 1989 denial of most-favored nation import status and other sanctions against China to protest the killing of pro-democracy protestors in Tiananmen Square.[7] In fact, U.S. foreign policy has been described as "sanctions based," because the United States has imposed over one hundred such schemes since President Wilson declared their efficacy in the wake of the First World War carnage, and has done so with no obvious normative motivation.[8] Although methods of gauging the effects of statecraft are controversial, a leading analyst estimates that the United States has achieved its purpose about one-third of the time.[9] At the turn of the century, some two-thirds of the world's population in seventy-five countries was subject to one U.S. economic sanction or another, from mislabeling cans of tuna to excessive deforestation to more serious human rights violations such as narcotics trafficking.[10]

Human rights violations have resulted in states jointly taking economic sanctions through the UN Security Council. For example, various North Atlantic Treaty Organization countries began in 1986 to impose sanctions against Libya as a result of Libyan leader Moammar Gaddafi's support for the terrorist killing of 279 passengers aboard an American airliner bombed over Lockerbie, Scotland.[11] The United Nations also imposed economic sanctions on Iraq in 1990 with UN Security Council Resolution 661,[12] calling on Member states to impose trade and financial sanctions against Iraq. The goal of the UN sanctions was to get Saddam Hussein to withdraw from Kuwait, which Iraq had recently invaded. The U.S. sanctions shared this goal, and in addition, were imposed to "condemn . . . gross violations of internationally recognized human rights in Kuwait, including widespread arrests, torture, summary executions, and mass extra-judicial killings."[13]

Another human rights aspect of economic sanctions is their effect on the civil society of the targeted country. By depriving citizens of the benefits of trade, sanctions have led to serious denials of human rights. We will explore both of these aspects in this chapter.

14.2 Human Rights Framework

Article 2(7) of the UN Charter provides that "nothing contained in the present Charter shall authorize the United Nations to intervene in matters which are essentially within the domestic jurisdiction of any state." By definition, the purpose of economic sanctions is to change a state's behavior, so the question in each case will be whether they meet the Charter's allowance by the Security Council of multilateral economic sanctions to preserve the peace and stability of the international system.[14] Article 56's obligation on Member states to respect human rights and fundamental freedoms and "to take joint and separate action in cooperation with the Organization for the achievement of [these] purposes" provides further support for positive action. A better interpretation of this combination of Charter prescriptions is that "economic measures are fully consistent with the Charter's goal of joint and separate action to achieve its human rights goals,"[15] although human rights advocates have taken the United States and other countries to task for turning the rhetoric of human rights on its head for domestic political ends.[16]

Because this book focuses on the Americas, it is pertinent to mention that the OAS Charter specifically prohibits the imposition of economic sanctions. Article 20 provides that "no State may use or encourage the use of coercive measures of an economic or political character in order to force the sovereign will of another State and obtain from it advantages of any kind." Thus, the framework for economic sanctions in the Americas is one of unqualified prohibition. Similarly, Article 19 forbids states to intervene in the affairs of another state and expressly notes that the prohibition addresses an interference or a threat against the state that includes but is not limited to armed force.

14.3 International Trade Framework

Thirty industrialized WTO Members have implemented the authority provided by the GATT's trade and development provisions to establish preference regimes, such as the U.S. Generalized System of Preferences (GSP), that grant unilateral, nonreciprocal, duty-free treatment to products imported from the 120 WTO Members considered to be LDCs.[17] Some Members operate these preference programs as part of their economic sanction policy. For example, in the United States and the EU, assistance to economic development and diversification of Emerging Market countries is conditioned on their satisfactory progress toward realization of certain human rights, including in particular worker rights and elimination of drug trafficking.[18] Worker rights enforcement in the United States includes a ban on entry of products of forced, indentured, or prison labor.[19] The U.S. law also authorizes withholding of development and security assistance and trade benefits from countries that engage in a "consistent pattern of gross violations of internationally recognized human rights."[20] An example of a law targeted to one country's human rights behavior, the Federal Burma Statute requires periodic reports to Congress on the progress toward democratization in that country.[21]

Europe's scheme grants additional preferences to LDCs that meet internationally recognized labor and environmental standards. The EU's differential preference scheme to promote human rights has been upheld as meeting the nondiscriminatory provisions of the WTO's special and differential treatment provisions.[22]

Beginning in the 1970s, the United States began to impose sanctions for human rights reasons in earnest. Burma, Suriname, Haiti, the Sudan, and Somalia all felt the reach of U.S. sanctions to protect human rights.[23] In 1991 the United States imposed economic sanctions on Haiti to encourage return of democratic rule in the face of a military coup that had resulted in extrajudicial executions, disappearances, torture, rape, and limitations on freedom of association and assembly.[24] The Comprehensive Anti-Apartheid Act of 1986 imposed an array of economic sanctions aimed at forcing South Africa to reverse apartheid.[25] In 1981 the United States imposed economic sanctions to cause Poland to "free those in arbitrary detention, to lift martial law, and to restore the internationally recognized rights of the Polish people to free speech and association."[26] In 2003, joined by many other nations, the United States imposed sanctions against Burma to protest the ruling regime's torture of objectors, conscription of child soldiers, ethnic cleansing of minorities, and government-sponsored use of forced and slave labor.[27]

14.4 Judging Economic Sanctions

Under what circumstances should we consider economic sanctions justified? This debate should entail consideration of four principal issues. First, is the sanction legal? Section 14.6 discusses whether such sanctions as the U.S. Helms-Burton law against Cuba are justified under various treaties or customary international law. Second, is the state morally justified in imposing the sanctions? It is more likely to find greater public support for refusing to trade with a government that persecutes religious minorities than with one that is financially corrupt. The third issue is normative. Does the state apply economic sanctions to enforce human rights policies and not as a disguised means to protect its industries or to accomplish other domestic political purposes? Unlike the second factor, this issue seeks a consistently applied standard that is not simply reactive to current political forces.

The final gauge of the propriety of an economic sanction is whether it accomplishes its objective without major adverse effects. The opportunity cost to business in the country imposing the sanction and the negative effects on the citizens of the sanctioned state are weighed against the likelihood that the sanctions will change the targeted behavior.

14.5 Human Rights Impact of Economic Sanctions

Analysis of the history of economic sanctions reveals a compelling reality. U.S imposition of economic sanctions for human rights purposes is an example of the divide between countries that embrace civil and political rights, on one hand, and those that favor economic, cultural, and social rights, on the other. The United States imposes economic sanctions principally to support civil and political rights. Where these sanctions cause severe human suffering, they jeopardize the economic, social, and cultural rights of civil society inside the sanctioned country by, for example, destroying jobs, contributing to poor health conditions, and increasing hunger and poverty. Thus, the same sanctions that are imposed to end human rights violations of a civil and political nature are causing human rights violations of an economic, social, and cultural nature in the same country.[28] For example, U.S. sanctions on Burma have "caused 400,000 layoffs . . . mainly women working in the textile industry."[29] Many women who have already lost their jobs in the textile industry have been forced into prostitution, a tragic end in itself as well as because it is a prescription for early death from AIDS. Sanctions against Haiti's military regime made food very expensive, reduced the availability of medicine and medical supplies, stopped garbage collection and the maintenance of sewage treatment plants, and decreased the supply of drinking water.[30] Economic sanctions with these kinds of results not only send the message that economic, social, and cultural rights inhabit a lower plane than civil and political rights, but also are themselves inhumane.

These examples, which are representative, argue that U.S. unilateral sanctions are inconsistent with the nature of international human rights as indivisible and interdependent. U.S. economic sanctions contribute to the setting of the civil and political human rights norms favored by the United States, but do so by subordinating and sometimes negatively affecting economic, social, and cultural rights that are a higher priority in other countries. This approach erodes the equal footing of both generations of rights.[31]

By no means are adverse effects on economic, social, and cultural rights limited to U.S. sanctions. Sanctions taken by the U.N. Security Council have caused disturbance of food distribution channels, interfered with the right to work, made provision of clean drinking water and quality food unreliable, disrupted delivery of drugs and medical supplies, and interfered with operation of education and public health systems.[32] Even the humanitarian exemptions built into these UN-sponsored sanctions did not fully alleviate the adverse effects.[33] States may not logically argue that full achievement of the objectives of the economic sanctions cannot be achieved without disturbance of certain human rights in the targeted country. Citizens of the targeted country do not forfeit their basic economic, social, and cultural rights by reason of violation by political leaders of their civil and political rights, or for that matter of international peace and security: "Lawlessness of one kind should not be met by lawlessness of another kind which pays no heed to the fundamental rights that underlie and give legitimacy to any such collection action."[34]

The principal study of the effects of economic sanctions on human rights bluntly concluded that "under sanctions, the middle class is eliminated, the poor get poorer, and the rich get richer as they take control of smuggling and the black market."[35] "In the long run," the report continued, "as democratic participation, independent institutions and the middle class are weakened, and as social disruption leaves the population less able to resist the Government, the possibility of democracy shrinks."[36] Reacting to these unacceptable human rights impacts, the United Nations has endorsed so-called smart sanctions that target the personal financial assets and access to financial markets of the ruling elite in ways that avoid harmful general effects on the populace and cannot easily be exploited by a despotic leader into "a pretext for eliminating domestic sources of political opposition."[37]

A retired foreign service officer with personal experience in the use of sanctions believes that the United States cannot afford to forgo the use of sanctions, leaving the choices only diplomacy or war:

> Sanctions can work. They proved critical to getting the Dayton Accords that ended the War in Bosnia. They convinced the Serbian Government to turn Milosevic over to the Hague for trial. They landed the Libyan

terrorists al-Megrhia and Fhimah in a Scottish Court. They played an important role in restoring democracy to Haiti and Nicaragua, and in ending apartheid in Rhodesia and South Africa. During the critical days after Iraq's invasion of Kuwait, sanctions held Saddam Hussein at bay, stopping him from taking advantage of Kuwaiti oil or fortifying his military to resist the international coalition that was raised against him.[38]

14.6 Conundrum of Cuba

(A) History

Although Cuba had been in the U.S. sphere of influence prior to Castro taking power in 1959, chilly relations commenced shortly after the revolution.[39] In 1960 President Eisenhower broke off relations with Cuba when the Cuban government nationalized enterprises and property of U.S. citizens. These nationalizations were a reaction by Castro to a July 6, 1960, amendment to the Sugar Act of 1948 that permitted the U.S. president unilaterally to reduce the quota of sugar imported from Cuba. The same day that Congress granted president Eisenhower this discretionary power, he exercised it.

In response, that same day the Cuban Council of Ministers adopted Law No. 851, which characterized the U.S. action as an "act of aggression" and gave the Cuban president and prime minister the power to nationalize, by forced expropriation, property or enterprises in which American nationals had an interest—a power that Castro, too, immediately exercised.

In addition to breaking off relations with Cuba, the U.S. reaction to the nationalizations was to seek the destabilization of the Castro regime. To achieve this goal, in 1960 the United States imposed an economic embargo on exports to Cuba and in 1962 imposed an embargo on imports. These actions were possible under the Trading with the Enemy Act of 1917,[40] which allowed the president to act during peacetime and wartime emergencies. In 1977 the Act was amended, prospectively, to apply only in wartime,[41] but any emergency declared prior to the enactment of the amendment could be extended year by year, thus allowing grandfathering in of the U.S. embargo against Cuba.[42] Every year since the passing of the amendment, U.S. presidents have extended the embargo in the national interest.

In 1992, thirty years after the initial embargo, the Cuban Democracy Act[43] (CDA or "Torricelli Law") marked the tightening of U.S. economic policy toward Cuba. The extraterritorial reach of the CDA's provisions is at the heart of the virtually universal challenge to their legality under accepted international norms. The most controversial of the CDA's provisions is the restoration of an aspect of the 1962 embargo that had been repealed in 1975 prohibiting foreign subsidiaries of U.S. corporations from doing business with Cuba.

The international community has opposed the embargo, and this provision in particular, on the basis of impermissible interference with state sovereignty. Annually, since 1992 when the CDA was only pending in Congress, the European Community (as the EU was then known) has objected in the UN General Assembly to the prohibition of foreign-owned subsidiaries, incorporated and domiciled outside the United States, from trading with Cuba.[44] The basis of the objection is that, under international law, the nationality of a corporate entity is the state of its incorporation. By including wholly owned subsidiaries of U.S. corporations in its jurisdictional reach, through the CDA the United States is seeking to exercise jurisdiction over corporate entities that, pursuant to international law, are foreign (i.e., non-U.S. corporations).

Every year since then, the General Assembly has adopted resolutions entitled "Necessity of Ending the Economic, Commercial and Financial Embargo Imposed by the United States of America Against Cuba," which provide that the General Assembly is "concerned about the promulgation and application by Member States of laws and regulations whose extraterritorial effects affect the sovereignty of other States and the legitimate interests of entities or persons under their jurisdiction, as well as the freedom of trade and navigation."[45] The resolutions call on "States to refrain from promulgating and applying laws and measures of the kind" and urge the repeal of such laws.[46]

On March 12, 1996, President Bill Clinton signed into law the Cuban Liberty and Democratic Solidarity Act (Libertad),[47] commonly known as the Helms-Burton Act. This Act codified the economic sanctions against Cuba imposed by executive orders issued by previous presidents. Besides strengthening the embargo, it establishes a cause of action for former Cuban nationals who have become U.S. citizens, as well as U.S. nationals who lost property or assets in the nationalization. It also prohibits trafficking in confiscated property and allows the denial of visas for entry into the United States to anyone who traffics in nationalized property.

The United States is not the only country that has enacted an economic embargo against Cuba. The 1962 Proclamation of the Meeting of Ministers of Foreign Affairs of the OAS, at Punta del Este, Uruguay, allowed for the United States and other countries to impose an economic embargo against Cuba.[48] In 1975, at the sixteenth meeting of the Consultation of Ministers of Foreign Affairs of the OAS, however, the group adopted a resolution to permit individual Members to reestablish relations with Cuba pursuant to national interests and policy.[49] Since that resolution was passed, virtually every OAS Member has established relations with Cuba—both diplomatic and economic. Moreover, in August 1996, an OAS Committee declared that the Helms-Burton Act was illegal as it sought to exercise jurisdiction in a manner contrary to international norms.

(B) Legality of the Helms-Burton Act Under Customary International Law

The controversial provisions of the Helms-Burton Act include Title III, which allows U.S. nationals to seek compensation in U.S. courts for property losses from Castro's seizures, and Title IV's denial of U.S. entry to foreign nationals who "traffic" in expropriated property of a U.S. citizen. In this case, the legality of a unilateral economic sanction turns on the nature of the legal system—civil or common law—that we employ in the analysis. In common law systems, application of national law to activities that occur outside state territory depends on whether there is a substantial relationship between the law and the foreign activity. Civil law doctrine would never find appropriate the application of national laws outside the national territory without some national interest nexus.

Customary international law supports the "objective territorial principle" taken by the *Baker*[50] case. A country can take action under its laws when a foreign activity has substantially negative impacts within its territory. An American Bar Association (ABA) Recommendation on the subject agrees that the substantial effects test is part of the territorial principle.[51] The Recommendation does not challenge basing sanctions on extraterritorial action, only on applying those sanctions to a company that is, in fact, a national of another state through its incorporation elsewhere, even if it is a wholly owned subsidiary of a U.S. company.

(C) WTO Legality of U.S. Sanctions Against Cuba

Title IV's effects on the ability of European corporations doing business in Cuba—most of them subsidiaries of U.S. firms—thereafter to trade with the United States, led the European Commission to challenge Helms-Burton as violative of the nondiscrimination provisions of the GATT's Four Pillars (see section 2.3). The United States announced that its actions were justified under GATT Article XXI as national security measures and that, because that Article left national security measures to the sole discretion of each Member, a WTO dispute settlement panel would have nothing to decide.[52]

Article XXI(b)(iii) provides that "nothing in this Agreement shall be construed . . . to prevent a [WTO Member] from taking any action which *it* considers necessary for the protection of its essential security interests . . . taken in time of war or other emergency in international relations" (emphasis added). Legal experts disagree about whether this standard is self-judging. One side contends that the drafters could not have intended to leave to the complete discretion of Members any action taken under Article XXI because the term "emergency in international relations" describes an extreme and unusual occurrence that is eminently subject to analysis by dispute panels.[53] In the absence of a declaration of war against Cuba, the United States must establish an emergency in international relations, which, under this theory, must be interpreted as having a close relationship to war. Another reason to suggest that no emergency in international relations exists is the consistent vote by the UN General Assembly against the U.S. embargo of Cuba. In this view, Cuba's shooting down of an aircraft flown by Cuban exiles in 1996 is a relatively minor incident that cannot be considered an international wrong by that country. Another view is that, because Article XXI is on its face self-judging, there can be no interpretive role for a dispute panel, and assumption of jurisdiction over such a measure thus serves no purpose.[54]

These theories of the appropriate interpretation of GATT Article XXI were not adjudicated. The United States and Europe settled the dispute by U.S. agreement that the president would waive application of Title IV, as the U.S. Congress had authorized him to do.

(D)   Effectiveness of Sanctions Against Cuba

Trade sanctions hurt workers and industries, not the officials who authored the policies that are the target of the sanctions. The countries most likely to face sanctions are those run by undemocratic governments least likely to let the pain of their population sway them.

While in nearly fifty years of the embargo the purported goal of achieving democracy in Cuba has not been met, the embargo has had deleterious effects on Cuba and the Cuban people. In 1958 the United States accounted for 67 percent of Cuba's exports and 70 percent of its imports,[55] placing it seventh on both export and import markets of the United States.[56] In 1999, by contrast, official U.S. exports to Cuba totaled $4.7 million, mainly donations of medical aid, pharmaceuticals, and other forms of charitable assistance,[57] and Cuba ranked 184th of 189 importers of U.S. agricultural products in the year 2000.[58] The relaxation of sanctions against food and medicines beginning in 2000 found Cuba rising to 138th in 2001 and to 26th in 2004.[59] By 2006, Cuba's ranking had fallen slightly to become the 33rd largest market for U.S. agricultural exports (exports totaling $328 million).[60] The U.S. International Trade Commission estimates an ongoing annual loss to all U.S. exporters of approximately $1.2 billion for their inability to trade with Cuba.[61]

The Cuban government estimates that the total direct economic impact caused by the embargo is eighty-six billion dollars, which includes loss of export earnings, additional costs for import, and a suppression of the growth of the Cuban economy.[62] Various economic researchers and the U.S. State Department, however, discount the effect of the embargo and suggest that the Cuban problem is one of lack of hard foreign currency, which renders Cuba unable to purchase goods that it needs in the open market.[63]

That there has been an economic impact of the embargo is evident to anyone who visits Cuba. For example, there is a minuscule number of modern automobiles on the roads of Cuba. Most are American vehicles from the late 1950s—prior to the embargo. To be sure, because the law prohibits ships from entering U.S. ports for six months after making deliveries to Cuba, the policy effectively denies Cuba access to the U.S. automobile market.[64]

As noted above in section 14.1, however, the impacts of economic sanctions are greater than lack of access to goods. In the case of Cuba, some argue that the U.S. embargo has had a deleterious impact on nutrition and health with a lack of availability of medicine and equipment, as well as decreased water quality.[65] Indeed, the American Association for World Health (AAWH), in a 1997 report, concluded that "the U.S. embargo of Cuba has dramatically harmed the health and nutrition of large numbers of ordinary Cuban citizens. . . . [I]t is our expert medical opinion that the U.S. embargo has caused a significant rise in suffering—and even deaths—in Cuba. . . . A humanitarian catastrophe has been averted only because the Cuban government has maintained a high level of budgetary support for a health care system designed to deliver primary and preventive health care to all of its citizens."[66] Thus, AAWH concludes that the embargo, limiting availability of food, medicine, and medical supplies, has a deleterious effect on Cuban society. Significantly, religious leaders, including the late Pope John Paul II, opposed the embargo and called for its end.[67] The gravamen of the objection is the humanitarian and economic hardships that the embargo cause.

(E)   The Irony of Remittances

The purpose of the embargo is to strangle Cuba's economy; yet, remittances play a large role in holding up the economy of Cuba: "At more than $50 billion a year, family remittances are central to economic growth, national expenditures, and balance of payments for many countries in Latin America and the Caribbean. Remittances now exceed portfolio investment, foreign aid, and government or private borrowing, and they have proven to be remarkably stable, often increasing when economies falter."[68] The U.S. State Department estimates that remittances to Cuba range from $600 million to $1 billion per year, with the great bulk coming from families in the United States.[69] A 2004 report on Cuban economic development confirms this range, estimating that remittances to the island from U.S. residents totaled approximately $900 million in 2003, which represented about 3 percent of the country's GDP. This amount of money would have "determinative influence on the country's financial stability and on the level of consumption of households."[70] These figures contrast with survey of individuals which placed the remittances in $460 million range.[71]

In 2004, U.S. regulations changed so as to narrow the allowed remittances that can be sent as well as the people to whom they can be sent. Regulations now permit remittances to be sent only to immediate family; there is a prohibition on remittances to certain government officials and members of the Communist Party. The total amount of remittances that may be taken to Cuba is currently only three hundred dollars, dramatically down from three thousand.[72] Interestingly, a study showed that a year after the new, more restrictive regulations were implemented, the flow of funds to Cuba remained unchanged.[73] Although the more restrictive regulations may not have decreased the flow of funds to Cuba, polls reveal that some Cubans believe that they are receiving less money. The most likely explanation for this phenomenon is that the Cuban government is finding means to capture a greater percentage of the money that is being sent.[74]

In light of the embargo, the existence and level of remittances is significant. The Cuban government benefits from the remittances by permitting Cubans to shop in state-operated "dollar stores," which sell food and other household necessities that are otherwise unavailable in Cuba. These stores' sales are at high markups—sometimes estimated at over 240 percent of face value.[75]

In an action consistent with the embargo policy and goals, the administration's June 2004 tightening of restrictions on remittances also tightened allowed travel, potentially cutting off another source of funds to the island. It is estimated that in 2003 there were 125,000 family visits to Cuba, which resulted in approximately ninety-six million dollars in hard currency for the Cuban government.[76] Thus, the tightened travel restrictions in both family and education categories work along with the embargo in limiting the funds that reach the island.

Remittances can be reconciled with the official policy of the embargo—even the limited remittances under the new, more restrictive regulations—on the premise that the sending of remittances is a private, family affair.[77] Thus, while the embargo seeks to strangle the weak Cuban economy, allowing private parties to make remittances to families can be viewed as a private affair into which government should not intrude. Such perspective notwithstanding, one has to reconcile the changing regulations with respect to remittances. To be sure, the current decrease in levels of remittances allowed permit the United States to acknowledge the private nature of the actions while seeking to maintain a coherent foreign policy of not providing economic support to the government of Cuba. Nonetheless, "Remittances are helping to stabilize a society hurt by economic crisis and the inequalities generated by a bureaucratic power structure."[78] The impact on family members in Cuba, as with remittances sent to other parts of Latin America (see section 12.6), is to help people, especially family members, out of poverty—helping them "cope with austerity and scarcity" as well as indirectly to strengthen the emerging market economy.[79]

14.7 Final Thoughts: Value of Economic Sanctions

Section 14.5 shows that the human rights fallout from economic sanctions is not limited to the Cuban embargo. Nonetheless, economic sanctions can play a valid role in ending human rights abuse, especially when undertaken as agreed multilateral action by the UN Security Council. As section 14.5 noted, sanctions can work and, in any event, will be preferable to war if diplomatic solutions fail. Because they can reach financial assets in all UN states, UN actions are likely to be more successful in limiting effects through a "smart sanctions" approach aimed at the perpetrators of the human rights violations and not the state's innocent civil society.

Targeting the financial assets in other countries of human rights despots also may cause the economic hardships to the state's civil society to increase as the leaders seek substitutes for their lost caches. The alternative of economic embargoes, however, even with food and medicine exceptions (which in any event are essential), so clearly has adverse human rights consequences that it should stand as a last resort. Even multilateral sanctions should not be undertaken unless they pass the test outlined in section 14.4. One wonders how many sanctions states would undertake if they considered carefully whether the proposed action accords with international law, whether it is morally justified by the acts or omissions of the target state's leaders, whether it fits the state's well-vetted normative framework for sanctions, and whether the action will accomplish its purpose without causing major adverse effects on civil society. The Cuban embargo could not survive that inquiry, nor could many other sanctions that states have imposed in the heat of the moment.

15

Recognizing Indivisibility, Bridging Divides

Visions and Solutions for the Future of the Trade and Human Rights Relationship

15.1 Overview

As the forces of globalization continue to explode into ever more intrusive corners of our lives, the splendid isolation of the human rights and trade regimes is in fact no longer possible, even if it were desirable. The question that we have tried to answer in this volume is whether that integration will be purposeful, conspicuous, proactive, and ingenious—that is, splendid in both design and reach, or more of the ad hoc mélange of superficial and isolated duct-tape "solutions" that we have had so far to endure. Economic expansion not only is consistent with responding to human rights obligations, but is emboldened precisely to the extent of that response. Well-fed, healthy, educated, enfranchised, rested, comfortably clothed, non-oppressed, non-marginalized, trusting workers are the essence of efficient, reliable, and loyal humanized engines of business. Such individuals also are more active in the political sphere, where democratic participation will reduce public corruption and promote social justice, which in turn will spur both internal growth and foreign investment. The social well-being of the individual is inseparable from the economic well-being of the world.

Our Final Thoughts sections have suggested specific ways of pursuing a holistic vision of trade and human rights in order to make social and economic well-being synergistic. For example, in discussing the changing nature of citizenship, we urge that we not forget the individual voice as we listen to the powerful economic actors. Similarly, in scrutinizing the global persistence of poverty and women's subordination, we propose the "mainstreaming" of the woman and poverty questions in order to account for such concerns in trade policy and in trade agreements.

In analyzing the related issues of labor and trafficking, we note that neither legal nor policy bases permit TNCs to engage in exploitative labor practices even if they can be blamed on a perverted perspective on comparative advantage. Workers cannot be asked to shoulder such a burden or to labor under substandard conditions. It is trade's success that has created vacuums in labor forces of unskilled or semiskilled workers. It is unacceptable, however, to fill these vacuums with persons trafficked for labor. It is also intolerable to expect workers to surrender the human rights to freedom of association, freedom from discrimination, to fair wages, healthy working conditions, and dignity in the workplace.

In the analysis of the closely related human rights to health, to indigenous cultures, and to a healthy environment, we urge the United States and other recalcitrant developed countries to confirm their oft-stated commitment to these key concerns by ratifying promptly the CBD and its Biosafety Protocol. These treaties at once offer specific solutions to controversial food safety issues arising from GMOs, protect traditional knowledge of indigenous populations, and preserve the shrinking biodiversity on which we rely for health and sustainable development, and on which first peoples depend for their livelihoods and their culture.

As to the human right to health, developed countries must refrain from filing WTO or FTA challenges to good faith attempts by LDCs to bring in essential medicines for epidemics faced by their citizens, such as HIV/AIDS, malaria, tuberculosis, and dengue fever. The rules in this area are highly technical; for example, in the revision to the TRIPS Agreement to permit WTO Members without generic drug industries to obtain generic medicines from other countries, members must seek licensing on a drug-by-drug, country-by-country basis that slows relief and minimizes economies of scale. Splitting hairs with legal niceties in this area is little more than playing technical games with life-threatening consequences when all civilized nations recognize that keeping drug prices high in the face of epidemics is unconscionable. Moreover, developed countries must stop imposing "TRIPS-plus" provisions on emerging market nations through FTAs, which these countries need to take advantage of trade's promise. These provisions, which lengthen periods of patent protection and delay development of generic substitutes, create new and unjustifiable impediments to timely dissemination of essential medicines.

As to protecting the environment, much of the work lies in the hands of the WTC. The Appellate Body from the start has demonstrated its sensitivity to the place of trade law within the larger body of international law. It has elevated trade's exceptions for human rights policies to the same plane as trade's fundamental nondiscrimination principles. The WTC must continue to integrate WTO rules with the human rights *acquis*. Because PPMs are the lifeblood of human rights, the WTC also must reverse GATT's legally unjustifiable PPM distinction, which has been destructive of opportunities over the years for successful integration of trade law's economic growth with human rights law's improvement of the human condition.

To this same end, the WTC must continue to bring customary human rights norms to bear on interpretation of provisions in WTO Agreements and to trump those inconsistent WTO provisions that hold a lower place in the international law hierarchy. To resurrect for human rights restrictions the GATT Article III safe harbor, the WTC must be vigilant in instructing panels to take account of the human rights impact of an imported product as part of the consideration of the product's "likeness" with other products.

15.2 Human Rights Approach to Trade, Trade Approach to Human Rights

(A) Synchronicity or Conflict?

Not only are there few direct contradictions between international human rights law and international trade law, at bottom there is greatly more synchronicity than conflict. The Marrakesh Agreement, which established the WTO, does not seek economic growth as an end, but as a means to raise standards of living, to ensure full employment, to help developing countries secure a share in the growth engendered by trade, to grow consistently with sustainable development, and to protect the environment. These are objectives focused on individuals, on human beings, not transnational corporations. Ultimately, these goals bespeak the same ends as do human rights: increasing human dignity.[1]

A special responsibility to seek consistency between trade and human rights rules exists because of the universal recognition that human rights treaties define the standards of right and wrong treatment of civil society.

The many public welfare clauses in the GATT and in other WTO Agreements provide meaningful opportunities to meet this responsibility.[2] Until recently, the UNCHR has been content to condemn the WTO as a "veritable nightmare" for developing countries and women for the reasons that we have discussed, including that the WTO's founding instruments make only oblique reference to human rights and its rules are gender-insensitive.[3] In response to criticism of the antimarket bias of these "nightmare" reports,[4] recent UNCHR analyses examine the human rights dimensions of trade rules and suggest explicit WTO recognition that promotion of human rights is a trade objective.[5] Rather than simply vilifying the WTO as anathema to realization of human rights, the UNCHR has begun to seek this "soft law" approach to interpretation of WTO provisions, in pursuit of "consistency between the progressive liberalization of trade and the progressive realization of human rights."[6] As Professor Petersmann has observed: "Human rights must guide the interpretation, not only of GATT's 'exceptions' and safeguards clauses, but also of the interpretation of the basic WTO guarantees of freedom, non-discrimination, property rights and the rule of law which protect corresponding human rights values of individual liberty, non-discrimination, private property and access to courts."[7] Former WTO legal affairs officer Professor Joost Pauwelyn reminds us that the WTO "was not negotiated for the benefit only of exporters or free traders" and "must consequently take account of interests in favor of both trade liberalization and nontrade values necessitating trade restrictions."[8]

Many of the human rights that intersect with trade are customary. Moreover, every WTO Member has ratified at least one of the major UN human rights conventions and has, through these treaties and through the UN Charter itself, taken on the obligation to promote and protect human rights. Three-fourths have ratified the 1966 ICESCR and all but one—the United States—have ratified the CRC. The WTO would enhance its democratic legitimacy by an explicit recognition of the human rights obligations of its Members and agreement that these obligations serve as relevant legal context for the interpretation and implementation of WTO rules.[9]

At first glance, such recognition would seem only to restate the obvious, that the WTO Agreements do not exist in a vacuum. Rather, they reside among all other public international law, including human rights treaties and custom. With respect to interpretation of WTO Agreements, such a commitment would only reinforce the direction already securely mapped by the WTO Appellate Body in a line of uncompromising decisions that squarely position global trade rules to be conversant with other international law. With respect to state implementation of WTO Agreements, requiring a human rights approach would have significant consequences. International human rights law must be the blueprint used to design new trading rules and it must be the yardstick by which the success of these rules is measured.

The necessity that trade agreements and their interpretation take account of human rights does not mean that the human rights field cannot learn much from trade. Trade is often criticized for being utilitarian— willing to compromise to reach agreement. Because they spring from natural law, human rights are less subject to compromise, if at all. How does one choose between elimination of the worst forms of child labor and bringing additional jobs to a poverty-stricken people? Is a dictator who deprives civil society of its human rights in order to participate in political life justified because he implements a larger social safety net for marginal members of society?

(B) Common Normative Foundations of Human Rights and Trade Law

Section 4.2(B) explained the similar inspirations and paths of modern international human rights and international trade law. In pursuit of splendid integration, we now emphasize their common normative foundations in the concept of nondiscrimination. Discrimination plays a prominent role in every human rights convention as the first enemy of whatever right is being protected. One cannot envision achieving the goals of the treaties without promoting equality and fairness in society by protecting the marginalized, the socially excluded, minorities, women, and civil society's other vulnerable members. Interestingly, as presented in chapter 2, global trading rules also rest on a foundation of nondiscrimination, of equal treatment of goods and services like those in other WTO Members or within the importing Member's bounds. If nothing else, these shaping principles demonstrate a shared foundation in equality, democratic governance, and the rule of law. Neither human rights nor free markets may be realized without democratic governance, as discussed in chapter 13, and nondiscrimination is an essential element. An in-depth review of the disciplines' underlying foundational premises reveals that trade and human rights do not, after all, speak different languages or spring from alien cultures. Their nonintegration results primarily from a simple lack of serious dialogue.

Pessimists might observe that although the nondiscrimination foundations are the same, the beneficiaries are not. Because trade rules accord higher priority to nondiscrimination in trade than to nondiscrimination in the treatment of individuals, trade in fact discriminates in favor of the rich, the West, men, and the educated. Nondiscrimination in trade can also be a two-edged sword, allowing a Member to deny to foreign products and services what it chooses not to provide to its own citizens, instead of requiring the minimum standards set out in human rights treaties. Indeed, trade's nondiscrimination persona can harm or help human rights objectives, depending on how governments use it. No modern government can deny knowledge of trade's creation of both winners and losers, enormous profits to transnational companies and other businesses that catch trade's sweeping wave, but increasing inequality, exclusion, and marginalization for the majority of civil society—whether in emerging or developed trading partners—whose skill sets fail to match the present needs of the global market.

Economists remind us that trade naturally tends to create a wider dispersion of wealth out from the averages—every OECD country is now experiencing this effect. The rich get richer and the poor get poorer, even if overall fewer people are living in poverty because of new and better jobs—jobs not available to the geographically immobile (such as women) or to indigenous populations or the undereducated. Economists can properly treat these domestic redistribution effects as someone else's problem. Trade negotiators, however, cannot, but must grapple during actual negotiations with their remediation.[10]

We have for this reason repeatedly emphasized that no responsible government should enter into a trade agreement or otherwise participate in the global market without committing to maintain a fully funded (proportionate to its wealth) safety net for trade's displaced industries, workers, and towns. Although the United States spends proportionally less per capita on general labor adjustment programs than most developed nations, its Trade Adjustment Assistance Program, while nominal until the American public finally noticed trade's effects after the NAFTA entered into force, has evolved into a model of what nations must strive to accomplish when jobs are lost as a result of trade. Gaps remain, including coverage for loss of service jobs, but the U.S. program marks the path for addressing not only compensation for income lost through trade's creative destruction (including job insurance that pays one-half the lost job's salary), but also in securing reeducation in alternate skills and replacement of the tax base lost when major sources of a town's employment move offshore as a result of competition from comparatively advantaged foreign producers.[11] Admittedly, the Program's existence stems less from eleemosynary intentions than from the need to overcome endemic opposition to trade liberalization from a nation not yet dependent on exports. The linkage of trade agreements with a social safety net—that is, with concern for the human rights implications of increased trade—is an important archetype for developed and developing nations alike. Attention to this linkage must become an explicit aspect of negotiation of trade agreements, not simply an afterthought when predictable job discombobulation occurs.

15.3 Small Steps: Ending Trade's Splendid Isolation from Human Rights

(A) The Place of Human Rights Law in WTO Rules

With the unremitting and inevitable intersections described throughout this volume, trade and human rights would seem ideal candidates for natural alliance to accomplish their complementary goals.[12] Trade's guarantees of collective freedom, nondiscrimination, property rights, and the rule of law protect the corresponding human rights to individual liberty, protection from discrimination, the right to private property, and guaranteed access to the judicial system.[13] We have seen the tragic reality—neither alliance nor coordination; often even simple recognition of the other policy is lacking.

Three propositions portend for us the way to end trade's splendid isolation from human rights. First, global trade rules contain an abundance of effective but unexplored safe harbors to shelter human rights measures from sanctions for violation of trade's nondiscrimination and other defining pillars. Second, the unheralded indirect effects of both the WTO and FTAs in forcing governments to act with greater transparency and accountability have resulted in substantial advancement of human rights compliance. Finally, we can no longer seriously question that governments have an obligation to include in trade agreements enforceable provisions that ensure compliance by signatories with fundamental human rights.

WTO rules routinely are linked to the inability of nations to make meaningful progress in sharpening environmental and other human rights protections. The dictates of free trade are increasingly viewed as determinative of the limits of human rights law.[14] Global trade rules aim to allow nations to profit from their comparative advantage, their ability to deliver a product or service at lower opportunity cost than other nations.[15] WTO rules accomplish this purpose by removing impediments to the free movement of goods, primarily through nondiscrimination provisions. Nevertheless, even as these comprehensive rules break down market barriers, GATT's Public Health and Welfare Clause shelters trade constraints taken to protect public morals; to conserve exhaustible natural resources; to protect human, animal, or plant life or health; or to preserve national treasures. The WTO SPS and TBT agreements proclaim that no country should be prevented from taking trade measures needed to protect human life or health or the environment at the level that the country itself considers appropriate. The TRIPS Agreement authorizes specific remedies to prevent patent rights from adversely affecting the transfer of technology that is vital to medical care and economic development of lesser-developed nations. It also permits Members to deny patents if necessary to protect public morals, public health, or to prevent serious prejudice to the environment. These provisions clearly sound in human rights law.

Exceptions based on public health and protection of natural resources have received the most attention and will continue to be used to protect human rights restrictions from GATT's fundamental proscription of discriminatory governmental restrictions on trade. As mentioned in section 2.4, however, Article XX(a)'s protection of public morals provides an especially fertile source of discretion to apply human rights law. A wide range of trade restrictions over the years has been based on the "immorality" of governmental activities, from prohibitions of trade with countries practicing slavery to bans on child pornography.[16] Article XX(a) likely would also support trade barriers erected to address other immoral acts by a foreign government against its citizens, such as by indentured child labor, denial of freedom of the press, prohibition of the right to emigrate, or a consistent pattern of gross violations of human rights. Each of these reasons has been used by the United States and its trading partners to justify trade restrictions.[17]

We acknowledge the special care that the WTC must exercise to ensure that Members do not use claims of protection of public morals to discriminate against a virtually unlimited list of government activities. For example, a Member that seeks on morality grounds to use trade sanctions in response to a country's universal but substandard educational system or its choice of foods cries out for more objective—but pluralistic—assessment of the Public Morality clauses in GATT Article XX(a) for trade in goods, Article XIV(a) of GATS, and in regional trade agreements. These clauses must not be interpreted, as some Members have interpreted GATT Article XXI's National Security Clause, as entirely self-judging. They would then, by definition, become doctrinally sterile and effectively unusable. A Public Morality Clause without objective benchmarks would trump all other trade rules, an absurd and thus unthinkable result. The WTC's definition in the *U.S.-Gambling* decision—"standards of right and wrong conduct maintained by or on behalf of a community or nation"—seems to us a starting point to protect against the slippery slope of unilateral conferral of moral underpinnings on trade restrictions by one of the extraordinarily diverse body of 150-plus WTO Members. We believe that the parameters for these standards reside in the fundamental human rights that we address as trade "benchmarks" in section 15.3(C).

In addition to these substantive WTO provisions, the rules that govern dispute settlement procedures confirm the WTO's place within the corpus of public international law,[18] which brings the Vienna Convention into the room with dispute settlement panels. "The GATT," as the WTC confirmed in its first decision, "is not to be read in clinical isolation from public international law."[19] WTO panels have used rules of general international law independently of interpreting a particular WTO provision in such areas as deciding a panel's jurisdiction, drawing adverse inferences, the role of amicus curiae briefs, and judicial economy.[20]

WTO dispute panels have been highly deferential to Members when the human right to health is at stake,[21] emphasizing the importance of the discretion accorded WTO Members to choose their own level of health protection.[22] From this record we can see that WTO Members have both given themselves wide berth to pursue human rights law and also have directed dispute panels interpreting these provisions to be guided by general international law in their interpretations of claims under the WTO covered agreements.

Trade rules have made a start, which should be considered reasonable under the circumstances, in attempting to set priorities for national pursuit of human rights principles. Aggressive implementation of the WTO's human rights policies can lead to purposeful integration of human rights into the WTO system.

(B) The Human Rights Face of Regional Trade Agreements

The rule of law, including the substantive ingredients of justice and fairness, is basic to enjoyment of human rights.[23] In our experience FTAs in the Hemisphere have had pronounced effects on attainment of rules-based governance.[24] These secondary and mostly unheralded effects include provisions that encourage transparency, accountability, and due process by governments. Dispute settlement systems in FTAs similarly promote timeliness, inclusive record keeping, and impartiality in the administrative decisional process. These are strong incentives for national authorities to follow a decision process open not solely to the trading community, but to civil society generally. The downsides of FTAs—those that invoke vehement protests—are precisely those provisions that appear to trammel human rights, that take away freedoms from workers, that degrade the environment, and that get in the·way of state protection of its citizens by having its health and safety regulations trumped by corporate fiscal interests.

(C)   Incorporation of Fundamental Human
      Rights into Trade Agreements

At GATT's inception in 1947, we could forgive negotiators their failure to appreciate trade's inevitable effects on human rights. We may no longer countenance such ignorance in the crafting of trade treaties that have transformed the world over the past thirty years into an unstoppable engine of economic growth with near fathomless potential to change the standard of living of every global citizen. Each new treaty is not only born into the corpus of existing public international law, including human rights treaties and custom, but each new trade negotiation must accept the facts that half a century of ever-broader trade rules have revealed.

Trade's inexorable growth has, as economists predicted, created winners and losers. Austrian economist Joseph Schumpeter called this eminently predictable process "creative destruction," the perpetual cycle by which capitalism destroys old, less efficient products and services and replaces them with new, more efficient ones. Technological change, Schumpeter noted, "incessantly revolutionizes the economic structure from within."[25]

Trade's winners mostly have been transnational corporations able to reduce their costs by seeking out countries with a comparative advantage in their products, usually without concern either for the human lives or the natural resources abused in that search. Trade's biggest losers have been the human rights of workers, of environmental and thus human health, of women, of indigenous populations, of the poor, and of development and developing countries generally.

For the same reasons that a developing country cannot today justify the worst forms of child labor by citing similar U.S. and European abuses during industrialization of those countries in the 19th century, trade negotiators cannot fail to use the unique power of globalization to eliminate poverty, to make a reality of nondiscrimination, to protect the traditional knowledge of indigenous populations, to ensure the raising of women out of second-class status, and to protect core labor rights. Trade's right to regulate for human rights purposes must become trade's obligation to regulate consistently with human rights law.[26]

We applaud the insistence of developed countries in recent trade pacts on a modicum of protection for workers and the environment, recognizing trade's intimate relationship with human rights and the enforceability of trade agreements because of the severe financial sanctions that follow from their violation. Countries with the largest markets are the natural leaders of the purposeful intersection of trade and human rights law because their transnational corporations are the primary beneficiaries of market openings. To those who would argue that it is not trade's place to assume the responsibility of human rights enforcement, we respond that we are asking no more than that repeated and universal recognition of the importance of human rights be extended to trade instruments that inevitably will have overwhelming impacts on the human rights of the citizens of each trading partner. To those who claim that it is not within the jurisdiction of trade to decide which human rights to enforce, we agree. UN and regional human rights agencies must tell trade negotiators which fundamental human rights are so closely tied to trade that they must be counted among trade's benchmarks. This volume, we hope, has provided the resources for that dialogue.

With respect to labor rights, the accomplishment of that task is underway. While we could wish for more complete inclusion, the ILO by overwhelming majority has definitively identified in its Work Declaration those human rights that must become part of trade's rules.[27] With respect to nondiscrimination, the specifics have been decided by the Universal Declaration, ICCPR, ICESCR, CERD, CEDAW, and custom so that none could deny the ability to draft appropriate language for a trade agreement. The same may be said for noneconomic protections for women. Beyond these subjects of human rights abuse, agreement on which rights with respect to, for example, poverty, indigenous populations, health, or the environment are so fundamental that trade rules must become enforcement partners of the UN and individual states is far less clear. With respect to poverty eradication, a human rights goal closely linked to trade, it is clear that the global consensus exists. Hence, including appropriate provisions in trade agreements ought not be problematic. Yet, regarding the environment, another area in which some level of consensus exists, successive FTAs that require enforcement only of each country's existing environmental rules in reality are a step backward from developing custom with regard to the most basic of environmental rights, including the Precautionary Principle, the Polluter Pays Principle, the Extraterritorial Harm Principle, environmental equity, and sustainable development.[28] Human rights advocates need to agree on the fundamental principles for these and other subjects of human rights treaties that may simply be inserted into trade agreements; it will be more difficult for trade negotiators to resolve those battles in the midst of a trade negotiation. The shared minimum standards, however, can still work as a base so that there is no environmental degradation for lack of absolute, across-the-board agreement on norms.

15.4   *Reparations for Human Rights Violations*

(A)   Global Harm Principle

States must assume responsibility to deliver through their trade agreements the human rights promised by a dozen UN treaties. States have been careful in couching their human rights commitments to avoid, with respect to many critical needs of individuals, binding and measurable actions to ensure the human rights either of their own citizens or those in other countries. Yet, the question of whether, nonetheless, states, in particular economically powerful states, may be held to human rights observance is not solely moral in nature, but has taken on penumbral legal or rules-based governance characteristics through a combination of treaties, customs, and historical fact.

There are two sources of this penumbral legal obligation. The first is the customary international law principle of Global Harm. Reasoning from John Stuart Mill that "the only purpose for which power can be rightfully exercised over any member of a civilized community, against his will, is to prevent harm to others,"[29] Thomas Pogge, in a series of essays from the 1990s, concludes that each of us has a *negative duty* to refrain from caus- ing harm to others, and that this duty applies equally to states. When we harm others through our actions, we become liable to rectify the damage that we have caused.[30]

The Global Harm Principle finds reflection in customary international environmental law emanating from the *Trail Smelter Arbitration*, which affirmed Canada's responsibility for the damage from copper smelter fumes that transgressed the border into the state of Washington. Bas- ing its conclusion on general principles of international law, the tribunal found in 1941 that "no state has the right to use or permit the use of its territory in such a manner as to cause injury by fumes in or to the ter- ritory of another or the properties or persons therein."[31] Recognition of a cross-border harm principle carved out an important exception to the long-standing customary international law principle—a touchstone of traditional international law—that states have unfettered national sover- eignty over natural resources and absolute freedom of the seas beyond the three-mile territorial limit.[32] Three decades later, the concept had become so widely accepted that Stockholm Declaration Principle 21 provided global scope to the *Trail Smelter* Principle by confirming that states have sovereign rights to exploit their natural resources, but may not do so in a manner that causes harm to other states. States have the "responsibility to ensure that activities within their jurisdiction or control do not cause damage to the environment of other States or of areas beyond the limits of national jurisdiction."[33]

This customary international environmental law principle must also find universal acceptance by state practice in the wake not only of environmen- tal, but a fortiori with respect to other human rights harm. In this regard, the United Nations implicitly recognized the Global Harm Principle in 1989 in its declaration that, with respect to activities carried out in the territory of a State, "States of origin shall take appropriate measures to prevent or, where necessary, to minimize the risk of transboundary harm," and, if such harm nonetheless occurs, "the State of origin shall make reparation for ap- preciable harm."[34] To this end, Frank Garcia argues that the same moral ob- ligations that require a state to be just in the social contract with its domes- tic civil society "attach with equal force with respect to that state's . . . trans- national economic relations."[35] Garcia reasons from the general conception of justice articulated by John Rawls to assert that "international social and economic inequalities are just only if they result in compensating benefits for all states, and in particular for the least advantaged states."[36] Thus situated as an element of distributive justice, Rawlsian theory offers additional support for the Global Harm Principle, which we posit as the penumbral legal debt that the economically powerful states owe to those elements of civil society harmed by the global activity of these states.

In the aftermath of the Second World War, the major powers imposed the present global institutional order known as the Bretton Woods System, consisting of the IMF to regulate exchange rates, the World Bank to finance development, and the GATT (now WTO) to regulate trade. To manage the peace and prevent future war, these powers also created the United Nations. While these institutions at their creation foretold a stable economic and financial system in which every nation had an equal opportunity to develop to its full potential, the actual face of development, poverty, disease, regional conflict, genocide, and other human rights disasters now are undeniable. Presented with these now foreseeable and avoidable effects on human rights, the affluent states have maintained this same institutional order, despite the existence of viable alternatives that do not cause these human rights harms.

The WTO has enabled the continuation of global poverty "through monetary agreements that favour affluent states at the cost of poor states."[37] Protectionist exemptions and huge agricultural subsidies by First World states have created unemployment, reduction in incomes, and lower tax revenues in the Third World.[38] Corporate search for maximization of profit by exploiting comparative advantage—cheap labor—also has resulted in unemployment and depressed wages, indeed the emasculation of the middle class in First World states. By perpetuating a global order whose foreseeable effects are widespread human rights harms and whose ramifications are avoidable because viable alternatives exist that do not cause these human rights harms, affluent states have caused harm to others—have in fact committed human rights violations. For these reasons, the major trade powers have a negative duty to ameliorate the human rights harm that their global institutional order has caused.

To the rebuttal that some human rights conventions limit the responsibility of a state to protecting the rights of its own citizens, we rely on cases that find jurisdiction for violation of the human rights of civil society outside a state's territory if the state was in fact exercising jurisdiction over those persons when it committed the violation. Even without recourse to the broader definition of "territory" that we address in the next section, the European Commission of Human Rights looks to a relational concept of jurisdiction. An obvious example is the exercise of control by a state's armed forces, as in the case of Turkey and Turkish-occupied Northern Cyprus.[39] The global economic order exercises no less control over the daily lives of civil society in every state, from the value of their work, the buying power of their wages, the availability and conditions for receiving a loan, and the financial consequences of their noncompliance with international trading rules. A state that has "effective overall control" over another state's citizens is bound by human rights obligations that otherwise are confined to acts on the state's own territory.[40]

(B) Pacta Sunt Servanda

The second source of the quasi-legal obligation to use trade instruments for the advancement of human rights flows from the principle of *pacta sunt servanda*, the good faith obligation of states to implement the commitments that they have assumed by acceding to particular human rights treaties.[41] At a minimum, they have an obligation through the UN Charter to promote human rights, including through international institutions—"to reaffirm faith in fundamental human rights, in the dignity and worth of the human person, in the equal rights of men and women" (preamble). The Universal Declaration in addition contributes to the increasingly customary status of many human rights.

Two factors argue for broad application of the good faith principle with regard to human rights. In the first place, human rights treaties inherently require global effect. Of course, the objectives of any treaty will be undermined if major players in the arena refuse to be bound. The natural, theological, humanist, positive law, near-spiritual origin of human rights law makes illogical the claim that, for example, CRC could protect children in the North, but not in Nicaragua. Exempting certain states undermines the essence, the very logic, of human rights treaties, not simply their effectiveness. The same incoherency attends such an argument regarding a treaty prohibiting genocide, racial discrimination, torture, forced labor, and so forth.

The second factor favoring broad application of *pacta sunt servanda* is the changing nature of the concept of "territory." We recognize that a signatory is bound to ensure application of its international obligations only within its own territory, and that the usual meaning of "territory" is the geographical reach of the state's political boundaries. A different meaning must obtain in the face of the inevitably extraterritorial effect of trade agreements, however, just as the concept of universal jurisdiction would apply in the case of peremptory norms.

Just as the Vienna Convention would find invalid a reservation to a treaty that is incompatible with the treaty's object and purpose,[42] we must find suspect the contention of signatories to human rights treaties that the treaty's scope is by definition limited to the geographical territory under full control of the signatories. Analysts have documented extensively the adverse effects of trade agreements on both the political and economic human rights of civil society of the Members of such treaties.

Without detracting from the positive effects of trade agreements in gradually reducing poverty (at least for some), increasing environmental awareness, and overcoming infrastructural and institutional obstacles to the advancement of human rights, the adverse effects are common knowledge to nations that have taken on both human rights and trade obligations. In fact, these adverse effects of trade's liberalization transform the meaning of the effects doctrine with respect to the extent of each signatory's human rights obligation. For example, when the United States negotiates a chapter in a trade agreement with Costa Rica that brings broad protections to U.S. investment in the telecommunications market of Costa Rica, U.S. human rights obligations extend to the telecommunications workers in Costa Rica adversely affected by the investment chapter because of the trade instrument's necessary and inevitable effects.

This global projection of state action taken within its geographical boundaries has led to the emergence of objective territorial principles. If a state may use these principles to extend its traditional jurisdictional reach, the principles also must support expansion of the state's traditional international obligations.[43] In addition, the very nature of globalization has forced transformation of the concept of territory. Geographical boundaries as a result have become less relevant not only for measuring delivery of social justice, but also for determining the extent of a state's obligations under international law. Globalization has forced us to rethink our usual notions of both time and space and has made reconception of law's relationship to territorial boundaries the central challenge of international law.[44]

We may also distinguish the general international law definition of jurisdiction, which relies on territory, from that of jurisdiction for human rights violations based on the different objects and purposes of relevant treaties. General state jurisdiction seeks to protect the sovereign equality and independence of states. Territorial limits best accomplish this purpose. Human rights treaties seek, on the other hand, to protect the individual from acts or omissions of the state. Territorial limits to jurisdiction are not relevant to these objects and we are thus instructed by Article 31 of the Vienna Convention to eschew the limitations of a territorial premise for state jurisdiction.[45]

WTO case law is similar: early trade dispute settlement panels reasoned that GATT Members could not act under the Public Health and Welfare exceptions to GATT's nondiscrimination prescriptions if doing so projected the Member's policies beyond its borders.[46] The WTO Appellate Body rejected this line of thinking on the unassailable ground that the GATT and other WTO Agreements necessarily have effects beyond any one Member's borders. Limiting access to GATT's important human rights exceptions solely to those social purposes achievable within a Member's territory would eviscerate the safe harbors guaranteed by the trading system's Public Health and Welfare exceptions.[47] In the case, the WTC conceded that conservation of endangered sea turtles that roam thousands of miles into the ocean was impossible through the intra-territorial action of a single WTO Member. Although the WTC required the United States to engage in good faith negotiations to seek accomplishment of its environmental protection purpose without violating the nondiscrimination principles of the WTO, the WTC in the end approved the border restrictions on shrimp caught without turtle protective devices, thus projecting the U.S. objective to every nation that either caught or processed shrimp and wished access to the large U.S. market.

(C)   Corporate Responsibility for Reparations

(1)   CORPORATIONS AS STATE ACTORS

We first noted in section 5.5 that TNCs often exercise greater control over the individual in civil society than states. For purposes of the Global Harm and *Pacta Sunt Servanda* principles, we argue here that TNCs should be treated as states, not as individuals with respect to their obligation to ensure that their actions comply with established human rights norms. These powerful actors cause substantial human rights violations by polluting air and water, by using natural resources beyond the ability of these resources to sustain themselves, by securing patents to the traditional knowledge of indigenous populations without compensation, by co-opting governments of smaller economies into selling rights to the future livelihood of their civil societies, and by violating the core labor rights of their workers. Amy

Sinden has argued that the ability of TNCs to exercise such extensive control over the well-being of civil society requires that we treat TNCs not as private individuals, but as government entities.[48] Nestlé SA would not by this logic somehow literally be bound by human rights treaties signed by Switzerland. The theory would require that the country of registration be held responsible for human rights violations committed by its TNCs, wherever those violations may occur. Failure of the state to employ the civil and criminal jurisdiction that international law authorizes the state to exercise over its corporations would amount to state-sanctioned violation of human rights by the TNC.

By reference again to the Vienna Convention's prohibition of reservations inconsistent with a treaty's object and purpose, treaty signatories could not have intended to escape responsibility for the human rights violations of their citizens on the grounds that the state simply chooses not to regulate the TNC with respect to a particular activity.[49]

(2)   HUMAN RIGHTS COURT JURISDICTION
       OVER TNC VIOLATIONS

This penumbral or constructive state responsibility for the human rights violations of TNCs arguably confers jurisdiction on the Inter-American Court of Human Rights for human rights violations committed by TNCs. In fact, the state signatory to ACHR has violated the Convention by failing to police and prevent the violation by an entity within its control. As outlined in the previous section, enforcement is not thereby automatically ensured, because many important countries of registration of TNCs, such as the United States and Canada, have not ratified ACHR, much less its Protocol of San Salvador. The fact remains that the state has committed a violation of its human rights obligation, imposed by the Global Harm and *Pacta Sunt Servanda* principles, through its transnational corporate agent.

(D)   National Remedies for Human Rights Violations

The recently revived U.S. Alien Tort Statute (ATS)[50] is available to litigants in U.S. federal courts to enforce certain duties of states and corporations to protect human rights. The ATS calls on the concepts of customary international law and *pacta sunt servanda* to establish positive law prohibiting human rights violations, such as those that occur as a direct result of the global trading system created and perpetuated by states and corporations. By its resurrection as an instrument of human rights enforcement, the ATS joins a line of precedent extending from the 18th century, more recently reconstituted after the Second World War in the form of the Nuremberg Trials and other reparation arrangements sought soon thereafter from the Soviet Union, Castro's Cuba, and South Africa for human rights violations. More recent reparations claims involve slave labor; forced prostitution and sterilization; torture; illegal occupation; looting of art works; and expropriation of land.

Latin America has a particularly strong history of judicially enforced reparation in the form of its *amparo* suit, which permits federal courts to provide remedies to citizens for violations by the state of their constitutional rights. Many of these constitutional protections sound in human rights; these explain the basis for the guarantee of the *amparo* suit by the American Convention on Human Rights.[51]

Landmark decisions in *Filartiga v. Pena-Irala*[52] and *Sosa v. Alvarez-Machain*[53] brought a flood of ATS human rights cases to U.S. federal courts.[54] Although many questions remain unanswered, the courts have provided certain parameters. As the statute itself makes clear, an ATS claim must meet three conditions: (1) the plaintiff is an "alien"—not an U.S. citizen; (2) the violation is tortious; and (3) the tort violates the law of nation, which can be either customary law or a treaty of the United States.[55] It seems that the advice that held true in *Paul v. Avril* remains valid—a well-pleaded tort that violates the law of nations is sufficient to provide a cause of action.[56] The good news for the human rights community is that many human rights violations that arise from the global trading system meet this standard.

The Federal Circuit Court in the *Rio Tinto* case made an important analysis of ATS requirements. As summarized in the General Introduction, *Rio Tinto* contains both egregious abuses of *jus cogens* norms and violations that encompass grayer areas of customary international law, all based on trade and investment activities. The District Court found that the complaint stated actionable ATS claims of racial discrimination, violations of the laws of war, and violation of the UN Convention on the Law of the Sea (UNCLOS). Based primarily on a Statement of Interest filed by the U.S. Department of State, however, the District Court dismissed all claims on grounds of nonjusticiable political questions and, alternatively, on the basis of international comity and the act of state doctrine.[57]

The Ninth Circuit, noting that its review of the appeal of the lower court's dismissal required only a finding that one of the claims was a non-frivolous violation of the law of nations, separated the alleged violations into three categories: (1) war crimes and crimes against humanity, (2) racial discrimination, and (3) environmental destruction. Because the first set of allegations involved well-established violations of international norms, the Appellate Court adjudged them actionable under the ATS and did not analyze them in detail.[58] The *Rio Tinto* opinion thus primarily focused on the customary nature of the racial and environment claims.

The District Court had dismissed claims of racial discrimination under the act of state doctrine. The Appellate Court reversed this decision based on its view that racial discrimination, like war crimes and crimes against humanity, constituted "the least controversial core" of today's ATS jurisdiction. The Court found systematic racial discrimination to be a *jus cogens* violation that cannot seek international law protection as a sovereign act.[59]

The Appellate Court did not view the environmental devastation claim, based on the UNCLOS, as rising to the level of a *jus cogens* violation, but ruled that the act of state doctrine did not for that reason necessarily shield the state from prosecution. Because approximately 150 nations have ratified UNCLOS, the Appellate Court found that the treaty thereby codified customary international law and permitted an ATS claim.[60]

Although the nature of ATS jurisdiction is a work in progress, it doubtlessly reaches extreme violations of human rights, such as war crimes, systematic racial discrimination, torture, forced labor, and other *jus cogens* human rights violations. Moreover, the courts now seem willing seriously to analyze whether other human rights abuses, such as health and environment questions, should be actionable as equally fundamental. The *Rio Tinto* Court turned to the Restatement of the Foreign Relations Law of the United States and a multilateral environmental agreement as a basis for determining today's law of nations. We anticipate that courts in the United States will look to other international agreements in placing the ATS among other national judicial remedies, including the important *amparo* action, for human rights violations that may be unenforceable at the international level.

15.5 Mr. Ricardo, Meet the 21st Century

Despite two hundred years of increasingly more sophisticated advancement of economic theory, the disarmingly minimalist Ricardian model of comparative advantage continues today to explain why trade increases both world welfare and the real incomes of the countries engaged in that trade. Ricardo's assumptions of balanced trade, full employment, and free movement of labor between industries make as much sense from an economic perspective in the 21st century as they did in the 19th.[61] To be sure, ever-shifting trade balances, employment rates, and labor costs cause real human suffering from outsourcing, currency manipulation, and unfavorable current account deficits. Section 15.2(B) insists that governments maintain strong, trade-related safety nets to relieve this suffering. These effects, however, do not undermine the economic strength of comparative advantage. External economies that arise from today's high-technology world require qualifications to the theory, but these externalities, too, leave undisturbed Ricardo's insights.

Even with the continued relevance of comparative advantage to understanding the present global market, we believe that Ricardo would not have disapproved of our formulation—a Ricardo-plus version. We contend that properly valued human rights compliance increases comparative advantage and thus leads to further welfare increases. As we confirmed throughout this volume, human rights–compliant treatment of workers—and civil society in general, including conservation of the environment through sustainable development—increases worker productivity, ensures future resource inputs, strengthens brand loyalty, reduces health care costs, builds trade-expanding infrastructure, and stabilizes democratic institutions that nurture vigorous markets.

States and companies that work to implement human rights treaties thereby gain an edge in the global market by increasing their comparative advantage. In the field of the human right to a healthy environment, Amy Sinden reminds us that, "in a world of ubiquitous [environmental] spillover and global commons effects, a welfare maximizing trading scheme is not one in which all trade barriers are removed, but one in which carefully targeted trade barriers are imposed in order to internalize the externalities associated with transboundary environmental harms." Failure to do so perpetuates an economically inefficient market, one that is inconsistent with the fundamental welfare economics on which the world trading system is based.[62]

By the same analysis, countries that wish to exert maximum leverage for their own interests in the global market must rely not solely on economic theory, but also on the often begrudgingly approached regional and global human rights framework. Fundamental human rights law becomes in this way a credible factor in a state's economic growth plan. The state's investment in the human rights of its civil society thus pays

multiple dividends. In other words, compliance with human rights standards is a variable that must be used in creating measures of efficiency—
ascertaining a country's comparative advantage.

15.6 *Linking Trade and Human Rights in the Americas*

Efforts to accomplish through an FTAA more complete economic integration of the Hemisphere, discussed in section 2.6(F), also must complete
the linkage of trade and human rights. An FTAA must require all signatories to adhere to the OAS system of human rights, including ACHR, and
to accept the now-controversial jurisdiction of the Inter-American Court
of Human Rights. Despite the limited number of adherents to its binding jurisdiction (twenty-one of the thirty-four OAS signatories), the Inter-
American Court is an active instrument of human rights progress in the
Hemisphere and all OAS countries will benefit if its reach is extended.

The Santiago Summit of the Americas in 1998 began an important step
toward using the FTAA to spur ratification of ACHR by the United States,
Canada, and other OAS states that have hesitated to make that commitment: "Respect for and promotion of human rights and the fundamental
freedoms of all individuals is a primary concern of our governments. In
commemorating the fiftieth anniversary of the American Declaration of
the Rights and Duties of Man and the Universal Declaration of Human
Rights, we agree on the need to promote the ratification and implementation of the international agreements aimed at preserving them and to continue strengthening the pertinent national and international institutions."

In the Quebec Summit in 2001, FTAA heads of state went further in
their commitment to linking Hemisphere-wide economic integration with
the human rights system of the Americas: "We support strengthening and
enhancing the effectiveness of the inter-American human rights system,
which includes the Inter-American Commission on Human Rights and
the Inter-American Court of Human Rights. We mandate the thirty-first
regular session of the General Assembly of the OAS to consider an adequate increase in resources for the activities of the Commission and the
Court in order to improve human rights mechanisms and to promote the
observance of the recommendations of the Commission and compliance
with the judgments of the Court."[63] These pronouncements present the
United States and other laggard OAS Members the opportunity to serve
their civil societies more completely by participating fully in the Inter-
American human rights system. The mandates also foreshadow provision,

within the FTAA itself, of the missing link between trade and human rights that must precede fulfillment of the half-century old promises of the UN and OAS human rights declarations.

15.7 Afterword

In this volume, we have demonstrated the desirability, viability, and absolute necessity that states pursue both human and economic well-being as a single, integrated ideal. The synchronicity between human rights and trade—their common foundations and goals—is patent. Increasingly, states in the Americas embrace and acknowledge both the coexistence of these fields as well as the need for both to flourish for the betterment of humankind. We hope the blueprint for integration that we have drafted in this work is useful in future conversations to promote the social well-being of the individual alongside the economic well-being of the world.

In sum, *Just Trade* proposes a paradigmatic shift in the examination of the myriad significant intersections of the trade and human rights conundrum. The new covenant is as uncomplicated in theory as it is complex in its execution: with respect to every trade agreement, negotiators must ask the human rights question. That is, in the crafting of any agreement, a proactive, positive inquiry must be made into what are the likely human rights consequences of the potential accord. It is a new commitment by trade and human rights representatives and advocates to prepare in effect a human rights impact statement prior to the conclusion of any trade agreement to ascertain what must be done in order for those involved—states, corporate entities, and individuals alike—to benefit from trade's promise of prosperity. The new covenant then demands action on this analysis in the form of modified agreement provisions, implementing legislation, financial and technical assistance, and other measures to deliver, finally, on that promise.

Notes

INTRODUCTION

Epigraph. Homer, *The Odyssey*, trans. Robert Fagles (New York: Penguin, 1997), 215.

1. In India, the reference to middle class is to those with disposable income— that is, workers earning between two thousand dollars and four thousand dollars annually, in an economy in which an annual income of three thousand dollars is the starting point for automobile purchases. *See* Indrajit Basu, "India's Growing Urge to Splurge," *Asia Times*, Aug. 22, 2003, http://www.atimes.com/atimes/ South_Asia/EH22Df01.html; Scott Bauldaff, "Boom Splits India's Middle Class," *Christian Science Monitor*, May 13, 2004, http://www.csmonitor.com/2004/0513/ p01s04-wosc.html.

2. Amy Chua, *World On Fire: How Exporting Free Market Democracy Breeds Ethnic Hatred and Global Instability* (New York: Doubleday, 2003), 54–56.

3. HRW, "Turning a Blind Eye: Hazardous Child Labor in El Salvador's Sugarcane Cultivation," *HRW Report* 16, no. 2(b) (June 2004): http://hrw.org/re-ports/2004/elsalvador0604/index.htm.

4. "La Oroya: Lead Poisoning and the Doe Run Lead Smelter in Peru," Asociación Interamericana para la Defensa del Ambiente (AIDA), http://www. aida-americas.org/aida.php?page=laoroya (accessed May 22, 2007). The Inter-American Court of Human Rights has accepted AIDA's petition on behalf of La Oroya's people.

5. *Sarei v. Rio Tinto*, 487 F.3d 1193 (9th Cir. 2007). See discussion of the case in the summary of the ATS, section 15.4(D).

6. Paul Collier and David Dollar, *Globalization, Growth, and Poverty: Building an Inclusive World Economy* (New York: Oxford University Press, 2001), 1, as summarized on the World Bank Web site at http://publications.worldbank.org/ ecommerce/catalog/product?item_id=370788.

7. Andrei A. Levchenko and Quy Toan Do, "Trade, Inequality, and the Political Economy of Institutions" (Jan. 26, 2006), http://papers.ssrn.com/sol3/papers. cfm?abstract_id=879746 (accessed Dec. 21, 2006).

8. Chua, *World on Fire*, 6.

10. "Colombian Rebel Group Demands Government Scrap FTA With US," *Latin American Advisor,* May 23, 2007 (Inter-Amer. Dialogue), 2.

11. Derived from Organisation for Economic Co-Operation and Development data, http://www.oecd.org/statsportal/0,2639,en_2825_293564_1_1_1_1_1,00.html.

12. *Compare* "HIV/AIDS & Emergencies: Compounding Crises" (June 2006), UN World Food Programme, http://www.wfp.org/food_aid/doc/39149_Emergencies.pdf, *with* "Breaking Out of the Poverty Trap," UN World Food Programme, http://www.wfp.org/food_aid/introduction/index.asp?section=12&sub_section=1. *See also* Ofeibea Quist-Arcton, "For Niger, Improved Health Care May Cut Famine," *National Public Radio* ("Morning Edition," Oct. 31, 2005), http://www.npr.org/templates/story/story.php?storyId=4982368 (accessed July 2, 2007).

13. "Hunger Map," UN World Food Programme, http://www.wfp.org/country_brief/hunger_map/index.asp?section=9&sub_section=hunger (accessed Sept. 25, 2006).

14. Duncan Brack, "Multilateral Environmental Agreements: An Overview," in *Trade, Investment and the Environment: Proceedings of the Royal Institute of International Affairs Conference,* eds. Halina Ward and Duncan Brack (London: Earthscan, 2000), 125.

15. *See, e.g.,* Tim Connor, "Rerouting the Race to the Bottom? Transnational Corporations, Labor Practice Codes of Conduct, and Workers' Right to Organize—The Case of Nike, Inc.," in *Moral Imperialism: A Critical Anthology,* ed. Berta E. Hernández-Truyol (New York: New York University Press, 2002), 166.

16. Kristin Wintersteen, "Poverty, Trade and Development, and the WTO" (1999), University of Washington, http://lic.law.ufl.edu/~hernandez/Trade/Winterst.pdf.

17. Clive Crook, "Globalisation and Its Critics," *The Economist,* Sept. 29, 2001, 3.

18. Xavier Sala-i-Martin, "The Disturbing 'Rise' of Global Income Inequality," Columbia University Department of Economics Discussion Paper No. 0102-44 (Apr. 2002), 76, http://www.papers.nber.org/papers/w8904.pdf; *see* William Watson, "A Global World Is a More Equal World," *National Post Online,* May 29, 2002, http://www.columbia.edu/~xs23/papers/worlddistribution/NationalPost Comment_files/printer.htm.

19. Watson, "A Global World."

20. *Id.*

21. This defining phrase first was used by professors Robert Howse and Makua Mutua in "Protecting Rights in a Global Economy: Challenges for the World Trade Organization" (2000), Rights and Democracy (International Centre for Human Rights and Democratic Development), http://www.ichrdd.ca/english/commdoc/publications/globalization/wtoRightsGlob.html (accessed Dec. 21, 2006).

22. Stephen J. Powell, "The Place of Human Rights in World Trade Organization Rules," *Florida Journal of International Law* 16 (2004): 219.

23. UN Development Programme (UNDP), *Human Development Report 2005* (New York: UNDP, 2005), 113, http://hdr.undp.org/reports/global/2005/.

CHAPTER 1

1. Statute of the International Court of Justice, 3 Bevans 1179, 59 Stat. 1031, T.S. No. 993 (1945). *See* Lori F. Damrosch, Louis Henkin et al., *International Law: Cases and Materials* (St. Paul, Minn.: West, 2001), xxvii–xxviii; Covey T. Oliver and Joseph M. Sweeney, *Cases and Materials on the International Legal System* (St. Paul, Minn.: West, 1995), 1390.

2. Damrosch, Henkin et al., *International Law.*

3. James Friedberg, "An Historical and Critical Introduction to Human Rights," in *Human Rights in Western Civilization: 1600 to the Present,* ed. John Maxwell and James Friedberg (Dubuque, Iowa: Kendall/Hunt, 1994), 2.

4. J. L. Brierly, *The Law of Nations: An Introduction to the International Law of Peace,* ed. Humphrey Waldock (New York: Oxford University Press, 1963), 1.

5. Restatement (Third) of the Foreign Relations Law of the United States (1987), § 101.

6. *Id.* at § 102.

7. *Id.* at § 102 cmt. d.

8. *Id.* at § 102 cmt. k.

9. *Id.* at § 702(a–f); § 702 cmt. n.

10. *See The Paquete Habana,* 175 U.S. at 700 (holding that "international law is part of our law. . . . For this purpose, where there is no treaty and no controlling executive or legislative act or judicial decision, resort must be had to the customs and usages of civilized nations").

11. *See, e.g.,* the *Fisheries Jurisdiction Case,* 1974 I.C.J. at 18 (noting art. 62 of the Vienna Convention ["may . . . be considered as a codification of existing customary law" on treaty terminations]); *see also U.S.-Section 301,* ¶ 7.21 (showing that WTO's Dispute Settlement Body treats the Vienna Convention as "rules of customary international law").

12. *See* S. Exec. Doc. L., 92d Cong. 1st Sess. (1971), at 1 (Department of State stating, in submitting treaty to the Senate, that the Vienna Convention "is already recognized as the authoritative guide to current treaty law and practice").

13. The CRDS provides other requirements for the valid conclusion of treaties, including a requirement of full powers to represent the states (art. 7); a requirement of consent of the state and a two-thirds vote of states present and voting for the adoption of the text (art. 9); authentication of the text (art. 10); and ways of expressing consent to be bound (arts. 11–15). *See also* Restatement (Third), § 201.

14. *United States v. Pink,* 315 U.S. 203 (1942).

15. Pub. L. No. 92-403, § 1, Aug. 22, 1972, 86 Stat. 619 (codified as amended at 1 U.S.C.A. 112b (2004)).

16. *See* 22 C.F.R. § 181.7(a) (providing for transmittal to Congress of "international agreements other than treaties").

17. 1 U.S.C.A. 112b(b) (2004).

18. Robert E. Dalton, "National Treaty Law and Practice: United States," in *National Treaty Law and Practice: Austria, Chile, Colombia, Japan, The Netherlands, United States*, Studies in Transnational Legal Policy, No. 30, eds. Monroe Leigh et al. (Washington: American Society of International Law, 1999), http://www.asil.org/dalton.pdf.

19. *Made in the USA Foundation,* 56 F.Supp.2d at 1226.

20. Bureau of Oceans and International Environmental and Scientific Affairs, "Supplementary Handbook on the C-175 Process: Routine Science and Technology Agreements," Appendix A: "Handbook on Treaties and Other International Agreements (The C-175 Handbook)," § 721.2(b)(1–3), U.S. Department of State, http://www.state.gov/g/oes/rls/rpts/175/1319.htm.

21. *See Made in the USA Foundation,* 56 F.Supp.2d at 1323 n.354, *quoting* Memorandum, Walter Dellinger, Asst. Atty. Gen. to [trade] Ambassador Michael Kantor, Nov. 22, 1994 (noting that some international agreements "may have to be ratified as treaties").

22. *See,* e.g., Trade Act of 2002, Pub. L. No. 107-210; 116 Stat. 933; 19 U.S.C. § 3803–5 (also called the U.S. Trade Promotion Authority Act).

23. *See* Restatement (Third), § 111 cmt. I.

24. *See* Barry E. Carter and Phillip R. Trimble, *International Law* (Gaithersburg, Md.: Aspen, 1995), 245.

25. *See* Restatement (Third), § 115.

26. *Crosby,* 530 U.S. at 363.

CHAPTER 2

1. We have drawn in part for this chapter from the teachings of professors John Jackson, Raj Bhala, and Paul Krugman. John H. Jackson, William J. Davey, and Alan O. Sykes, Jr., *Legal Problems of International Economic Relations: Cases, Materials, and Text on the National and International Regulation of Trasnational Economic Relations* (St. Paul, Minn.: West, 2008), chs. 1, 6–13; Raj Bhala, *International Trade Law: Theory and Practice* (New York: Lexis, 2007), chs. 7–15; Paul R. Krugman and Maurice Obstfeld, *International Economics: Theory and Policy* (Boston: Pearson Addison-Wesley, 2006), ch. 3; and *see* Stephen J. Powell and Mark A. Barnett, "The Role of United States Trade Laws in Resolving the Florida-Mexico Tomato Conflict," *Florida Journal of International Law* 11 (1997): 319, 359.

2. Adam Smith, *An Inquiry into the Nature and Causes of the Wealth of Nations,* ed. Edwin Cannan (New York: The Modern Library, 1937), Book IV, 414.

3. Thomas Cottier and Matthias Oesch, *International Trade Regulation: Law and Policy in the WTO, the European Union, and Switzerland* (London: Cameron May, 2005), 34.

4. *Id.* at 346.

5. An early GATT dispute settlement panel involved an Italian banking measure that required banks to loan money on terms more favorable to farmers who bought domestically made tractors than to farmers who bought imported tractors. Although Italy argued that the law regulated only Italian banks, the GATT Panel found a violation of Article III:4. The panel concluded that the banking law was a regulation "affecting the internal sale" of imported tractors (a farmer will be more likely to purchase domestic tractors if only such tractors qualify for the lower loan interest rate), and imported tractors were treated less favorably under that law than domestic tractors. Report of the Panel, "Italian Discrimination Against Imported Agricultural Machinery," L/833 (Oct. 23, 1958), GATT B.I.S.D. (7th Supp.), 60.

6. Most studies conclude that trade diversion from less-preferred suppliers worked by regional preference agreements is outweighed by their trade creation among FTA partners, but that the overall impact of FTAs is minor in comparison to the WTO. *See* OECD, *The Development Dimension—Agriculture and Development: The Case for Policy Coherence* (Paris: OECD, 2006), 47.

7. Our descriptor for the WTO's inelegantly named "Appellate Body" more accurately situates the entity within the international law dispute settlement system.

8. *U.S.-Gambling,* ¶ 296.

9. *Id.* at ¶¶ 266–67.

10. *U.S.-Shrimp-Turtle I,* ¶¶ 156, 159.

11. *Id.* at ¶¶ 129–30.

12. The subject of the disagreement was the panel's finding that the subsidy must be repaid, which is inconsistent with the general view among Members that WTO relief is prospective only. *Aust.-Leather,* ¶ 6.48.

13. WTO DSU, art. 3.2.

14. Raj Bhala and David A. Gantz, "WTO Case Review 2000," *Arizona Journal of International and Comparative Law* 18 (2001): 1, 19.

15. We have drawn in this section from Thomas A. O'Keefe, *Latin American Trade Agreements* (Irvington-on-Hudson, N.Y.: Transnational, 2004), ch. 1.

16. Berta E. Hernández-Truyol, "The Rule of Law and Human Rights," *Florida Journal of International Law* 16 (2004): 167, 188.

17. Declaration of Principles, First Summit of the Americas, OAS, Dec. 9-11, 1994, 2-4, http://www.summit-americas.org/miamidec.htm.

18. Endangered Species Convention; Basel Convention on Hazardous Wastes; Montreal Protocol on Ozone Layer. The parties can agree to add other agreements.

19. "Data and Research," The World Bank, http://econ.worldbank.org/WB-SITE/EXTERNAL/EXTDEC/0,,menuPK:476823~pagePK:64165236~piPK:6416514 1~theSitePK:469372,00.html (accessed Oct. 12, 2006); Bureau of Economic Analysis (BEA), U.S. Department of Commerce, "Gross Domestic Product: Second Quarter 2006 (Final); Corporate Profits: Second Quarter 2006 (Final)," News Release, BEA, http://bea.gov/bea/newsrelarchive/2006/gdp206f.pdf.

20. Stephen J. Powell, "Regional Economic Arrangements and the Rule of Law in the Americas: The Human Rights Face of Free Trade Agreements," *Florida Journal of International Law* 17 (2005): 59, 82–94.

21. Venezuela's flirtation with MERCOSUR in 2006 appears ready to fizzle like a cheap Roman candle, foundering on Brazil's unwillingness to cede its pack-leader status to a Hugo Chávez–style "Bolivarian revolution." *See* Ed Taylor and David Haskell, "New Dispute Between Chavez and Brazil Threatens Venezuela's Entry into Mercosur," *International Trade Reporter* 24 (July 12, 2007): 992. Mexico seems poised to make a political statement about its NAFTA membership, and create trading alternatives to the United States, by joining MERCOSUR. *See* Ioan Grillo, "Brazilian, Mexican Presidents Insist Mexico Will Be Joining Mercosur Bloc," *International Trade Reporter* 24 (August 9, 2007): 1153.

22. Javier Corrales, "The Logic of Extremism: How Chávez Gains by Giving Cuba So Much," in *Cuba, Venezuela, and the Americas: A Changing Landscape,* Working Paper (Washington: Inter-American Dialogue and Cuban Research Institute, Dec. 2005) 3, http://www.igloo.org/libraryservices/download-nocache/Library/gi/interame/cubavene.

23. Tim Padgett and Dolly Mascarenas, "Why Raúl Castro Could End Up a Reformer," *Time,* Aug. 1, 2006, http://www.time.com/time/world/article/0,8599,1222009,00.html.

24. Diana Bronson and Lucie Lamarche, *A Human Rights Framework for Trade in the Americas* (Montreal: Rights and Democracy, 2001), n.2, http://www.ichrdd.ca/english/commdoc/publications/globalization/wto/frameworkFinal.html.

25. Powell, "Regional Economic Arrangements," 59.

CHAPTER 3

1. *See generally* Berta E. Hernández, "To Bear or Not to Bear: Reproductive Freedom As an International Human Right," *Brooklyn Journal of International Law* 17, no. 17 (1991): 309; *see also* Rebecca M. M. Wallace, *International Law: A Student Introduction* (London: Sweet and Maxwell, 1986), 175 ("Human Rights . . . are regarded as those fundamental and inalienable rights which are essential for life as a human being"). We have drawn in part for this chapter from Berta E. Hernández-Truyol, "Human Rights Through a Gendered Lens: Emergence, Evolution, Revolution," in *Women and International Human Rights Law, Vol. 1,* eds. Kelly D. Askin and Dorean M. Koenig (Ardsley, N.Y.: Transnational, 1999), 3.

2. Restatement (Third) of the Foreign Relations Law of the United States (1987), § 701 cmt. b (noting that the origins can be traced to "natural law [and] contemporary moral values").

3. *See generally* Hernández, "To Bear"; Wallace, *International Law*.

4. *See* Berta E. Hernández-Truyol, "Women's Rights as Human Rights—Rules, Realities, and the Role of Culture: A Formula for Reform," *Brooklyn Journal of International Law* 21 (1996): 605, 657 n.201.

5. Burns H. Weston, "Human Rights," *Human Rights Quarterly* 6 (1984): 257, 258.

6. *Id.*

7. *Id.*

8. *Id.* at 259 (citing Locke).

9. Lori F. Damrosch, Louis Henkin et al., *International Law: Cases and Materials* (St. Paul, Minn.: West, 1993), xxx (citing Aquinas).

10. Michael J. Bazyler, "Reexamining the Doctrine of Humanitarian Intervention in Light of the Atrocities in Kampuchea and Ethiopia," *Stanford Journal of International Law* 23 (1987): 547, 571 (citation omitted).

11. Covey T. Oliver and Joseph M. Sweeney, *Cases and Materials on the International Legal System* (St. Paul, Minn.: West, 1995), 1390–91; *see also* Damrosch, Henkin et al., *International Law*, xxiv.

12. http://www.state.gov/s/l/treaty/faqs/70139.htm. See also Damrosch, Henkin et al., *International Law*, 454.

13. Oliver and Sweeney, *Cases and Materials*, 1391.

14. Bazyler, "Reexamining the Doctrine" (quoting Hugo Grotius [citation omitted]).

15. Case-Zablocki Act, 1 U.S.C. § 112(b).

16. *Id.*

17. *See* Myres S. McDougal, Harold D. Laswell, and Lung-chu Chen, *Human Rights and World Public Order: The Basic Policies of an International Law of Human Dignity* (New Haven, Conn.: Yale University Press, 1980), 68–71, 73–75, *excerpted in* Frank Newman and David Weissbrodt eds., *International Human Rights: Law, Policy, and Process* (Cincinnati: Anderson, 1990), 211–12.

18. I. L. Oppenheim, *International Law: Treatise* (New York: Longmans, Green, 1912), § 288, *reprinted in* Louis B. Sohn and Thomas Buergenthal, *International Protection of Human Rights* (Indianapolis: Bobbs-Merrill, 1973), 1.

19. Oppenheim (1912), § 290, *reprinted in* Sohn and Buergenthal, *International Protection*, 3.

20. James Friedberg, "An Historical and Critical Introduction to Human Rights," in *Human Rights in Western Civilization: 1600 to the Present*, eds. John Maxwell and James Friedberg (Dubuque, Iowa: Kendall/Hunt, 1994), 2 (quoting Hugo Grotius).

21. See Circular 175 Procedure, referenced at 22 CFR 181.4, http://www.state.gov/s/l/treaty/c175/.

22. *Id.* at 596–97.

23. Gerhard von Glahn, *Law Among Nations: An Introduction to Public International Law* (New York: Macmillan, 1981), 185.

24. Ahmed M. Rifaat, *International Aggression: A Study of the Legal Concept—Its Development and Definition in International Law* (Stockholm: Almqvist and Wiksell International, 1979), 41–42; *see also* D. W. Bowett, *The Law of International Institutions* (London: Stevens, 1982), 17–18.

25. The adjudicative organ of the League of Nations was the PCIJ, which functioned from 1920 to 1939. Modeled after the PCIJ, the ICJ was created in 1945 as an organ of the United Nations. *See* Ray August, *Public International Law* (Englewood Cliffs, N.J.: Prentice Hall, 1995), 448; *see, e.g., Minority Schools in Albania,* for an example of a decision upholding a treaty protecting minorities.

26. Tom Farer, "Human Rights Before the Second World War," in Inter-American Commission on Human Rights, *Inter-American Commission on Human Rights: Ten Years of Activities, 1971–1981* (Washington: OAS, 1982), v–vi, *reprinted in* Richard B. Lillich, *International Human Rights: Problems of Law, Policy, and Practice* (New York: Little, Brown, 1991), 1.

27. *See German Settlers in Poland,* 20; *Treatment of Polish Nationals,* 17. The statute of the PCIJ adhered to the traditional view that only states could be parties to international proceedings. Nevertheless, the Court noted that other international instruments, such as the minority treaties, recognized the legal standing of individuals and itself recognized that there was no international principle standing in the way of individuals directly receiving or acquiring rights under a treaty provided that the state parties so intended. *See* Marjorie M. Whiteman, ed., *Digest of International Law, Vol. 1* (Washington: U.S. Department of State, 1963), 52, § 2 (quoting the Secretary-General, *Survey of International Law in Relation to the Work of Codification of the International Law Commission,* UN Doc. A/CN.4/1/rev.1 (1949), 19–21).

28. *See* International Convention for the Suppression of the Traffic in Women and Children; International Convention for the Suppression of the Traffic in Women of Full Age; Protocol to Amend the Convention for the Suppression of the Traffic in Women of Full Age.

29. Oppenheim (1912), § 292, *reprinted in* Sohn and Buergenthal, *International Protection,* 4.

30. *Id.* The evolution of the role of the individual in international law can clearly be seen in Lauterpacht's revision of Oppenheim's work. *See* I. L. Oppenheim, *International Law: A Treatise,* ed. H. Lauterpacht (New York: D. McKay, 1955), 632–42, *reprinted in* Sohn and Buergenthal, *International Protection,* 5.For example, in revising § 289, Lauterpacht concluded that "states may, and occasionally do, confer upon individuals . . . international rights stricto sensu, i.e., rights which they acquire without the intervention of municipal legislation and which they can enforce in their own name before international tribunals." *Id.*

31. *See generally* Whitney R. Harris, *Tyranny on Trial: The Evidence at Nuremberg* (Dallas: Southern Methodist University Press, 1954); Werner Maser, *Nuremberg: A Nation on Trial* (New York: Scribner, 1979); Bradley F. Smith, *The Road to Nuremberg* (London: Andre Deutsch, 1981); Telford Taylor, *The Anatomy of the Nuremberg Trials, A Personal Memoir* (New York: Knopf, 1992).

32. *Nuremberg Trial*, 6 F.R.D. 69, 110 (1946).

33. *See* Whiteman, *Digest, Vol. 1*, 51 (citing Charles De Visscher, *Theory and Reality in Public International Law*, trans. P. E. Corbett [Princeton, N.J.: Princeton University Press, 1957], 125 n.8).

34. *See* Michael Akehurst, *A Modern Introduction to International Law* (Boston: Allen and Unwin, 1984), 75–76.

35. *See also* UN Charter, art. 1(3).

36. Louis B. Sohn, "The New International Law: Protection of the Rights of Individuals Rather than States," *American University Law Review* 32 (1982–83): 1, 17.

37. UN Charter, art. 1(3) (stating that a purpose of the Charter is to "promot[e] and encouag[e] respect for human rights and for fundamental freedoms for all without distinction as to race, sex, language, or religion").

38. *See Re Drummond Wren; see also* Violation by the USSR of Fundamental Human Rights, Traditional Diplomatic Practices and Other Principles of the Charter, G.A. Res. 285 (III), UN Doc. A/900 (Apr. 25, 1949), 34–35 (the resolution stated that the measure taken by the USSR was thought not to be in conformity with the Charter provisions at §§ 13, 16).

39. *See Sei Fuji*, 217 P.2d at 481 (the Appellate Court opinion held that the Alien Land Law was invalid because of conflicts with Charter human rights provisions, but the California Supreme Court, while invalidating the statute under the 14th Amendment, rejected the status of the Charter as the supreme law of the land and held that the human rights provisions in the Charter were not self-executing. The Court stated that the provisions lacked the mandatory nature necessary to show an intent to create enforceable rights.). For other cases holding that the human rights provisions of the UN Charter are not self-executing, see *Frolova*, 761 F.2d at 374 n.5 and cases cited therein. *See also Oyama*, 332 U.S. at 633 (holding that the Alien Land Law is unconstitutional under the 14th Amendment, with four Justices referring to the inconsistency of the law with the UN Charter).

40. *Legal Consequences—Namibia*, ¶ 129. *See also* Question of South West Africa, G.A. Res. 2145 (XXI), UN Doc. A/6316 (Oct. 27, 1966), 2 (terminating South Africa's mandate over South West Africa [Namibia]).

41. *Legal Consequences—Namibia*, ¶ 131.

42. *See* Egon Schwelb, "The International Court of Justice and the Human Rights Clauses of the Charter," *American Journal of International Law* 66 (1972): 337; *see generally* Jordan J. Paust, "Customary International Law: Its Nature,

Sources, and Status as Law of the United States," *Michigan Journal of International Law* 12 (1990–91): 59.

43. *See, e.g.,* Beijing Declaration (gender concerns); Copenhagen Declaration (development concerns).

44. Whiteman, *Digest, Vol. 13,* 663, § 11 (quoting UN ECOSOC Res. 1/5, Feb. 16, 1946).

45. There were eight abstentions: Byelorussia, Czechoslovakia, Poland, Saudi Arabia, Ukraine, USSR, Union of South Africa, and Yugoslavia. The communist states that had abstained from signing the Universal Declaration accepted it in 1975 Helsinki Declaration.

46. Whiteman, *Digest, Vol. 13,* 663 (citing Universal Declaration).

47. M. Cherif Bassiouni and Alfred M. De Zayas, eds., *The Protection of Human Rights in the Administration of Criminal Justice: A Compendium of United Nations Norms and Standards* (Irvington-on-Hudson, N.Y.: Transnational, 1994), xxiv (essentially, *jus cogens* are peremptory norms so fundamental that contrary treaties or customs are invalidated).

48. "Statement by Mrs. Franklin D. Roosevelt on Dec. 9, 1948," *Department of State Bulletin* 19 (1948): 751, 751–52.

49. *See* Sohn and Buergenthal, *International Protection,* 518–19, 522.

50. Restatement (Third), pt. VII intro. n.

51. Whiteman, *Digest, Vol. 13,* 663.

52. *Id.* at 664–65 (citing Preparation of Two Drafts International Covenants on Human Rights, G.A. Res. 543 [VI], UN Doc. A/2119 [Feb. 5, 1952], 36; Inclusion in the International Covenant or Covenants on Human Rights of an Article Relating to the Right of Peoples to Self-Determination, G.A. Res. 545 [VI], UN Doc. A/2119 [Feb. 5, 1952], 36).

53. A second optional protocol to the ICCPR was adopted in 1989.

54. ICCPR, arts. 6, 7, 8(1)–(2), 15, 16, 18. Such rights include the right to life; freedom from torture or cruel, inhuman, or degrading treatment or punishment; freedom from slavery and servitude; non-applicability of retroactive laws; right to recognition as a person before the law; and the right to freedom of thought, conscience, and religion.

55. The OAS was established in May 1948 during the 9th Inter-American Conference, which was held in Bogota, Colombia.

56. ACHR, art. 41(a).

57. Significantly, at Article 19(6), this Protocol makes the right to organize trade unions and the right to education subject to the system of individual petition under the Convention. For an extensive treatment of the Inter-American human rights systems, see generally Thomas Buergenthal and Dinah Shelton, *Protecting Human Rights in the Americas: Cases and Materials* (Arlington, Va.: N. P. Engel, 1995).

58. Significantly, it was based on this notion of indivisibility and interdependence of rights that the UN General Assembly had called on the UN Commission on Human Rights to adopt a single convention on human rights. Draft International Covenant on Human Rights and Measures of Implementation: Future Work of the Commission on Human Rights, G.A. Res. 421 (V), UN Doc. A/1775 (Dec. 4, 1950), 42.

59. Stephen P. Marks, "Emerging Human Rights: A New Generation for the 1980s?" *Rutgers Law Review* 33 (1981): 435, 437 (stating that "the commonly recognized starting point for the emergence of international human rights as we know them today is the movement for the 'rights of man' in eighteenth-century Europe"). Significantly, notwithstanding these origins, Marks notes that he does not suggest "that the concept of human rights is exclusively or even essentially Western. All cultures and civilizations in one way or another have defined rights and duties of man in society on the basis of certain elementary notions of equality, justice, dignity, and worth of the individual (or of the group)." *Id.* (citing Jeanne Hersch, UN Educational, Scientific and Cultural Organization [UNESCO], *Birthright of Man: A Selection of Texts* [Paris: UNESCO, 1969]; UNESCO, *Human Rights: Comments and Interpretations* [New York: A. Wingate, 1949], for illustrations of universality of rights). *See also* Sohn, "The New International Law," 33.

60. Marks, "Emerging Human Rights," 438. Property is considered a civil and political right because it was central to the interest fought for in the French and American revolutions. *Id.*

61. In fact, there are states where women cannot travel without their husband's consent. Moreover, the right to travel includes issues of refugees, particularly refugee women who have been documented as suffering particularly harshly and being very vulnerable to sexual violence and abuse. *See generally* UN High Commissioner of Refugees (UNHCR), *Sexual Violence Against Refugees: Guidelines on Prevention and Response* (Geneva: UNHCR 1995).

62. Marks, "Emerging Human Rights," 438.

63. *Id.; see also* Sohn, "The New International Law," 33.

64. *See generally* Asbjørn Eide and Allan Rosas, "Economic, Social, and Cultural Rights: A Universal Challenge," in *Economic, Social, and Cultural Rights: A Textbook*, eds. Asbjørn Eide, Catarina Krause, and Allan Rosas (Boston: M. Nijhoff, 1995), 16.

65. *See generally id.; see also* Asbjørn Eide, "Cultural Rights as Individual Human Rights," in Eide et al., eds., *Economic, Social and Cultural Rights*, 229–30.

66. President Franklin Delano Roosevelt's "Four Freedoms" speech, in which he discussed "four essential human freedoms," established the third freedom as the "freedom from want, which translated into world terms, means economic understandings which will secure to every nation a healthy peacetime life for its

inhabitants everywhere in the world." Franklin D. Roosevelt, Annual Message to Congress (Jan. 6, 1941), *reprinted in* John Woolley and Gerhard Peters, "The American Presidency Project" [online], http://www.presidency.ucsb.edu/ws/index.php?pid=16092. The "Four Freedoms" speech provided:

> In the future days, which we seek to make secure, we look forward to a world founded upon four essential human freedoms.
> The first is the freedom of speech and expression everywhere in the world.
> The second is the freedom of every person to worship God in his[/her] own way everywhere in the world.
> The third is the freedom from want, which translated into world terms, means economic understandings which will secure to every nation a healthy peacetime life for its inhabitants everywhere in the world.
> The fourth is freedom from fear—which translated into world terms, means a world-wide reduction of armaments to such a point and in such a thorough fashion that no nation will be in a position to commit an act of physical aggression against any neighbor—anywhere in the world. (*Id.*)

Later in his State of the Union message to Congress delivered January 11, 1944, President Roosevelt articulated many of these economic rights as part of his vision for a truly free United States. He noted that "true individual freedom cannot exist without economic security and independence . . . People who are hungry and out of a job are the stuff of which dictatorships are made." Franklin D. Roosevelt, State of the Union Message to Congress (Jan. 11, 1944), *reprinted in* John Woolley and Gerhard Peters, "The American Presidency Project" [online], http://www.presidency.ucsb.edu/ws/index.php?pid=16518. The president emphasized: "The best interests of each Nation, large and small, demand that all freedom-loving Nations shall join together in a just and durable system of peace. . . . [A] basic essential to peace is a decent standard of living for all individual men and women and children in all Nations. Freedom from fear is eternally linked with freedom from want." *Id.* The president called for "the establishment of an American standard of living higher than ever before known. We [presumably meaning U.S. citizens] cannot be content, no matter how high that general standard of living may be, if some fraction of our people—whether it be one-third or one-tenth—is ill-fed, ill-clothed, ill-housed, and insecure." *Id.* President Roosevelt presented a long list of rights, including the right to a job; to earn enough to provide food, clothing, and recreation; to a decent home for a family; to adequate medical care and the opportunity to achieve and enjoy good health; to adequate protection from the economic fears of old age, sickness, accident, and unemployment; and to a good education. *Id.*

67. *See* Marks, "Emerging Human Rights," 439 (citing Declaration on the Establishment of a New International Economic Order, G.A. Res. 3201 [S-VI], UN Doc. A/9559 [May 1, 1974], 3–4).

68. *See* Stockholm Declaration, princ. 1 ("[wo/]man has the fundamental right . . . [to] an environment of a quality that permits a life of dignity and well-being, and [s/]he bears a solemn responsibility to protect and improve the environment for present and future generations"); Rio Declaration, princ. 9; African Charter, art. 24 ("all peoples shall have the right to a general satisfactory environment favorable to their development"); Beijing Declaration, ch. IV, § K ("women and the environment"); Copenhagen Declaration, ¶ 8 ("people . . . are entitled to a healthy and productive life in harmony with the environment").

69. International Conference on Population and Development, Cairo, Egypt, Sept. 5–13, 1994, *Report*, UN Doc. A/CONF. 171/13 (1994), princ. 3 ("the right to development is a universal and inalienable right"); Copenhagen Declaration, commitment 1(n) (referring to right to development as "universal, indivisible, interdependent and interrelated" human rights); ICESCR, art. 1(1); CEDAW, pmbl.; Development Declaration; Vienna Declaration, pt. 1, para. 10; Beijing Declaration, ¶ 220; DEVAW; DRRP (right to development defined as "the right of every human being and group to full development . . . implies equal access to the means of personal and collective advancement and fulfillment in a climate of respect for the values of civilizations and cultures, both national and world-wide"); UN Educational, Scientific, and Cultural Organization (UNESCO), *Educational, Scientific, and Cultural Organization at Its 20th Session* (Paris: UNESCO Press, 1981), *reprinted in* UNESCO, *UNESCO's Standard-setting Instruments* (Paris: UNESCO, 1981), § III.C.1 (stating that freedom means the supremacy of human rights everywhere).

70. *See generally* Marks, "Emerging Human Rights," 445–46 and sources cited therein; Sohn, "The New International Law," 56–59 and sources cited therein. The 1976 UN Commission on Human Rights also said that "everyone has the right to live in conditions of international peace and security and fully to enjoy economic, social and cultural rights and civil and political rights." UN Commission on Human Rights, 32nd Session, UN Doc. E/5768 (Mar. 5, 1976); African Charter, art. 23(1) ("all peoples shall have the right to national and international peace and security").

71. *See* Marks, "Emerging Human Rights," 442; Sohn, "The New International Law," 59–60; Allan Rosas, "The Right to Development," in Eide et al., eds., *Economic, Social, and Cultural Rights*, 247–55.

72. Vienna Declaration, ¶ 5.

CHAPTER 4

1. Steve Charnovitz, "The Globalization of Economic Human Rights," *Brooklyn Journal of International Law* 25 (1999): 113 (quoting Frank Garcia).

2. *Id.*, text at n.2.

3. *See generally*, Nathanial Berman, "Economic Consequences, Nationalist Passions: Keynes, Culture, and Policy," *American University Journal of International Law and Policy* 10 (1995): 619.

4. James T. Gathii, "Construing Intellectual Property Rights and Competition Policy Consistently with Facilitating Access to Affordable AIDS Drugs to Low-end Consumers," *Florida Law Review* 53 (2001): 727, 737.

5. Articles of Agreement of the International Bank for Reconstruction and Development, Dec. 27, 1945, 2 UNTS 134, 158 (1947), art. III, § 5(b).

6. Ibrahim Shihata, "The World Bank and Human Rights: An Analysis of the Legal Issues and the Record of Achievements," *Denver Journal of International Law and Policy* 17 (1988): 39.

7. Joseph Gold, *Political Consequences Are Prohibited by Articles of Agreement When the Fund Considers Requests for Use of Resources*, IMF Survey 146–48 (Washington: IMF, May 23, 1983).

8. *See generally* Jeffrey L. Dunoff, "The Death of the Trade Regime," *European Journal of International Law* 10 (1999): 733.

9. GATT, arts. XX(b), (e), (g).

10. John H. Jackson, William J. Davey, and Alan O. Sykes Jr., *Legal Problems of International Economic Relations* (St. Paul, Minn.: West, 2008), 217–22; John H. Jackson, *World Trade and the Law of GATT* (Indianapolis: Bobbs-Merrill, 1969), 59; Gathii, "Construing," 741.

11. *See, e.g.,* "Investing in Development: A Practical Plan to Achieve the Millennium Development Goals," Millennium Project, http://www.unmillennium-project.org/reports/index.htm (accessed June 27, 2007).

12. *U.S.-Gasoline*, 17.

13. Joost Pauwelyn, "The Role of Public International Law in the WTO: How Far Can We Go?" *American Journal of International Law* 95 (1995): 535, 538.

14. UN Charter, pmbl. and art. 1. *See* Winston P. Nagan and Craig Hammer, "The Changing Character of Sovereignty in International Law and International Relations," *Columbia Journal of Transnational Law* 43 (2004): 141, 155.

15. Jeremy C. Marwell, "Trade and Morality: The WTO Public Morals Exception After Gambling," *New York University Law Review* 81 (2006): 802, 808.

16. Thomas Cottier and Matthias Oesch, *International Trade Regulation: Law and Policy in the WTO, the European Union, and Switzerland* (London: Cameron May, 2005), 523.

17. Pauwelyn, "The Role," 540–41.

18. Many of these mandates find parentage in chapter 18 of NAFTA, entitled "Publication, Notification, and Administration of Laws," Oct. 7, 1992, 107 Stat. 2057, 32 I.L.M. 289 (1993). For details of this and a burgeoning number of other rules-based provisions, see sections VI to VIII of Stephen J. Powell, "Regional Economic Arrangements and the Rule of Law in the Americas: The Human Rights Face of Free Trade Agreements," *Florida Journal of International Law* 17 (2005): 59.

19. Powell, "Regional Economic Arrangements," 60, 62 (quoting Gabriela Llobet Yglesias, then-Costa Rican vice minister of trade).

20. Joost Pauwelyn, *Conflict of Norms in Public International Law: How WTO Law Relates to other Rules of International Law* (New York: Cambridge University Press, 2003), 95.

21. Pauwelyn, "The Role," 535.

22. *U.S.-Gasoline*, 17.

23. *Korea-Procurement*, ¶ 7.96.

24. Vienna Convention, arts. 2(1)(g), 30(4). Findings and recommendations of WTO dispute settlement panels apply only to the issues and Members before the panel.

25. *Id.* at art. 30(2).

26. *See U.S.-1916 Act*, ¶ 54, n.30 (*la competence de la competence*); *Canada-Aircraft*, ¶ 202 (adverse inferences); *U.S.-Shrimp-Turtle I*, ¶ 107 (amicus briefs); *U.S.-Wool*, 19 (judicial economy).

27. *U.S.-Shrimp-Turtle I*, ¶¶ 130–32. The case involved the ultimately successful use by the United States of a GATT General Exception to support a discriminatory ban on importation of shrimp caught without use of excluder devices to avoid ensnaring endangered sea turtles in nets.

28. *EC-Computers*, ¶ 84. *See* Vienna Convention, art. 31(3)(c).

29. Vienna Convention, art. 31(3)(c). *See* Pauwelyn, "The Role," 575.

30. As but two examples, the 1994 WTO Agreement on Application of SPS builds on Article XX(b) of the GATT 1947; the 1998 ILO Work Declaration builds on eight earlier conventions addressing particular labor rights.

31. Vienna Convention, arts. 34–38.

32. Pauwelyn, "The Role," 554; *see* Convention Against Torture.

33. As but one of many examples, the TRIPS Agreement (art. 27.1) permits Members to deny a patent if necessary to protect human, animal, or plant life or health; public morality; or serious prejudice to the environment.

34. The Public Morals Clause of GATS Article XIV(a) immunizes restrictions "necessary to protect public morals or to maintain public order." The Public Morals Clause applicable to trade in goods, GATT Article XX(a), does not contain the public order phrase, for reasons we need not explore.

35. *U.S.-Gambling*, ¶¶ 6.459–465. No party appealed this aspect of the panel's decision.

36. WTO panels continue to reject the narrow view of the United States that non-WTO law is pertinent only insofar as it aids textual interpretation of WTO provisions. *See, e.g., EC-Biotech Products*, ¶¶ 7.57–68.

37. *See EC-Tariff Preferences*, ¶ 7.211. *Compare* Tatjana Eres, Note, "The Limits of GATT Article XX: A Back Door for Human Rights?" *Georgetown Journal of International Law* 35 (2004): 597, 616 (WTO jurisprudence requires proof of nexus between condemned behavior and imported product) *with* Argument of the European Communities in *EC—Tariff Preferences*, ¶ 15 (WTO allows Members to adopt policy objectives separate and distinct from those of the WTO Agreements).

38. *EC-Tariff Preferences,* ¶ 7.211.

39. *EC-Asbestos,* ¶ 172.

40. NAAEC, art. 24.1; NAALC, art. 29.1; CAFTA-DR-US.

41. A WTO Member need not show trade harm from a violation to initiate a WTO dispute process, although the absence of such harm may limit the complaining Member's ability to "retaliate" if the responding Member loses and fails to bring its laws into compliance with the WTO Agreements. *EC-Bananas,* ¶ 132; WTO DSU, art. 22.4.

42. Cottier and Oesch, *International Trade Regulation,* 524.

43. While the human rights illegality of torture has reached customary status, this is not to say that an agreed definition exists, as we learned during the 2004 Abu Ghraib, Iraq, prisoner abuse scandal. *See* Jane Stromseth, "Post-conflict Rule of Law Building: The Need for a Multi-layered, Synergistic Approach," *William and Mary Law Review* 49 (2008): 1443, 1462.

44. Powell, "Regional Economic Arrangements," 70.

45. Kevin Watkins, *The OXFAM Poverty Report* (Oxford: OXFAM, 1995), 109.

46. *See* Hannah L. Meils, "A Lesson from NAFTA: Can the FTAA Function as a Tool for Improvement in the Lives of Working Women?" *Indiana Law Journal* 78 (2003): 877, 882.

47. *See* John S. Gordon, *An Empire of Wealth: An Epic History of American Economic Power* (New York: HarperCollins, 2004), xxx; Robert J. Samuelson, "The Republic of Turmoil," *Newsweek,* Nov. 29, 2004, 45.

CHAPTER 5

1. We have drawn in part for this chapter from Berta E. Hernández and Matthew Hawk, "Traveling the Boundaries of Statelessness: Global Passports and Citizenship," *Cleveland State Law Review* 52 (2005): 97.

2. Universal Declaration, art. 15; ICCPR, art. 24(3); American Declaration, art. XIX; ACHR, art. 20.

3. Universal Declaration, art. 22.

4. Universal Declaration, art. 27; ICCPR, art. 27; ICESCR, art. 15; American Declaration, art. XIII; Protocol of San Salvador, art. 14; OAS Charter, art. 45.

5. ICCPR, art. 1; ICESCR, art. 1.

6. ICCPR, art. 25; American Declaration, art. XX (referring to a person's right to participate); ACHR, art. 23; OAS Charter, art. 45.

7. *See* Will Kymlicka and Wayne Norman, "Return of the Citizen: A Survey of Recent Work on Citizenship Theory," *Ethics* 104 (1994): 352, 353; *see also* Kim Rubenstein, "Citizenship in a Borderless World," in *Legal Visions of the 21st Century: Essays in Honour of Judge Christopher Weeramantry,* eds. Antony Anghie and Garry Sturgess (Boston: Kluwer Law International, 1998), 183.

8. *See* Rubenstein, "Citizenship."

9. *See* Ursula Vogel, "Marriage and the Boundaries of Citizenship," in *The Condition of Citizenship*, ed. Bart van Steenbergen (Thousand Oaks, Calif.: Sage, 1994), 79.

10. *See* Jürgen Habermas, "Citizenship and National Identity," in van Steenbergen, ed., *The Condition of Citizenship*, 22.

11. Ralf Dahrendorf, "The Changing Quality of Citizenship," in van Steenbergen, ed., *The Condition of Citizenship*, 16.

12. *Id.* at 17.

13. Keith Faulks, *Citizenship* (New York: Routledge, 2000), 3.

14. *Id.* at 4.

15. Bryan S. Turner, *Citizenship and Capitalism: The Debate over Reformism* (Boston: Allen and Unwin, 1986), xxi.

16. Kymlicka and Norman, "Return of the Citizen," 370 (citing Iris M. Young, "Polity and Group Difference: A Critique of the Ideal of Universal Citizenship," *Ethics* 99 [1989]: 250, 258) (developing notion of "differentiated citizenship," pursuant to which group members would belong to and participate in communities based not only on their individual status but also as group members).

17. Kymlicka and Norman, "Return of the Citizen," 352.

18. *See* Mary G. Dietz, "Context Is All: Feminism and Theories of Citizenship," *Daedalus* (Fall 1987): 1, 5.

19. Engin F. Isin and Patricia K. Wood, *Citizenship and Identity* (Thousand Oaks, Calif.: Sage, 1999), 4.

20. Marshall's classic essay "Citizenship and Social Class" (1949) describes three types of citizenship that developed since the 18th century: first, the 18th-century conception of civil citizenship, contemporaneous with the French and U.S. declarations, established rights requisite for individual, personal freedom (of men), such as rights to liberty, justice, and property; second, in the 19th century the concept of political citizenship developed and focused the right to participate in political processes; third, the 20th-century concept of social citizenship emphasized social and economic rights, which became the foundation of the so-called welfare state in Western societies. *See* Bart van Steenbergen, "The Condition of Citizenship: An Introduction," in van Steenbergen, ed., *The Condition of Citizenship*, 2; Nancy Fraser and Linda Gordon, "Civil Citizenship Against Social Citizenship? On the Ideology of Contract-Versus-Charity," in van Steenbergen, ed., *The Condition of Citizenship*, 90 (discussing Marshall's three stages of citizenship).

21. van Steenbergen, "An Introduction," 1–2 (noting Marshall's definition of ideal of citizenship).

22. *Id.*

23. Consequently, this work, like others, disagrees with Marshall's conclusion that social citizenship marked the end point of the development of citizenship theory. *See id.* at 3 ("in this book, the notion of social citizenship as the *final* stage is not accepted"); *see also* Dahrendorf, "The Changing Quality"; Richard

Falk, "The Making of Global Citizenship," in van Steenbergen, ed., *The Condition of Citizenship*, 127; Habermas, "Citizenship"; Bryan S. Turner, "Postmodern Culture/Modern Citizens," in van Steenbergen, ed., *The Condition of Citizenship*, 153.

24. *See* Dietz, "Context Is All," 5; Kymlicka and Norman, "Return of the Citizen," 297; Young, "Polity and Group Difference."

25. Dietz, "Context Is All," 2 (citations omitted).

26. *Id.* at 5 (citation omitted); *see also* Kathleen B. Jones, "Citizenship in a Woman-friendly Polity," *Signs* 15, no. 4 (1990): 781, 786.

27. *See* Ruth Lister, "Women, Economic Dependency, and Citizenship," *Journal of Social Policy* 19 (1990): 445, 453.

28. Anne Phillips, *Democracy and Difference* (University Park: Pennsylvania State University, 1993), 77.

29. *Id.*

30. *Id.* at 78.

31. Dietz, "Context Is All," 2.

32. Ronald Beiner, "Introduction: Why Citizenship Constitutes a Theoretical Problem in the Last Decade of the Twentieth Century," in *Theorizing Citizenship*, ed. Ronald Beiner (Albany: State University of New York Press, 1995), 20 n.2.

33. *See* Joseph H. Carens, "Aliens and Citizens: The Case for Open Borders," in Beiner, ed., *Theorizing Citizenship*, 229.

34. *See* Dahrendorf, "The Changing Quality," 13–14; Michael Ignatieff, "The Myth of Citizenship," in Beiner, ed., *Theorizing Citizenship*, 75.

35. *See* Carens, "Aliens and Citizens," 237 (suggesting that "in the original position . . . one would insist that the right to migrate be included in the system of basic liberties for the same reasons that one would insist that the right to religious freedom be included: it might prove essential to one's plan of life").

36. *Nottebohm* (court ruled that because there did not exist a genuine link between Nottebohm—originally of German nationality and a longtime resident of Guatemala, which was at war with Germany and treated him as an alien enemy—and Liechtenstein, Guatemala did not have to recognize his Liechtenstein nationality, which he acquired during a brief trip to the state).

37. *See, e.g.*, Martha C. Nussbaum, "Nature, Function, and Capability: Aristotle on Political Distribution," in *Oxford Studies in Ancient Philosophy*, eds. Julia Annas and Robert H. Grimm (New York: Oxford University Press, 1988), 145; *see also* Kymlicka and Norman, "Return of the Citizen," 359 n.11 (noting some liberals' recognition of the need for civic virtue).

38. *See* Habermas, "Citizenship," 31; *see also* Hans Adriaansens, "Citizenship, Work, and Welfare," in van Steenbergen, ed., *The Condition of Citizenship*, 66 (suggesting that the discussion of citizenship move from a moral order to the "social structural prerequisites underlying the moral discourse" and urging the individualization of the wage structure, which was geared to traditional and gendered visions of work divisions).

39. T. H. Marshall defined citizenship as a status bestowed on those who are full members of a community, and in so doing, he expanded citizenship to include social rights as well as political and civil rights, with social citizenship including health, education, and welfare. T. H. Marshall, *Citizenship and Social Class* (New York: Cambridge University Press, 1950). This view would appear to be in accord with President Franklin D. Roosevelt's vision for the United States as expressed in his "Four Freedoms" speech. President Roosevelt's 1941 "Four Freedoms" Speech, 87-1 Cong. Rec. 44, 46-67 (1941), *reprinted in* Frank Newman and David Weissbrodt, *International Human Rights: Law, Policy, and Process* (Cincinnati: Anderson, 1990), 50 (addressing freedom of speech and expression, freedom of religion, freedom of want, and freedom from fear). *See also* Dietz, "Context Is All," at 14 (suggesting that a "democratic vision does not legitimize the pursuit of every separate, individual interest . . . democratic citizenship . . . has a distinctive set of relations, virtues, and principles . . . [and] its relation is that of civic peers; its guiding virtue is mutual respect; its primary principle is the 'positive liberty' of democracy and self-government, not simply the 'negative liberty' of noninterference").

40. Nathan Thornburgh, "Inside the Life of the Migrants Next Door," *Time*, Feb. 6, 2006, 34, 38 (Figure).

41. Jorge Nef, "Globalization and the Crisis of Sovereignty, Legitimacy, and Democracy," *Latin American Perspectives* 29 (2002): 59, 60.

42. M. Patricia Fernández-Kelly, "Immigration, Poverty, and Transnationalism: The Changing Terms of Citizenship in a Global Economy," in *Moral Imperialism: A Critical Anthology*, ed. Berta E. Hernández (New York: New York University Press, 2002), 342.

43. *Id.*

44. *See* "About the FTAA," FTAA-ALCA, http://www.ftaa-alca.org/View_e.asp (accessed June 5, 2007).

45. *See* Douglas S. Massey, Jorge Durand, and Nolan J. Malone, *Beyond Smoke and Mirrors: Mexican Immigration in an Era of Economic Integration* (New York: Russell Sage Foundation, 2003), 2.

46. Donald L. Barlett and James B. Steele, "Who Left the Door Open?" *TIME*, Sept. 12, 2004, 53.

47. Peggy Levitt, *The Transnational Villagers* (Berkeley: University of California Press, 2001), 19.

48. *Id.*

49. Nina Glick Schiller, "Transmigrants and Nation-States: Something Old and Something New in the U.S. Immigrant Experience," in *The Handbook of International Migration*, eds. Charles Hirschmann, Philip Kasinitz, and Josh DeWind (New York: Russell Sage Foundation, 1999), 99.

50. Nef, "Globalization."

51. *Id.* at 62.

52. Immanuel Wallerstein, *The Modern World-System: Capitalist Agriculture and the Origins of The European World-Economy in the Sixteenth Century* (New York: Academic Press, 1976), 230.

53. Mark Weisbrot, "CAFTA Not Likely to Do Better than NAFTA," *Chicago Tribune*, Dec. 18, 2003.

54. "Race to the bottom" is "the constant search for cheaper wages, lower taxes and weaker environmental and other regulations, [which] produces a downward spiral in socio-economic conditions in the United States and in countries around the world. For example, jobs moved from Detroit to Mexico in pursuit of lower wages, and now jobs are being moved from Mexico to China." "Glossary of International Trade Terms," American Friends Service Committee, http://www.afsc.org/trade-matters/learn-about/glossary.htm (accessed June 5, 2007). "Race to the bottom" is also "the idea that, if one country provides a *competitive advantage* to its firms by lax regulation (of the environment, for example), then competing firms in other countries will demand even weaker regulation by their governments, and regulation will be reduced to minimal levels everywhere." Alan V. Deardorff, "Deardorff's Glossary of International Economics" (2001), http://www-personal.umich.edu/~alandear/glossary/r.html (accessed June 5, 2007). *See also* Tim Connor, "Rerouting the Race to the Bottom? Transnational Corporations, Labor Practice Codes of Conduct, and Workers' Right to Organize—The Case of Nike, Inc.," in Hernández-Truyol ed., *Moral Imperialism*, 166.

55. Jorge Nef, "The Political Economy of Globalization, Exclusion, and Human Insecurity in the Americas: Historical and Structural Perspectives" (paper presented at Global Blues and Sustainable Development: The Emerging Challenges for Bureaucracy, Technology, and Governance Conference, University of South Florida, Sept. 23–24, 2005), 4, http://www.patelcenter.usf.edu/assets/pdf/IPSA-Nef.pdf ("in this complex exchange system, [the same way as] capital, technology, and ideology flow south[, . . .] profits and population[s] flow north").

56. Saskia Sassen, "Economic Globalization and the Redrawing of Citizenship," in Hernández-Truyol ed., *Moral Imperialism*, 135.

57. *Id.* at 137.

58. *Id.* (emphasis in original).

59. *Id.* at 141 (footnotes omitted) ("Given the properties of the systems through which the market operates . . . and the magnitude of orders it can produce, it can exercise undue pressure to get the right types of policies instituted, which is precisely what is happening"). *See also id.* at 144 (noting that "a new and increasingly institutionalized framework designed to embrace various objectives that lie largely in the domain of markets and firms . . . allows firms and markets to exercise enormous influence in shaping what the 'proper' government policy ought to be").

60. *Id.* at 146.

61. *See* Michael Walzer, "The Civil Society Argument," in *Dimensions of Radical Democracy: Pluralism, Citizenship, and Community*, ed. Chantal Mouffe (New York: Verso, 1992), 162–63.

62. *See id.* at 163 (suggesting that "once incorporated into civil society . . . citizenship . . . can [n]ever again be all-absorbing").

63. For the ideas of citizenship proposed by civil society theorists, see Kymlicka and Norman, "Return of the Citizen," 363.

CHAPTER 6

1. An extreme example is David Weissbrodt, Joan Fitzpatrick, and Frank Newman, *International Human Rights: Law, Policy, and Process* (Ottawa: Anderson, 2002), which does not address environmental protection at all.

2. *See, e.g.*, David Hunter, James Salzman, and Durwood Zaelke, *International Environmental Law and Policy* (New York: Foundation Press, 2007), 1365.

3. *Id.* at 1367 (exploring the use of "a human rights approach" as "an independent legal strategy for protecting the environment"). *See also* Michael R. Anderson, "Human Rights Approaches to Environmental Protection: An Overview," in *Human Rights Approaches to Environmental Protection*, eds. Alan E. Boyle and Michael R. Anderson (New York: Clarendon, 1996), 1–4, 21–23.

4. J. G. Merrills, *Environmental Protection and Human Rights: Conceptual Aspects*, in Boyle and Anderson, eds., *Human Rights Approaches*, 40.

5. A Commission of Experts appointed by Costa Rica's Environmental Court issued its factual report in early 2004: *Evaluating Report, Comisíon de Peritos para la Valoración del Daño Ambiental de los Sectores Canal Battan, Barra del Pacuare, Lagunas Madre de Dios y Santa María* (2004). *See also* Modest Kwapinski, "Case Study of Docket No. 11-03, Standard Fruit Company of Costa Rica, S.A.," 1–2 (MS, student seminar paper on Tribunal Ambiental Administrativo investigation, on file with authors).

6. 28 I.L.M. 161 (1988), O.A.S. T.S. No. 69 (1988).

7. CAFTA-DR-US, art. 21.1.1.

8. Richard L. Herz, "Litigating Environmental Abuses Under the Alien Tort Claims Act: A Practical Assessment," *Virginia Journal of International Law* 40 (2000): 545, 547.

9. *See* Clifford Rechtschaffen and Eileen P. Gauna, *Environmental Justice: Law, Policy, and Regulation* (Durham, N.C.: Carolina Academic Press, 2002), 3.

10. *See* Secretariat, Commission for Environmental Cooperation (CEC), *Metales y Derivados: Final Factual Record* (Montreal: CEC, July 2, 2002), 21, http://www.cec.org/files/pdf/sem/98-7-FFR-e.pdf (accessed June 28, 2007).

11. *See* "Letter to President of Chile's Human Rights Commission from the Mapuche Peoples" (Aug. 22, 1998), http://members.aol.com/mapulink2/english-2/

letter-06.html (accessed June 29, 2007). The effect of similar government-transnational projects on indigenous populations is discussed in chapter 11.

12. Duncan Brack, "Multilateral Environmental Agreements: An Overview," in *Trade, Investment, and the Environment: Proceedings of the Royal Institute of International Affairs Conference*, eds. Halina Ward and Duncan Brack (London: Earthscan, 2000), 125.

13. Carmen G. Gonzalez, "Trade Liberalization, Food Security, and the Environment: The Neoliberal Threat to Sustainable Rural Development," *Transnational Law and Contemporary Problems* 14 (2004): 419, 423, 469–70.

14. *U.S.-Tuna-Dolphin II,* ¶ 5.8.

15. *E.g., U.S.-Gasoline,* ¶ 6.9 (the United States chose not to appeal the panel finding that imported and domestic gasoline were like products under GATT Article III:4 despite different pollution effects in their production). Two dispute panels convened under the NAFTA in the late 1980s first alerted the environmental community to the potential for conflict between trade rules and environmental protection. These cases explored another basis for denying environmental regulations the protection of GATT Article III's safe harbor. An "internal regulation" (which Article III will shelter if it is nondiscriminatory) may be treated as a border regulation (prohibited outright by Article XI) if the regulation adversely affects imports. These cases address fishery size limits, but the internal regulation/border restriction issue has far broader implications. *See* the discussion of this seemingly dormant distinction in Chris Wold, Sanford Gaines, and Greg Block, *Trade and the Environment: Law and Policy* (Durham, N.C.: Carolina Academic Press, 2005), 148–64.

16. Robert Howse and Donald Regan, "The Product/Process Distinction—An Illusory Basis for Disciplining 'Unilateralism' in Trade Policy," *European Journal of International Law* 11 (2000): 249, 253–61.

17. GATT art. III:1. Article X:1 refers to regulations affecting a product's "processing, mixing, or other use." *See* Steve Charnovitz, "Green Roots, Bad Pruning: GATT Rules and Their Application to Environmental Trade Measures," *Tulane Environmental Law Journal* 7 (1994): 299, 322.

18. John H. Jackson, "Comments on *Shrimp/Turtle* and the Product/Process Distinction," *European Journal of International Law* 11 (2000): 303, 304.

19. As to China's Laogai system of 1,500 prison labor camps, one observer noted that, "with the exception of shipments here and there being turned away at U.S. Ports because they can be traced to forced labor, most goods make it to market. Christmas tree lights, auto parts, textile goods are only some of the items to be considered. And this, of course, ignores the fact that a lot of the forced labor goods stay in country and support the system of legitimate export goods." Patricia Pylman, "Forced Prison Labor in China," Eternal Perspective Ministries, http://www.epm.org/articles/laogai.html (accessed Jun. 16, 2007).

20. Laurence Boisson de Chazournes, "Unilateralism and Environmental Protection: Issues of Perception and Reality of Issues," *European Journal of International Law* 11 (2000): 315, 317, 325; Philippe Sands, "'Unilateralism,' Values, and International Law," *European Journal of International Law* 11 (2000): 291, 300.

21. *Compare Japan-Lumber*, 167 (lumber from different species of trees are unlike) *with Spain—Coffee*, 102 (coffees of all bean types are like).

22. The WTC held that consideration of the difference in physical characteristics such as health risk must take account of the purpose of Article III as a whole, especially its prohibition of discrimination "so as to afford protection to domestic industry." Consideration of consumer preferences alone offers a wide berth for introduction of human rights aspects of a product's creation. *EC-Asbestos*, ¶ 128. *See* the excellent elaboration of these issues in Michael J. Trebilcock and Robert Howse, *The Regulation of International Trade* (New York: Routledge, 2005), 105, 539.

23. The other exceptions are mostly of historic interest. Paragraph (c) covers import and export of gold or silver; Paragraph (h) deals with intergovernmental commodity agreements; Paragraph (i) permits limits on exports to ensure domestic supply; and Paragraph (j) is a more general short supply provision.

24. The reference to "general" reminds us that other, specific exceptions to the Four Pillars are contained within articles I, II, III, and XI themselves, as we discuss in section 2.3.

25. *U.S.-Shrimp-Turtle I*, ¶¶ 156–59.

26. *Id*. at ¶ 120.

27. The New York draft of Paragraph (b) originally required that "corresponding domestic safeguards . . . exist in the importing country." The more reasonable conclusion from this language is that if a Member chooses to protect human or animal health outside its jurisdiction by a restrictive import measure, the Member also must impose similar protections on the conduct of its domestic producers.

28. *Thailand-Cigarettes*, ¶ 75. In fact, the case found that "necessary" means "the least GATT-inconsistent measure" that the Member "could reasonably be expected to employ to achieve its health policy objective." To be sure, the Necessity Test in this view elevates trade over the social purpose of the exception, but does not require that any trade restriction be "unavoidable."

29. *U.S.-Tuna-Dolphin I*, ¶ 5.27. The panel's second alternative holding does not suffer from these same logical shortcomings. The panel found that even if an import prohibition were the only reasonably available choice to protect dolphins outside its territory, it was not "necessary" to require as a condition of import that Mexico's rate of killing dolphins not exceed the U.S. rate for the year that the tuna were imported. Mexico's tuna captains could not know what benchmark applied because the U.S. rate would only be calculated after the period ended.

The panel's analysis in this respect is sound and the WTC in fact resurrects it in the *U.S.-Shrimp-Turtle I* decision some seventeen years later, as noted in section 6.5(C). The actual holding of *U.S.-Tuna-Dolphin I* nonetheless remained that Paragraph (b) did not permit extraterritorial protection of animal life or health. The United States and Mexico exiled the decision to GATT limbo as an unadopted report because neither agreed with its reasoning. They settled their dispute through negotiation of a dolphin-protection treaty. Agreement for the Reduction of Dolphin Mortality in the Eastern Tropical Pacific, 33 I.L.M. 936 (1994).

30. The existence of other GATT provisions that apply extraterritorially does not prove that the treaty in all instances permits such reach, in the same way that finding provisions of clearly limited application would not prove the opposite. *See* Lorand Bartels, "Article XX and the Problem of Extraterritorial Jurisdiction: The Case of Trade Measures for the Protection of Human Rights," *Journal of World Trade* 36 (2002): 353, 358. Although the WTC has declined to pass on this question, *U.S.-Shrimp-Turtle I*, ¶ 133, WTO Members have not since raised the extraterritorial argument.

31. *U.S.-Tuna-Dolphin II*, ¶ 5.38.

32. *EC-Asbestos*, ¶ 172.

33. *See supra* note 30.

34. *Canada-Herring and Salmon*, ¶ 4.6.

35. *U.S.-Gasoline*, ¶ 19.

36. *U.S.-Shrimp-Turtle I*, ¶ 141.

37. *U.S.-Gasoline*, ¶ 21.

38. *U.S.-Shrimp-Turtle I*, ¶¶ 163-66.

39. *Id.* at ¶¶ 180-81.

40. "We observe that, although the *TBT Agreement* is intended to 'further the objectives of GATT 1994,' it does so through a specialized legal regime that applies solely to a limited class of measures. For these measures, the *TBT Agreement* imposes obligations on Members that seem to be *different* from, and *additional* to, the obligations imposed on Members under the GATT 1994." *EC-Asbestos*, ¶ 80 (*dictum*).

41. Article 2.5 provides that if the technical regulation is in pursuit of a listed objective, the regulation benefits from a presumption that it meets the Necessity Test of Article 2.2: it is not more trade-restrictive than necessary, at least if the regulation also "is in accordance with relevant international standards."

42. Satisfactory reasons might include that the Member possessed inadequate testing equipment or that the standard would not have worked in the extreme cold of its climate.

43. National Research Council, *Standards, Conformity Assessment, and Trade into the 21st Century* (Washington: National Academy of Sciences, 1995), Executive Summary, http://books.nap.edu/readingroom/books/stand/summary.html#3.

44. The General Interpretative Note to Annex 1 of the Marrakesh Agreement Establishing the WTO commands that, in the event of a conflict between the GATT and another WTO Agreement, the other WTO Agreement prevails.

45. *EC-Sardines,* ¶ 275. The complaining Member also must establish that the challenged measure is not "based on" the international standard.

46. Example from Elliot B. Staffin, "Trade Barrier or Trade Boom: A Critical Evaluation of Environmental Labeling and Its Role in the 'Greening' of World Trade," *Columbia Journal of Environmental Law* 21 (1996): 205, 238.

47. Doaa A. Motaal, "The Agreement on Technical Barriers to Trade, the Committee on Trade and the Environment, and Eco-Labelling," in *Trade, Environment, and the Millennium,* eds. Gary P. Sampson and W. Bradnee Chambers (New York: UN University Press, 2002), 267, 272.

48. The narrow interpretation of the PPM language is logical on one level. While GATT's "physical characteristics and uses" test for whether two products are "like" is anything but scientifically objective, still it is far more objective than some of the production processes that could be used by a country as a disguised form of protection for its own industry. For example, a Member might specify that imported coffee must have been roasted in one of a dozen ways that may be marginally more environmentally friendly when that method happens also to be used exclusively by the Member's domestic coffee growers. We addressed this "slippery slope" argument in section 6.4(A).

49. Those who adhere to the narrow interpretation also find no new coverage from the second sentence of the definition of "technical regulation": "It may also include or deal exclusively with terminology, symbols, packaging, marking or labeling requirements as they apply to a product, process, or production method." The "it" that begins this sentence supposedly is simply shorthand for the longer phrase at the start of the first sentence and thus does not change the requirement that the PPM must relate to the product's physical characteristics for the TBT Agreement to apply. The argument for the broader reading applies a fortiori to the second sentence: it is illogical for the drafters to add an entire sentence simply to repeat what already was included in the first sentence.

50. Curiously, the definition of "standard" in Annex 1.2 omits the word "their" before "related processes and production methods." A "standard" is a "document . . . that provides . . . characteristics for products or related processes and production methods, compliance with which is not mandatory." Because the disagreement is whether the PPM refers to the product or to its characteristics, the omission of this word contributes nothing to resolving the ambiguity.

51. The restrictive interpretation finds support in the negotiating history. Mexico inserted "their related" before "processes and productions methods" so that the TBT Agreement could lend its seal of approval only to a limited class of PPMs (in fact, it imposes additional requirements on covered measures). The EC supports the limited interpretation for opposite reasons than developing

countries such as Mexico, which view ecolabels as other means for developed countries to exclude developing country imports and protect their own industries. The EC favors voluntary ecolabels and takes the position that neither the GATT nor the TBT covers them.

52. Jan McDonald, "Domestic Regulation, International Standards, and Technical Barriers to Trade," *World Trade Review* 5 (2005): 249, 255, http://journals. cambridge.org/action/displayAbstract;jsessionid=6E57A0932687FCDE3772270D8 1270E72.tomcat1?fromPage=online&aid=340369 (accessed Jun. 16, 2007).

53. World Commission on Environment and Development, *Our Common Future* (New York: Oxford University Press, 1987), 43–46.

54. UN Report of the World Summit on Sustainable Development (Sept. 4, 2002), ¶ 15, ch. IX, http://daccessdds.un.org/doc/UNDOC/GEN/N02/636/93/ PDF/N0263693.pdf?OpenElement (accessed Aug. 10, 2006).

55. Arthur E. Appleton, "Environmental Labelling Schemes Revisited: WTO Law and Developing Country Implications," in Sampson and Chambers, eds., *Trade, Environment, and the Millennium*, 259.

56. Daniel C. Esty, *Greening the GATT: Trade, Environment, and the Future* (Washington: Institute for International Economics, 1994), 134.

57. Developing countries, at a minimum, will consider discarding the PPM distinction significant because it would imply that not only ecolabels, but also such policies as U.S. measures to protect dolphins and sea turtles, comply with the strictures of the TBT. *See* Peter L. Lallas and Andreas R. Zeigler, "International Occupational and Environmental Medicine," in *International Environmental Law and Policy*, eds. Edith B. Weiss et al. (New York: Aspen, 1998), 1077.

58. Wold et al., *Trade and the Environment*, 425.

59. Esty, *Greening the Gatt*, 216–18.

60. Paul Hawken, Amory Lovins, and L. Hunter Lovins, *Natural Capitalism: Creating the Next Industrial Revolution* (Boston: Little, Brown, 1999), 4, 19, 21.

61. *Id.* at 10–11.

62. *Id.* at 82–83.

63. "Who Benefits: Financial Institutions," International Finance Corporation, http://www.ifc.org/equatorprinciples (accessed Aug. 9, 2006).

64. "The 'Equator Principles': A Financial Industry Benchmark for Determining, Assessing, and Managing Social and Environmental Risk in Project Financing" (July 2006), princ. 2, 3, 5, The Equator Principles, http://equator-principles. com/documents/Equator_Principles.pdf.

65. Al Gore and David Blood, "For People and Planet," *San Francisco Chronicle*, Apr. 4, 2006.

66. "Experts: Climate Change Hurts Poorest," *Associated Press*, Mar. 21, 2006 (quoting Michel Jarraud, secretary-general, World Meteorological Organization).

67. *EC-Hormones*, ¶¶ 103–4; *EC-Sardines*, ¶ 275. In *EC-Biotech Products*, ¶¶ 7.2977–79, the panel applied Appellate Body decisions to find that, with respect

to SPS Article 5.7's precautionary approach to food safety measures, "in cases where a complaining party alleges that an SPS measure is inconsistent with Article 5.1, it is incumbent on the complaining party, and not the responding party, to demonstrate that the challenged measure is inconsistent with at least one of the four requirements set forth in Article 5.7." The USTR has said that this same reversal of the burden of proof applies to TBT measures as well. *The GATT Uruguay Round Agreements: Report on Environmental Issues* (Washington: USTR, Aug. 1994), 51, *reprinted in Uruguay Round Table Agreements*, H.R. Doc. No. 103-316, vol. 1, 1233 (Sept. 27, 1994) ("It was understood during the negotiation of the TBT Agreement that the second sentence of Article 2.2 would operate in a manner similar to Article 5.6 of the S&P Agreement").

CHAPTER 7

1. J. P. Smith, "Healthy Bodies and Thick Wallets: The Dual Relation between Health and Economic Status," *Journal of Economic Perspectives* 13 (1999): 145, 166.

2. M. Gregg Bloche and Elizabeth R. Jungman, "Health Policy and the WTO," *Journal of Legal Medicine and Ethics* 31 (2003): 529.

3. Universal Declaration, arts. 3, 23, 25.

4. UNCHR Res. 2001/33.

5. American Declaration, art. VII.

6. Protocol of San Salvador, arts. 10, 11, 12.

7. Ratifications are recorded on the OAS Web site at http://www.oas.org/main/main.asp?sLang=E&sLink=http://www.oas.org/DIL/treaties_and_agreements.htm.

8. Tina Rosenberg, "Look at Brazil," *New York Times*, Jan. 28, 2001, http://query.nytimes.com/gst/fullpage.html?sec=health&res=9D05E5DB113CF93BA15752C0A9679C8B63. *See* Web site of Pan American Health Organization *at* http://www.paho.org.

9. Joanna Theiss, "When Trade Shifts Its Weight: Creating a Balance Between Public Health and Private Rights in the Area of Access to HIV/AIDS Medicines," 4 (MS on file with authors).

10. *Id.*

11. Alan Beattie, "Farmers Say EU Rules Feed a Hunger for Trade Barriers: Poor Countries Allege that Food Standards Offer Backdoor Protectionism," *Financial Times UK*, Oct. 10, 2005, 20.

12. The evidentiary basis for Japan's later restrictions on imported fruit to protect against fire blight failed even the initial step of constituting what the Appellate Body would accept as a risk assessment under SPS Agreement Article 5.1. *Japan-Apples*, ¶¶ 189–97.

13. *Japan-Agricultural Products*, ¶ 4.2.

14. *Australia-Salmon*, ¶ 124.

15. *Id.* at ¶¶ 162–64.

16. *EC-Hormones*, ¶¶ 186, 196–97.

17. Biosafety Protocol, arts. 10.6, 11.8.

18. Although many iterations of the principle have been fashioned by entities seeking to "improve" one or more of its conditions, the statement widely accepted as definitive is contained in the Rio Declaration, princ. 15. Article 1 of the Biosafety Protocol explicitly labels its "precautionary approach" as that of the Rio Declaration's Principle 15.

19. *See* Terence P. Stewart and David S. Johanson, "A Nexus of Trade and the Environment: The Relationship Between the Cartagena Protocol on Biosafety and the SPS Agreement of the World Trade Organization," *Colorado Journal of International Environmental Law* 14 (2003): 1, 38.

20. *EC-Biotech Products,* ¶ 7.75.

21. *Id.* at ¶ 7.89.

22. *Id.* at, *e.g.,* ¶¶ 7.3258–62 (as to Austria's ban of T25 maize; the panel elsewhere in its decision applied identical reasoning with respect to other countries and products).

23. Frederick H. Degnan, "The Food Label and the Right-to-Know," *Food Drug Law Journal* 52 (1997): 49, 49, 55–56.

24. CBD, art. 27, ann. 2.

25. Bloche and Jungman, "Health Policy," 530; M. Gregg Bloche, "WTO Deference to National Health Policy: Toward an Interpretive Principle," *Journal of International Economics Law* 5 (2002): 825, 827.

26. *See, e.g.,* U.S.-*Wheat,* ¶¶ 69–70.

27. *EC-Asbestos,* ¶¶ 173–74.

28. Bloche, "WTO Deference," 848.

29. Cristiana Bastos, *Global Response to AIDS: Science in Emergency* (Bloomington: Indiana University Press, 1999), 68.

30. Carlos Passarelli and Veriano Terto Jr., "Good Medicine: Brazil's Multifront War on AIDS," *NACLA Report on the Americas* 35 (2002): 35, 37.

31. Ellen. T. Hoen, "TRIPS, Pharmaceutical Patents, and Access to Essential Medicines: A Long Way from Seattle to Doha," *Chicago Journal of International Law* 3 (2002): 27, 28.

32. Bloche and Jungman, "Health Policy," 534.

33. DHHS Panel on Antiretroviral Guidelines for Adults and Adolescents, Office of AIDS Research Advisory Council (OARAC), U.S. National Institutes of Health, *Guidelines for the Use of Antiretroviral Agents in HIV-1-Affected Adults and Adolescents* (Bethesda, Md.: OARAC, Oct. 10, 2006), 40, http://aidsinfo.nih.gov/contentfiles/AdultandAdolescentGL.pdf.

34. Taimoon Stewart, "The Functioning of Patent Monopoly Rights in Developing Countries: In Whose Interests?" *Social Studies* 49 (2000): 1.

35. World Health Organization (WHO), *Report on Infectious Diseases: Removing Obstacles to Healthy Development,* WHO/CDS/99.1 (Geneva: WHO, 1999), ch. 1.

36. Winston P. Nagan, "International Intellectual Property, Access to Health Care, and Human Rights: South Africa v. United States," *Florida Journal of International Law* 14 (2002): 155, 162.

37. "Abbott Laboratories Agrees to Cut in Price for AIDS Drug in Brazil" (July 5, 2007), 2, Inter-American Dialogue.

38. "Brazilian Government Set to Break Patent Today on HIV/AIDS Drug," *Latin American Advisor*, May 4, 2007, 3.

39. Passarelli and Terto, "Good Medicine," 37.

40. Amendment of the TRIPS Agreement, Decision of December 8, 2005, WT/L/641.

41. "Amendment to WTO TRIPS Agreement Makes Access to Affordable Medicines Even More Bleak," Press Release (Dec. 7, 2005), Médicins Sans Frontières, http://www.accessmed-msf.org/prod/publications.asp?scntid=712200514255 22&contenttype=PARA (accessed June 28, 2007).

42. Rahul Rajkuman, "CAFTA Will Hurt People with HIV," *Boston Globe*, May 26, 2005, http://www.boston.com/news/globe/editorial_opinion/oped/ articles/2005/05/26/cafta_will_hurt_people_with_hiv/.

43. Note from Richard Stern, of the HIV/AIDS advocacy group Agua Buena, based in Costa Rica (Mar. 30, 2006) (on file with authors).

44. Lucien O. Chauvin, "Peru's Congress Approves Amendments to Free Trade Agreement with United States," *International Trade Reporter* 24 (July 5, 2007): 957; Rosella Brevetti, "United States, Panama Sign Free Trade Pact Under TPA; Colombia Accepts Changes to FTA," *International Trade Reporter* 24 (July 5, 2007): 957.

45. Hoen, "TRIPS," 28.

46. Melinda F. Gates, "What Women Really Need," *Newsweek*, May 15, 2006, 66–67.

47. Christopher R. Hedican, Jason M. Hedican, and Mark P. A. Hudson, "McDonnell Douglas: Alive and Well," *Drake Law Review* 52 (2004): 383, 423, n.199.

48. Imani Perry, "Buying White Beauty," *Cardozo Journal of Law and Gender* 12 (2006): 579, 582, 606.

49. Edward E. Telles and Edward Murguia, "Phenotypic Discrimination and Income Differences Among Mexican Americans," *Social Sciences Quarterly* 71 (1990): 682, 682–83.

50. Christina Gomez, "The Continual Significance of Skin Color: An Exploratory Study of Latinos in the Northeast," *Hispanic Journal of Behavioral Science* 22 (2000): 94, 94.

51. James A. Auerbach and Barbara K. Krimgold, "Improving Health: It Doesn't Take a Revolution," in *Income, Socioeconomic Status, and Health: New Research Initiatives*, eds. James A. Auerbach and Barbara K. Krimgold (Washington: National Policy Association, 2001), 12.

CHAPTER 8

1. Ernst-Ulrich Petersmann, "Challenges to the Legitimacy and Efficiency of the World Trading System: Democratic Governance and Competition Culture in the WTO, Introduction and Summary," *Journal of International Economics Law* 7 (2004): 585, 589.

2. Sidney Weintraub, "The United States and the Future of Free Trade in the Americas," *Law and Business Review of the Americas* 6 (2000): 303, 304. We might have greater willingness to accept such union advocacy as an example of international union solidarity, not domestic protectionism, but for near-universal union opposition to trade liberalization of any sort. Thomas J. Manley and Luis Lauredo, "International Labor Standards in Free Trade Agreements of the Americas," *Emory International Law Review* 18 (2004): 85, 95–96. At the rank-and-file level, many workers do indeed support better working conditions for their counterparts in other nations. This motivation is reflected in the keying of wage proposals to living standards in the LDC, not in the developed market.

3. Claire M. Dickerson, "The Recognition of the Individual: A Human Rights Perspective for International Commerce," in *Moral Imperialism: A Critical Anthology*, ed. Berta E. Hernández-Truyol (New York: New York University Press, 2002), 161.

4. Manley and Lauredo, "International Labor Standards," 91.

5. Petersmann, "Challenges," 590.

6. The eight treaties considered fundamental by the ILO are Freedom of Association and Protection of the Right to Organise (Ratified 1948, No. 87); Right to Organise and Collective Bargaining Convention (1949, No. 98); Equal Remuneration Convention, (1951, No. 100); Forced Labor Convention (1930, No. 29); Discrimination (Employment and Occupation) Convention (1958, No. 111); Abolition of Forced Labor Convention (1957, No. 105); Minimum Age Convention (1973, No. 138); CEWFCL.

7. ILO Work Declaration, pmbl. and art. 2.

8. We remind readers of the point made in chapter 3 that the WTO is a statist body that does not question the legitimacy of extant government officials to represent the best interests of their citizens.

9. WTO, Ministerial Declaration of December 13, 1996, Singapore, WT/MIN(96)/DEC, ¶ 4, http://docsonline.wto.org. We would hardly have expected developed countries to admit complicity in protectionist practices and the desire to deny LDCs their comparative advantage, particularly in the midst of multilateral negotiations styled the "Doha Development Agenda."

10. Minimum Age Convention, art. 2.4. The Convention permits "light work" that does not interfere with schooling at age thirteen (twelve for LDCs). *Id.* at arts. 7.1, 7.4.

11. Juan Forero, "In Ecuador's Banana Fields, Child Labor Is Key to Profit," *New York Times*, Jul. 13, 2002 (quoting U.S. House of Rep. George Miller, D-CA), http://www.clrlabor.org/alerts/2002/updateonnoboabananacampaign.html#5.

12. ILO Work Declaration, pmbl; *see* "About the Declaration," ILO, http://www.ilo.org/dyn/declaris/DECLARATIONWEB.ABOUTDECLARATIONHOME?var_language=EN (accessed June 28, 2007).

13. Although the United States normally is the *demandeur* in promoting the linkage of trade and labor rights, it has ratified only the child labor and forced labor conventions. "Ratifications of the ILO Fundamental Conventions" (June 29, 2007), ILO, http://webfusion.ilo.org/public/db/standards/normes/appl/appl-ratif8conv.cfm?Lang=EN (accessed June 28, 2007).

14. Berta E. Hernández-Truyol, "Human Rights, Globalization, Culture: Centering Personhood in International Narrative," in *Moral Imperialism: A Critical Anthology*, ed. Berta E. Hernández-Truyol (New York: New York University Press, 2002), 357.

15. "How the ILO Works," ILO, http://www.ilo.org/public/english/depts/fact.htm.

16. Kimberly A. Elliot, "The ILO and Enforcement of Core Labor Standards," *International Economics Policy Briefs*, No. 00-6 (Jul. 2000), 1, 2–4, http://www.iie.com/publications/pb/pb00-6.pdf. Article 26 of the ILO Constitution authorizes complaints by Members that will be investigated by a Commission of Inquiry, whose report may be appealed to the ICJ. Article 33's authorization of economic sanctions, however, has been used but once, to ban Burma, found to have committed repeated violations of the forced labor prohibitions, from ILO meetings. *Id.* at 5–6.

17. This apt term is used by Marisa A. Pagnattaro, "The 'Helping Hand' in Trade Agreements: An Analysis of and Proposal for Labor Provisions in U.S. Free Trade Agreements," *Florida Journal of International Law* 16 (2004): 845.

18. WTO, "Cross-cutting and New Issues," in *Understanding the WTO* (Geneva: WTO, 2007), 63, 75, http://www.wto.org/english/thewto_e/whatis_e/tif_e/understanding_e.pdf.

19. Petersmann, "Challenges," 588.

20. In accordance with the ICCPR, work or service that is not "normally required of a person who is under detention in consequence of a lawful order of a court" would lose the protection of Article 3(c)'s exemption from violation of the human right to be free from forced or compulsory labor.

21. *U.S.-Shrimp-Turtle I*, ¶ 141.

22. *U.S.-Gasoline*, ¶ 19 (discussing the leading GATT case, *Canada-Herring and Salmon*, which held at para. 4.6 that the border restriction must be "primarily aimed at" the conservation of exhaustible natural resources. This test would disqualify an array of actions with multiple extraterritorial purposes, such as the U.S. Clean Water Act).

23. Steve Charnovitz, "Environmental and Labour Standards in Trade," *World Economy* 15 (May 1992), *reprinted in* Steve Charnovitz, *Trade Law and Global Governance* (London: Cameron May, 2002), 59, 63.

24. The Business Roundtable, *Preparing for New WTO Trade Negotiations to Boost the Economy* (Washington: The Business Roundtable, May 1999), iv, http://www.businessroundtable.org/pdf/321.pdf.

25. Steve Charnovitz, "Triangulating the World Trade Organization," *American Journal of International Law* 96 (2002): 28, n.67.

26. Minimum Age Convention.

27. ICECSR, art. 7(b).

28. *Id.* at arts. 12.2(b), (c).

29. *EC-Asbestos*, ¶ 114.

30. *Id.* at ¶¶ 168, 171.

31. *U.S.-Gambling*, ¶¶ 6.459–61.

32. Steve Charnovitz, "The Moral Exception in Trade Policy," *Virginia Journal of International Law* 38 (1998): 689, 694.

33. *U.S.-Gambling*. We have drawn for our analysis of the case from Jeremy C. Marwell, "Trade and Morality: The WTO Public Morals Exception After Gambling," *New York University Law Review* 81 (2006): 802.

34. The GATS Clause adds permission also "to maintain public order," a cause not pertinent to our analysis.

35. *U.S.-Tuna-Dolphin I*, ¶ 5.28; *U.S.-Tuna-Dolphin II*, ¶¶ 5.20, 5.24.

36. Charnovitz, "The Moral Exception," 723.

37. Elissa Alben, "GATT and the Fair Wage: A Historical Perspective on the Labor-Trade Link," *Columbia Law Review* 101 (2001): 1410, 1416, 1422.

38. *U.S.-Shrimp I*, ¶¶ 156, 159.

39. Marrakesh Agreement Establishing the World Trade Organization, Apr. 15, 1994, 1867 U.N.T.S. 154; 33 I.L.M. 1154 (1994) (Marrakesh Agreement), at General Interpretative Note to Annex 1A, 33 I.L.M. 1154 (1994).

40. *Korea-Beef*, ¶ 162.

41. NAALC. The background of the side agreement is somewhat more complex. *See* Raj Bhala, *International Trade Law: Theory and Practice* (New York: Lexis, 2007), 840.

42. *Compare* NAALC, arts. 21, 22, *with* NAFTA, chs. 19, 20.

43. NAALC, art 41.1.

44. Pub. L. No. 107-210, 116 Stat. 933, 19 U.S.C. 2004 (2002).

45. 19 U.S.C. §§ 3802(a)(6), (7), (9) (2002).

46. 19 U.S.C. § 3802(b)(12) (2002).

47. 19 U.S.C. § 3802(b) (2002).

48. U.S.-Chile FTA, art. 18.1(1).

49. In the WTO, failure of the losing Member to implement a dispute panel's recommendations leads to authorization by the WTO for the winning

Members to impose trade penalties "equivalent to the level of nullification or impairment"—that is, to match the trade value lost as a result of the WTO Agreement violations. WTO DSU, art. 22.5.

50. Manley and Lauredo, "International Labor Standards," 85.

51. CAFTA-DR-US.

52. "Central America has been the scene of continuing abuses of workers' rights," including ongoing suppression of worker rights to organize, beatings and even assassinations of union leaders, child labor in dangerous jobs, and employment discrimination against both women and indigenous peoples. Sandra Polaski, "Central America and the U.S. Face Challenge—and Chance for Historic Breakthrough—on Workers' Rights," Carnegie Endowment for International Peace: Trade, Equity, and Development Project, *Issue Brief* (Feb. 2003), http://carnegieendowment.org/publications/index.cfm?fa=view&id=1187&prog=zgp&proj=zted.

53. CAFTA-DR-US, art. 16.1.2, 16.8.

54. Manley and Lauredo, "International Labor Standards," 110; CAFTA-DR-US, arts. 16.4–6.

55. Office of the USTR, "Real Results on Labor Rights: Facts About Peru's Labor Law Protection and Enforcement," *Peru TPA Facts* (Dec. 2005), http://www.ustr.gov/assets/Document_Library/Fact_Sheets/2005/asset_upload_file163_8548.pdf.

56. Rosella Brevetti, "Democratic, GOP Lawmakers Reach Agreement with Administration on FTAs," *International Trade Reporter* 24 (May 17, 2007): 674.

57. Larry Rohter, "South American Trading Bloc Frees Movement of Its People," *New York Times*, Nov. 24, 2002, sec. 1, 6.

58. Ministerial Declaration of San Jose, Summit of the Americas, Fourth Trade Ministerial Joint Declaration, San Jose, Costa Rica (Mar. 19, 1998), ¶ 11. The nine negotiating groups address market access; investment; services; government procurement; dispute settlement; agriculture; intellectual property rights; subsidies, anti-dumping, and countervailing duties; and competition policy.

59. Bipartisan Trade Promotion Act of 2002, Pub. L. No. 107-210, 116 Stat. 933 (2002).

60. Pagnattaro, "The 'Helping Hand,'" 891.

61. Jordana Timerman, "Chávez and Maradona Lead Massive Rebuke of Bush," *The Nation*, Nov. 5, 2005, http://www.thenation.com/doc/20051121/timerman.

62. James F. Hollifield and Thomas Osang, "Trade and Migration in North America: The Role of NAFTA," *Law and Business Review of the Americas* 11 (2005): 327, 339.

63. María P. Fernández-Kelly, "Maquiladoras: The View from the Inside," in *The Women, Gender, and Development Reader*, eds. Nalini Visvanathan et al. (Atlantic Highlands, N.J.: ZED, 1997), 203, 204.

64. William C. Gruben, "NAFTA, Trade Diversion, and Mexico's Textiles and Apparel Boom and Bust," *Southwest Economy* 5 (Sept./Oct. 2006): 11, 13.

65. Philip Martin, "NAFTA and Mexico-US Migration," (Dec. 16, 2005), 7, http://giannini.ucop.edu/Mex_USMigration.pdf.

66. Pia Orrenius and Madeline Zavodny, "Immigration Policy: What Are the Consequences for an Amnesty for Undocumented Immigrants?" *Georgetown Public Policy Review* 9 (2004): 21, 24–25.

67. Howard F. Chang, "Migration as International Trade: The Economic Gains from the Liberalized Movement of Labor," *University of California-Los Angeles Journal of International Law and Foreign Affairs* 3 (1999): 371, 373.

68. *See* WTO Secretariat, Background Note, "Presence of Natural Persons (Mode 4)," S/C/W/75 (Dec. 8, 1998). The first three modes of supply are (1) cross-border supply (if Member A is opening its financial services sector, an example is a Member B bank making a loan to a customer in Member A by telephone or other means that finds both the banker and the customer remaining in their home countries); (2) consumption abroad (the Member A customer travels to the bank in Member B to get the loan); and (3) commercial presence (Member B's bank establishes a branch in Member A). Mode 4 in this example would entail an employee of the Member B bank traveling to Member A to meet with the customer.

69. Julia Nielson, "Current Regimes for Temporary Movement of Service Providers: Labour Mobility in Regional Trade Agreements," at the Joint WTO-World Bank Symposium on Movement of Natural Persons (Mode 4) Under the GATS (Apr. 11–12, 2002).

70. WTO Secretariat, Background Note.

71. Daniel Pruzin, "Developing Countries Decry Absence of Mode 4 Offers in WTO Service Talks," *WTO Reporter*, July 15, 2003.

72. USTR inclusion of immigration allowances in the Chile and Singapore FTAs caused Senate Finance Trade Committee Chair Sensenbrenner to include in the Bipartisan Trade Promotion Authority Act of 2002 a prohibition on addressing immigration matters in FTAs. WTO negotiations are not yet covered by this ban.

73. Christopher S. Rugaber, "Business Groups Consult with House Panel on Talks over Temporary Entry Provisions," *WTO Reporter*, April 18, 2005.

74. F. James Sensenbrenner, *Letter to USTR*, May 19, 2005, http://insidetrade.com/secure/dsply_nl_txt.asp?f=wto2002.ask&dh=14262543&q=Sensenbrenner.

75. Daniel Pruzin, "Developing Countries Decry Absence of Mode 4 Offers in WTO Services Talks," *WTO Reporter*, July 15, 2003.

76. *Id.*

77. Rugaber, "Business Groups Consult."

78. "House Presses Snow for Active Engagement in WTO Service Talks," *Inside U.S. Trade*, Apr. 22, 2005.

79. Rugaber, "Business Groups Consult."

80. Daniel Pruzin, "Developing Nations Offer Mode 4 Demands in Services, Focus on Independent Workers," *WTO Reporter*, Mar. 16, 2006.

81. *See* Tomer Broude, "The WTO/GATS Mode 4, International Labour Migration Regimes, and Global Justice," Hebrew University International Law Research Paper No. 7-07 (May 18, 2007), 26–27, http://papers.ssrn.com/sol3/papers.cfm?abstract_id=987315.

82. Berta E. Hernández-Truyol, "Building Bridges—Latinas and Latinos at the Crossroads: Realities, Rhetoric, and Replacement," *Columbia Human Rights Law Review* 15 (1994): 369, 376.

83. Michael Hughes and Bradley R. Hertel, "The Significance of Color Remains: A Study of Life Chances, Mate Selection, and Ethnic Consciousness Among Black Americans," *Social Forces* 68 (1990): 1105.

84. Itabari Njeri, "Colorism in American Society, Are Light-skinned Blacks Better Off?" *Los Angeles Times*, Apr. 24, 1988, 1 (27 percent v. 15 percent); Verna M. Keith and Cedric Herring, "Skin Tone and Stratification in the Black Community," *American Journal of Sociology* 97 (1991): 760, 768.

85. Leonard M. Baynes, "If It's Not Just Black and White Anymore, Why Does Darkness Cast a Longer Discriminatory Shadow Than Lightness? An Investigation and Analysis of the Color Hierarchy," *Denver University Law Review* 75 (1997): 131, 133; Carlos H. Arce, Edward Murgia, and W. Parker Frisbee, "Phenotype and Life Chances Among Chicanos," *Hispanic Journal of Behavioral Sciences* 9 (1987): 19, 32.

86. F. James Davis, *Who Is Black? One Nation's Definition* (University Park: Pennsylvania State University Press, 1991), 101.

87. Larry Rohter, "Soccer Skirmish Turns Spotlight on Brazil's Racial Divide," *New York Times*, Sept. 19, 2006.

88. Mirta Ojito, "Best of Friends: Worlds Apart," *New York Times*, June 5, 2000.

89. Imani Perry, "Of Desi, J. Lo, and Color Matters: Law, Critical Race Theory, and the Architecture of Race," *Cleveland State Law Review* 52 (2005): 139, 145.

90. Larry Rohter, "Multiracial Brazil Planning Quotas for Blacks," *New York Times*, Oct. 2, 2001, A3.

91. Carl Degler, *Neither Black Nor White: Slavery and Race Relations in Brazil and the United States* (New York: Macmillan, 1971), 98–112, 226.

92. John J. Putman, "Cuba," *National Geographic*, June 1999, 20.

93. Tanya K. Hernández, "An Exploration of the Efficacy of Class-based Approaches to Racial Justice: The Cuban Context," *University of California-Davis Law Review* 33 (2000): 1135, 1145.

94. Tanya K. Hernández, "Pioneering the Lens of Comparative Race Relations in Law: A. Leon Higginbotham Jr. As a Model of Scholarly Activism," *Yale Law and Policy Review* 20 (2002): 331, 335. *See also* Robert J. Cottrol, "The Long,

Lingering Shadow: Law, Liberalism, and Cultures of Racial Hierarchy and Identity in the Americas," *Tulane Law Review* 76 (2001): 11, 40.

95. Baynes, "If It's Not Just Black," 185.

96. Jennifer Bol, "Using International Law to Fight Child Labor: A Case Study of Guatemala and the Inter-American System," *American University International Law Review* 13 (1998): 1135, 1137.

97. Mathias Busse, "Do Labour Standards Affect Comparative Advantage? Evidence for Labour-Intensive Goods" (Nov. 2001), 7, http://www.hwwa.de/Forschung/Handel_&_Entwicklung/docs/Archiv/Labour%20Standards.pdf (accessed June 28, 2007).

98. Beth Stephens, "The Amorality of Profit: Transnational Corporations and Human Rights," *Berkeley Journal of International Law* 20 (2002): 45, 47.

99. Stephen G. Woods and Brett G. Scharffs, "Applicability of Human Rights Standards to Private Corporations: An American Perspective," *American Journal of Comparative Law* 50 (2002): 531, 539.

100. Detlev F. Vagts, "The Multinational Enterprise: A New Challenge for Transnational Law," *Harvard Law Review* 83 (1970): 739, 756.

101. Isabella D. Bunn, "Global Advocacy for Corporate Accountability: Transatlantic Perspectives from the NGO Community," *American University International Law Review* 19 (2004): 1265, 1271–72.

102. *Id.* Some of the first U.S. companies to develop corporate codes of conduct were General Dynamics, General Electric, and Martin Marietta. *Id.*

103. Institute of Contemporary Observation (ICO), *Day and Night at the Factory: Working Conditions of Temporary Workers in the Factories of Nokia and Its Suppliers in Southern China* (Shenzhen, China: ICO, Mar. 2005), 12, http://www.vientiluotto.net/en_kiina-raportti.pdf (accessed June 28, 2007).

104. Ryan P. Toftoy, "Now Playing: Corporate Codes of Conduct in the Global Theater: Is Nike Just Doing It?" *Arizona Journal of International and Comparative Law* 15 (1998): 905, 918.

105. Kamil Ahmed, "International Labor Rights: A Categorical Imperative?" *Revue de Droit (Universite de Sherbrooke)* 35 (2004): 145, 170.

106. Ramon Mullerat, "Global Responsibility of the Global Business," at the ABA Section of International Law Fall Meeting (Nov. 2006) (MS, on file with authors).

107. *See* Busse, "Do Labour Standards," 7. Codes of conduct are voluntary commitments by enterprises, associations, or other entities that set principles and standards for the conduct of market activities. Rasmus A. Kristensen, Danish Institute for Human Rights (DIHR), *Corporate Codes of Conduct in Denmark: An Examination of Their CSR Content* (Copenhagen: DIHR, 2005), 9, http://www.humanrightsbusiness.org/pdf_files/Corporate%20Codes%20of%20Conduct%20in%20Denmark.pdf.

108. "Codes of Conduct for Multinationals," ILO, Bureau for Workers' Activities, http://www.itcilo.it/english/actrav/telearn/global/ilo/guide/main.htm#Summ (accessed June 28, 2007).

109. "Corporate Codes of Conduct," ILO, Bureau for Workers' Activities, http://www.itcilo.it/english/actrav/telearn/global/ilo/code/main.htm (accessed June 28, 2007).

110. Ahmed, "International Labor Rights," 170.

111. Bunn, "Global Advocacy."

112. Drafters of the U.S. Constitution created a tension in negotiation of trade agreements through the Foreign Commerce Clause powers of the Congress in Art. I, Sec. 8, and the Foreign Affairs Clause powers of the Executive in Art. II, Sec. 2, which requires cooperation between the two branches as to trade matters.

113. Trade Act of 1974, Pub. L. No 93-618, pt. 2, 88 Stat. 1978, *classified principally to* ch. 12, tit. 19 U.S.C. (1974). The program actually was instituted in the Trade Expansion Act of 1962, but was little utilized until the 1974 law expanded its coverage. Committee on Ways and Means, U.S. House of Representatives, *Overview and Compilation of U.S. Trade Statutes*, Committee Print No. WMCP 101-14 (Washington: U.S. Government Printing Office, 1989), 81.

114. *See generally* "Programs and Opportunities: Trade Adjustment Assistance," U.S. Department of Agriculture, http://www.fas.usda.gov/itp/taa/taa.asp (accessed June 28, 2007).

115. *See* "Program Benefits," Trade Adjustment Assistance for Firms, http://taa-centers.org/benefits.html#costsharing (accessed June 28, 2007).

116. Employment and Training Administration, U.S. Department of Labor, "If Imports Cost You Your Job . . . Apply for Trade Adjustment Assistance," Fact Sheet, http://www.doleta.gov/programs/factsht/taa.htm (accessed June 28, 2007).

117. *E.g.,* the state of California is engaged fully in the retraining of workers located in that state; *see* "Employment Development Department: Unemployment Insurance—Trade Adjustment Assistance (TAA)," http://www.edd.ca.gov/uirep/uinafta.htm (accessed June 28, 2007).

118. Trade Adjustment Assistance Reform Act of 2002, Pub. L. No. 107-210, 116 Stat. 933 (Aug. 6, 2002).

119. Carlos Patrón, "Globalization and Neo-nationalism Through the Lens of the Peru—United States Free Trade Agreement," Lecture at University of Florida College of Law (Feb. 24, 2006) (MS, on file with authors).

120. Clive Crook, "Globalization and Its Critics," *Economist*, Sept. 27, 2001, 3; Patrón, "Globalization."

121. John Williamson, Institute for International Economics, "After the Washington Consensus: Latin American Growth and Sustainable Development," Keynote Speech at the Seminar on Latin American Financing and the Role of Development Banks (Mar. 30–31, 2006), 8, http://www.iie.com/publications/papers/williamson0306.pdf (accessed June 28, 2007).

122. Michael Wines, "Africa Adds to Miserable Ranks of Child Workers," *New York Times*, Sept. 22, 2006.

CHAPTER 9

1. Article 36 of the CRC further provides that "state parties shall protect the child against all other forms of exploitation prejudicial to any aspect of the child's welfare." Article 32(2)(a)–(b) commits state parties to taking steps to ensure the child's well-being, including establishing minimum-age provisions and regulating hours and conditions of employment.

2. *See* table 9.1 for the list of state ratifications to these conventions.

3. ILO Convention No. 29, art. 2(1).

4. David Tuller, *Freedom Denied: Forced Labor in California* (Berkeley: Human Rights Center (HRC), University of California, Berkeley, 2005), 3, http://www.hrcberkeley.org/download/freedomdenied.pdf.

5. HRW, *Fingers to the Bone: United States Failure to Protect Child Farmworkers* (New York: HRW, 2000), pt. III, http://www.hrw.org/reports/2000/frmwrkr/index.htm#TopOfPage.

6. Free the Slaves, Washington, D.C., and HRC, *Hidden Slaves Forced Labor in the United States* (Berkeley: HRC, Sept. 2004), 16.

7. OUSGA, U.S. Department of State, *Trafficking in Persons Report: June 2006*, DOS Publ. No. 11335 (Washington: OUSGA, rev. June 2006), 6, http://www.state.gov/documents/organization/66086.pdf (citing ILO estimates).

8. Ann D. Jordan, "Human Rights or Wrongs? The Struggle for a Rights-based Response to Trafficking in Human Beings," *Gender and Development* 10, no. 1 (2002): 28; M. Patricia Fernández-Kelly, "Immigration, Poverty, and Transnationalism: The Changing Terms of Citizenship in a Global Economy," in *Moral Imperialism: A Critical Anthology*, ed. Berta E. Hernández-Truyol (New York: New York University Press, 2002), 337.

9. Andrew Cockburn, "21st Century Slaves," *National Geographic*, Sept. 2003, 2.

10. David Shirk and Alexandra Webber, "Slavery Without Borders: Human Trafficking in the U.S.-Mexican Context," *Hemisphere Focus* XII, no. 5 (2004): 1, 2, http://www.csis.org/media/csis/pubs/hf_v12_05.pdf.

11. Lucinda Vargas, "Maquiladoras 2000: Still Growing," *Business Frontier* 3 (2000), http://www.dallasfed.org/research/busfront/bus0003.html.

12. *Id.*

13. *Id.*

14. María P. Fernández-Kelly, "Maquiladoras: The View from the Inside," in *The Women, Gender and Development Reader*, eds. Nalini Visvathanan et al. (Atlantic Highlands, N.J.: Zed, 1997), 204.

15. Cirila Q. Ramírez, "Unions, Collaboration, and Labour Conditions in Mexican Maquiladoras" (July 2001), International Studies Association.

16. Southwest Center for Environmental Research and Policy (SCERP), "The U.S.-Mexican Border Environment: A Road Map to a Sustainable 2020," Border

Environment Research Reports No. 5 (May 1999), 12, http://www.scerp.org/
SCERPborder_institute.pdf.

17. Shirk and Webber, "Slavery Without Borders," 1.

18. OUSGA, *Trafficking*, 8.

19. *Id.* at 6 (citing ILO estimates).

20. Tuller, "Freedom Denied," 1.

21. Free the Slaves and HRC, *Hidden Slaves*, 10.

22. *Id.*; Report of the Director-General, International Labour Office, *A Global Alliance Against Forced Labour: Global Report Under the Follow-up to the ILO Declaration on Fundamental Principles and Rights at Work 2005*, Report I(B) (Geneva: International Labour Office, 2005), 9, http://www.ilo.org/dyn/declaris/ DECLARATIONWEB.DOWNLOAD_BLOB?Var_DocumentID=5059; "The World Fact Book: Field Listing—Trafficking in Persons," Central Intelligence Agency, https://www.cia.gov/library/publications/the-world-factbook/fields/2196. html (accessed June 25, 2007) (listing women and girls as main sources for most forms of human trafficking).

23. "The World Fact Book."

24. A 1999 report states that an estimated forty-five thousand to fifty thousand women and children are trafficked annually to the United States. Amy O'Neill Richard, Center for the Study of Intelligence (CSI), *International Trafficking in Women to the United States: A Contemporary Manifestation of Slavery and Organized Crime* (Washington: CSI, Nov. 1999), iii, http://citeseer.ist.psu. edu/cache/papers/cs/18373/http:zSzzSzwww.cia.govzSzcsizSzmonographzSz-womenzSztrafficking.pdf/international-trafficking-in-women.pdf (citing Central Intelligence Agency). Yet another government report states that "the U.S. Government estimates that 18,000 to 20,000 people are trafficked annually into the United States." U.S. Department of Justice, "Assessment of U.S. Activities to Combat Trafficking in Persons" (Aug. 2003), 3, http://www.state.gov/g/tip/rls/ rpt/23495.htm. Unfortunately, none of the data gives the methodology or information explaining how the figures were obtained, so it is difficult to obtain an accurate estimate.

25. Free the Slaves and HRC, *Hidden Slaves*, 5.

26. *Id.*

27. Shirk and Webber, "Slavery Without Borders," 1.

28. *Id.* at 2.

29. Kevin Bales and Becky Cornell, "The Next Step in the Fight Against Human Trafficking: Outlawing the Trade in Slave-made Goods," *Intercultural Human Rights Law Review* 1 (2006): 211, 217.

30. Shirk and Webber, "Slavery Without Borders," 2.

31. Kathryn Farr, *Sex Trafficking: The Global Market in Women and Children* (Portland: Worth, 2005), 139–44.

32. *Id.* Farr explicitly asserts that colonial rulers introduced their own gender inequities into seized territories, which lead to further devaluation and economic disfranchisement of women.

33. Tuller, "Freedom Denied," 7, 11.

34. Free the Slaves and HRC, *Hidden Slaves*, 16.

35. *Id.* at 17.

36. *Id.* at 5, 8; Peter Landsman, "The Girls Next Door," *New York Times*, Jan. 25, 2004.

37. Landsman, "The Girls"; Free the Slaves and HRC, *Hidden Slaves*, 5.

38. Shirk and Webber, "Slavery Without Borders," 1.

39. Elizabeth Hopper and José Hidalgo, "Invisible Chains: Psychological Coercion of Human Trafficking Victims," *Intercultural Human Rights Law Review* 1 (2006): 185, 196.

40. *Id.* at 200.

41. Free the Slaves, Washington, D.C., and HRC, "Hidden Slaves Forced Labor in the United States," *Berkeley Journal of International Law* 23 (2005): 47, 48–49.

42. *Id.*

43. Michael Wines, "Africa Adds to Miserable Ranks of Child Workers," *New York Times*, Aug. 24, 2006.

44. *Id.*

45. "Child Protection from Violence, Exploitation, and Abuse: Child Labour," UNICEF, http://www.unicef.org/protection/index_childlabour.html (last accessed June 18, 2008).

46. HRW, *Fingers to the Bone* (citing United Farm Workers estimates); UNICEF Child Protection.

47. *Id.*

48. *Id.* (defining "source states [as those] from which migrant streams flow seasonably up and out into other parts of the country").

49. Wines, "Africa."

50. *Id.*

51. Report of the Director-General, *A Global Alliance.*

52. Wines, "Africa"; "Human Rights News—Backgrounder: Child Labor in Agriculture," HRW, http://hrw.org/backgrounder/crp/back0610.htm (accessed July 2, 2007).

53. Landsman, "The Girls."

54. *Id.*

55. Dorchen A. Leidholdt, "Strategies for Combating Human Trafficking Within the United States, Canada, and Mexico," *Intercultural Human Rights Law Review* 1 (2006): 91, 92.

56. Center for the Advancement of Human Rights (CAHR), Florida State University, *Florida Responds to Human Trafficking* (Tallahassee: CAHR, 2003), 9, http://www.cahr.fsu.edu/the%20report.pdf.

57. Leidholdt, "Strategies."

58. Landsman, "The Girls."

59. *See* Barbara Kralis, "Slavery as Domestic Servitude" (July 24, 2006), http://www.renewamerica.us/columns/kralis/060724. "According to our survey data, the second highest incidence of forced labor takes place in domestic service in U.S. homes. Every year U.S. citizens and foreign nationals living in the U.S. bring thousands of domestic workers into the country, and many of them suffer abuse. Visas normally require that domestic service workers remain with their original employer or face deportation. This requirement tends to discourage workers from reporting abuses. Additionally, some perpetrators are foreign nationals who rely on diplomatic immunity to shield themselves from punishment if their use of forced domestic labor is uncovered." *Id.* (quoting Dr. Kevin Bales, http://www.freetheslaves.net).

60. Free the Slaves and HRC, "Hidden Slaves," 62 (citation omitted).

61. *Id.* at 55–56.

62. *Id.* at 56.

63. Michael Bochenek, *El Salvador: Abuses Against Child Domestic Workers in El Salvador* (New York: HRW, 2004), http://www.hrw.org/reports/2004/elsalvador0104/elsalvador0104.pdf (citing ILO, *Child Labour: Tolerating the Intolerable* (Geneva: ILO, 1996)).

64. *Id.*

65. Kralis, "Slavery" (other "wealthier" nations include France and those of the Persian Gulf and Asia).

66. Free the Slaves and HRC, "Hidden Slaves," 62.

67. *Id.* (citing National Labor Relations Act, 29 U.S.C. § 152(3) (2003) ["the term 'employee' . . . shall not include any individual employed . . . in the domestic service of any family or person at his home"]).

68. *Id. See* 8 C.F.R. § 214.2(h)(6) (requiring that employment of temporary nonagricultural workers last for at least one year and a given employer can petition for additional extensions for a total of three years).

69. Victims of Trafficking and Violence Protection Act of 2000, Pub. L. No. 106-386, Oct. 28, 2000.

70. *Id.*, § 103(8)(B). The Act also defines "coercion" (§ 103(2)), "involuntary servitude" (§ 103[5]), and "debt bondage" (§ 103(4)).

71. OUSGA, *Trafficking*, 53.

72. *Id.*

73. *Id.* at 6.

74. *Id.* at 29–30. Although this U.S. State Department study uses domestic U.S. standards for its analysis, it is useful because those definitions and prohibitions are in accord with the international definitions. *See* VTVPA.

75. OUSGA, *Trafficking*, 30.

76. *Id.* at 46.

77. *Id.* at 30.

78. *Id.* at 46.

79. *Id.* at 30–31.

80. *Id.* at 30.

81. *Id.* at 46.

82. *Id.* at 266.

83. *Id.* at 268–69.

84. *Id.* at 108.

85. We have drawn in part for this section from the OUSGA, *Trafficking*; Farr, *Sex Trafficking*; *In Modern Bondage: Sex Trafficking in the Americas*, eds. David E. Guinn et al. (Leiden, Brill Academic Publishers, 2002).

86. OUSGA, *Trafficking*; Guinn et al., eds., *In Modern Bondage*.

87. OUSGA, *Trafficking*, 93.

88. Guinn et al., eds., *In Modern Bondage*, 49.

89. Cockburn, "21st Century Slaves."

90. *Id.* This section is based on Cockburn's article.

91. Abigail Goldman, "Sweat, Fear and Resignation Amid All the Toys," *Los Angeles Times*, Nov. 26, 2004. This section is based on Goldman's article.

92. *Id.*

93. *Id.* (citing Alfredo Hualde, director, Department of Social Studies, at a research institution in Tijuana).

94. Shirk and Webber, "Slavery Without Borders," 1.

95. Free the Slaves and HRC, "Hidden Slaves," 63.

96. *Id.* "The Migrant and Seasonal Agricultural Worker Protection Act (MSPA) . . . and the Fair Labor Standards Act (FLSA) . . . mandate the payment of minimum wage and the regulation of deductions from workers' pay to ensure that workers are not paid below the federal minimum wage, regardless of their immigration status. The MSPA also mandates that migrant labor contractors—companies that supply farm labor to growers—must be registered with the Department of Labor. Both immigration and labor laws hold the labor contractor rather than the grower responsible for the legal rights of workers. It is common for growers to hire workers through farm labor contractors. The Department of Labor can revoke the permit of a contractor who has a history of violations. Legal advocates and government labor inspectors also can pursue civil suits against employers who use forced labor and violate the MSPA and FLSA." *Id.* at 63–64 (citations omitted).

97. FLSA, 29 U.S.C.A. § 201 *et seq.* (2007).

98. Occupational Safety and Health Act, 29 U.S.C.A. § 651 *et seq.* (2007).

99. John Lantigua, "Why Was Carlitos Born This Way?" *Palm Beach Post*, Mar. 13, 2005.

100. *See* 29 U.S.C.A. §§ 213(a)(6) (providing exemptions from minimum wage and overtime pay provisions for those employed in agriculture) and 213(b)(12) (giving an overtime exemption for anyone employed in agriculture).

101. HRW, *Fingers to the Bone*, pt. I (quoting Darlene Adkins, coordinator, Child Labor Coalition).

102. Immokalee means "my home" in Seminole. John Bowe, "Nobodies: Does Slavery Exist in America?" *The New Yorker*, Apr. 21, 2003.

103. *Id.*; Cockburn, "21st Century Slaves."

104. Bowe, "Nobodies."

105. *Id.*

106. *Id.*

107. *Id.* (citing U.S. Department of Labor figures).

108. Cockburn, "21st Century Slaves" (citing Kevin Bales, a slavery expert).

109. *Id.* (citing U.S. Department of State).

110. OUSGA, *Trafficking*, 22–23. Best practices include: "[1.] a government should proactively identify victims of trafficking . . . [; 2.] once identified, a suspected victim of trafficking should be afforded temporary care as a victim of a serious crime . . . [; 3.] confirmed trafficking victims should not be punished for crimes that are direct result of being trafficked . . . [; 4.] confirmed trafficking victims should be encouraged to cooperate with law enforcement authorities in the investigation of the crime committed against them . . . [; and 5.] a trafficking victim who is unwilling or unable to cooperate in a trafficking prosecution can be returned to her community of origin provided that this return is accomplished in a responsible manner, with preparations made in advance for the victim's safe return and reintegration." *Id.*

111. *Id.* at 34.

112. *Id.* at 35.

113. *Id.*

CHAPTER 10

1. August Bebel, *Woman: Past, Present, and Future*, trans. Meta L. Stern (New York: Boni and Liveright, 1918), *reprinted in Human Rights in Western Civilization 1600–Present*, eds. John A. Maxwell and James J. Friedberg (Dubuque, Iowa: Kendall/Hunt, 1994), 86–87 ("the women question demands our special consideration. What the position of woman has been in *ancient* society, what her position is today and what it will be in the coming social order, are questions that deeply *concern* at least one half of humanity").

2. World Conference on Human Rights, Vienna, Austria, June 14–25, 1993, *Report*, UN Doc. A/CONF.157/24 (pt. I) (Oct. 13, 1993); *see also* Vienna Declaration.

3. Additionally, Article 26 of the ICCPR provides for the equal protection of the law, which includes a guarantee of nondiscrimination on all the listed grounds.

4. CEDAW, art. 5(a) (requiring states "to modify the social and cultural patterns of conduct of men and women, with a view to achieving the elimination of

prejudices and customary and all other practices which are based on the idea of the inferiority or the superiority of either of the sexes or on stereotyped roles for men and women"").

5. Other concerns are that sex discrimination "is an obstacle to the participation of women, on equal terms with men, in the political, social, economic and cultural life of their countries, hampers the growth of the prosperity of society and the family makes more difficult the full development of the potentialities of women in the service of their countries and humanity; . . . [and] in situations of poverty [raises concerns about lack of] access to food, health, education, training and opportunities." CEDAW, pmbl.

6. "Economic, Social, and Cultural Rights (ESCR) and Women: A Fact Sheet" (July 20, 2005), Amnesty International USA, http://www.amnestyusa.org/women/pdf/economicrights.pdf (accessed June 6, 2007).

7. *See* Monica Gutestam, "A Look Back . . . 1980; INSTRAW—10 Years Old: Working Hard to Help Women—International Research and Training Institution for Women," *UN Chronicle*, Dec. 1990, http://findarticles.com/p/articles/mi_m1309/is_n4_v27/ai_9281080.

8. *See* "Women's Earnings as a Percentage of Men's 1951–2005," infoplease, http://www.infoplease.com/ipa/A0193820.html (accessed June 6, 2007) (ratio of female to male wages in 2005 is 77 percent, citing U.S. Women's Bureau and the National Committee on Pay Equity); "The Gender Wage Ratio: Women's and Men's Earnings," Fact Sheet IWPR #C350 (updated Apr. 2007), Institute for Women's Policy Research, http://www.iwpr.org/pdf/C350.pdf (accessed June 6, 2007) (ratio of female to men earnings is 77 percent); *see also* UN Statistic Division, *Statistics and Indicators on Women and Men*, UN Doc. ST/ESA/STAT/SER.K/WWW/16/Rev.5 (Apr. 22, 2005), http://unstats.un.org/UNSD/demographic/products/indwm/ww2005/tab5g.htm (ratio of female to male wages range from 44 percent [Bahrain] to 133 percent [Switzerland], averaging around 70 percent).

9. *See* María P. Fernández-Kelly, "Maquiladoras: The View from the Inside," in *The Women, Gender, and Development Reader*, eds. Nalini Visvanathan et al. (Atlantic Highlands, N.J.: Zed, 1997), 203; UN Department of Economic and Social Affairs, *1999 World Survey on the Role of Women in Development: Globalization, Gender and Work* (New York: UN, 1999).

10. WEDO, *A Gender Agenda for the World Trade Organization: A WEDO Primer on Women and Trade* (New York: WEDO, 1999), http://www.wedo.org/files/genderagendaWTO_primer.htm.

11. *Id.*

12. *Id.*

13. The Precautionary Principle "states that when there are threats of serious or irreversible damage to the environment or to human health, the lack of scientific certainty on any particular subject should not be used to postpone

protection measures." *Id.*; *see also* Kerry H. Whiteside, *Precautionary Politics: Principle and Practice in Confronting Environmental Risk* (Cambridge: MIT Press, 2006) (discussing its origins and development).

14. WEDO, *A Gender Agenda* (citing Conference on Environment and Development ["Earth Summit"], Rio de Janeiro, Brazil, June 3–14, 1992, *Agenda 21*, UN Doc. A/CONF.151/26/Rev.1 (1992); CBD; *Beijing Declaration and Platform for Action*, A/CONF.177/20 Annex I [1995], A/CONF.177/20/Add.1 Annex II (1995)).

15. WEDO, *A Gender Agenda*.

16. The Gerber Case in Guatemala is an example of trade rules triumphing over local health regulations. Guatemala, in order both to protect infants and lower mortality rates, in part by encouraging breast-feeding over artificial breast-milk substitutes, passed a law prohibiting pictures of healthy babies on baby food and juices aimed at children under two years of age. Gerber, arguing that the healthy baby picture was its trademark, refused to comply and, backed by the U.S. government, threatened action under CAFTA-DR-US, arguing that the intellectual property provisions of GATT would allow the trademark use over the local law prohibition. Gerber won the debate when the Guatemalan Supreme Court ruled that the domestic law did not apply to imports. *Id.*

17. WEDO, *A Gender Agenda*.

18. *Id.* (citing TRIPS Agreement and CBD).

19. We have drawn in part for this section from Americas Policy Group, Canadian Council for International Cooperation (CCIC), *Report from the Americas Policy Group Roundtable: Human Rights in Mexico at the 10th Anniversary of NAFTA: Opportunities and Challenges for Canada, Appendix A: APG Background Paper* (Ottawa: CCIC, Jan. 2004), 5–29, http://ccic.ca/e/docs/003_apg_mexico_nafta_roundtable_report.pdf; UN Development Fund for Women (UNIFEM), *Progress of the World's Women 2005: Women, Work, and Poverty* (New York: UNIFEM, 2005), 18 (box 1.1); and Fernández-Kelly, "Maquiladoras."

20. This is not, however, unique to Mexico. *See* Anne-Marie Mooney Cotter, *Gender Injustice: An International Comparative Analysis of Equality in Employment* (Burlington, Vt.: Ashgate, 2004).

21. Inter-American Development Bank (IDB), *Women in the Americas: Bridging the Gender Gap* (Washington: IDB, 1995).

22. Office of the Special Advisor on Gender Issues and Advancement of Women (OSAGI), "Gender Mainstreaming," Women Watch, http://www.un.org/womenwatch/osagi/gendermainstreaming.htm (accessed June 6, 2007) (emphasis omitted).

23. World Conference on Human Rights, *Report*.

24. *See* "History of Abuelas de Plaza de Mayo," Abuelas de Plaza de Mayo, http://www.abuelas.org.ar (accessed June 7, 2007) (a nongovernmental organization of *abuelas* [grandmothers] dedicated to locate and have returned the children of their own children, both of whom disappeared between 1976 and 1983 while Argentina was under a military dictatorship).

25. IDB, *Women in the Americas*, 2, 10–14.

26. *Id.* at 12.

27. Octavio Paz, *El Laberinto de la Soledad* (*The Labyrinth of Loneliness and Solitude*) (New York: Penguin, 1997), 35–36, author's translation.

28. Berta E. Hernández-Truyol, "Borders (En)gendered: Normativities, Latinas, and a LatCrit Paradigm," *New York University Law Review* 72 (1997): 882, 915 (quoting Rosa M. Gil and Carmen I. Vázquez, *The María Paradox: How Latinas Can Merge Old World Traditions with New World Self-Esteem* [New York: G. P. Putnam's Sons, 1996], 7).

29. Candace Hoyes, "Here Comes the Brides' March: Cultural Appropriation and Latina Activism," *Columbia Journal of Gender and the Law* 13 (2004): 328, 345–46 (citations omitted).

30. Fernández-Kelly, "Maquiladoras."

31. Civil Rights Act of 1964, Pub. L. No. 88-352, June 2, 1964.

32. Berta E. Hernández-Truyol, "Law Is Not Enough," *George Washington International Law Review* 37 (2005): 1031, 1051 (citation omitted).

33. *See* Berta E. Hernández-Truyol, "Latinas, Culture, and Human Rights: A Model for Making Change, Saving Soul," *Women's Rights Law Reporter* 23 (2001): 21.

34. IACHR, OAS, *Report of the Inter-American Commission on Human Rights on the Status of Women in the Americas, Part III: Analysis of the Information Received from Member States and Nongovernmental Organizations*, OEA/Ser.L./V/II.100 Doc. 17, Oct. 13, 1998, http://www.cidh.oas.org/countryrep/Mujeres98-en/Chapter%203.htm.

35. Hernández-Truyol, "Law Is Not Enough," 1052.

CHAPTER 11

1. We have drawn in this discussion from Naomi Roht-Arriaza, "Of Seeds and Shamans: The Appropriation of the Scientific and Technical Knowledge of Indigenous and Local Communities," *Michigan Journal of International Law* 17 (1996): 919, 926; Rosemary J. Coombe, "The Recognition of Indigenous Peoples' and Community Traditional Knowledge in International Law," *St. Thomas Law Review* 14 (2001): 275; S. James Anaya, *Indigenous Peoples in International Law* (New York: Oxford University Press, 1996); Srivdhya Ragavan, "Protection of Traditional Knowledge," *Minnesota Intellectual Property Review* 2 (2001): 1, 4; and Eric K. Yamamoto, Carrie A. Y. Shirota, and Jayna K. Kim, "Indigenous Peoples' Rights in U.S. Courts," in *Moral Imperialism: A Critical Anthology*, ed. Berta Hernández-Truyol (New York: New York University Press, 2002), 300.

2. Indigenous and Tribal Populations Convention, art. 1.

3. Ragavan, "Protection," 4.

4. Barbara Pando, "Guatemala-Maya Civil War," ICE Case Studies No. 15 (Nov. 1997), The Inventory of Conflict and Environment, http://www.american. edu/ted/ice/peten.htm (accessed May 19, 2007).

5. Chris von Spiegelfeld, "Cat's Claw: Possibilities for a Peruvian Geographic Indicator," TED Case Study No. 772 (2004), 1, Trade Environment Database, http://www.american.edu/ted/cats-claw.htm (accessed Jun. 26, 2007).

6. Roht-Arriaza, "Of Seeds and Shamans," at 926. "Indigenous and local communities long have excelled at identifying and classifying the names, properties, and uses of the biodiversity found on their lands, and they have often known how to take better advantage of that biodiversity than Western scientists. For example, by consulting indigenous peoples, bio-prospectors can increase the success ratio in trials for useful substances from one in 10,000 samples to one in two." *Id.*

7. *See* World Council of Indigenous Peoples (WCIP), "The Need for International Conventions," WCIP Concept Paper (Apr. 1981), text at n.2, http://www. halcyon.com/pub/FWDP/International/intconv.txt. (quoting the separate opinion of Judge Fouad Ammoun in the *Western Sahara Case*, 1975 I.C.J. 4) (accessed June 28, 2007).

8. James Anaya and Robert A. Williams, "The Protection of Indigenous Peoples' Rights Over Lands and Natural Resources Under the Inter-American Human Rights System," *Harvard Human Rights Journal* 14 (2001): 33; Siegfried Wiessner, "The Rights and Status of Indigenous Peoples: A Global Comparative and International Legal Analysis," *Harvard Human Rights Journal* 12 (1991): 57.

9. Nibutani Dam, 38 I.L.M. 399. The Japanese government appropriated land of Ainu native farmers for construction of a dam. The tribe sued in Sapporo District Court, relying primarily on its status as an "ethnic minority" under the Japanese constitution and Article 27 of ICCPR, which had been adopted by Japan in 1979. Despite its ruling that the taking was illegal, the Court dismissed the action as inconsistent with the constitution's view of the public welfare. 38 I.L.M. 428.

10. Lorie M. Graham, "Resolution of Claims to Self-Determination: The Expansion and Creation of Dispute Settlement Mechanisms," *ILSA Journal of International and Comparative Law* 10 (2004): 385, 391.

11. *Id.*

12. Proposed American Declaration on the Rights of Indigenous Peoples, art. XV(1).

13. *See* "Endangered Languages Data Summary: Introduction," Linguistic Society of America/Committee on Endangered Languages and Their Preservation, https://kuscholarworks.ku.edu/dspace/bitstream/1808/461/1/Endangered%20Languages%20Data%20Summary.pdf (accessed June 18, 2008).

14. Marcus A. Orellano, "Indigenous Peoples, Energy, and Environmental Justice: The Pangue/Ralco Hydroelectric Project in Chile's Alto BíoBío," 1 (MS, on file with authors).

15. *See* John H. Jackson, William J. Davey, and Alan O. Sykes, Jr., *Legal Problems of International Economic Relations* (St. Paul, Minn.: West, 2008), 226.

16. Pollyanna E. Folkins, "Has the Lab Coat Become the Modern Day Eye Patch? Thwarting Biopiracy of Indigenous Resources by Modifying International Patenting Systems," *Transnational Law and Contemporary Problems* 13 (2003): 339, 350.

17. In section 7.5, we examined the effect of the TRIPS Agreement on the ability of governments in developing countries to provide essential medicines to their citizens. The concern relevant to the present discussion is that the SPS Agreement carried forward antiquated interpretations of GATT Article XX(b), and made this soft law enforceable through the powerful dispute settlement mechanisms of the WTO. We learn in this section why the human rights community also criticizes the TRIPS Agreement for its impairment of the use of traditional knowledge by indigenous populations.

18. Estimated by authors from Stephen E. Siwek, *Copyright Industries in the U.S. Economy: The 2004 Report* (Washington: Economists Inc., 2004), 9, http://www.iipa.com/pdf/2004_SIWEK_FULL.pdf.

19. TRIPS Agreement, arts. 2, 3, 9.

20. *Id.* at art. 16.1.

21. *Id.* at art. 15.3.

22. *Id.* at art. 33. The TRIPS Agreement measures the twenty-year period from the time of application for the patent, whereas the prior U.S. term of seventeen years ran from the time of patent issuance.

23. Aaron Cosbey, International Institute for Sustainable Development, "The Sustainable Development Effects of the WTO TRIPS Agreement: A Focus on Developing Countries," in the Trade Observatory Digital Library, http://www.tradeobservatory.org/library.cfm?filename=Sustainable_Development_Effects_of_the_WTO_TRI.htm (accessed May 19, 2007).

24. TRIPS Agreement, art. 27.1.

25. *Id.* at art. 10.1.

26. *Id.* at art. 12.

27. *Id.* at arts. 38.1 and 45.2.

28. "Intellectual Property and Sustainable Development," CIEL, http://www.ciel.org/Tae/Trade_IntProperty.html (accessed May 19, 2007).

29. The first paragraph of the TRIPS Agreement's preamble identifies this need to watch that enforcement of IPR does not itself impede trade.

30. Edward O. Wilson, *The Diversity of Life* (New York: Norton, 1999), 181.

31. Catherine Farley and Daphne Field, "Healing Plants," *Toronto Star*, Jan. 8, 1995, B1.

32. Martin Teitel, "Selling Cells: The Thriving Business of Patenting Life," *Dollars and Sense*, Sept.–Oct. 1994, 24, 38.

33. "U.S. Cancels Patent on Sacred Ayahuasca Plant," *Environmental News Service*, Nov. 5, 1999, http://www.erowid.org/plants/banisteriopsis/banisteriopsis_media1.shtml.

34. Darshan Shankar, *Tribal and Rural Farmer-Conservers*, 14 *Agrobiodiversity and Farmers' Rights* (Chennai, India: Swaminathan Research Foundation, 1996), 170.

35. Chidi Oguamanam, "Localizing Intellectual Property in the Globalization Epoch: The Integration of Indigenous Knowledge," *Indiana Journal of Global Legal Studies* 11 (2004): 135, 140.

36. Kembrew McLeod, *Owning Culture: Authorship, Ownership, and Intellectual Property Law*, ed. Toby Miller (New York: Peter Lang, 2001), 171.

37. *See* Folkins, "Has the Lab Coat," 347, 353–60.

38. Oguamanam, "Localizing Intellectual Property," 143.

39. Terence N. D'Altroy, "Reinventing Unchanged Andean Traditions," *Cardozo Journal of International and Comparative Law* 12 (2004): 83, 89.

40. Julia Whitty, "Gone: Mass Extinction and the Hazards of Earth's Vanishing Biodiversity," Apr. 25, 2007, *Mother Jones*, http://www.motherjones.com/news/feature/2007/05/gone.html (accessed May 19, 2007).

41. Stephen J. Powell, "Regional Economic Arrangements and the Rule of Law in the Americas: The Human Rights Face of Free Trade Agreements," *Florida Journal of International Law* 17 (2005): 59, 66.

42. CBD, art. 8(j).

43. *Id.* at arts. 8(j), 10(c).

44. *Id.* at art. 15.

45. Stockholm Declaration, princ. 21.

46. CBD, at art. 15(5).

47. The authors are aware that the linkage between indigenous populations and biodiversity through the traditional knowledge issue is of critical importance to protection of the environment, which we discuss primarily in chapter 6. As the reader has observed, study of each trade and human rights intersection proves the inseparability of human rights that we recognize in chapter 2. We have chosen to address the tie between the CBD and traditional knowledge in this chapter, even though that traditional knowledge cannot exist unless we protect the environment.

48. David P. Kelly, "Trading Indigenous Rights: The NAFTA Side Agreements as an Impetus for Human Rights Enforcement," *Buffalo Human Rights Law Review* 6 (2000): 113, 122.

49. Judith Kimerling, "Indigenous Peoples and the Oil Frontier in Amazonia: The Case of Ecuador, ChevronTexaco, and Aguinda v. Texaco," *New York University Journal of International Law and Politics* 38 (2006): 413, 631.

50. *Id.* at 457–58.

51. *Id.* at 464.

52. Letta Tayler, "Amazon Tribe Sues Oil Giant-Texaco Ruined Environment, They Contend," *South Florida Sun-Sentinel*, June 11, 2005, 20A.

53. Terence Chea, "Chevron Accused of Human Rights, Environmental Abuses," *Merced Sun-Star* (CA), Jan. 3, 2006, B1.

54. Kimerling, "Indigenous People," 459.

55. Chea, "Chevron."

56. Kimerling, "Indigenous People," 528.

57. *Id.* at 629.

58. "Asian Logging Companies Move into Heart of Amazon Rainforest," Press Release, *Worldwide Forest/Biodiversity Campaign News* (Mar. 10, 1997), http://forests.org/archived_site/today/recent/1997/brasiapr.htm.

59. Rudy S. Salo, "When the Logs Roll Over: The Need for an International Convention Criminalizing Involvement in the Global Illegal Timber Trade," *Georgetown International Environmental Law Review* 16 (2003): 127, 136.

60. "Asian Logging Companies."

61. Zachary Lazarus, "A War Worth Fighting: The Ongoing Battle to Save the Brazilian Amazon," *Law and Business Review of the Americas* 9-SPG (2003): 399, 414.

62. Samara D. Anderson, "Colonialism Continues: A Comparative Analysis of the United States and Brazil's Exploitation of Indigenous Peoples' Forest Resources," *Vermont Law Review* 27 (2003): 959, 973.

63. *Id.* at 973–74.

64. Manuel Délano, "Unica: Endesa Smokes Peace Pipe with Pehuenches Over Dam," *El Pais*, Sept. 22, 2003, 7.

65. Orellana, "Indigenous Peoples," 1.

66. *Id.*

67. *Id.* at 10.

68. John A. Ragosta, "Trade and Agriculture, and Lumber: Why Agriculture and Lumber Matter," *Kansas Journal of Law and Public Policy* 14 (2005): 413, 416.

69. Elizabeth Royte, "Who Made a Difference?" *Smithsonian*, Nov. 2005, 35 (quoting Mark Plotkin, Amazon Conservation Team founder).

70. Emanuella Arezzo, "Struggling Around the Natural Divide: The Protection of Tangible and Intangible Indigenous Property," Duke Law School Legal Studies Paper No. 126, 2, http://papers.ssrn.com/sol3/papers.cfm?abstract_id=927991.

71. We define "bioprospecting" to mean the systematic search for new sources of compounds, genes, enzymes, whole organisms, and other products that have potential economic value and can be found in the earth's biodiversity. Ana Sittenfeld, "Biodiversity, Bioprospecting, and Intellectual Property: The Case of Costa Rica and Merck Pharmaceuticals," Lecture at University of Florida College of Law, Mar. 1, 2006 (MS, on file with authors).

72. Thomas J. Krumenacher, "Protection for Indigenous Peoples and Their Traditional Knowledge: Would a Registry System Reduce the Misappropriation of Traditional Knowledge?" *Marquette Intellectual Property Law Review* 8 (2004): 143, 155.

73. Anupam Chandler and Madhavi Sunder, "The Romance of the Public Domain," *California Law Review* 92 (2004): 1331, 1362.

74. Elizabeth Royte, "Mark Plotkin," *Smithsonian*, Nov. 2005, 38.

75. UNDP, *Human Development Report 1999* (New York: Oxford University Press, 1999). *See* McLeod, *Owning Culture*, 170.

76. Francesca T. Grifo and David R. Downes, "Agreements to Collect Biodiversity for Pharmaceutical Research: Major Issues and Proposed Principles," in *Valuing Local Knowledge: Indigenous Peoples' Intellectual Property Rights*, eds. Stephen B. Brush and Doreen Stabinsky (Washington: Island, 1996), 297–98.

77. Laurence R. Helfer, "Toward a Human Rights Framework for Intellectual Property," *University of California-Davis Law Review* 40 (2007): 971, 978.

78. TRIPS Agreement, art. 27.2.

79. Official Insignia of Native American Tribes; Statutorily Required Study, 64 Fed. Reg. 29841 (Jun. 3, 1999). *See* Cynthis M. Ho, "Bio-piracy and Beyond: A Consideration of Socio-cultural Conflicts with Global Patent Policies," *University of Michigan Journal of Law Reform* 9 (2006): 433, 537.

80. *Mayagna (Sumo) Awas Tingni Community*, ¶ 149.

81. Siegfried Wiessner, "Defending Indigenous Peoples' Heritage: An Introduction," *St. Thomas Law Review* 14 (2001): 271.

82. Emad Mekay, "Development: Latin America's Indigenous People Marginalised—World Bank," *Inter Press Service*, May 18, 2005, http://www.ipsnews.net/interna.asp?idnews=28734 (accessed Sept. 20, 2006).

83. "Indígenas Koguis y Arhuacos Buscan Apoyo en E.U. para Salvar la Sierra Nevada de Santa Marta" (Native Koguis and Arhuacos Look for Support in EU to Save the Sierra Nevada of Santa Marta), *El Tiempo*, Sept. 6, 2006, http://www.eltiempo.com/internacional/euycanada/noticias/ARTICULO-WEB-NOTA_INTERIOR-3232946.html (accessed May 19, 2007).

CHAPTER 12

Epigraph. The World Bank, *World Development Report 2000/2001: Attacking Poverty* (New York: Oxford University Press, 2001), 15.

1. Universal Declaration, art. 22; *see also* ICESCR, art. 9.

2. Universal Declaration, arts. 23, 25(1); ICESCR, arts. 6(1), (7).

3. World Summit for Social Development, Copenhagen, Denmark, Mar. 6–12, 1995, *Report of the World Summit for Social Development*, UN Doc. A/CONF.166/9 (Apr. 19, 1995).

4. Copenhagen Declaration, ¶ 8.

5. UN Millennium Declaration, ¶ 19.

6. UNESCO, Commission for Social Development, *Report on the Forty-third Session,* UN Doc. E/CN.5/2005/7 (Aug. 4, 2005), iii.

7. 2005 World Summit Outcome, G.A. Res. 60/1, UN Doc. A/RES/60/1 (Oct. 24, 2005).

8. David C. Korten, *When Corporations Rule the World* (San Francisco: Berrett-Koehler, 1997), 43 (quoting Mahbub ul Haq, former vice president, World Bank).

9. *Id.* at 43; *see also* Clive Crook, "Globalisation and Its Critics," *The Economist,* Sept. 29, 2001.

10. Korten, *When Corporations Rule,* 45.

11. Jean-Bertrand Aristide, former president of Haiti, in his book *Eyes of the Heart,* observes that "1.3 billion people [live] on less than one dollar a day. Three billion people, or half the population of the world, live on less than two dollars a day. Yet this same planet is experiencing unprecedented economic growth." Jean-Bertrand Aristide, *Eyes of the Heart: Seeking a Path for the Poor in the Age of Globalization* (Monroe, Maine: Common Courage, 2000), 5. A 2000 press release from WTO News, however, citing a recent study, *Trade, Income Disparity and Poverty,* provides that 1.2 billion people live on less than one dollar per day and an additional 1.6 billion people—more than a quarter of the world's population— exist on one dollar to two dollars per day. WTO, "Free Trade Helps Reduce Poverty, Says New WTO Secretariat Study," Press Release No. 181 (June 13, 2000), http://www.wto.org/english/news_e/pres00_e/pr181_e.htm (citing *Special Studies 5: Trade, Income Disparity and Poverty,* eds. Dan Ben-David, Håkan Nordström, and L. Alan Winters (Geneva: WTO, 1999)).

12. WTO, "Free Trade."

13. "The classic link between international trade and poverty in developing countries is via the labour market. If opening up to international trade allows a country to export more labour-intensive goods and replace local production of capital and skill-intensive goods by imports, it increases the demand for labour— typically in the formal sector. . . . If poverty is concentrated among people who are actually or potentially part of the labour market, increasing demand will help to alleviate poverty." L. Alan Winters, "Trade and Poverty: Is There a Connection?" in Ben-David et al. eds., *Special Studies 5,* 54 (box 3).

14. Håkan Nordström, "Trade, Income Disparity, and Poverty: An Overview," in Ben-David et al. eds., *Special Studies 5,* 5.

15. Dan Ben-David, "Trade, Growth, and Disparity Among Nations," in Ben-David et al. eds., *Special Studies 5,* 37.

16. Winters, "Trade and Poverty," 43.

17. Nordström, "Trade, Income Disparity, and Poverty," 1.

18. UNDP, *Human Development Report 2003* (New York: Oxford University Press, 2003), 37.

19. "These different dimensions of poverty interact in important ways. So do interventions to improve the well-being of poor people. Increasing education leads to better health outcomes. Improving health increases income-earning potential. Providing safety nets allows poor people to engage in higher-risk, higher-return activities. And eliminating discrimination against women, ethnic minorities, and other disadvantaged groups both directly improves their well-being and enhances their ability to increase their incomes." The World Bank, *World Development Report*, v.

20. Winters, "Trade and Poverty," 46.

21. The World Bank, *World Development Report*, v. It is significant that two of the Bretton Woods institutions (i.e., the World Bank and IMF) recognized that poverty is multidimensional, leaving methodologies to be defined by the countries themselves while they are carrying out their Bank-mandated Poverty Reduction Strategy Papers. *See also* "Frequently Asked Questions," Bretton Woods Project, http://www.brettonwoodsproject.org/faq/index. shtml#index-320747 (accessed June 5, 2007); "Poverty Reduction Strategy Papers (PRSP)," IMF, http://www.imf.org/external/np/prsp/prsp.asp (accessed June 5, 2007).

22. UNICEF, *The State of the World's Children 2005—Childhood Under Threat* (New York: UNICEF, 2004), inside cover.

23. UNDP, *Human Development Report 1999* (New York: Oxford University Press, 1999), 31.

24. *Id.* at 36.

25. UNDP, *Human Development Report 2000* (Oxford Univ. Press, 2000), 82 (box 4.7).

26. Oxfam International, *Make Trade Fair for the Americas: Agriculture, Investment, and Intellectual Property: Three Reasons to Say No to the FTAA*, Oxfam Briefing Paper 37 (2003), 1.

27. UNDP, *Human Development Report 2003*, 2.

28. *Id.*

29. *Id.* at 3.

30. *Id.*

31. Ben-David, "Trade, Growth, and Disparity," 37.

32. UNDP, *Human Development Report 2003*, 42 (box 2.3).

33. *Id.*

34. The World Bank, *World Bank Atlas* (Washington: World Bank, 2004), 13.

35. *Id.* at 14.

36. UNDP, *Human Development Report 2003*, 5.

37. *Id.* at 42 (box 2.3). One of the main problems with $1 a day poverty data derives from underlying adjustments of international price differences. Assuming that $1 a day is the correct average price of the subsistence consumption bundle in developing countries—a major assumption—the price of this bundle needs to

be translated into national currencies. The World Bank does this using purchasing power parity (PPP) rates: price indices that compare the price of a bundle of goods in one country with the price in another.

But the process for obtaining these rates is not entirely transparent. Moreover, they produce inaccurate poverty lines because many of the prices they are based on are for goods that poor people do not consume. Making matters worse, these conversions do not take into account the considerable price differences between countries' urban and rural areas. Moreover, poor people have to pay higher unit prices for many goods and services because they cannot afford to buy in bulk. (*Id.* [citations omitted])

38. Lucia C. Hanmer, Graham Pyatt, and Howard White, "What Do the World Bank's Poverty Assessments Teach Us about Poverty in Sub-Saharan Africa?" *Development and Change* 30 (1999): 795. In looking at the Bank's assessments for twenty-six countries, the authors argue that the assessments critique "income-poverty defined against an inevitably arbitrary poverty line." *Id.* at abstract.

39. *Id.* at 799.

40. *Id.* at 802.

41. *Id.* at 804.

42. Winters, "Trade and Poverty," 43.

43. Nordström, "Trade, Income Disparity, and Poverty," 1 (citing the World Bank, *Global Economic Prospects and the Development Countries* (Washington: World Bank, 2000)).

44. UNDP, *Human Development Report 2003*, 145.

45. *Id.* at 162.

46. *Id.* at 23.

47. Americas Policy Group, CCIC, *Report from the Americas Policy Group Roundtable: Human Rights in Mexico at the 10th Anniversary of NAFTA: Opportunities and Challenges for Canada, Appendix A: APG Background Paper* (Ottawa: CCIC, 2004), 5–29, http://ccic.ca/e/docs/003_apg_mexico_nafta_roundtable_report.pdf.

48. Oxfam International, "Make Trade Fair," 3 (citation omitted). We have drawn in part for this section from Stephen J. Powell and Andrew Schmitz, "The Cotton and Sugar Subsidies Decisions: WTO's Dispute Settlement System Rebalances the Agreement on Agriculture," *Drake Journal of Agricultural Law* 10 (2005): 287, 288.

49. *Id.* at 3–4 (citations omitted).

50. UNDP, *Human Development Report 2003*, 19.

51. Rome Declaration on World Food Security and World Food Summit Plan of Action (FAO Nov. 17, 1996), 1, http://www.fao.org/docrep/003/w3613e/w3613e00.htm.

52. Organisation for Economic Co-operation and Development (OECD), *Agriculture and Development: The Case for Policy Coherence* (Paris: OECD, 2005), 3.

53. Melaku G. Desta, *The Law of International Trade in Agricultural Products: From GATT 1947 to the WTO Agreement on Agriculture* (Boston: Kluwer Law International, 2002), 6.

54. Terence P. Stewart, *GATT Uruguay Round: A Negotiating History (1986–1992)* (Boston: Kluwer Law and Taxation, 1993), 134.

55. Paul C. Rosenthal and Lynn E. Duffy, "Reforming Global Trade in Agriculture," in *The World Trade Organization: The Multilateral Trade Framework for the 21st Century and U.S. Implementing Legislation*, ed. Terence P. Stewart (Chicago: ABA, 1996), 146.

56. Carmen G. Gonzalez, "Institutionalizing Inequality: The WTO Agreement on Agriculture, Food Security, and Developing Countries," *Columbia Journal of Environmental Law* 27 (2002): 433.

57. *See* Alan O. Sykes Jr., "Comparative Advantage and the Normative Economics of International Trade Policy," *Journal of International Economic Law* 1 (1998): 57.

58. Elizabeth Becker, "Lawmakers Voice Doom and Gloom on W.T.O. Ruling," *New York Times*, Apr. 28, 2004, C1.

59. Timothy Josling, "Agriculture and the Next WTO Round," in *The WTO After Seattle*, ed. Jeffrey J. Schott (Washington: Institute of International Economics, 2000), 92.

60. OECD, *Agricultural Policies in OECD Countries: At a Glance* (Paris: OECD, 2006).

61. Homi Kharas, "Lifting All Boats" (Jan./Feb. 2005), *Foreign Policy*, http://www.foreignpolicy.com/story/cms.php?story_id=2752.

62. Carin Smaller, Institute for Agriculture and Trade Policy (IATP), *Can Aid Fix Trade? Assessing the WTO's Aid for Trade Agenda* (Minneapolis: IATP, 2006), 4, http://www.tradeobservatory.org/library.cfm?refid=89070.

63. *See* Alvaro V. Llosa, "Lessons from the Poor" (Oct. 18, 2006), The Independent Institute, http://independent.org/newsroom/article.asp?id=1834.

64. WTO, "Decision on Measures Concerning the Possible Negative Effects of the Reform Programme on Least-developed and Net Food-importing Developing Countries," in *The Results of the Uruguay Round of Multilateral Trade Negotiations: The Legal Texts* (Geneva: GATT, 1994), 448.

65. Vandana Shiva, *Stolen Harvest* (Cambridge: South End, 2000), 82.

66. *Id.* at 7.

67. *Id.* at 13.

68. Oxfam International, "Make Trade Fair," 5 (citation omitted).

69. *Id.* at 7 (citation omitted).

70. Winters, "Trade and Poverty," 54.

71. UNDP, *Human Development Report 2003*, 89 (citing John Madeley, *Food for All: Can Hunger Be Halved?* (Washington: Panos Publications, 2001)).

72. Nathan Thornburgh, "Inside the Life of the Migrants Next Door," *TIME*, Feb. 6, 2006, 34, 41.

73. *Id.* at 36–37.

74. Donald L. Barlett and James B. Steele, "Who Left the Door Open?" *TIME*, Sept. 12, 2004 (quoting statement by construction worker to another reporter).

75. Geri Smith, *Work in the States*, "Build a Life in Mexico," *Business Week*, July 18, 2005, http://www.businessweek.com/magazine/content/05_29/b3943007_mz001.htm.

76. Barlett and Steele, "Who Left the Door Open?"

77. Pedro De Vasconcelos, IDB, and MIF, *Sending Money Home: Remittances to Latin America and the Caribbean* (Washington: IDB, May 2004), 11, http://idb-docs.iadb.org/wsdocs/getdocument.aspx?docnum=547263.

78. *Id.*

79. Andres Oppenheimer, "Latin America's Family Remittances—Heading South?" *Miami Herald*, Dec. 10, 2004 (citing IDB figures).

80. De Vasconcelos et al., *Sending Money Home*, 11.

81. Diego Cevallos, "Latin America: Remittances Rescue Millions from Poverty" (Nov. 25, 2005), Inter Press Service (IPS) News Agency, http://www.ipsnews.net/news.asp?idnews=31189 (citing an unnamed 2004 study by the OAS).

82. *Id.*

83. Thornburgh, "Inside the Life," 41 (quoting Roberto Suro, director, Pew Hispanic Center, Washington).

CHAPTER 13

1. Amartya Sen, "Freedom and Needs," *New Republic*, Jan. 10, 17, 1994.

2. Thomas M. Franck, "The Emerging Right to Democratic Governance," *American Journal of International Law* 86 (1992): 46, 46–47.

3. *See, e.g.,* Enhancing the Effectiveness of the Principle of Periodic and Genuine Elections, G.A. Res. 43/157, UN Doc. A/RES/43/157 (Dec. 8, 1988).

4. Harold H. Koh, "The Right to Democracy," *Issues of Democracy* 5 (May 2000): http://usinfo.state.gov/journals/itdhr/0500/ijde/koh.htm.

5. *Id.*

6. *Id.* ("where democracy flourishes, so too do[es] peace"); Harry Bliss and Bruce Russett, "Democracy and Trade: Ties of Interest and Community," in *Democratic Peace in Europe: Myth or Reality*, eds. Gustaf Geeraerts and Patrick Stouthuysen (Brussels: VUB University Press 1999), 75 (noting that "democracies engage in fewer militarized disputes with each other" and that "trade promotes peace").

7. Sen, "Freedom and Needs."

8. Universal Declaration, art. 19; ICCPR, art. 19; American Declaration, art. IV; ACHR, art. 13.

9. Universal Declaration, art. 26; ICESCR, art. 13; American Declaration, art. XII; Protocol of San Salvador, art. 13.

10. Universal Declaration, art. 20; ICCPR, art. 21; American Declaration, art. XXI; ACHR, art. 15.

11. Universal Declaration, art. 18; ICCPR, art. 18; American Declaration, art. III; ACHR, art. 12.

12. Universal Declaration, art. 18; ICCPR, art. 18; American Declaration, art. IV; ACHR, art. 13.

13. Universal Declaration, art. 19; ICCPR, art. 19; American Declaration, art. IV; ACHR, art. 13.

14. Koh, "The Right to Democracy."

15. Delegation of the United States, "The OAS, Democracy, and Trade" (document for the Dialogue of Heads of Delegation), OAS General Assembly 32d Regular Session, OEA/Ser.P AG/doc.4060/02 rev. 1 (June 4, 2002), http://oea.org/XXXIIGA/english/speeches/speech_us2.htm.

16. *Id.; see also* Koh, "The Right to Democracy" (observing that democracy "provides breathing room for civil society"); Daniel T. Griswold, Center for Trade Polity Studies, Cato Institute, *Trading Tyranny for Freedom: How Open Markets Till the Soil for Democracy* (Washington: Cato Institute, 2004), 1.

17. Delegation of the United States, "The OAS, Democracy, and Trade."

18. *See* Universal Declaration, art. 26; ICESCR, art. 13; American Declaration, art. XII; OAS Charter, art. 34(h); Protocol of San Salvador, art. 13.

19. Delegation of the United States, "The OAS, Democracy, and Trade."

20. *See* Tom J. Farer et al., "The Human Right to Participate in Government: Toward an Operational Definition," *American Society of International Law Proceedings* 82 (1988): 505, 506 (remarks by Jack Donnelly).

21. *Id.* at 516 (remarks by Kenneth Sharpe).

22. Daniel R. Williams, "After the Gold Rush-Part I: Hamdi, 9/11, and the Dark Side of the Enlightenment," Northeastern Univ. School of Law Research Paper No. 16-2007, http://papers.ssrn.com/sol3/papers.cfm?abstract_id=963754.

23. George Will, "Will Trade Change China?" *Gainesville Sun*, Apr. 27, 2007, 11A (quoting President George W. Bush).

24. Mark B. Baker, "No Country Left Behind: The Exporting of Legal Norms under the Guise of Economic Integration," *Emory International Law Review* 19 (2005): 1321, 1324.

25. Richard M. Ebeling, "Book Review, Global Fortune: The Stumble and Rise of World Capitalism" (March 2001), The Future of Freedom Foundation, http://www.fff.org/freedom/0301h.asp (quoting Peruvian politician Mario Vargas Llosa).

26. "Unbridled Capitalism Will Lead to Very Real Problems," *Spiegel*, http://www.spiegel.de/international/spiegel/0,1518,druck-411543,00.html (accessed June 24, 2007) (interview with Harvard economist Kenneth Rogoff).

27. Ebeling, "Book Review" (citing Indian free-market economist Deepak Lal).

28. Griswold, "Trading Tyranny," 1.

29. *Id.* at 8.

30. Bliss and Russett, "Democracy and Trade," 87.

31. *Id.* at 75.

32. Griswold, "Trading Tyranny," 1.

33. Mark Engler, "CAFTA: Free Trade vs. Democracy" (Jan. 30, 2003), http://americas.irc-online.org/commentary/2003/0301cafta-opp.html.

34. WTO, "Trade Liberalization Statistics: Poverty," http://www.gatt.org/trastat_e.html (accessed June 1, 2007) (citing CorpWatch, http://www.corpwatch.org/).

35. Engler, "CAFTA."

36. Sarah Anderson, "The Equity Factor and Free Trade: What the Europeans Can Teach Us," *World Policy Journal* XX(3) (2003): 45, 46, http://www.world-policy.org/journal/articles/wpj03-3/anderson.html ("poor four" refers to Ireland, Greece, Spain, and Portugal).

37. *Id.*

38. Central American Free Trade Agreement is "a treaty that would expand [North American Free Trade Agreement]–style trade barrier reductions to Central America. The first bargaining session for CAFTA convened in San José, Costa Rica on January 27 [2003]." Engler, "CAFTA."

39. *Id.*

40. HRW, "Corporations and Human Rights: Freedom of Association in a Maquila in Guatemala," *HRW Report* 9, no. 3(B) (Mar. 1997): http://www.hrw.org/reports/pdfs/g/guatemla/guatemal973.pdf.

41. HRW, "Mexico—No Guarantees: Sex Discrimination in Mexico, Maquiladora Sector," *HRW Report* 8, no. 6(B) (Aug. 1996): http://www.hrw.org/reports/1996/Mexio896.htm (Mexican maquiladoras); HRW, *World Report 2003: Events of 2002, November 2001–November 2002* (New York: HRW, 2003), 143 (Guatemalan maquiladoras).

CHAPTER 14

1. Raj Bhala, *International Trade Law: Theory and Practice* (New York: Lexis, 2007), 590.

2. "The Domestic Costs of Sanctions on Foreign Commerce" (Mar. 1999), 2, Congressional Budget Office, http://www.cbo.gov/ftpdocs/11xx/doc1133/tradesanc.pdf (accessed June 28, 2007).

3. *See* Gary C. Hufbauer et al., *Economic Sanctions Reconsidered: History and Current Policy* (Washington: Institute for International Economics [IIE], 1990), 65–67.

4. Bhala, "International Trade Law," 590.

5. Sarah H. Cleveland, "Norm Internalizations and U.S. Economic Sanctions," *Yale Journal of International Law* 26 (2001): 1, 11.

6. Gary C. Hufbauer et al., *Economic Sanctions Reconsidered: Supplemental Case Histories* (Washington: IIE, 1990), 434–63.

7. Gary C. Hufbauer et al., *Economic Sanctions Reconsidered* (Washington: IIE, 1990), 268–82 (hereinafter Hufbauer et al., *Economic Sanctions 1*).

8. *See* Bhala, "International Trade Law," 588–92.

9. Hufbauer et al., *Economic Sanctions 1*, 92–105.

10. *See* Robin Wright, "Powell Intends to Curb U.S. Use of Diplomatic Sanctions," *Los Angeles Times*, Jan. 22, 2001.

11. Allan Gerson, "Terrorism and Genocide: Determining Accountability and Liability," *Thomas Jefferson Law Review* 28 (2005): 79, 82; Hufbauer et al., *Economic Sanctions 1*, 140–52.

12. The Situation Between Iraq and Kuwait, S.C. Res. 661, UN Doc. S/RES/661 (Aug. 6, 1990), 19.

13. Amy Howlett, "Getting 'Smart': Crafting Economic Sanctions That Respect All Human Rights," *Fordham Law Review* 73 (2004): 1199, 1214 (quoting § 586A(7), 104 Stat. 1979, 2048).

14. UN Charter, art. 39 ("the Security Council shall determine the existence of any threat to the peace, breach of the peace, or act of aggression and shall make recommendations, or decide what measures shall be taken . . . to maintain or restore international peace and security"); art. 41 ("the Security Council may decide what measures not involving the use of armed force are to be employed . . . and it may call upon the Members of the United Nations to apply such measures. These may include complete or partial interruption of economic relations and of rail, sea, air, postal, telegraphic, radio, and other means of communication, and the severance of diplomatic relations").

15. Cleveland, "Norm Internalizations."

16. Philip Alston, "Labor Rights Provisions in U.S. Trade Law," in *Human Rights, Labor Rights, and International Trade*, eds. Lance A. Compa and Stephen F. Diamond (Philadelphia: University of Pennsylvania Press, 1996), 71.

17. GATT, pt. IV, esp. art. XXXVIII; H.R. Rep. No. 98-1090 on the Trade and Tariff Act of 1984, Pub. L. No. 98-573 (renewal of GSP initiated in 1968), 1 (Sept. 27, 1984). The Enabling Clause to the framework agreement resulting from the Tokyo Round of GATT negotiations granted a permanent waiver for nondiscriminatory GSP schemes. GATT, *Decision of the Contracting Parties of 28 November 1979*, L/4903, BISD 26S/203.

18. The U.S. GSP Program's benefits also require protection of intellectual property rights and reduction of trade-distorting investment practices. H.R. Rep. No. 98-1090, 5. The GATT Enabling Clause provides that concessions from LDCs shall not be inconsistent with the development, financial, or trade needs of the LDCs. GATT, *Decision*, ¶ 5.

19. Tariff Act of 1930, ch. 497, 46 Stat. 689, 19 U.S.C. § 1307 (2006).

20. Foreign Assistance Act §§ 116, 22 U.S.C. § 151n (development assistance); § 502(b), 22 U.S.C. § 2304(a)(1) (security assistance); Pub. L. No. 104-208, 110 Stat. 3009-113 (1996) (prohibiting U.S. assistance to foreign security force units "if the Secretary of State has credible evidence to believe such unit has committed gross violations of human rights").

21. 1997 Omnibus Consolidated Appropriations Act, Pub. L. No. 104-208, § 570(d), 110 Stat. 3009, 3116 (1996).

22. *EC-Tariff Preferences*, ¶ 165.

23. Hufbauer et al., *Economic Sanctions 1*, 6.

24. *See* Howlett, "Getting 'Smart,'" 1215.

25. *Id.* at 1213 (Pub. L. No. 99-440, 100 Stat. 1086).

26. *Id.* (quoting from President Reagan's 1981 Christmas address)(citation omitted).

27. *Id.* at 1215.

28. *Id.* at 1200.

29. Nicholas D. Kristof, "Our Man in Havana," *New York Times*, Nov. 8, 2003, at A15.

30. Margaret P. Doxey, *International Sanctions in Contemporary Perspective* (New York: St. Martin's Press, 1996), 32–33.

31. Howlett, "Getting 'Smart,'" 1201.

32. UN Committee on Economic, Social, and Cultural Rights (UNCESCR), "General Comment No. 8: The Relationship Between Economic Sanctions and Respect for Economic, Social, and Cultural Rights," UN Doc. E/C.12/1997/8 (Dec. 4, 1997), ¶ 3.

33. *Id.*, ¶¶ 4-5.

34. *Id.*, ¶ 16.

35. Marc Bossuyt, UN Economic and Social Council, "Working Paper: The Adverse Consequences of Economic Sanctions on the Enjoyment of Human Rights," UN Doc. E/CN.4/Sub.2/2000/33 (June 21, 2000), ¶ 50.

36. *Id.*

37. Kofi A. Annan, *"We the Peoples": The Role of the United Nations in the 21st Century* (New York: UN Department of Public Information, 2000), 50. *See also* UNCHR, Subcommission on Human Rights, Adverse Consequences of Economic Sanctions on the Enjoyment of Human Rights, Res. 1997/35 (Aug. 28, 1997); UNCESCR, "General Comment No. 14: The Right to the Highest Attainable Standard of Health," UN Doc. E/C.12/2000/4 (May 11, 2000).

38. Victor Comras, "Economic Sanctions and U.S. Foreign Policy" (Feb. 25, 2002), Remarks to the Open Forum, http://www.state.gov/s/p/of/proc/tr/9128. htm.

39. We have drawn in part for this section from Berta E. Hernández-Truyol, "Sanctions and Sovereignty: Analysis of the Embargo Under International Legal Norms," Special Pullout Section, *New York Law Journal* 215 (Feb. 20, 1996): S4 (col. 1).

40. 50 U.S.C. App. § 5 (1988).

41. Act of Dec. 28, 1977, Pub. L. No. 95-223, tit. I, §§ 101(a), 102, 103(b), 91 Stat. 1625, 1626 (codified at 50 U.S.C. App. § 5(b)).

42. *Id.*; *see Tagle*, 643 F.2d at 1059–60.

43. 22 U.S.C. §§ 6001–10 (1992).

44. Necessity of Ending the Economic, Commercial, and Financial Embargo Imposed by the United States of American Against Cuba, G.A. Res. 47/19, UN Doc. A/RES/47/19 (Nov. 24, 1992) (passed by a vote of 59-3-71; only states voting against the resolution were the United States, Israel, and Romania, with such traditional U.S. allies as Canada and France voting in favor of the resolution). *See also* United Nations, *Yearbook of the United Nations 1992* (Dordrecht: Martinu Nijhoff, 1993), 234.

45. G.A. Res. 47/19, pmbl. *See also* G.A. Res. 48/16, UN Doc. A/RES/48/16 (Nov. 3, 1993); G.A. Res. 49/9, UN Doc. A/RES/ 49/9 (Oct. 26, 1994); G.A. Res. 50/10, UN Doc. A/RES/50/10 (Nov. 2, 1995).

46. *See* note 45.

47. 22 U.S.C. § 6021–91 (1996).

48. Proclamation 3447 of Feb. 3, 1962, 27 Fed. Reg. 1085 (1962) (noting that "the present government of Cuba is incompatible with the principles and objectives of the Inter-American system").

49. Freedom of Action of the States Parties to the Inter-American Treaty of Reciprocal Assistance to Normalize or Conduct Their Relations with the Republic of Cuba at the Level and in the Form that Each State Deems Advisable, OAS Resolution, July 29, 1975, OAS Doc. OEA/Ser. G. C.P./Doc. 9/75, 14 I.L.M. 1354 (1975).

50. 609 F.2d at 138.

51. ABA, "Resolution and Report on Extraterritorial Economic Sanctions" (1998), 10 (MS, on file with authors).

52. "U.S. Government Continues to Seek Compromise with Europe on Cuba Affair (Helms-Burton Act) But, If It Fails, It Will Refuse WTO Panel Competence," *Reuter Agency Europe*, Feb. 22, 1997.

53. Kees J. Kuilwijk, "Castro's Cuba and the Helms-Burton Act—An Interpretation of the GATT Security Exception," *Journal of World Trade* 31 (1997): 49.

54. Raj Bhala, "National Security and International Trade Law: What the GATT Says and What the United States Does," *University of Pennsylvania Journal*

of International Economics Law 19 (1998): 263, 268. *See also* Peter Lindsay, "The Ambiguity of GATT Article XXI: Subtle Success or Rampant Failure?" *Duke Law Journal* 52 (2003): 1277, 1281.

55. James Stamp and Jonathan Coleman, U.S. ITC, *The Economic Impact of U.S. Sanctions with Respect to Cuba*, USITC Publ. 3398, Investigation No. 332–413 (Washington: U.S. ITC, 2001), 1–7, http://www.usitc.gov/publications/pub3398. pdf (citing U.N. Economic Commission for Latin America, *Economic Survival of Latin America 1963* [New York: UN Department of Public Information, 1965], 273).

56. *Id.* (citing "Direction of Trade Statistics—Database and Browser," IMF, http://www.imf.org/external/pubs/cat/longres.cfm?sk=20954.0).

57. *Id.* at 1–11 (citing data compiled by U.S. departments of Commerce and the Treasury).

58. "FASonline," Foreign Agricultural Service, U.S. Department of Agriculture, http://www.fas.usda.gov/ustrade/ (accessed June 13, 2007) (compiled from Agricultural Export Commodity Aggregations).

59. *Id.*

60. *Id.*

61. Stamp and Coleman, *The Economic Impact,* 2–19.

62. Felipe Pérez Roque, minister of foreign affairs, Cuba, "Statement to the U.N. General Assembly: Necessity of Ending the Economic, Commercial, and Financial Embargo Imposed by the United States of America Against Cuba" (Nov. 8, 2006), http://emba.cubaminrex.cu/Default.aspx?tabid=7298.

63. Stamp and Coleman, *The Economic Impact,* 2–17 (citing Jaime Suchlicki, Institute for Cuba and Cuban American Studies, University of Miami, "The U.S. Embargo of Cuba," Occasional Paper Series [June 2000], 14); Bureau of Inter-American Affairs, U.S. Department of State, "Zenith and Eclipse: A Comparative Look at Socio-Economic Conditions in Pre-Castro and Present Day Cuba" (Feb. 9, 1998, rev. June 2002), http://www.state.gov/p/wha/ci/14776.htm.

64. Manuel Roig-Franzia, "4 Legs Replacing 4 Wheels in Rural Cuba," *Washington Post*, Oct. 29, 2006.

65. AAWH, "Denial of Food and Medicine: The Impact of the U.S. Embargo on the Health and Nutrition in Cuba—An Executive Summary" (Mar. 1997), http://www.cubasolidarity.net/aawh.html.

66. *Id.*

67. Larry Rohter, "Pope Condemns Embargo; Castro Attends Mass," *New York Times,* Jan. 26, 1998.

68. "Making the Most of Family Remittances: Second Report of the Inter-American Dialogue Task Force on Remittances" (May 2007), 1, Inter-American Dialogue, http://www.thedialogue.org/PublicationFiles/family_remittances.pdf.

69. "Background Note: Cuba," U.S. Department of State, http://www.state. gov/r/pa/ei/bgn/2886.htm (accessed June 7, 2007).

70. Jorge Pérez-Lopéz and Sergio Díaz-Briquets, "Remittances to Cuba: A Survey of Methods and Estimates," *ASCE Proceedings* 15 (2005): 396, 396–97, http://lanic.utexas.edu/project/asce/pdfs/volume15/pdfs/diazbriquetsperezlopez.pdf (quoting Comisión Económica para América Latina y el Caribe, "Cuba: Evolución económica durante 2003 y Perspectivas para 2004," LC/MEX/L.622 [2004], 2).

71. *Id.* at 397 (citing Bendixen and Associates, "Remittances to Cuba from the United States" (May 25, 2005)); *see also* Nancy San Martin, "Flow of Funds to Cuba Holds Steady," *Miami Herald*, May 26, 2005 (citing Bendixen and Associates, "Remittances").

72. Pérez-Lopéz and Díaz-Briquets, "Remittances to Cuba," 406.

73. San Martin, "Flow of Funds."

74. *Id.* According to the survey, approximately 440,000 Cuban Americans send $150 on an average of seven times per year, translating to about $1,050 a year. This provides approximately $460 million cash to Cuba. As noted above, other estimates place the flow of all remittances as high as $1 billion. The heightened regulations allow only up to $1,200 in cash remittances a year and only to immediate family members, so no longer can monies be sent to grandparents, cousins, or more distant relatives. One analyst estimates that the Cuban government takes up to 20 percent of the remittances, partly from a 10 percent fee imposed in 2004 by the government on exchanges of dollars. Thus, 20 percent of an estimated $460 million in remittances amounts to $92 million that the remittances provide the government. *Id.* (citing Bendixen and Associates, "Remittances"). *See also* Commission for Assistance to a Free Cuba (CAFC), "Report to the President" (May 2004), 34, http://www.state.gov/documents/organization/32334.pdf (noting that U.S. cash remittances to Cuba account for estimated $400 million to $800 million per year, with some estimates ranging as high as $1 billion); Mark P. Sullivan, "Cuba: U.S. Restrictions on Travel and Remittances," Cong. Res. Serv. Rep. at CRS-9 (updated Feb. 27, 2007), http://fpc.state.gov/documents/organization/83002.pdf (noting that the restrictions on the remittances are regulated by the Cuban Assets Control Regulation, which, pursuant to June 16, 2004, amendments, limits the remittances to three hundred dollars per quarter to nationals of Cuba who are members of the immediate family, which comprises a spouse, child, grandchild, parent, grandparent, or sibling).

75. "Background Note: Cuba."

76. *See* CAFC, "Report to the President," 37.

77. "Making the Most of Family Remittances," 4.

78. Manuel Orozco, "Challenges and Opportunities of Marketing Remittances to Cuba" (July 27, 2002), 15, Inter-American Dialogue, http://www.thedialogue.org/PublicationFiles/Challenges%20and%20Opportunities%20of%20marketing%20remittances%20to%20.pdf.

79. *Id. See also* Lorena Barberia, "Working Paper #15: Remittances to Cuba: An Evaluation of Cuban and US Government Policy Measures," Rosemary Rogers

Working Paper Series (Sept. 2002), 1, http://web.mit.edu/cis/www/migration/ pubs/rrwp/15_remittances.doc (accessed June 28, 2007) (noting that "in absolute terms remittances are as important for Cuba's economy as they are for other countries in the Caribbean, roughly equivalent to those received by the Dominican Republic and twice as high as those received by Haiti. Indeed, a 1998 survey of Latin American immigrants' remittance behavior found that the percentage of Cuban-Americans sending remittances is higher than Mexican-Americans and lower than Dominican-Americans" [citation omitted]).

CHAPTER 15

1. Leana Bresnahan, "Final Examination in International Economic Law and Human Rights," 1–2 (MS submitted for St. Thomas University School of Law LL.M. in Intercultural Human Rights, Apr. 28, 2007) (on file with authors).

2. Ernst-Ulrich Petersmann, "Time for a United Nations 'Global Compact' for Integrating Human Rights into the Law of Worldwide Organizations: Lessons from European Integration," *European Journal of International Law* 13 (2002): 621, 645.

3. "Globalization and Its Impact on the Full Enjoyment of Human Rights," ECOSOC Doc E/CN.4/Sub. 2/20000/13, para. 15 (June 15, 2000), http:// www.unhchr.ch/Huridocda/Huridoca.nsf/(Symbol)/E.CN.4.Sub.2.2000.13. En?Opendocument.

4. Ernst-Ulrich Petersmann, "The 'Human Rights Approach' Advocated by the UN High Commissioner for Human Rights and by the International Labor Organization: Is It Relevant for WTO Law and Policy?" *Journal of International Economics Law* 7 (2004): 605, 614.

5. *See, e.g.,* "The Impact of the Agreement on Trade-related Aspects of Intellectual Property Rights on Human Rights," E/CN.4/Sub. 2/2001/13 (UNCHR, June 27, 2001), ¶ 28.

6. "Economic, Social, and Cultural Rights: Liberalization of Trade in Services and Human Rights," Report of the High Commissioner on Human Rights, E/ CN.4/Sub.2/2002/9 (UNCHR, June 25, 2002).

7. Petersmann, "Time," 645.

8. Joost Pauwelyn, "The Role of Public International Law in the WTO: How Far Can We Go?" *American Journal of International Law* 95 (2001): 535, 552.

9. *See* Petersmann, "Time," 607.

10. Kimberly A. Elliott, Debayani Kar, and J. David Richardson, "Assessing Globalization's Critics: 'Talkers Are No Good Doers???'" IIE Working Paper No. 02-5 (2002), 22, http://ssrn.com/abstract=360440 (the title is from Shakespeare's *Richard III*).

11. *See* Lori G. Kletzer and Howard Rosen, "Easing the Adjustment Burden on U.S. Workers," in *The United States and the World Economy: Foreign Economic*

Policy for the Next Decade, eds. C. Fred Bergsten and IIE (Washington: IIE, 2005), 316–19.

12. Professor Powell first discussed this issue in "The Place of Human Rights Law in World Trade Organization Rules," *Florida Journal of International Law* 16 (2004): 219.

13. Petersmann, "Time," 645. "Fundamental principles of trade law, in particular non-discrimination, are of equal and paramount importance in their own way and right. . . . They reflect equally important basic standards of justice, going beyond economic efficiency." Thomas Cottier and Matthias Oesch, *International Trade Regulation: Law and Policy in the WTO, the European Union, and Switzerland* (London: Cameron May, 2005), 522.

14. University of Florida Levin College of Law Professor Alyson Flournoy, "Memorandum to Curriculum Committee on Trade and Environment Course Proposal" (Feb. 16, 2003) (on file with authors). While the reference is to environmental law, human rights advocates in general would agree with the statement.

15. Paul R. Krugman and Maurice Obstfeld, *International Economics: Theory and Policy* (Boston: Pearson Addison-Wesley, 2006), 26.

16. Steve Charnovitz, "The Moral Exception in Trade Policy," *Virginia Journal of International Law* 38 (1998): 689, *reprinted in* Steve Charnovitz, *Trade Law and Global Governance*, (London: Cameron May, 2002), 346.

17. *Id.* at 332–33.

18. WTO DSU; *see* Pauwelyn, "The Role," 542.

19. *U.S.-Gasoline*, 10.

20. *See U.S.-1916 Act*, ¶ 54, n.30 (*la competence de la competence*); *Canada-Aircraft*, ¶ 202 (adverse inferences); *U.S.—Shrimp-Turtle I*, ¶ 107 (amicus briefs); *U.S.-Wool*, 19 (judicial economy).

21. *EC-Meat*, ¶ 8.157; *EC-Hormones*, ¶ 123.

22. *EC-Asbestos*, ¶¶ 168, 173-74.

23. Professor Powell first discussed this issue in "Regional Economic Arrangements and the Rule of Law in the Americas: The Human Rights Face of Free Trade Agreements," *Florida Journal of International Law* 17 (2005): 59.

24. Application of the rule of law is included, along with open and transparent civil institutions, in the list of the trappings of democracy, which was affirmed as a human right by the United Nations in 1999. UNCHR Res. 1999/57, UN Doc. E/CN.4/1999/57 (1999). *See* David Weissbrodt, Joan Fitzpatrick, and Frank Newman, *International Human Rights: Law, Policy, and Process* (Cincinnati: Anderson, 2001), 540.

25. Joseph Schumpeter, *Capitalism, Socialism, and Democracy* (New York: Harper and Brothers, 1942), 83.

26. Petersmann, "The 'Human Rights Approach,'" 615.

27. The ILO Work Declaration exists because WTO Members in the 1996 Singapore Declaration embraced worker rights and asked the ILO to set down

those most closely tied to trade. Petersmann, "The 'Human Rights Approach,'" 617.

28. *See* Larry A. DiMatteo et al., "The Doha Declaration and Beyond: Giving a Voice to Non-trade Concerns Within the WTO Trade Regime," *Vanderbilt Journal of Transnational Law* 36 (2003): 95, 105–7.

29. J. S. Mill, *On Liberty*, ed. Elizabeth Rapaport (Indianapolis: Hackett, 1978), 9.

30. Thom Brooks, "Is Global Poverty A Crime?" (Nov. 9, 2006), 17, http://ssrn.com/abstract=943762.

31. *Trail Smelter Arbitration*, 3 R.I.A.A. at 1965.

32. *See* Edith B. Weiss, "Global Environmental Change and International Law: The Introductory Framework," in *Environmental Change and International Law: New Challenges and Dimensions*, ed. Edith B. Weiss (Tokyo: UN University Press, 1992), § II, http://www.unu.edu/unupress/unupbooks/uu25ee/uu25ee04.htm#ii.%20the%20development%20of%20international%20environmental%20law; *see also* Permanent Sovereignty over Natural Resources, G.A. Res. 1803 (XVII), UN Doc. A/5217 (Dec. 14, 1962).

33. Stockholm Declaration, princ. 21.

34. Draft Articles on International Liability for Injurious Consequences Arising Out of Acts Not Prohibited by International Law, May 30, 1989, International Law Commission, UN GAOR, 44th Sess., Supp. No. 10, UN Doc. A/44/10 (1989), 222, arts. 1, 8 and 9, *reprinted in* Lakshman D. Guruswamy et al., *Supplement of Basic Documents to International Environmental Law and World Order: A Problem Oriented Coursebook* (St. Paul, Minn.: West, 1999), 81–83.

35. Frank J. Garcia, *Trade, Inequality, and Justice: Toward a Liberal Theory of Just Trade* (Ardsley, N.Y.: Transnational, 2003), 70.

36. *Id.* at 134.

37. Thomas W. Pogge, *World Poverty and Human Rights: Cosmopolitan Responsibilities and Reforms* (Cambridge: Polity, 2002), 19; Brooks, "Is Global Poverty A Crime?" 11.

38. Pogge, "World Poverty," 18.

39. *Chrysostomos and Papachrysostomou v. Turkey*, 26.

40. *Cyprus v. Turkey*, ¶ 77; *see* Nicola Venneman, "Application of International Human Rights Conventions to Transboundary State Acts," in *Transboundary Harm in International Law: Lessons from the Trail Smelter Arbitration*, eds. Rebecca M. Bratspies and Russell Miller (New York: Cambridge University Press, 2006), 295, 297.

41. Vienna Convention, art. 26.

42. *Id.* at art. 19(c).

43. *Alcoa*, 148 F.2d at 416; *see* Lori F. Damrosch et al., *International Law: Cases and Materials* (St. Paul, Minn.: West, 2001), 1095.

44. Frank J. Garcia, "The 'Fair' Trade Law of Nations, or A 'Fair' Global Law of Economic Relations?" (presentation at Fifth Annual International Law

Symposium, University of Idaho, Coeur d'Alene, Mar. 1, 2007) (on file with authors).

45. Venneman, "Application," 302.

46. *U.S.-Tuna-Dolphin I*, ¶ 5.27. The second *Tuna-Dolphin* panel rejected this approach, although it reached the same result by finding that U.S. projection of its environmental policy beyond its borders undermined GATT's multilateralism. *U.S.-Tuna-Dolphin II*, ¶¶ 5.32, 5.38.

47. *U.S.-Shrimp-Turtle I*, ¶ 156.

48. Amy Sinden, "The Power of Rights: Imposing Human Rights Duties on Transnational Corporations for Environmental Harms," Temple University Legal Studies Research Paper No. 2006-22, http://ssrn.com/abstract=925679 (accessed May 29, 2007).

49. Vienna Convention, art. 19(c).

50. 28 U.S.C.S. § 1350 (2000) ("the district courts shall have original jurisdiction of any civil action by an alien for a tort only, committed in violation of the law of nations or a treaty of the United States"). We will refer to this legislation as the ATS, although others call it the Alien Tort Claims Act (ATCA).

51. ACHR, art. 25.1; Habeas Corpus in Emergency Situations (Arts. 27(2), 7(6) of the American Convention on Human Rights), Advisory Opinion OC-8/87, January 30, 1987, at ¶ 32, Inter-Am. Ct. H.R. (Ser. A) No. 8 (1987).

52. 630 F.2d 876 (2d Cir. 1980).

53. 542 U.S. 692 (2004).

54. Carolyn A. D'Amore, "*Sosa v. Alvarez-Machain* and the Alien Tort Statute: How Wide Has the Door to Human Rights Litigation Been Left Open?" *Akron Law Review* 39 (2006): 593, 600. Courts granted ATS jurisdiction in only two of twenty cases filed between 1789 and 1980.

55. ATS, 28 U.S.C.S. § 1350 (2000). *See also Hanoch Tel-Oren v. Libyan Arab Republic*, 517 F.Supp 542, 548 (1981).

56. *Paul v. Avril*, 812 F.Supp. 207, 212 (S.D. Fla. 1993) (the plain language of the statute, with phrases such as "committed in violation" of the law of nations, implies a cause of action).

57. *Sarei v. Rio Tinto*, 221 F.Supp.2d 1116, 1139–63, 1199–1209 (C.D. Cal. 2002).

58. *Rio Tinto*, supra note 42, at *5.

59. *Rio Tinto*, supra note 42, at *11 (quoting from *Siderman de Blake v. Republic of Argentina*, 965 F.2d 699, 718 [9th Cir. 1992], the Foreign Relations Law Restatement "identif[ies] jus cogens norms prohibiting . . . systematic racial discrimination," and "international law does not recognize an act that violates jus cogens as a sovereign act").

60. *Rio Tinto*, supra note 42, at *11–12.

61. *See* Paul Krugman, "Ricardo's Difficult Idea," The Official Paul Krugman Web Page, http://web.mit.edu/krugman/www/ricardo.htm (accessed June 7, 2007).

62. Amy Sinden, "Accounting for the Environmental Costs of the Softwood Lumber Trade" (paper presented at 5th Annual International Law Symposium, University of Idaho, Coeur d'Alene, Mar. 1–3, 2007) (MS, on file with authors).

63. Declaration of Quebec City, Third Summit of the Americas, Apr. 22, 2001, http://www.summit-americas.org/Documents%20for%20Quebec%20City%20 Summit/Quebec/Declaration%20of%20Quebec%20City%20-%20Eng%20-%20 final.htm (accessed June 1, 2007).

Index

Abuse: beating, 176, 179, 331n. 52; physical, 140, 173, 176, 182; and trafficking, 171–72, 176, 200. *See also* Rape; Sexual, abuse

Acquis: human rights, 87, 277; public international law, 228

African Charter on Human and Peoples' Rights, 56, 61, 311nn. 68, 70

Agreement on Agriculture (WTO), 242–44, 246, 352nn. 48–49, 353nn. 53, 56

Agreement on Application of Sanitary and Phytosanitary Measures. *See* Sanitary and Phytosanitary Measures Agreement (SPS), WTO

Agreement on Subsidies, WTO, 38

Agreement on Technical Barriers to Trade (TBT), WTO, 33, 38, 103–8, 110, 113, 117, 128, 149–50, 282, 322n. 40, 323nn. 49, 51, 324nn. 57, 67

Agriculture: export, 6, 27, 89, 117, 159, 244–46, 71; import, 119, 159, 186, 246, 271, 303n. 5; reform, 46, 89, 241–47, 232–34; sector, 156, 158, 196, 241–42; subsidy, 6, 8, 27, 45, 47, 196, 204–41, 240–47, 288, 352n. 48; work, 2, 174, 181, 183–85, 190–91, 197–98, 247, 339n. 68, 340n. 100. *See also* Farms; Food; Poverty

Aguinda v. Texaco, 224, 347n. 49, 348n. 56

AIDS. *See* HIV/AIDS

Alcoa, United States v., 290, 364n. 43

Alien Tort Statute (Alien Tort Claims Act), U.S., 54, 292–94, 299n. 5, 365n. 50

Amazon rainforest, 4, 61, 88, 183, 223–24

American Association for World Health (AAWH), 271–72

American Bar Association (ABA), 269

American Convention on Human Rights (ACHR), 56, 58, 115, 142, 171, 194, 232, 252, 292–93, 296, 308n. 56, 314nn. 2, 6, 355nn. 8, 10–13, 365n. 51

American Declaration on the Rights and Duties of Man, 58, 77, 115, 194, 232, 252, 296, 314nn. 2, 4, 6, 325n. 5, 355nn. 8–13, 18

American Revolution, 59, 309n. 60

Amparo, 293–94

Analysis. *See* Cost-benefit analysis; Econometric approach

Andean Community of Nations (CAN), 43–45

Animal: diversity, 123, 221; life/health of, 88, 94, 96, 98, 104, 108, 116–19, 121–23, 127, 148, 196, 224, 229, 282, 313n. 33, 321nn. 27, 30; resources, 98, 109, 118–20, 217, 221, 243

Anti-dumping, and WTO agreement, 38, 130, 215, 331n. 58
Anti-Dumping Act of 1916, U.S., 47, 247
Aquinas, St. Thomas, 51, 305n. 9
Arbitrary detention, 16, 20, 264
Assembly, freedom of, 252, 264
Association, freedom of, 6, 61, 73, 139, 141, 143, 166, 169, 253, 260, 264, 276, 328n. 6
Australia—Leather, WTO, 303n. 12
Australia—Salmon, WTO, 120–21, 137, 325nn. 14–15

Baker, United States v., 269
Balancing test, WTO nondiscrimination rules and exceptions, 38, 95, 98–99, 122, 148, 150
Banjul charter. *See* African Charter on Human and Peoples' Rights
Basel Convention on the Control of Transboundary Movements of Hazardous Wastes and Their Disposal, 90, 303n. 18
Batey. See Shantytown
Beauty hierarchy, 134, 161. *See also* Colorism
Bebel, August, 192, 341n. 1
Beijing Declaration and Platform for Action, 196, 205, 308n. 43, 311nn. 68–69, 343n. 14
Biodiversity, 89, 109, 113, 124, 129–30, 196, 221–22, 224, 226, 348n. 71; indigenous, 206, 218, 221–22, 226, 228, 230, 276, 345n. 6, 347n. 47. *See also* Biosafety, Protocol on; Convention on Biological Diversity; Ecosystem, degradation of
Biological diversity. *See* Biodiversity
Biomimicry, 111
Biopiracy of traditional knowledge, 208, 218–20, 229

Bioprospecting for traditional knowledge, 218–19, 223, 226–27, 229, 348n. 71
Biosafety, Protocol on. *See* Cartegena Protocol on Biosafety
Bipartisan Trade Promotion Act of 2002, U.S., 152–53, 332n. 72
Black/white paradigm, 162. *See also* Colorism
Bolivarian Alternative, 155, 304n. 21
Bonafide occupational qualification (BFOQ), 202
Bondage. *See* Debt bondage; Forced labor; Trafficking
Bretton Woods institutions, 26–27, 47, 64–65, 228, 351n. 21
Brierly, J. L., on defining international law, 14, 301n. 4
Brundtland Report (on sustainable development), 109–10
Bush, George W., U.S. President, 133, 150, 154, 256–57, 355n. 23

Canada—Aircraft, WTO, 68, 283, 313n. 26, 363n. 20
Canada—Herring and Salmon, WTO, 99–100, 322n. 34, 329n. 22
Canadian Council for International Co-Operation (CCIC), 343n. 19
Capitalism, 74, 231, 250, 257, 284; natural, 110–12; sustainable, 257, 277, 286, 291. *See also* Equator Principles
Caribbean Basin Initiative, U.S., 142
Cartagena Protocol on Biosafety, 7, 123–29, 135, 276, 326nn. 17–19. *See also* Biodiversity; Convention on Biological Diversity
Case-Zablocki Act, U.S., 22, 305nn. 15–16
Castro, Fidel, Cuban President, 45–46, 252, 267, 269, 293. *See also* Cuban Embargo

Center for International Environmental Law (CIEL), 217
Center for the Advancement of Human Rights (CAHR), 338n. 56
Central America-Dominican Republic-United States Free Trade Agreement (CAFTA-DR-US), 82, 133, 136, 154–55, 260, 314n. 40, 319n. 7, 331nn. 51, 53–54, 343n. 16, 356n. 38
Central American Common Market (MCCA), 44–45
Chapeau Test, 94–96, 101–3, 110, 119, 148; and discrimination, 96, 101–2, 110, 119, 147–48; and disguised trade restriction, 92, 95–96, 101, 110, 119–21, 123, 147–48, 323n. 48. See also GATT; General Exceptions, GATT Art. XX
Charnovitz, Steve, 215, 311n. 1, 320n. 17, 330nn. 23, 25, 32, 36, 353n. 16
Chávez, Hugo, Venezuelan President, 44–45, 155, 254–55, 304n. 21
Children: disappeared, 343n. 24; health of, 2, 109, 115, 171, 241, 343n. 16; forced labor, 173, 175–76, 177–80; labor, 2, 4, 137, 139, 142–43, 15, 151, 157, 165–66, 169, 279, 285, 329n. 13, 331n. 52; labor, exploitation of, 63, 137, 146, 170, 190–91, 336n. 1; labor, indentured, 5–6, 8, 37, 282; labor, source state for, 178, 338n. 48; and pornography, 37, 171, 282; and poverty, 236–37; rights of, 85, 115, 139, 141–43, 169, 170–71, 289, 309n. 66, 329n. 13, 336n. 1; and sex tourism trade, 182, 190–91; sexual exploitation of, 181–82, 190–91; special protection of, 115, 194; and sex, 37, 170; trafficking of, 177–180. See also Convention on the Rights of the Child; Convention concerning the Prohibition and Immediate Action for the Elimination of the Worst Forms of Child Labour
Chile. See Ralco Dam
Chlorofluorocarbon (CFC), 106–7
Chrysostomos and Papachrysostomou, ECHR, 364n. 39
Chua, Amy, on globalization and democracy intersection, 3, 299nn. 2, 8
Citizenship, 8, 11, 154, 158, 249, 259–60, 275, 315nn. 16, 20–21, 23, 316n. 38, 317n. 39, 319nn. 62, 63; desirable activity model, 75–76; economic, 83–84; global, 112, 164, 284; and globalization, 75–85; heterogeneous, 76; legal status model, 75–76; transnationalization, 4, 81, 83–85, 317nn. 42–43, 336n. 8
Civil: law, 40–41, 269; rights, 12, 56–59, 77–78, 141–42, 250, 258, 260, 265–66, 309n. 60, 311n. 70, 317n. 39; society, 3, 6, 11, 47, 50, 63, 66–67, 74, 76, 85, 118, 167, 186–87, 199, 253, 256, 258–59, 262, 265, 274, 277, 279–80, 284, 287–292, 295–96, 319nn. 62–63, 355n. 16. See also First generation (civil and political) rights; International Covenant on Civil and Political Rights (ICCPR); Negative, rights
Civil Rights Act of 1964, U.S., 202
Classification of human rights, 58–61. See also First generation (civil and political) rights; Second generation (social, economic, cultural) rights; Third generation rights
Climate change, 4, 28, 106, 109, 113, 135
Clinton, Bill, U.S. President, 47, 150–51, 268
Coalition of Service Industries, 159
Codex Alimentarius Commission, 121–22, 196

Collective: bargaining, 137, 139,
166, 328n. 6; rights, 210. *See also*
Solidarity rights; Third generation
rights; Union
Color caste system. *See* Colorism
Colorism: discrimination, 134, 160,
208; and health, 133–34; hierarchy,
134, 160–61, 333n. 85; and labor
rights; 160–62; and racism, 134, 160.
See also "One drop" rule
Commission for Assistance to a Free
Cuba (CAFC), 361nn. 74, 76
Common heritage, right to, 61
Common Market of the South. *See*
MERCOSUR
Communication, right to, 61, 258
Communications theory, 52
Comparative advantage: effect on
workers rights, 136–39, 169, 226,
276, 281, 288, 295; food security,
242; and immigration, 157; and
natural resources, overuse of, 4,
89, 285; and poverty, 288; primacy
of human rights, 101; Ricardian
model of, 27–29, 123, 157, 242,
295; Ricardo-plus version, 295
Compulsory labor. *See* Debt bondage;
Forced labor
Conference on Environment and Development, Rio de Janeiro (1992),
108–9, 196, 343n. 14; Declaration
of, 110, 125, 311n. 68, 326n. 18
Conference on Security and Cooperation in Europe, Helsinki (1975),
Declaration of, 308n. 45
Conference on the Human Environment, Stockholm (1972): 109;
Declaration of, 287, 311n. 68,
347n. 45
Constitution. *See* International Labour
Organisation (ILO); Mexico, consti-
tution of; United States

Convention Against Torture and
Other Cruel, Inhuman or Degrading Treatment or Punishment, 56,
68–70, 313n. 32
Convention concerning Forced or
Compulsory Labour (ILO Convention 29), 171, 175, 189, 328n. 6,
336n. 3
Convention concerning Indigenous
and Tribal Peoples in Independent
Countries (ILO Convention 107),
206, 209, 344n. 2
Convention concerning Minimum Age
for Admission to Employment (ILO
Minimum Age Convention), 139,
328n. 10
Convention concerning the Abolition
of Forced Labour (ILO Convention
105), 171, 175, 189, 328n. 6, 363n. 27
Convention concerning the Prohibi-
tion and Immediate Action for the
Elimination of the Worst Forms
of Child Labour (CEWFCL)(ILO
Convention 182), 152–53, 171, 175,
189, 328n. 6
Convention for the Suppression of
the Traffic in Persons and of the
Exploitation and the Prostitution of
Others, 171
Convention on Biological Diversity
(CBD), 7, 123, 126–27, 129, 135,
196–97, 210, 220–22, 226–27, 230,
276, 326n. 24, 343nn. 14, 18, 347nn.
42–44, 46–47. *See also* Biosafety,
Protocol on
Convention on Rights and Duties of
States (CRDS), 301n. 13
Convention on the Elimination of All
Forms of Discrimination Against
Women (CEDAW), 56, 61, 66, 170,
193–94, 205, 285, 311n. 69, 341n.
4, 342n. 5

Convention on the Elimination of All Forms of Racial Discrimination (CERD), 56, 61, 170, 285

Convention on the Prevention and Punishment of the Crime of Genocide, 56. *See also* Genocide

Convention on the Rights of the Child (CRC), 56, 61, 170, 278, 289, 336n. 1

Copenhagen Declaration on Social Development. *See* World Summit for Social Development, Copenhagen

Copyright protections. *See* Trade-related Aspects of Intellectual Property Rights, WTO Agreement on

Core-periphery exploitation, 80, 82

Corporate codes of conduct: and labor rights, 163; and social responsibility, 162–64, 166, 291–92

Cost-benefit analysis, 98, 123, 125

Coyote, 176, 183, 185. *See also* Trafficking

Creative destruction of trade, 280–81, 284

Crook, Clive, 6, 300n. 17, 335n. 120, 350n. 9

Crosby v. National Foreign Trade Council, 25, 302n. 26

Cross-border flow, 70, 85, 258, 287; of goods, 81, 157; of people, 157. *See also* Immigration; Indigenous peoples

Cuban Democracy Act (CDA), U.S., 267–68, 359n. 43

Cuban embargo, by U.S., 45–47, 267–74

Cuban Liberty and Democratic Solidarity Act (Libertad), U.S., 268, 359n. 47

Culture: concerns, 77, 78, 173, 249; heritage, 218; and human rights, 49–50, 55; identity, 10, 41, 80, 210, 217; life, 75, 85; minority, 60, 209, 213; right to, 56–60, 75, 78, 115, 141–42, 151, 164, 212, 220, 256, 265–66, 309nn. 64–65, 311nn. 70–71, 342n. 5; traditions, 60, 70, 78, 146, 193; uniformity, 2–3, 66, 130, 193, 223, 257. *See also* Gender; Indigenous peoples; Women

Cyprus v. Turkey, 289, 364n. 40. *See also* European Commission of Human Rights

de Vitoria, Francisco, on natural law, 51

Debt bondage, 176–77, 180, 183, 191, 339n70. *See also* Forced Labor; Trafficking

Declaration of Independence, U.S., 59, 315n. 20

Declaration of Principles Concerning Multinational Enterprises and Social Policy, ILO, 164

Declaration on Environment and Development (Rio Declaration). *See* Conference on Environment and Development, Rio de Janeiro

Declaration on Fundamental Principles and Rights at Work (Work Declaration), ILO, 139–41, 153, 166, 285, 313n. 30, 329n. 12, 337n. 22, 363n. 27

Declaration on Race and Racial Prejudice (DRRP), 311n. 69

Declaration on the Elimination of Violence Against Women (DEVAW), 311n. 69

Declaration on the Right to Development. *See* International Conference on Population and Development, Cairo

Declaration on the Rights of Man and of the Citizen, French, 59, 315n. 20

Declaration on World Food Security (Rome Declaration), 352n. 51

Democratic governance, 88, 250–52, 256, 279

Democracy, right to, 61, 232, 250–60, 278–79, 317n. 39, 363n. 24

Detention. *See* Arbitrary detention

Destination state. *See* Trafficking

Deterritorialization, 66, 78, 80, 82. *See also* Extraterritorial/ity; Territory

Development, right to, 311nn. 69, 71. *See also* Sustainable development

Dignity, right to, 55, 75, 79, 172, 193–94, 232–33, 276–77, 289, 309n. 59, 311n. 68

Disappearance of persons, 16, 20, 199, 264, 343n. 24. *See also* Children

Discrimination. *See* Chapeau Test; Colorism; National Treatment Clause, GATT Art. III; Most-favored Nation Clause, GATT. Art. I; Nondiscrimination; Racial; Sexual

Disguised trade restriction/protection, 136–37, 264. *See also* Chapeau Test

Dispute Settlement Body, WTO. *See* World Trade Court

Dispute settlement panel, 67, 243; of GATT, 33, 37, 95–96, 291, 303n. 5. *See also* World Trade Court

Dispute Settlement Understanding (DSU), WTO, 40, 246, 303n. 13, 314n. 41, 330n. 49, 363n. 18

Diversity. *See* Animal diversity; Biodiversity; Genetic; Plant

Divide: bridging the, of trade and human rights, 9, 11, 226–28; North-South, 82, 156–57; public/private, 184

Doctors Without Borders, 132

Doha Development Round, WTO, 47–48, 196, 244, 246, 328n. 9

Domestic work, 174–75, 179–81, 199–200, 339n. 59, 339n. 67. *See also* Products; Servitude

Domestic Restrictions Test, WTO, 100, 103

Due process, 53, 284; and trade, 67, 102, 167

Drugs. *See* Medicine

Earth Summit, 1992. *See* Conference on Environment and Development, Rio de Janeiro

Ecolabels, and TBT Agreement (WTO), 107–8, 110, 150, 323nn. 51, 57. *See also* Labeling of products

Econometric approach, 6, 238–39, 240, 258

Economic: means test, 159; rights, 12, 56–60, 75, 78, 83–84, 115, 142, 164, 209–10, 231, 250–51, 260, 265–66, 309n. 66, 311n. 70, 315n. 20; sanctions, 4, 12, 252, 261–74, 329n. 16; well-being, 11–12, 75, 83–84, 204, 259, 261, 275, 292, 297. *See also* International Covenant on Economic, Social, and Cultural Rights; Second generation (social, economic, cultural) rights

Economy. *See* Market economy

Ecosystem, degradation of, 86–113, 221, 225. *See also* Biodiversity

Education, right to, 50, 60, 193, 235, 252, 254, 308n. 57, 310n. 66, 317n. 39, 342n. 5

Eisenhower, Dwight D., U.S. President, 267

Elections, genuine, 251–252, 254–255, 260

Eli Lilly, 217

Elkington, John, and "triple bottom line," 112

Embargo. *See* Cuban embargo, by U.S.

Endesa, 225, 348n64

Environmental equity, 112, 286. *See also* Healthy environment, right to; Multilateral, environmental agreement

Equal protection, right to, 193–94, 341n. 3

Equality, right to, 50, 53, 55, 61, 194, 233, 260, 270, 309n59. *See also* Gender

Equator Principles, 110–12, 324nn. 63–64

Equity. *See* Environmental equity; Gender

Esty, Daniel, on "greening the GATT," 110, 324nn. 56, 59

Ethnic/ity: 76, 78, 162; identity, 210, 333n. 83; minority, 53, 85, 171, 264, 345, 351n. 19; origin, right to, 56, 59

European Commission of Human Rights (ECHR), 228, 270, 288. *See also Chrysostomos and Papachrysostomou; Cyprus v. Turkey*

European Communities (EC), 34, 36, 97, 105, 126, 259, 268, 313n. 37; and regional human rights system, 58. *See also* European Commission on Human Rights; European Convention for the Protection of Human Rights and Fundamental Freedoms; *individual EC cases*

European Communities—Asbestos, 33–35, 71, 93–94, 98–99, 104, 118, 130, 134, 145–46, 313n. 39, 321n. 22, 322n. 32, 326n. 27, 330nn. 29–30, 363n. 22

European Communities—Bananas, 314n. 41

European Communities—Biotech Products, 117, 119, 126–29, 135, 313n. 36, 324n. 67, 326nn. 20–22

European Communities—Computers, 313n. 28

European Communities—Hormones, 99, 121, 127, 129, 196, 324n. 67, 325n. 16, 363n. 21

European Communities—Meat, 363n. 21

European Communities—Sardines, 105, 323n. 45, 324n. 67

European Communities—Tariff Preferences, 313n. 37, 324n. 38, 358n. 22

European Convention for the Protection of Human Rights and Fundamental Freedoms, 56

European Union. *See* European Communities

Exception. *See* General Exceptions, GATT Art. XX

Exhaustible natural resource. *See* Natural, resources, exhaustible

Exploitation: at core-periphery, 80, 82; and first generation rights, 59; of labor, 174–76, 180–82, 184–85, 190–91, 276, 288; of migrants, 80, 183; of natural resources, 217, 225, 287; of the poor, 80, 183; sexual, 170, 172–73, 180–82, 184, 190–91. *See also* Children; Forced labor; Indigenous peoples; Trafficking; Women

Extraterritorial Harm Principle, WTO, 286

Extraterritorial/ity, 95, 97–98, 103, 148, 268–69, 289, 321n. 29, 322n. 30, 329n. 22. *See also* Extraterritorial Harm Principle, WTO

Fair Labor Standards Act (FLSA), U.S., 340nn. 96–97

Family: right to, 59, 172, 193–94, 310n. 66; role of, 50

Famine. *See* Fear, and famine; Hunger

Farms, 43, 89, 94, 156, 167, 174–75, 177–78, 185–86, 199, 242; indigenous, 208, 212, 218, 223, 225, 345n. 9; and poverty, 242, 247; subsistence, 43, 87, 204, 211, 230, 247. *See also* Agriculture

Fear, and famine, 250–60; freedom from, 260, 309n. 66, 317n. 39; and poverty, 236, 249; of trafficking, 176–77, 180, 185

First generation (civil and political) rights, 58–61, 141, 266. *See also* Civil, rights; Classification of human rights; International Covenant on Civil and Political Rights; Negative, rights; Political, rights

First peoples. *See* Indigenous peoples

Fisheries Jurisdiction Case, ICJ, 301n. 11

Food: right to, 60, 84, 87, 235, 309n. 66, 342n. 5; safety, 63, 99, 114, 118, 121–22, 134, 276, 325n. 67; sanctions, 265–66, 271–74; security, 3, 6, 204, 242, 244, 246–47, 325n. 51. *See also* Biosafety, Protocol on; Declaration on World Food Security

Food and Drug Administration (FDA), U.S., 128

Forced labor, 139, 141–42, 145–46, 166, 169–82, 185, 189–91, 252–63, 289, 294, 320n. 19, 328n. 6, 329nn. 13, 16, 20, 339n. 59, 340n. 96. *See also* Children; Products

Foreign investment: and labor laws, 151; and gender mainstreaming, 204; and trafficking, 176. *See also* Investment; Principles for Responsible Investment

Forum non conveniens, 224

Four Freedoms Speech, 309n. 55, 317n. 39

Four Pillars of GATT, 4, 30–36, 68, 89, 94–96, 106, 113–14, 137, 150, 270;

exceptions to, 36–39, 70–71, 92, 96, 113, 145, 148, 321n. 24. *See also* General Exceptions, GATT Art. XX

Fox, Vincente, Mexican President, 81, 248, 309n. 60

Franck, Thomas, on right to democracy, 251, 354n. 2

Free speech, right to, 59, 264, 309n. 66, 317n. 39

Free Trade Area of the Americas (FTAA): hemispheric integration, 47; citizenship, 81; labor rights, 155–56; democracy, 41, 253; linking trade and human rights, 296–97, 317n. 44

French Revolution, 59, 255. *See also* Declaration on the Rights of Man and the Citizen

Frolova v. U.S.S.R., 307n. 39

Gabcíkovo-Nagymaros Case, ICJ, 87

Gandhi, Indira, 109

Garcia, Frank, 287, 311n. 1, 364nn. 35

GATS, 37, 70, 136, 146–47, 157–60, 283, 313n. 34, 330n. 34. *See also* Mode 4, GATS

GATT, 24; basic purpose, 33; and Bretton Woods system, 27; Four Pillars, 30; greening of, 110; and GSP, 357n. 17; human rights priorities, 63; and PPMs, 89, 91, 323n. 48; as self-contained entity, 65; and SPS agreement 346n. 17. *See also* Dispute settlement panel; General Exceptions, GATT Art. XX

Gender: cultural trope, 173, 193, 203, 239; equality, 8, 50, 60, 66, 173, 193–94, 199, 202–5; equity, 50, 342n. 8; gap, 192; mainstreaming, 199, 204–5, 249, 276; neutral, 179, 198, 200, 202–3; and poverty, 173,

198, 236, 241, 275–76, 342n. 5, 351n.
18; role, 173, 202, 236, 341n. 4; subordination, 10, 60, 66, 173, 236, 239,
275; trope, 173, 193, 203, 239. *See
also* Women
General Exceptions, GATT Art. XX,
36–38, 70, 72, 88, 89–95, 97, 99, 101,
103–4, 108, 110, 113–14, 134, 143, 278,
282, 321nn. 23–24. *See also* Four
Pillars of GATT; *and individual
exception/clause*
General Motors, 162, 323n. 46, 326nn.
56, 59
Generalized System of Preferences
(GSP), U.S., 263, 357n. 17, 358n. 18
Generational construct of human
rights. *See* Classification of human
rights; First generation (civil and
political) rights; Second generation
(social, economic, cultural) rights;
Third generation rights
Genetic: diversity, 89, 220; modification (GM), 7, 116, 124, 126–28,
135, 229; genetically-modified organism (GMO), 124, 127–29, 137,
196–97, 276; resource, 208, 217,
220–22, 226, 228–30
Genocide, 4, 16, 20, 56, 67, 73, 210,
288–89. *See also* Convention on
the Prevention and Punishment of
the Crime of Genocide; Humanity,
crimes against
German Settlers in Poland (PCIJ),
306n. 27
Global Harm Principle, 286–89
Governance, rules-based, 73, 284, 286.
See also Democratic governance
Green consumers, 107–8, 110. *See also*
GATT, greening of
Gross domestic product (GDP), 3–4,
29, 42, 47, 207, 240, 272
Grotius, Hugo, and the development

of international law, 51–52, 305nn.
14, 20
Group rights. *See* Collective, rights;
Solidarity rights; Third generation
rights
Guidelines for Multinational Enterprises, OECD, 164

Harassment. *See* Sexual, harassment
Hartford Fire Ins. Co. v. California, 74
Health: right to, 87, 114–15, 118–19,
129–30, 133–34, 194, 276, 283; risk
assessment of, 35, 93–94, 133, 173
Healthy environment, right to, 61,
86–88, 90, 115, 149, 276, 295
Helms-Burton Act (1996), U.S., 46,
264, 268–70
Helsinki Declaration, 308n. 45
Heritage, right to, 61. *See also* Culture;
Indigenous peoples
Heterogeneous. *See* Citizenship;
Women
Hierarchy. *See* Beauty hierarchy; Colorism; International law; Legal hierarchy; Racial, hierarchy
HIV/AIDS, 114–16, 130–33, 173, 229,
265, 276
Housing, right to, 50, 60, 233
Human rights: abuse of, 2, 12, 55, 273,
286, 294; framework, 49, 75–76,
86–88, 114–15, 136–42, 170–73,
193–94, 206–11, 231–34, 251–53,
262–63, 295; fundamental, 55–56,
68, 86, 132, 136, 140, 193–94, 251,
253, 263, 266, 281, 283–86, 289,
294–96, 304n. 1, 307n. 37; indivisibility of, 9, 58, 61, 78–79, 141, 265,
309n. 58, 311n. 69; interdependency
of, 58, 61, 78–79, 141, 309n. 58, 311n.
69; reparation for violation, 286–94;
violations, 4, 37, 71, 138, 140, 256,
261–62, 265, 274, 282, 294, 358n. 20;

Human rights (*continued*): universality, of, 49–50, 55, 61, 138, 140, 277, 285, 309n. 59. *See also* Classification of human rights; Sustainable development; Territory; Trade-related Aspects of Intellectual Property Rights; Universality
Human Rights Watch (HRW), 260, 299n. 3, 336n. 5, 338nn. 46–48, 52, 339n. 63, 341n. 101, 356nn. 40–41
Human bondage. *See* Debt bondage; Forced labor; Slavery, Trafficking
Humanitarian assistance, right to, 61, 266
Humanitarianism, 63. *See* also Human rights
Humanity, crimes against, 52, 54, 294; war, 52, 54, 135, 294. *See also* Genocide
Hunger, 4, 236–237, 265, 300n. 13; freedom from, 232, 260

Identity: cultural, 10, 41, 80, 210, 217; ethnic, 210, 333n. 83. *See also* Indigenous peoples
Immigration, 23; illegal, 184, 340n. 96; law, 176–77, 180; policy, 157–60, 180, 332nn. 66, 72; and poverty, 247–48, 317nn. 42–43; and undocumented workers, 154, 156, 174, 176–77, 181, 184, 186, 190, 235, 241, 332n. 66; and the United States, 159, 180, 185–86, 332n. 66, 340n.96. *See also* Debt bondage; Mode 4, GATS; Trafficking
Immokalee, Florida, and debt bondage, 185–86, 341n. 102
Immorality. *See* Morality/morals; Public Morals Clause, GATT Art. XX(a)
Income/wealth gap, 4, 43, 80, 174, 231, 238, 259

Indigenous peoples: and colorism, 161; culture, 209–12, 218, 220, 222–23, 225–26, 228–30; exploitation of, 227–28, 241; and globalization, 206, 211, 22, 226; intellectual property rights of, 208, 210, 213, 217–19, 226–30, 348n. 71; land, 4, 207–10, 223–25, 230; language, 207, 211–13, 218–19, 227; lifestyles, 3, 207, 211–13, 222–25, 228; medicine, 10, 208, 217–19, 227; vs. nonindigenous, 208; population, 11, 206, 209, 345n. 9, 349nn. 79, 73; rights, 8, 42, 47, 208–12, 217, 223, 228, 230, 276, 285–86, 331n. 52; sovereignty, 207; and sustainable development, 88, 206, 210, 217, 222, 276; tribes, 207, 209, 211–12, 217–18, 223–25, 227, 229–30, 34n. 9; and TRIPS, 197, 208, 216–19, 222, 226–29, 240, 346n. 17. *See also* Biodiversity; Biopiracy of traditional knowledge; Bioprospecting for traditional knowledge; Convention concerning Indigenous and Tribal Peoples in Independent Countries; Farms; Informed consent of indigenous peoples; Plant; Territory; Traditional knowledge
Industrial revolution, 113, 137, 168, 201, 217
Informal sector, 197–98, 241
Informed consent, of indigenous peoples, 210–11, 222, 227–28
Institute for International Economics (IIE), 168, 324n. 56, 335n. 121, 353n. 59, 357nn. 3, 6–7, 362nn. 10–11
Intellectual property, 23, 213–17; right to, 208, 226, 228, 331n. 58, 343n. 16, 358n. 18. *See also* Indigenous peoples; Trade-related Aspects of Intellectual Property Rights; World Intellectual Property Organization;

World Trade Organization, intellectual property rights of

Inter-American Commission on Human Rights (IACHR), 58, 188, 210, 212, 225, 296

Inter-American Court of Human Rights, 188, 292, 296, 299n. 4. See also *Mayagna (Sumo) Awas Tingni Community*

Inter-American Development Bank (IADB), 248, 343n. 21, 344nn. 25–26, 354nn. 77–79

Interdependency of human rights, 58, 61, 78–79, 141, 309n. 58, 311n. 69

International Bill of Human Rights, 56, 64, 141, 193

International Agreement for the Suppression of the White Slave Trade (1904), 171

International Conference on Population and Development, Cairo (1994), 311n. 69; Declaration of, 311nn. 69, 71

International Convention for the Suppression of the Traffic in Women of Full Age, 171, 306n. 28

International Convention for the Suppression of the Traffic in Women and Children, 171, 306n. 28

International Convention for the Suppression of the White Slave Traffic (1910), 171

International Court of Justice (ICJ), 55, 145; statute of, 14. See also *Gabcíkovo-Nagymaros*; *Fisheries Jurisdiction Case*; *Legal Consequences—Namibia*; *Nottebohm Case*

International Covenant on Civil and Political Rights (ICCPR), 56–58, 60, 87, 141, 170, 193, 208–9, 213, 251–52, 254, 285, 308nn. 52–54, 314nn. 4–6, 319n. 20, 341n. 3, 345n. 9, 355nn. 8, 10–13

International Covenant on Economic, Social, and Cultural Rights (ICESCR), 56–57, 60, 141, 170, 193, 208–9, 220, 232, 251–52, 278, 285, 311n. 69, 314nn. 4–5, 349nn. 1–2, 355nn. 9, 18

International Finance Corporation (IFC), WTO, 112, 225, 324n. 63

International Labour Organization (ILO), 59, 138–42, 154–55, 164, 166, 175, 179, 209, 328n. 6, 329nn. 13, 15, 336n. 7, 337n. 19, 339n. 63; Constitution of, 59, 329n. 16; core labor standards, 148, 152–54, 160, 164, 166–69, 329n. 16, 334n. 108, 335n. 109. See also *specific declarations and conventions*

International law: hierarchy, 11, 62, 66–73, 277; history, 13–17; individual as object of, 49, 52–54, 306n. 30; law-making, 18–20; public, 40, 62, 64–65, 67, 69, 84, 112, 153, 214, 228, 278, 283; sources, 13–16, 19, 24, 62, 67–69, 72–73; as U.S. law, 20–25; and the WTO, 38–40. See also International law, customary

International law, customary, 56, 57, 68, 73, 127–28, 264, 269, 286–87, 292–94, 301n. 11; persistent objector to, 15–16, 49, 79, 84, 138, 141, 177, 187, 193, 255, 329n. 14

International Monetary Fund (IMF), 26, 47, 64–65, 111, 288, 312n. 7, 351n. 21, 360n. 56

International Office of Epizootics, 121

International Organization for Standardization (ISO), 104

International Plant Protection Convention, 121

International Trade Commission (ITC), U.S., 271, 360nn. 55–57

Investment, 63, 82, 158, 163, 166–67, 210, 237, 245, 249, 290, 331n. 58, 358n. 18. *See also* Foreign investment; Principles for Responsible Investment

Jackson, John H., WTO scholar, 93, 302n. 1, 312n. 10, 320n. 18, 346n. 15
Japan, 6, 31, 117, 119–20, 162, 216, 218, 243, 302n. 18. See also *Nibutani Dam*; *specific cases*
Japan—Agricultural Products, WTO, 122, 125–26, 325n. 13
Japan—Apples, WTO, 325n. 12
Japan—Lumber, WTO, 321n. 21
John Paul II, Pope, and Cuban embargo, 272
Juarez, Mexico, and maquiladoras, 201
Jus civile, 14
Jus cogens, 15–16, 19–20, 24, 57, 67–71, 146, 290
Jus gentium, 14
Just trade, 1, 5, 297

Koh, Harold, 251–52, 354nn. 4–6, 355nn. 14, 16
Korea—Beef, WTO, 150
Korea—Procurement, WTO, 313n. 23

Labeling of products, 98, 104–5, 117, 128, 150, 196–97, 262, 323n. 49
Labor: rights, abuse of, 83, 112, 136, 154, 162, 164, 285, 331n. 52, 338n. 45, 339nn. 59, 63; rights, core, 136, 144, 153, 285, 291; standards, core, 138–41, 148, 152, 155, 168. *See also* Comparative advantage; Debt bondage; Forced labor; Prison Labor Exception, GATT Art. XX(e)
Language, 9, 41, 84–85, 160–61, 177; right to, 53, 55, 59, 194, 208, 307n. 37. *See also* Indigenous peoples

LatCrit, 52
League of Nations, 53, 147, 171, 306n. 25
Legal Consequences—Namibia, ICJ, 55–56, 307nn. 40–41
Legal hierarchy, between human rights and trade law, 66–73, 129
Lex posterior, 69
Lex specialis, 69
Life: right to, 49–50, 53–55, 87–88, 114, 172, 193, 233, 242, 257, 304n. 1, 308n. 54; protection of, 58, 63, 77, 88, 94, 96–98, 104, 114, 117–18, 122–23, 143, 145, 229, 276, 282, 309n. 66, 311n. 68, 313n. 33. *See also* Public life, right to
Lifestyle, 192, 211, 226, 233. *See also* Indigenous peoples
Like products, relation to trade non-discrimination, 31–35, 91–94, 101, 106, 320n. 15, 323n. 48
Living standard. *See* Standard of living
Living modified organism (LMO), 124. *See also* Genetic
Llosa, Mario Vargas, on value of a free market, 257, 355n. 25
Locke, on the rights of "man," 50, 305n. 8

Made in the USA Foundation v. United States, 42, 45, 302nn. 19, 21
Mainstreaming. *See* Gender
Malnutrition, 241. *See also* Food
Man, rights of. *See* American Declaration on the Rights and Duties of Man; Declaration on the Rights of Man and of the Citizen (French); Rights of man
Maquiladora, 7, 88, 156, 174–75, 184, 195, 198, 201, 241, 260
Mar del Plata, Argentina. *See* Summit of the Americas, Mar del Plata

Marianista/Machista culture, 200–201

Marine Mammal Protection Act of 1972 (MMPA), U.S., 90–91, 96–97

Market economy, 84, 168, 273

Marrakesh Agreement Establishing the World Trade Organization, 118, 277, 323n. 44, 330n. 39

Marry/marriage, right to, 194

Marshall, T. H., on citizenship, 76–77, 315nn. 20–23, 317n. 39

Mattel, Inc., 183–84, 187

Mayagna (Sumo) Awas Tingni Community, IACHR, 248, 349n. 80

Medicine: essential/lifesaving, 63, 114–16, 130–33, 222, 240, 276, 346n. 17; generic, 132–33, 276; patent of, 116, 130–33, 214, 216–17, 229–30, 276, 282; sanctions involving, 265–66, 271–72, 274. *See also* HIV/AIDS; Indigenous peoples

Merck Pharmaceuticals, 132, 348n. 71

MERCOSUR: first Latin "free trade" pact, 43–45; and labor rights, 154–55; and Mexico, 304n. 21; Southern Cone Common Market, 154–55; and Venezuela, 45, 304n. 21

Mexico, constitution of, 59, 151, 223. *See also* Juarez, Mexico, an maquiladoras

Miami, Florida, U.S. *See* Summit of the Americas, First

Migrant and Seasonal Agricultural Worker Protection Act (MSPA), U.S., 340n. 96

Migration. *See* Immigration

Mill, John Stuart, 286, 364n. 29

Millennium Development Declaration, UN, 233–34, 239, 312n. 11

Minimum Age Convention, 139, 328n. 10

Minority Schools in Albania (PCIJ), 306n. 25

Mode 4, GATS, and immigration policy, 157–60, 332nn. 68–71, 75–76, 333nn. 80–81

Monroe Doctrine, and Cuba, 46

Montreal Protocol on Substances that Deplete the Ozone Layer, 106, 303n. 18

Morales, Evo, Bolivian President, 44, 254

Morality/morals, 19, 70, 146, 148–49, 177, 200, 229–30, 282, 313n. 33, 330n. 33, 334n. 98. *See also* Public Morals Clause, GATT Art. XX(a)

Most-favored Nation Clause (MFN), GATT Art. I, 30–32, 38, 70, 90, 101, 104, 108, 149, 159. *See also* Four Pillars of GATT; General Exceptions, GATT Art. XX

Mothers, right to special protection, 115, 202

Multilateral, 9, 19, 36, 97, 103, 244, 353n. 55; environmental agreement, 7, 42, 68, 87, 89–90, 99, 103, 113, 294, 30n. 14, 320n. 12, 365n. 46; negotiation, 27, 38, 48, 64, 116, 328n. 9, 353n. 64; sanctions, 263, 273–74. *See also* Multilateral Investment Fund; Economic, sanctions

Multilateral Investment Fund (MIF), 248, 354nn. 77–78

Multinational corporation. *See* Transnational, corporation

Murder, 20, 140, 200

Namibia. See *Legal Consequences—Namibia*

National Institute for Children and Family, 187

National Labor Relations Act, U.S., 339n. 67

National Treatment Clause, GATT
Art. III, 31–36, 89–94, 96, 100–101,
103–4, 108, 145, 277, 303n. 5, 320n.
15, 321n. 22. *See also* Four Pillars of
GATT; General Exceptions, GATT
Art. XX
Nationality: right to, 75, 193–94; state
of, 54–55
Nations: community of, 29, 38,
147–48, 332nn. 68–69; law of,
14–16, 51–52, 54, 293–94, 364n. 44,
365nn. 50, 56; will of, 51. *See also*
League of Nations
Native. *See* Indigenous peoples
Natural: law, 14, 19, 50–51, 55, 57, 70,
76, 279, 289, 305n. 2; persons, 136,
157–58, 160; resources, 4, 41, 57, 63,
68, 148, 210, 217, 219, 222, 225, 282,
285, 287, 291; resources, exhaust-
ible, 37, 71–72, 95–96, 99, 101, 282,
329n. 22; rights, 50–51, 55. *See also*
Capitalism; Comparative advantage;
Mode 4, GATS
Natural Resources Exception, GATT
Art. XX(g), 37, 63, 71–72, 95–97,
99–102, 144, 148, 281, 329n. 22. *See
also* General Exceptions, GATT.
Art. XX
Nazi, 49, 52, 54, 255
Necessity Test: GATT Art. XX(a),
36–39, 71–72, 95–99, 103–4, 108;
GATT Art. XX(b), 108, 119, 130,
144, 146, 150, 32n. 28, 322n. 41
Negative: duty, 287–88; rights, 59, 66,
133, 317n. 39. *See also* Civil, rights;
Political, rights
Nexus. *See* Trade Nexus Test, GATT
Art. XX
Nibutani Dam litigation, 209, 345n. 9
Nondiscrimination: right to, 57, 59–60,
67, 78, 101, 134, 193–94, 204,
208–10, 213, 279–80, 281, 285, 341n.

3; and trade law, 4, 30–31, 38, 42,
86, 89, 95, 101, 103–4, 107, 109, 113,
143, 149, 159, 196, 204, 264, 270, 277,
278–82, 291, 320n. 15, 357n. 17, 363n. 13
Nonreciprocal trade. *See* Trade
Non-self-executing agreement. *See*
United States
North American Agreement on Environmental Cooperation (NAAEC),
314n. 40
North American Agreement on Labor
Cooperation (NAALC), 150–52,
314n. 40, 330nn. 41–42
North American Free Trade Agreement (NAFTA), 7, 22–23, 36,
42–43, 45–46, 72, 81–82, 136,
150–53, 155–57, 168, 174, 197–98,
240–41, 259–60, 280, 304n. 21,
312n. 18, 320n. 15, 330n. 42, 343n. 19
North Atlantic Treaty Organization, 262
North-South. *See* Divide
Nottebohm Case, ICJ, 79, 316n. 36
Nuremberg Trial/Tribunal, 49, 52, 54,
293

"Objective" Territorial Principle, 269,
290. See also *Baker, United States v.*
Occupational Safety and Health Act,
U.S., 185
Office of the Special Adviser on Gen-
der Issues and Advancement of
Women (OSAGI), UN, 343n. 22
Office of the Under Secretary for
Global Affairs (OUSGA), U.S., 189,
191, 336n. 7, 337nn. 18–19, 339nn.
71–76, 340nn. 77–87, 341nn. 110–13
"One drop" rule, 161. *See also*
Colorism
Opinion juris sive necessitatis, 15
Oppenheim, I. L., and "rights of man-
kind," 54, 305nn. 18–19, 306nn.
29–30

Optional Protocol to the Convention on the Rights of the Child on the involvement of children in armed conflicts, 171, 189

Optional Protocol to the Convention on the Rights of the Child on the sale of children, child prostitution and child pornography, 171, 189

Optional Protocol to the International Covenant on Civil and Political Rights, 56–57

Ordre public. See Morality/Morals; Public Morals Clause GATT Art. XX(a)

Organisation for Economic Co-operation and Development (OECD), 164–65, 244, 280, 300n. 11, 303n. 6, 353nn, 52, 60

Organism. *See* Genetic; Living modified organism

Organization of American States (OAS), 46, 58, 115, 142, 248, 252–54, 269, 296–97, 306n. 26, 308n. 55, 325n. 7, 344n. 34, 354n. 81, 355nn. 15–17, 19, 359n. 49; Charter, 58, 194, 232–33, 252, 254, 263, 314nn. 4, 6, 355n. 18

Originalism, 147

Originality test, and traditional knowledge, 219

Otherness, 171

Own property (land), right to, 50, 54, 61, 193–94, 203, 208, 230, 232, 278, 281, 309n. 60, 315n20. *See also* Intellectual property

Oyama v. California, 307n. 39

Pacta sunt servanda, 19, 289–92

Pacta tertiis, 68

Palermo Protocol. *See* Protocol to Prevent, Suppress and Punish Trafficking in Persons, Especially Women and Children

Paquete Habana, The, 301n. 10

Paradigm. *See* Black/white paradigm

Paris Convention for the Protection of Industrial Property (1883), WIPO, 215–16

Participation, right to, 59, 75, 78–80, 85, 88, 210, 251–52, 255, 279, 314n. 6, 315n. 20, 342n. 5, 355n. 20

Paul v. Avril, U.S., 365n. 56

Pauwelyn, Joost, and the WTO, 278, 312nn. 13, 17, 313nn. 20–21, 29, 32, 362n. 8, 363n. 18

Peace, 64, 266, 311n. 70, 354n. 6, 357n. 14; right to, 61, 108, 233, 251–52, 260, 263, 267, 288, 309n. 66, 354n. 6

Peremptory norm. *See Jus cogens*

Periphery. *See* Core-periphery exploitation

Permanent Court of International Justice (PCIJ), 53, 306nn. 25, 27. *See also German Settlers in Poland; Minority Schools in Albania; Treatment of Polish Nationals*

Persistent objector to customary international law, 15–16, 49, 79, 84, 138, 141, 177, 187, 193, 255, 329n. 14

Personhood, right to, 61, 170

Petersmann, Ernst-Ulrich, and GATT, 278, 328nn. 1, 5, 329n. 19, 362nn. 2, 4, 7, 9, 363nn. 13, 26–27

Phytosanitary, 137. *See also Japan— Apples*, WTO; Sanitary and Phytosanitary Measures Agreement

Pink, United States v., 21, 301n. 14

Plant: diversity, 88, 109, 123, 217, 221, 224; indigenous, 217–19, 226–27; life/health, 88, 94, 98, 104, 117–19, 121–23, 229, 282, 313n. 33. *See also* Food; Genetic, modification; International Plant Protection Convention

Plotkin, Mark, and Amazon indigenous peoples, 227, 348n. 69, 349n. 74

Pogge, Thomas, and "negative duty," 286, 364nn. 37–38

Political: life, 193, 249, 279; rights, 12, 56–59, 78, 142, 129, 250, 255, 258, 260, 265–66, 309n. 6, 311n. 70, 317n. 39. *See also* First generation (civil and political) rights; International Covenant on Civil and Political Rights; Negative, rights

Polluter Pays Principle, 286

Poor, the. *See* Poverty

Pornography, as violation of Public Morals Clause, 37, 282. *See also* Children

Port Hope Environmental Group v. Canada, UN, 87

Positive rights, 59, 66, 289, 292, 317n. 39. *See also* Culture, rights; Economic, rights; Social, rights

Positivism, 51

Poverty: abject, 178; absolute, 2, 6, 240; and agricultural reform, 241–47; extreme, 232–34, 236–41, 254; line, 238–39, 351n. 37, 352n. 38; measuring, 6, 235–41, 249, 259, 350n. 11, 351nn. 21, 37; reducing/eradicating, 6, 41, 47, 63, 109, 140, 155, 204, 232–35, 239, 248–49, 254, 285–86, 290, 351n. 21; and sanctions, 265, 273; and trafficking, 174, 178, 279. *See also* Gender; Immigration

Precautionary Principle, and SPS Agreement, 119, 124; relation to human rights 123; as customary law 127; and women's health, 196

Pregnancy, 115, 194, 198, 260

Principle 21. *See* Conference on Environment and Development, Rio de Janeiro

Principles for Responsible Investment, UN, 111–12. *See also* Foreign Investment; Investment

Prison Labor Exception, GATT Art. XX(e), 71, 92, 95–97, 99, 143–45, 148

Prisoners: of war, 21, 145; right of, 65; torture of, 71, 145, 314n. 43. *See also* Products

Processes or production methods (PPMs), 89–94, 96, 106–8, 110, 113, 118, 145, 277

Products, 5, 35, 86, 93, 104, 106–8, 117, 149, 323nn. 49–50; domestic, 3, 27–31, 33–34, 90, 92–93, 99, 100–101, 303n. 5, 320n. 15, 321nn. 22, 27, 323n. 48; of forced/prison labor, 71–72, 92, 95–97, 99, 143–45, 148, 263, 320n. 19; standards, 27, 33, 103–8, 117, 127, 165, 196–97, 232, 236. *See also* Genetic; Labeling of products; Like products; Production

Production: costs, 28–30, 38, 111–12, 162, 166–67, 169, 211, 214, 247, 282, 284; methods, 86, 112. *See also* Processes of Production Methods; Products

Property: nationalization of, 21, 46, 255, 266–69; reform, 46, 233. *See also* Intellectual property

Proposed American Declaration on the Rights of Indigenous Peoples, IACHR, 210, 345n. 12

Prostitution, 170–73, 175, 179, 183, 189–91, 200, 265, 293

Protectionism, 26, 82, 92–93, 136, 138, 240, 328n. 2; trade policies, 6, 8, 26–27, 33, 47–48, 61, 82, 90, 92–93

Protocol of Amendment to the Charter of the Organization of American States (Protocol of Buenos Aires), 58

Protocol of San Salvador (right to healthy environment) (1988), 58, 88, 115, 142, 194, 232, 292, 314n. 4, 355n. 9, 355n. 18

Protocol to Amend the Convention for the Suppression of the Traffic in Women of Full Age, 306n. 28

Protocol to Prevent, Suppress and Punish Trafficking in Persons, Especially Women and Children (Palermo Protocol), 171–72, 189

Public Health and Welfare Clause, GATT Art. XX, 35, 37, 63, 65, 72, 88, 94–103, 105, 108, 114, 118–19, 122, 130, 134, 143, 145–46, 148, 270, 282, 291, 313n. 30, 321nn. 22, 29, 346n. 17. *See also* General Exceptions, GATT Art. XX; Necessity test

Public life, right to, 67, 76, 199. *See also* Life

Public morality. *See* Morality/morals; Public Morals Clause, GATT Art. XX(a)

Public Morals Clause, GATT Art. XX(a), 37–38, 63, 70–72, 94, 96, 136, 143, 146–49, 282–83, 312n. 14, 313n. 34, 330nn. 33–34. *See also* General Exceptions, GATT Art. XX; Morality/morals

Pull factors. *See* Trafficking

Purchasing power parity (PPP), 231, 238, 351n. 37

Push factors, of trafficking, 173–74, 187

Quality of life, 55, 240, 248, 257, 311n. 68

Quebec Summit. *See* Summit of the Americas

"Race to the bottom," 5, 43, 82, 155, 318n. 54

Racial: discrimination, 16, 20, 67, 73, 81, 134, 141, 160–62, 289, 293–94, 365n. 59; hierarchy, 171, 333n. 94; minorities, 53, 78, 85, 171; racialized rights, 59. *See also* Colorism

Racism. *See* Racial discrimination

Rainforest. *See* Amazon rainforest

Ralco Dam, Chile, 212, 225

Rape, 2, 140, 173, 176, 179, 193, 200, 264. *See also* Abuse

Rawls, John, and concept of justice, 287–88

Re Drummond Wren, 307n. 38

Reagan, Ronald, U.S. President, 254, 257, 358n. 26

Reciprocal trade. *See* Trade

Regional human rights system, 58, 82, 87, 233–52, 285, 295; African, 58; European, 58; Inter-American, 58, 194, 252, 296, 308n. 57, 334n. 96, 345n. 8, 359n. 48

Relationship test, in GATT Art. XX(g), 71–72, 99–100, 103, 144

Religion, 49, 51, 53, 70, 76, 78–79, 85, 146, 192, 194, 199–200, 217, 229, 250, 264, 272; freedom of, 54–55, 59, 87, 208, 213, 252–53, 307n. 37, 308n. 54, 316n. 35, 317n. 39

Remittances, 81–82, 248, 272–73, 361nn. 74, 79

Reparations, for human rights violations, 286–94

Responsible Investment Principles. *See* Principles for Responsible Investment, UN

Rest, right to, 115

Restatement (Third) of Foreign Relation Law, U.S., 14–15, 57, 294, 301n. 13, 302nn. 23, 25, 305n. 2, 308n. 50, 365n. 59

Restaveks practice. *See* Trafficking

Retaliation, financial, in WTO disputes, 39, 89, 153, 155, 314n. 41
Retraining, 235, 335n. 117; through trade adjustment assistance, 167–68. *See also* Trade adjustment assistance
Ricardo, David, and the Ricardian model, 1, 27–32, 36, 123, 157, 242, 294–95. *See also* Comparative advantage
Rights of man, 54, 58, 309n. 59. *See also* American Declaration on the Rights and Duties of Man; Declaration on the Rights of Man and of the Citizen (French)
Rio Declaration. *See* Conference on Environment and Development, Rio de Janeiro
Rio Tinto. See Sarei v. Rio Tinto
Risk: assessment, under SPS Agreement, 116, 118–19, 196, 287, 321n. 22, 325n. 12. *See also* Health
Rogoff, Kenneth, and unbridled capitalism, 257, 356n. 26
Role of government, 50, 73–74, 250. *See also* Family; Corporate codes of conduct; Culture; Gender; Women
Rome Declaration. *See* Declaration on World Food Security
Roosevelt, Eleanor, 56, 308n. 48
Roosevelt, Franklin D., 21, 60. *See also* Four Freedoms Speech

Safe: harbor, of GATT Art. III, 89–92, 96, 103, 145, 277, 281, 291, 320n. 15; house, and trafficking, 183. *See also* Food; Social, safety net
Samuelson, Paul, and comparative advantage, 29
Sanctions: economic, 4, 12, 252, 261–74, 329n. 16; multilateral, 263, 273–74

Sanitary and Phytosanitary Measures Agreement (SPS), WTO, 7, 38, 63, 99, 113–14, 116–30, 134–35, 196, 213, 215, 282, 313n. 30, 324n. 67, 325n. 12, 346n. 17; least-restrictive standard, 97, 122, 321n. 28, 322n. 41
San Salvador, Brazil. *See* Protocol of San Salvador
Sao Paulo, Brazil, and trafficking, 186
Sarei v. Rio Tinto, 2, 293–94, 299n. 5, 365nn. 57–60
Sassen, Saskia, on economic citizenship, 83–84, 318nn. 57–60
Schumpeter, Joseph, on creative destruction, 284, 363n. 25
Second generation (social, economic, cultural) rights, 58–61, 266. *See also* Culture; Economic, rights; Social, rights
Second Optional Protocol to the International Covenant on Civil and Political Rights, Aiming at the Abolition of the Death Penalty, 308n. 53
Sei Fuji v. California, 307n. 39
Self-determination, right to, 57, 60, 141, 203, 209–10, 212, 251–52
Sen, Amartya, on famines and democracy, 250–51, 354n. 1
Sensenbrenner, F. James, on immigration, 159, 332nn. 72, 74
Servitude, 2, 145, 170, 174–75, 185, 308n. 54; domestic, 175, 179–80, 183–86, 190–91, 339n. 59; indentured, 172, 177, 263; involuntary, 172–73, 176, 180–82, 191, 339n. 70; sexual, 173, 175. *See also* Children; Debt bondage; Forced Labor; Slavery
Sex tourism. *See* Children
Sexual: abuse, 170, 179, 200, 309n. 61; discrimination, 73, 175, 193; harassment, 140, 175, 193, 198. *See also* Children

Sexuality, 76, 199

Shantytown, 7, 182, 190

Sinden, Amy, and transnational corporations, 292, 295, 365n. 48, 366n. 62

Singapore Declaration of 1996, WTO, 138–39, 142, 329n. 9, 363n. 27. *See also* Declaration on Fundamental Principles and Rights at Work

Slavery, 50, 67, 112, 134, 161, 170, 172, 177, 183, 185–87; abolishment of, 49, 54; freedom from, 16, 20, 37, 54, 61, 73, 143, 146, 171–72, 180, 185, 282, 308n. 54; labor, 112, 145, 173, 264, 293; slave-like, 2, 172–75, 186. *See also* Servitude

Smith, Adam, on absolute advantage, 28–29, 302n. 2

Smuggling, 172, 175–76, 183–84, 191, 266. *See also* Trafficking

Social: justice, 77, 233, 275, 290; rights, 60, 77, 83, 135, 265, 317n. 39; safety net, 12, 82, 204, 207, 235, 237, 245, 250, 259, 279–81, 295, 351n. 19; well-being, 115, 275. *See also* Corporate codes of conduct; International Covenant on Economic, Social, and Cultural Rights; Second generation (social, economic, cultural) rights

Socialism, 59, 61, 66, 264; revolution, 59

Social security, right to, 60, 231–33

Societal: concept, 146; value, 67, 178

Socio-economics, 318n. 54, 360n. 63

Sole executive agreement. *See* United States

Solidarity rights, 58, 60–61. *See also* Collective, rights; Third generation rights

Source state. See Children; Trafficking

Southern Cone Common Market. *See* MERCOSUR

Sovereignty, 14, 17–18, 30, 53–55, 66, 83, 85, 204, 258–59, 268, 287, 312n. 14, 317n. 41, 359n. 39, 364n. 32

Spain—Coffee, WTO, 321n. 21

Speech. *See* Free speech

Splendid: integration, 9, 11, 279; isolation, 7, 9, 11, 62–74, 77, 95, 129, 213, 250, 256, 275, 281–86

Standard of living, 6, 55, 73, 94, 155, 197, 231, 235, 257, 284, 328n. 2; right to adequate, 60, 115, 232, 309n. 66

Standards: labor, core, 138–41, 148, 152, 155, 168; product, 27, 33, 103–8, 117, 127, 165, 196–97, 232, 236; technical, under TBT Agreement, 27, 103

Statute of International Court of Justice. *See* International Court of Justice

Stockholm Declaration. *See* Conference on the Human Environment, Stockholm

Strike, right to, 141, 154

Suárez, Francisco, on natural law, 51

Subaltern community/group, 78, 85, 220

Subjugation, 59, 201. *See also* Subordination

Subordination: and human law, 51, 67, 232, 265–66; of others, 171, 236. *See also* Gender; Women

Subsidy of goods, 27, 38, 45, 117, 130, 303n. 12, 331n. 58. *See also* Agreement on Subsidies, WTO; Agriculture; Anti-dumping, and WTO agreement

Subsistence, right to, 60, 209

Sugar, 45–46, 142, 151, 207, 244; -cane, 2, 143, 182, 190. *See also* Children

Sugar Act of 1948, U.S., and Cuba, 267

Sui generis system, and traditional knowledge protection, 228–29

Summit of the Americas: First, Miami (1994), 41, 47, 303n. 17; Mar del Plata, Argentina (2005), 3; Quebec City (2001), 296, 331n. 58, 366n. 63; Santiago (1998), 47, 296

Supplementary Convention on the Abolition of Slavery, the Slave Trade, and Institutions and Practices Similar to Slavery, 54

Supremacy Clause. *See* United States

Supreme court. *See* United States; World Trade Court

Sustainable development: definition, 109; of the environment, 5, 63, 89–90, 93, 112, 234; and Equator principles, 112; as human right, 87; and IPR, 217, 222; Rio Conference adoption, 108. *See also* Indigenous peoples

Sweatshop, 4, 137–38, 162, 175; anti-, 164

Tagle v. Regan, 359n. 42

Technical: assistance, 225, 246, 297; regulation under TBT Agreement, 104, 106–8, 149–50, 276, 322n. 41, 323n. 49; standard under TBT Agreement, 27, 103

Territory, 18–19, 31, 158, 269, 287–91, 338n. 32; and human rights, 70, 72, 78, 82–83, 85, 103, 120; indigenous, 208, 210, 224–25, 229. *See also* Deterritorialization; Extraterritorial Harm Principle; Extraterritorial/ity; Global Harm Principle; "Objective" Territorial Principle

Thailand—Cigarettes, WTO, 97–98, 321n. 28

Third generation rights, 58, 60–61. *See also* Collective, rights; Solidarity rights

Torricelli Law. *See* Cuban Democracy Act (CDA)

Torture, 4, 53, 63, 67, 70–71, 264, 289, 293; freedom from, 16, 20, 68, 71, 73, 87, 262, 294, 308n. 54, 314n. 43. *See also* Convention Against Torture

Trade: just, 1, 5, 297; nonreciprocal, 244, 246, 263; reciprocal, 31–32. *See also* Chapeau Test; Disguised trade restriction/protection; Doha Development Round, World Health Organization; Generalized System of Preferences; Most-favored Nation Clause

Trade Act of 1974, U.S., 335n. 113

Trade adjustment assistance, 158, 245

Trade Adjustment Assistance Reform Act of 2002, U.S., 167, 280, 335nn. 114–18

Trade Nexus Test, GATT Art. XX, 71–72

Trade Promotion Authority Act (2002), U.S., 152–53, 302n. 22, 331n. 59, 332n. 72

Trade-related Aspects of Intellectual Property Rights (TRIPS), WTO Agreement on, 62–63, 114, 116, 276, 282, 313n. 33, 343n. 18, 346n. 17; copyright protections added, 214–16, 346n. 18; and health, 130–33; and human rights, 213–16, 228–30; TRIPS-plus, 133, 228, 276. *See also* Copyright agreement; Indigenous peoples; Intellectual property

Trading with the Enemy Act of 1917, U.S., and Cuba, 267

Traditional knowledge, 10, 197, 204, 206–10, 213, 216–30, 240–41, 276, 285, 291, 345n. 6, 346n. 17, 347n. 47. *See also* Biopiracy of traditional knowledge; Bioprospecting for traditional knowledge; Indigenous peoples

Trafficking, 8, 11–12, 170–91; destination state for, 180–82, 190–91; and globalization, 174–75; prohibitions against, 54, 170; *restaveks* practice, 181–82; pull factors of, 173, 187; source state for, 175, 181–82, 184, 189–91, 241; transit state for, 180–82, 184, 190–91. *See also* Children; Debt bondage; Forced labor; Smuggling; Women

Trail Smelter Arbitration, UN, 287, 364n. 40

Transit state. *See* Trafficking

Transnational: commerce, 110, 112, 114, 261, 287, 319n. 11; community, 78, 85, 317nn. 47–48; corporation (TNC), 2–4, 12, 82, 83–84, 89, 174, 176, 112, 121, 133, 162–66, 206, 210, 215, 217–18, 229, 247, 259, 276–77, 280, 284–85, 291–92, 300n. 14, 318n. 54, 334nn. 98, 100, 108, 365n. 48; individual, 79–82, 85. *See also* Citizenship

Transparency, 67, 82, 102, 167, 223, 253, 255–56, 260, 281, 284, 351n. 37, 363n. 24

Travaux preparatoires; 19

Travel, freedom to, 59, 309n. 61. *See also* Cuban embargo

Treatment of Polish Nationals (PCIJ), 264, 306n. 27

Treaty: ratification, 20–21; reservation, 18–19

Tribe. *See* Indigenous peoples

"Triple bottom line," 112, 164

TRIPS Agreement. *See* Trade-related Aspects of Intellectual Property, Agreement on

U.K. v. Iceland. See Fisheries Jurisdiction Case

Understanding on Rules and Procedures Governing the Settlement of Disputes. *See* Dispute Settlement Understanding

Union: organizing, 137, 154, 175, 328n. 2, 331n. 52; right to form, 61, 141, 149, 308n. 57, 331n. 52. *See also* Solidarity rights

United Nations (UN): Charter, 14, 37, 55–57, 66, 72–73, 251, 262–63, 278, 289, 307nn. 35, 37–39, 357n. 14; Commission on Human Rights (UNCHR), 56–57, 87, 115, 278, 309n. 58, 311n. 70, 325n. 4, 358n. 37, 362nn. 5–6, 353n. 24; Committee on Economic, Social, and Cultural Rights (UNCESCR), 358nn. 32–34, 37; Development Fund for Women (UNIFEM), 343n. 19; Development Programme (UNDP), 301n. 23, 349n. 75, 350n. 18, 351nn. 23–25, 27–30, 32–33, 36–37, 352nn. 44–46, 50, 354n. 71; Educational, Scientific and Cultural Organization (UNESCO); General Assembly, 56–57, 251, 268, 270, 309n. 58, 360n. 62; Office of Drugs and Crime, 187; Security Council, 262–63, 266, 273, 357n. 14. *See also Nibutani Dam* litigation; *Port Hope Environmental Group v. Canada; Trail Smelter Arbitration*, UN; *specific convention, covenant, or declaration*

United States: Constitution, 16,
20–25, 307n. 39, 335n. 112; Department of Agriculture, 335n. 114,
360n. 58; Department of Commerce, 9, 304n. 19; Department
of Health and Human Services
(DHHS), 180, 326n. 33; Department of Justice, 337n. 24; Department of Labor, 165, 186, 335n. 116,
340n. 96, 341n. 107; Department
of State, 23, 189, 191, 293, 301n. 12,
302n. 20, 306n. 27, 336n. 7, 341n.
109, 360nn. 63, 69; executive-
congressional co-determination
agreement, 20–23; non-self-
executing agreement, 24, 307n. 39;
Senate role in treaty approval, 16;
in immigration, 159; sole executive
agreement, 21–23, 25, 150; Supremacy Clause, 24; Supreme Court, 16,
21, 74; trade adjustment assistance
program, 158, 245; Trade Representative (USTR), 159, 324n. 67, 331n.
55, 332nn. 72, 74. *See also specific
cases, laws, or acts*
United States—*1916 Act*, WTO, 68,
283, 313n. 26, 363n. 20
United States—Chile Free Trade
Agreement, 23, 136, 152–55, 330n.
48, 332n. 72
United States—*Gambling*, WTO,
37–38, 70, 146–47, 283
United States—*Gasoline*, WTO,
99–100, 144, 320n. 15, 312n. 12,
313n. 22, 329n. 22
United States—*Jordan*, WTO, 151–54
United States—*Section 301*, WTO,
301n. 11
United States—*Shrimp-Turtle I*, WTO,
68, 95, 100–103, 145, 148, 283,
313n. 27, 321n. 29, 322n. 30, 330n.
38, 363n. 20, 365n. 47

United States—*Shrimp-Turtle II*, WTO,
102–3
United States—*Tuna-Dolphin I*, GATT,
90–91, 95–99, 103, 108, 148, 321n.
29, 330n. 35, 365n. 46
United States—*Tuna-Dolphin II*,
GATT, 91, 95–99, 103, 108, 148,
330n. 35, 365n. 46
United States—*Wheat*, WTO, 326n. 26
United States—*Wool*, WTO, 283, 313n.
26, 363n. 20
Universal Declaration on Human
Rights, 7, 47, 56–57, 73, 87, 115,
141, 170, 193, 208–9, 212–13, 232,
251, 254, 285, 289, 296, 308n. 45
Universalism, and public morals, 147,
149
Universality of rights, 49–50, 55, 61,
138, 140, 277, 285, 309n. 59
Universal jurisdiction, 290
Unjustifiable discrimination. *See* Cha-
peau Test
Uruguay Round of Multilateral Trade
Negotiations, 117, 121, 133, 324n.
67, 353nn. 54–64

Victims of Trafficking and Violence
Protection Act (VTVPA), U.S.,
180–81, 339n. 74
Vienna Convention on the Law of
Treaties, 16–21, 24, 69–70, 93,
100, 126, 129, 283, 290–92, 301nn.
11–12, 313nn. 24–25, 28–29, 31,
364nn. 41–42, 365n. 49
Vienna Declaration and Programme of
Action, 61, 311n. 69, 341n. 2
Vote, right to, 193, 251–52, 255

W. R. Grace and Co., 218–19
Washington Consensus, 5, 335n. 121
Weeremantry, Christopher, Judge, ICJ,
87, 314n. 7

Well-being: human, 114–35, 204, 260, 297; and poverty, 231, 236–37, 351n. 19; right to, 60, 66, 87, 194, 259–60, 336n. 1; of workers, 145, 180, 187. *See also* Economic; Social

Wilson, Edward O., on bio-extinction rates, 221, 346n. 30

Women: culture of, 192, 199, 204, 341n. 4, 342nn. 5–6; exploitation of, 170, 181, 190–91; heterogeneity, 199, 204; role of, 10, 41, 192, 200, 204, 342n. 9; subordination of, 10, 60, 66, 173, 236, 239, 275; "woman" question, 52, 192–205, 276, 341n. 1. *See also* Convention on the Elimination of All Forms of Discrimination Against Women (CEDAW); Domestic work; Gender; Servitude

Women's Environment and Development Organization (WEDO), 195

Work. *See* Domestic work; Labor

Work Declaration, ILO. *See* Declaration on Fundamental Principles and Rights at Work

World Conference on Human Rights (1993), Vienna, 192, 196–97, 342nn. 10–12, 343nn. 14–15, 17

World Conference on Women (Fourth), Beijing (1995), 199

World Conservation Union, 220

World Food Programme, UN, 4, 300nn. 12–13

World Food Summit (1996), Rome, 242

World Health Organization (WHO), 2, 326n. 35

World Intellectual Property Organization (WIPO), 131, 213–14, 216

World Summit for Social Development, Copenhagen (1995), 233, 349n. 3; Declaration of, 233–34, 308n. 43, 311nn. 68–69, 350n. 4

World Summit on Sustainable Development, (2002), Johannesburg, 109, 324n. 54

World Summit Outcome 2005, 234, 350n. 7

World Trade Court (WTC): and health, 94, 130; and human rights road map, 103, 113; and Necessity Test, 98, 146; and PPMs, 92–93; and the Precautionary Principle, 128; and protecting environment, 277; and public international law, 38, 40; and Relationship Test, 99, 144; rules-based approach, 100, 105; use of ICJ decisions, 148; role of WTO's Appellate Body, 37

World Trade Organization (WTO), Charter, 27. *See also* Dispute settlement panel; World Trade Court

World Trade Organization, intellectual property rights of, 27, 131–33, 154, 226–30, 346n. 29. *See also* Indigenous peoples; Trade-related Aspects of Intellectual Property Rights, WTO Agreement on; World Intellectual Property Organization

About the Authors

BERTA ESPERANZA HERNÁNDEZ-TRUYOL is Levin Mabie and Levin Professor of Law at the University of Florida Levin College of Law and editor of *Moral Imperialism: A Critical Anthology* (NYU Press).

STEPHEN J. POWELL is Lecturer in Law and Director of the International Trade Law Program at the University of Florida Levin College of Law.